Publishing, Printing,
and the Origins of
Intellectual Life
in Russia

Publishing, Printing, and the Origins of Intellectual Life in Russia, 1700–1800

BY GARY MARKER

PRINCETON UNIVERSITY PRESS
PRINCETON, NEW JERSEY

Copyright © 1985 by Princeton University Press

Published by Princeton University Press, 41 William Street,
Princeton, New Jersey 08540
In the United Kingdom: Princeton University Press, Guildford, Surrey

All Rights Reserved

Library of Congress Cataloging in Publication Data will be
found on the last printed page of this book

ISBN 0-691-05441-X

This book has been composed in Linotron Sabon

Clothbound editions of Princeton University Press books
are printed on acid-free paper, and binding materials are
chosen for strength and durability

Printed in the United States of America by Princeton University Press
Princeton, New Jersey

TO ANN AND JOSHUA

CONTENTS

LIST OF TABLES

PREFACE

LIKE many first books, this study began as a doctoral dissertation far too many years ago and with expectations that, from hindsight, appear manifestly unrealistic. I became interested in the history of printing through a circuitous process that began with an uneasiness with what I took to be a failure in the existing literature to give Russian intellectual history an adequate social grounding. Granted, scholars had extensively studied most movements of significance, prominent intellectuals, and noteworthy schools of thought. We also knew a great deal about the membership of various groups and about social and educational backgrounds, and even something about choices of careers and vocations. But few scholars had seen fit to write anything concrete about how these representatives of the intelligentsia had been received as writers or thinkers once they presented themselves to prospective audiences. Since Russian intellectuals relied almost exclusively on the written word to communicate with their publics and to influence the course of Russian society, at least until the emergence of genuinely social movements in the last third of the nineteenth century, this failure struck me as being quite fundamental. Without an understanding of how, or whether, the ideas of leading writers circulated within the society, Russian intellectual history was left in something of a vacuum.

I decided, therefore, to write a general social history of ideas in Russia that would cover the entire period between Peter the Great and the era of the great reforms. After several months spent in furious pursuit of quantitative evidence on the circulation of books and magazines, I realized that the project was both far too large and fatally misconceived. Not only were there few numbers available in the published sources, but most of these were undocumented and, in the end, unverifiable. More critically, I slowly became aware that even verifiable numbers were, in themselves, of little significance because we (or at least I) knew very little about the circumstances in which books were published and disseminated. If the networks of distribution were undeveloped, or if they lay outside the reach of writers, circulation figures would tell us next to nothing concerning the affinities between writers and publics.

This new realization led me away from the pursuit of numbers, at least for the moment, and toward the study of the social and institutional development of Russian publishing and bookselling. At that point it became clear that printing history raised quite enough questions in itself, few of which had been discussed by historians, and that these questions took logical precedence over the social history of ideas. Hence, I emerged after an extended journey as an initiate to the history of printing.

This serpentine pilgrimage could not have been accomplished without considerable assistance, however. My advisor at the University of California at Berkeley, Nicholas V. Riasanovsky, has given generously of his time and his inexhaustible knowledge of Russian history. From the very first months of this project through all of the numerous revisions and modifications, he was always available for even the most extended consultations and advice. I would also like to thank S. S. Dmitriev and V. A. Vdovin of the history faculty of Moscow State University, who provided valuable assistance and advice while I was doing research in the Soviet Union during the academic year 1974–75. In addition, special appreciation must go to Reginald Zelnik, Brenda Meehan-Waters, David Griffiths, Martin Malia, Reinhard Bendix, Fred Weinstein, Jeremy Popkin, and others too numerous to list, who read parts of this manuscript at various stages of preparation and who made very helpful suggestions along the way.

I wish to extend a word of thanks to Linda Edmondson of the University of London for her continued interest and encouragement, and to the members of the now-defunct Berkeley Intellectual History Group, whose high level of discourse and critique improved this study immeasurably.

I also want to acknowledge the International Research and Exchanges Board and the Research Foundation of the State of New York for providing support at various stages of my research and writing, and I owe a deep debt of gratitude to Barbara Haegele for typing the entire manuscript.

Finally, I want to give a very special word of thanks to my wife, Ann, who has lived with Russian printing for well over a decade now, who has suffered through endless monologues on the most minute facets of Russian book publishing, and who through it all has devoted countless hours of time to reading drafts, typing, and making helpful and important suggestions that have made this book a much better work than it otherwise would have been.

NOTE ON TRANSLITERATION

In general, I have used System II of J. Thomas Shaw, *The Transliteration of Modern Russian for English-Language Publications* (Madison, Wis., 1967). For Russian personal names, I have followed the standard practice of transliterating directly from the Russian rather than employing the English equivalent. Hence, I use "Nikolai" rather than "Nicholas" and "Mikhail" rather than "Michael." There are two exceptions to this, however. The given names of Russian rulers are presented in their English-language equivalents ("Catherine," not "Ekaterina"); and names such as "Peter" and "Alexander," for which the Russian and English are essentially the same and for which there exists a common English spelling, are also presented in their English forms. Non-Russian names are rendered by strict transliteration for persons who were actually native Russians—"FonVizin." not "von Wiesen." In the case of persons who were not born in Russia or who maintained regular contact with a native non-Russian culture or heritage, the names are rendered as they would have appeared in the original language of the person in question—"Stählin," not "Shtelin."

Publishing, Printing,
and the Origins of
Intellectual Life
in Russia

INTRODUCTION

THE HISTORY of printing in Russia, it is safe to say, has never inflamed the passions of scholars of Russian history. Many historians, to be sure, are familiar with the biographies of certain prominent figures in the history of the Russian book, such as Ivan Fedorov, Nikolai Novikov, and Alexander Smirdin, whose individual achievements have long since found a place in the mainstream of historical narrative. But the place of printing as a system of communications and the role of printed books within the overall development of Russian culture and society remain largely unexplored as topics of significant inquiry by the historical profession.

This neglect should not be taken to suggest that the history of the Russian book has lacked recognition as a serious topic, however. Just the opposite is true. Bibliographers, antiquarians, literary historians, amateur bookmen, and even Soviet "archaeographers" have been writing about the subject, often quite brilliantly, for a long time.[1] At the present time, moreover, the subject has blossomed anew among Soviet bibliographers and archivists, with such ventures as the journal *Kniga* (The Book) and the History of the Russian Book project, which the research staff of the rare-book division of the library of the Academy of Sciences in Leningrad has been conducting for several years.[2] This outpouring of publications notwithstanding, an all but impenetrable barrier has steadfastly divided the study of book history in Russia from Russian history in general. Despite the abundance of secondary literature on the history of the Russian book, there exists no accepted conceptual structure or even periodization, beyond the usual dynastic demarcations, around which one can raise significant questions or develop a point of view.

Soviet book scholars, to be sure, are not uninterested in history. Many of the contemporary bibliographers who have written informative studies of books, including Sergei Luppov and Ivan Martynov, received their graduate training in history, and virtually all of them have attempted to treat the history of the Russian book with specific reference to time and place. But little of this historical consciousness has lent itself to speaking in any precise way about where the importance of printing or publishing lay in the unfolding of Russian history. Rather, most Soviet specialists either have chosen to ignore questions of historical significance altogether or, more commonly, they have embedded their own researches rather loosely in an implied theory of cultural progress that looks at the development of publishing largely as part of the march of enlightenment in the seventeenth and eighteenth centuries.

In its most general outlines, the theory assumes that there existed a historical polarity between secularization, enlightenment, and progress on the one hand and religion, reaction, and backwardness on the other.[3] The period between the middle of the seventeenth and the beginning of the nineteenth century, in this view, is characterized by an inexorable and spontaneous movement away from the Russian Orthodox church and from religious domination of the communication of ideas in the direction of secularism and progress. The state, as the bearer of educational opportunities and reform, was the initial agent of progress in the late seventeenth and early eighteenth centuries, but as the eighteenth century proceeded the intellectuals took responsibility for secularizing Russian culture. The Russian people, in turn, benefited from and approved of this onset of enlightenment because it gave them access to useful and interesting books which they naturally preferred to the purely religious publications of the church or the narrowly statist publications of the government.[4]

This vision has led Soviet scholars to look for evidence of the advance of secularization wherever they might find it and to place particular emphasis on episodes in which the writings of literary and philosophical heroes, such as Novikov, Radishchev, and Lomonosov, turn up in the hands of people outside of the literary elite. Since the course of secularization is assumed to be inexorable, except to the extent that the church or state could obfuscate or impede it, a great deal of literature has been written in the search for the origins of the process. One reads, for example, that literate culture was becoming more secular in the late seventeenth century not because of a nominal change in the church's control of the printing presses, but because many books that were on the surface religious were paying increased attention to teaching practical or this-worldly skills.[5] Thus, any examples of religious literature that included practical information are deemed to be the beginnings of the secular transformation.

Implicit in this argument is a model which assumes that publishing played a central but essentially neutral role as an instrument of enlightenment. In the final analysis, the printing press was nothing more than a medium, a vehicle through which the march of progress worked its will in bringing the people into contact with the intellectuals. The institution or technology of printing, therefore, played only a subordinate role in a larger drama.

As a general description of the evolution of intellectual history, this theory makes a certain amount of sense. Clearly some sort of transition was taking place from church-controlled to lay-controlled publishing between the late seventeenth and the late eighteenth centuries, and this transition more or less paralleled the emergence of a lay intellectual elite and the unfolding in Russia of the ideas of the Enlightenment. But identifying this process with progress has all of the logical pitfalls of any teleological argument that searches for the beginnings of something modern. The assumption, moreover, that printing was simply a neutral implement in the service of a larger process precludes inquiry into the possibility that printing, publishing, or bookselling had an independent effect upon social and cultural developments.

Most recent Soviet works, it should be noted, have reduced their reliance on this theory to little more than a general predisposition that shows up as a prelude to the far richer factographic research that follows.[6] Yet only occasionally have Soviet scholars expressed any reservations about the printing-as-secularizer idea, and their readiness to give detailed accounts of narrower factual subjects concerning eighteenth-century Russian books implicitly accepts both the inexorable march of secular progress and the notion that publishers and printing presses were essentially dependent agents of enlightenment.

This study, it will come as no surprise, attempts something different. Rather than focusing narrowly on the question of whether eighteenth-century printing was an instrument of progress, it seeks to construct a coherent narrative, a basis of periodization, and meaningful lines of analysis within which the internal evolution of Russian printing can be understood.

At a second level, it examines the affinities between the development of Russian printing and other aspects of Russian life, such as politics, education, and literary life. Certain obvious mutual influences affected the parallel evolutions of printing and both primary and secondary education, for example, and these, in turn, had important ramifications for broad segments of Russian society. Moreover, while the fact that officialdom had a monopoly over printing throughout much of the eighteenth century is well established, the use to which the autocracy put its monopoly and the consequences of its actions are far from clear. Such issues, I hope, will be elucidated during the course of my discussion.

Another goal of this study is to pinpoint the place of printing among all the other media available in eighteenth-century Russia, including hand copying, woodblock prints, and verbal communication. Once again, Soviet scholars have done a creditable job of describing the manuscript tradition and of showing its vitality even into the nineteenth century.[7] But the changing symbiosis between printing and hand copying and the circumstances under which printing shaped a role for itself and at what pace, and how it took over the leading role for public written communications from hand copying, are still little understood. Yet an understanding of this proccess is crucial in elucidating the importance of printing in Russian culture and society as a whole. It also helps to highlight the critical ways in which the evolution and significance of Russian printing differed from that of printing in the West.

The final and perhaps the most ambitious aim of this study is to comment on the place of printing in eighteenth-century Russia generally. Granted, the eighteenth century was a time in which the internal evolution of publishing underwent an intense transformation, what might even be termed a maturation, from a small church-dominated phenomenon into a much larger, more complex, more pluralistic set of institutions in which church, state, intellectuals, educated society, merchants, and artisans figured prominently. But what difference did this transformation make for Russian history? Was printing simply an object of larger developments or did the process and structure of printing come to influence important features of Russian society?

Since the prevailing model of cultural progress provides us with few usable answers to these questions, we must begin the inquiry by turning to histories of printing outside of Russia, not so much for the purpose of discovering an alternative model that will make everything clear as to see what sorts of approaches other historiographical traditions have found useful. To suggest that there currently exists a well-defined, readily accessible historical debate concerning the impact of printing in European culture and society would be misleading, however, since— notwithstanding Elizabeth Eisenstein's recent remarkable and much-debated study of early western printing[8]—much of the standard scholarship has remained content to speak of the revolutionary significance of printing without actually telling us what that significance was.

In spite of the scholarly reluctance to cross swords over theoretical approaches to printing and history, much literature of deep historical importance has nevertheless recently been written on the subject, including books by Robert Darnton, Lucien Febvre and Henri-Jean Martin, Robert Mandrou, Robert Altick, and Miriam Chrisman, that demonstrates an implicit awareness of the utility of the history of printing in elucidating aspects of popular culture, cultural diffusion, and the rise of popular ideologies.[9] Without doing too much damage to their respective arguments, furthermore, one can distill from them certain discrete models concerning how printing has functioned in various societies and, in particular, which features of society or of the communications process were most responsible for developing the ties between printing and society. Put in very simple terms, the leading candidates appear to be—in no particular order—technology, popular demand, political power, lay intellectual or religious elites, publishers and printers, and booksellers and colporteurs.

The first of these candidates, printing technology, has been the subject of sociological speculation by such luminaries as James Innis and Marshal McLuhan, who have argued in brief that the inherent technological properties of movable type represented such an enormous improvement over previous writing technologies that they brought the world to a new level of cultural development, what McLuhan has termed the "Gutenberg galaxy."[10] Unfortunately, sociologists of communication have had little taste for historicism, and their arguments consequently are not very clear concerning just when, where, or how this cultural transformation took place. Recently, however, the technology-centered argument has received a brilliant historical exposition in Elizabeth Eisenstein's two-volume study of early western printing, *The Printing Press as an Agent of Change.*[11]

Eisenstein believes that historians can effectively apply McLuhan's speculations to Europe between the mid-fifteenth century and the mid-seventeenth century, a period whose cultural history she sees as being deeply influenced by a "printing revolution" that thoroughly transformed the communication of the written word in Europe. When compared to fifteenth-century hand copying or woodblock printing, she demonstrates, movable type was a cheap, labor-efficient, and strikingly rapid means of reproducing the written word. It could create unlimited and uniform copies of a given text; it could, consequently, make identical copies available to all interested readers, regardless of their separation from the original publication by time or distance.

These inherent properties of limitless copies and uniformity of text allowed the printing press to expand throughout most of Europe with astonishing speed and enabled movable type soon to eclipse older means of reproduction as the primary medium of written communication. Among other consequences, argues Eisenstein, the circulation of printed books had an immediate and profound impact on Renaissance scholarship. Printing could be used to reproduce classical texts that had previously existed only in haphazardly distributed and often inaccessible manuscript copies. Humanist scholars now had at their disposal a much wider range of books to read and compare. Technological innovation, in other words, ipso facto set off a revolutionary ripple in European culture.

Once old texts came together within the same study, diverse systems of ideas and special disciplines could be combined. Increased output directed at relatively stable markets, in short, created conditions that favored, first, new combinations of old ideas, and, then, the creation of entirely new systems of thought.[12]

Eisenstein illustrates this thesis very effectively by weaving together numerous historical episodes in which she is able to pinpoint the impact of printing upon ongoing activities. The question arises, however, whether her thesis relates to the advent of printing everywhere or only in the West. To be sure, she does make passing reference to the fact that the emergence of movable type in Europe was different from what it was in China, for example.[13] Her approach to printing, nevertheless, places almost all its explanatory emphasis on technological innovation and virtually none on the special character of Renaissance Europe as a cultural or social setting for printing's advent.

Such an approach leads to the inference that movable type might be expected to work its will wherever it appeared. Yet even the most cursory glance at the history of early printing in Russia demonstrates that this is not so. Movable type was available for more than a hundred years in Europe before it appeared in Muscovy. Indeed, in the first century of European printing, presses proliferated by the hundreds and printed books by the tens of millions, before a single press came to Moscow. This chronology alone indicates that something existed in western culture and society to push printing forward that was not present in Russia. Even after printing did arrive in Russia, its development was slower and far more modest than in the West, at least until the eighteenth century, when Russian printing experienced something of a takeoff. Thus, although a number of Eisenstein's specific observations do have striking resonances in later Russian history, once printing finally did get going, technological determinism is not a useful general model for understanding Russian printing.[14]

Most of the other relevant literature, by contrast, has returned movable type and communications in general back to the broader outlines of cultural and social history; and, instead of placing special emphasis on technology, it has sought to link its evolution to the activities of specific social groups or institutions. One widely held position, for example, perceives the fate of communications as being dependent ultimately on the level of literacy and the contours of reading. According to this view, the interests of the reading public—whether it was an elite or mass public—had a controlling influence on what sorts of materials were printed, which ideas circulated successfully in Europe, and how the institutions of printing developed. This proposition is nowhere stated in so many words, but reflections of it can be found in a number of recent works. Robert Mandrou's study of French colporteurs and the broadsheets and pamphlets which they peddled in the provinces suggests a certain authenticity and spontaneity to their activities. They sold what people wanted to read; they informed their suppliers, who informed bookshops and presses, and so on down the line back to the point of publication. Ultimately, those publishers who satisfied these spontaneously expressed interests were rewarded monetarily.[15] Thus, the market system and the profit motive allowed readers to play a decisive role in the evolution of printing and books, and printing, for its part, introduced capitalism into cultural life.

Similar expressions of the power of readership can be found in several other recent monographs. Jeremy Popkin's study of right-wing journals during the French Revolution, for example, has shown that over the course of only a few years, the interests of subscribers, whether expressed in sales fluctuations or in letters to the editor, had a clear influence on the contents and ideological direction of the journals—more so than did the course of politics, the attitudes of the editors, or the demands of censorship.[16]

In a very different setting, Robert Altick's classic work, *The English Common Reader*, presents a similar if much more mediated and elongated image. The emergence of a mass reading public—i.e., the fact that a majority of Englishmen could read—slowly but inexorably forced those who oversaw cultural, political, and intellectual institutions to take note and respond.

> No longer were books and periodicals written chiefly for the comfortable few; more and more, as the century progressed, it was the ill-educated mass audience with pennies in its pocket that called the tune to which writers and editors danced.[17]

Thus Altick, like Mandrou and Popkin, concluded that the readership, whatever its size and social characteristics, could, through the system of the market for books, deeply influence the media, the role of printing in English society, and the contents of books.

Other scholars, however, have taken exception to this model of demand-pull. Social and literary theorists from the Frankfurt school in particular have suggested that the market and the rise of capitalism had a profoundly political character that ultimately requires shifting the emphasis from reading publics to the political powers who gained control of the media. Jürgen Habermas, for example, in his book *Strukturwandel der Öffentlichkeit*, argues that the notion of a self-conscious public arose with the emergence of the bourgeoisie as the leading class in civil society.[18] In precapitalist Europe, the communication of ideas took place in a smaller and more immediate set of relationships, in which there was little attempt to engage the interests of readers beyond those with whom one had direct contact. The emergence of the bourgeoisie, however, brought forth the expansion of an aggressive literate public and imposed market conditions on the flow of the printed word. Communications, therefore, became a more indirect and impersonal phenomenon.

The market economy did not bring about a free market of ideas, however. The bourgeoisie, as it gained control of the governmental apparatus, also took control of the communications mechanism to ensure that critical ideas did not gain broad circulation. In place of a true free market of ideas, the bourgeoisie substituted the myth of a "public" that collectively arbitrated the flow of ideas by the exercise of "public opinion." This "public," in Habermas's view, was nothing more than a universalized image of the bourgeoisie itself, and "public opinion" was merely the set of ideas that the articulate bourgeoisie chose to legitimize. Real social cleavages and conflicts, therefore, were obscured by this myth of a classless public, as the media became an effective instrument for inseminating false consciousness.[19]

In its specifics, Habermas's thesis has little applicability to eighteenth-century Russia, since Russia's bourgeoisie, if one can be said to have existed, was in no position to voice any collective expressions, much less to impose its will on society as a whole. The argument is further restricted by the fact that Russia, despite its economic backwardness, did have a self-conscious educated public, or *obshchestvo*, in the eighteenth century. At a more abstract level, however, much of what Habermas suggests about the role of power and the limits of the market has a good deal of relevance to the history of printing in Russia.

There is no doubt about the connection between the quest for power and influence in Russia on the one hand and the desire to control printing on the other. During most of the eighteenth century, lay printing was a governmental monopoly, and for much of that time Russia's rulers aggressively attempted to use the printing press to convey their own absolutist vision of politics and society to the entire populace. None of this activity, as we shall see, was carried out in response to market conditions or popular demand, a fact which demonstrates the need to look closely at who controlled the press before we conclude that publishers responded inexorably to the force of capital.

The government, it should be noted, was not alone in trying to press its views on Russian society in the eighteenth century. From the middle of the century onward, a self-conscious group of intellectuals, or literati, labored assiduously to transform their own newly acquired moral vision into the vision of all Russia.[20] These literati identified themselves in some way with the interests of the nation as a whole—"the fatherland"—and they saw themselves as being the conscience of the educated public and, for all practical purposes, the herald of public opinion. This tendency to identify themselves with an abstracted universal whole, while at the same time bemoaning the reluctance of flesh-and-blood readers to follow in their footsteps, is characteristic of many leading figures among the eighteenth-century literati, and it conforms rather well with what Habermas has described. If we accept the position of such historians as Marc Raeff and Andrzej Walicki, who have described the educated service gentry from which most of the literati emerged as something of a Russian functional equivalent of a middle class or third estate, largely because of their tendency to conflate their own ideals, doubts, and modernizing hopes with those of the entire nation, Habermas's argument looks all the more relevant.

What all of this tells us about printing, however, is not quite so clear. One could anticipate that the struggle for the attention of the Russian people would involve a struggle to control the media or to have access to them. Whoever controlled the media would be able to determine the composition of the books, pamphlets, and magazines that appeared and, to a certain extent, would be able to direct their dissemination. Both of these characteristics in fact are very prominent features of the history of printing in Russia. But there are clear drawbacks in expecting that the pursuit of power and influence can tell the whole story. During the course of the eighteenth century, control over the media passed through several hands and ended up largely under the purview of schools, merchants, and writers. Why should the state have given up its monopoly, and willingly at that, if the pursuit of power was the determining issue? Unless one is prepared to argue that these passages were a product of class struggle—hardly a promising approach to the relationships between state, schools, and service gentry—this behavior makes little sense from Habermas's perspective. What we discover, in fact, is that at some point the publishing system even in Russia does have to rely upon income from sales, and this reliance introduces—or reintroduces—publishers, booksellers, and readers as potential democratic influences on the course of publishing.

To a certain extent, the counterpoint of reader-centered and power-centered paradigms is a problem of research. Given sufficient evidence, one could presumably determine whether under specific circumstances popular taste, through its power of the purse, affected the direction of the press, or whether the universalizing masters of the media succeeded in imposing their own views on the readership as a whole.

In the final analysis, however, the issue remains primarily one of theory. Are the widespread dissemination and republication of a given title evidence of its popularity and the efficacy of spontaneous demand, or are they evidence of effective influence or manipulation from above? Clearly the answer need not rest with either of these sharp alternatives, since presumably influence and demand interacted at some level. In this context, those studies of dissemination that have focused less on the issue of political control and more on the question of intellectual aspirations for influence have been most instructive.

In their social and cultural role, printing and the institutions of communications function not as forces of democratic control but as elements of and even hostages to political power. A. S. Collins's two books on the life of letters in England, Edward Shils's essays on intellectuals contained in *The Intellectual and the Powers*, Lewis Coser's *Men of Ideas*, and Ian Watt's splendid book, *The Rise of the Novel*, see writers as struggling to play a leading role in determining what was written, what was printed, and how the media and the cultures of print developed.[21] For intellectuals, moreover, ideas and moral influence were at least as important as politics, profit, or technology. Access to printing was one means to those ends and, as a result, the study of printing could profitably be written as a history of the pursuit of intellectual standing and influence in modern society. Scholars of the Renaissance and Reformation, for example, have long understood that religious thinkers were greatly interested in taking advantage of printing as a means of spreading the word. Martin Luther's printing of hundreds of thousands of German bibles is the most prominent example of this phenomenon, but hardly the only one.[22] In more modern times, intellectuals have resorted to pamphlets and newspapers as a means of wedding ideas to the technology of mass media.

Yet intellectuals did not live in a vacuum. As relatively powerless individuals, they required the cooperation of the people who physically controlled the media—publishers, printers, and booksellers—and these people, more often than not, were in it for the money. Surely these middlemen had a hand in determining whose works were published and whose were sold. According to Robert Darnton, who has discussed publishers and traders in numerous articles and books, the contribution of these middlemen was, in fact, decisive.

The sociologists and quantifiers have demonstrated the importance of interpreting the Old Regime's literary culture in more than merely literary terms. Books have a social life and an economic value. All the aspects of their existence—literary, social, economic, and even political—came together with the greatest force in the publishing history of the eighteenth century. So sociocultural history . . . might gain a great deal from the study of publishers.[23]

Darnton's exposition is especially interesting in its vivid evocation of the underworld of pirate publishers of the *Encyclopédie* and other works and of the world of Grub Street, in which the lines between high-minded intellectuals, hacks, literary panderers, and profiteers were utterly obliterated. In the process, it brings out the importance of what might be termed the network, or infrastructure, of communications. Merchants, printers, hack writers—all rather unremarkable and obscure people—come to life in Darnton's work as major influences in the history of printed communications, yet among these groups the publishers and printers had the clearest perception of what the people wanted, what would sell, and what needed to be written. It was the publishers, therefore, who could set the terms for what would be printed and what would not.[24]

Darnton's work makes a compelling case for paying attention to publishers and booksellers not only in western Europe but anywhere that printing has appeared. But his specific argument, like so many others, does not fare so well when it is transplanted to Russian soil. Darnton's Swiss and French publishers, after all, were economically sensitive to the market for literature, and they had the means, experience, and contacts that allowed them to mobilize their presses, capital, and writers for profit maximization. But most of Russia's publishers could hardly be characterized as capitalists, since they expended little effort to uncover or develop markets for books until the middle of the eighteenth century. Still, all but the most official institutional presses were obliged to make their own way financially, and this requirement led them to search for means of increasing their income. This search set in motion a process that resulted in the emergence of a small but active corps of publishers for profit in the 1780s.

Profits, then, were very much an issue for Russian publishing, but rather than presupposing that publishers possessed an a priori knowledge of or interest in what the market looked like, as Darnton assumes for France, we need to explain the evolution of that consciousness as part of the historical narrative. What were the specific steps that led publishers from merely balancing the books by financial conservatism in the 1720s and 1730s to raising revenue by responding to the market in the 1780s? Insofar as they were successful at this, moreover, what were the consequences for the relationships between readers and publishers, readers and writers, and books and society?

This brief sojourn into the literature clearly has not yielded a ready-made heuristic structure on which to drape the history of Russian printing. If anything, it has highlighted the extent to which the cultural and social context that historians of Western printing tend to take for granted simply did not exist in Russia. But, as has been noted in a cursory fashion, some of the characteristic interactions between printing and society in the West that have been posited in this literature do appear in eighteenth-century Russia. Thus, from these various arguments it is possible to anticipate probable points of contact between eighteenth-century printing and other transformations that were taking place in Russian society. In particular, they suggest that the circumstances in which the technological properties of printing took on a cultural and social form involved the interplay of an ideologically aggressive officialdom, the broadening of literacy, the emergence in midcentury of a corps of self-conscious literati, the changing structure of the economy for books, and the penetration of merchant capital into publishing and bookselling from the 1760s onward. All of this took place in a culture in which literacy and reading remained highly exceptional and in which the struggle for the attention of the Russian public was directed and largely waged at the top of society, among the relatively small educated elites residing in Moscow and St. Petersburg. One could, of course, make similar statements about other cultures in the eighteenth century, but the geographic and social centralization of leisure lay culture was far more extreme in Russia than it was elsewhere in Europe.

This study, then, begins with the premise that the pursuit of an effective public voice by political, religious, and literary elites became synonymous with the struggle to create, to control, or to have access to the printed media. To a large extent, publishing became the lens through which the separate elites viewed the broader society. As a consequence, their separate confrontations with printing or publishing had a profound impact upon how these elites related to each other and to Russian society in general. I would argue, therefore, that the unfolding dialectic between elites and publishing—and, by extension, between elites and literate society—established the institutional parameters for the evolution of Russian intellectual life as a whole in the eighteenth century, and it is in this area, consequently, where the primary significance of eighteenth-century Russian printing lay.

Before beginning the actual narrative, it may be helpful to say a few words about the sources upon which this study relies. The eighteenth century is an ideal period for the study of Russian publishing, in large measure thanks to the excellent materials available on it. In spite of the expansion and growing pluralism of the publishing system, the century as a whole saw only about ten thousand titles in print; the system was thus small enough to describe comprehensively, yet large enough to make the inner history of printing meaningful to broader social and cultural developments. Soviet bibliographers have succeeded in compiling an array of marvelous catalogues of eighteenth-century Russian books, led by the multivolume *Union Catalogue of Russian Books in the Civil Orthography in the Eighteenth Century, 1725–1800.*[25] These catalogues include all or nearly all books printed in Russian or Church Slavonic in the eighteenth century as well as extensive commentary on print runs, publishers, censorship, textual variations, and patronage. As far as I know, there exists no catalogue for any other country that combines the comprehensiveness and attention to detail of these materials.

Not surprisingly, the availability of such first-rate reference materials has attracted a great deal of recent literary and archival research to eighteenth-century books, which over the past two decades has greatly expanded our fund of basic information on the history of publishing. One aspect of this research has been an extensive mapping of holdings of major archival collections by the Academy of Sciences chancellery, the chancellery of the Holy Synod of the Russian Orthodox Church, and the Public School Commission, without which foreign specialists could not even hope to conduct their own research in archival sources. Advantages such as these made possible the writing of a book with a wide topical and chronological scope.

I make no pretense, however, to having exhausted the archival records for this book. In places, I have turned to certain previously unexamined or little-used documents, such as booksellers' catalogues and various bookshop orders and business reports, but more frequently I have reexamined documents that other scholars have unearthed. Even this overlay of new and newly reconsidered sources cannot be considered complete, however, as is made clear by the continued outpouring of new information from well-known but incompletely digested collections, such as the seemingly unlimited records of the Academy chancellery and entirely new documentary collections. Thus, A. A. Zaitseva's recent research in the tax records of the St. Petersburg merchantry has augmented and substantially revised our knowledge of the bookselling establishment in the 1790s, and Moscow University's recent preliminary volume of printed material from its archaeographic surveys of various villages promises to have a profound impact upon current notions of provincial book culture and popular culture in the eighteenth and nineteenth centuries (see chapters 6 and 7). This book, then, is essentially a first attempt to give a coherent assessment of what has been learned to date and to bridge the gap between book history and history in general.

ONE

Printing and the Petrine Revolution

MODERN RUSSIAN INTELLECTUAL LIFE, so the consensus has it, began with Peter the Great. As a corollary to that maxim, one might profitably suggest that Peter's accession also transformed printing into a significant aspect of life in Russia. During his reign, the number of printed titles burgeoned from about six a year in the second half of the seventeenth century to nearly fifty a year in the early 1720s, and the number of Russian or Church Slavonic presses* grew from three in late Muscovite Russia to ten in operation at various times in Peter's reign.[1] All of the new presses, moreover, were placed under the direct control of the government rather than under that of the church. Not surprisingly, therefore, the topical composition of books shifted as well—and quite abruptly—away from works of faith and prayer and toward works with more secular concerns.

On the surface, these transitions seem to point to a precipitous decline in the status of the church and devotional publishing and a corresponding rise in the importance of the state and civic affairs. But before we can accept at face value what appears to be a sweeping cultural transformation, we need to examine the particular character of Petrine publishing more deeply. Changes of this magnitude required the active involvement of the tsar, the acquiescence of the church, and the cooperation of the people who produced and distributed the new books and, to some degree, of those who read them. In addition, they cost a great deal of money to bring about. The questions, then, are: Why did such dramatic changes take place, and, secondly, what were their effects on Russian culture?

Most scholars, plausibly enough, have placed the primary responsibility squarely on the shoulders of Peter himself. In the most recent study of Petrine printing, for example, S. P. Luppov, the leading authority on the eighteenth-century Russian book, has suggested that the transformation of printing was one important feature of a more general modernization of society and politics which, although it began earlier, gained rapid momentum under Peter. Peter's insistence upon new schools,

---

* The word "press" here, and throughout the text, refers to a publishing operation or publishing house, rather than to the physical machine that prints books. When it is necessary to make the distinction, the latter will be referred to as a "printing press."

new technologies, curricular advances, greater foreign contacts, and the growth of enlightenment came together to give printing a greater role in Russian society. In particular, the creation of primary and secondary schools throughout the empire, although motivated by narrowly practical considerations, did increase literacy, expand the popular interest in both utilitarian and general knowledge, and thereby increase the demand for printed books.[2]

One can discern in this pattern the emerging outline of some sort of structure that was initiated and largely controlled by Peter himself. Rather than being a one-sided reflection of the tsar's will, however, the publishing system, in Luppov's view, managed to establish a symbiosis in which the interests of the state as the producer of the printed word and those of the society as the consumer somehow coalesced around a shared rejection of religious superstition and an interest in modernity and secular affairs. It was this symbiosis that prepared the ground for the subsequent flowering of Russian printing.[3]

Luppov's thesis, if one may call it that, clearly succeeds in integrating printing into a broader context of political innovation, educational reform, and social change. And while it treats the emperor as the major domo of publishing, it eschews an overemphasis on Peter's role in favor of a more modulated picture of interaction between state and society. It achieves all this, moreover, with a wealth of newly uncovered and carefully studied evidence.

The image of a successful adaptation of secular printing to Russian society is not without its difficulties, however. It depends, first of all, on an overly optimistic characterization of reading in Russia, in that it presumes widespread literacy and a demand for secular books that cut across geographic and social boundaries. It fails to explain why, if the Petrine system was so successful and progressive, the secular printing network faced near-collapse and bankruptcy upon his death. Why, moreover, did those in charge of the presses subsequently choose to abandon the essential premises of Peter's printing system and, in essence, start over on a different institutional footing once Peter died? Why, finally, if secularization took such firm root in the society, did the religious presses fare so much better financially than the state presses did?

All of these questions suggest a rather different experience for printing than the one which Luppov and most other contemporary scholars have described. In fact, a review of the entire publishing network from the seventeenth century onward reveals that the social, cultural, and institutional bases for such a dramatic rise in secular publishing were quite limited and, consequently, that the impact of Peter's reform was far more muted than Luppov and others generally assert.

THE SEVENTEENTH-CENTURY BACKGROUND

When Peter came to power in 1689, he inherited a small church-controlled printing system which had had only an episodic impact on Russian culture.[4] Between the late 1550s, when printing first came to Muscovy, and the end of the seventeenth century, Muscovite authorities had established only one major publishing house (*pechatnyi dvor*) in Moscow, and a handful of small presses in monasteries on the western borderlands.[5] According to the most recent published estimates, these presses collectively printed fewer than 500 titles during the entire seventeenth century, most of which came out in moderate print runs of 1,200 or 2,400 copies.[6]

In spite of the appearance of occasional secular publications, such as alphabet books (*azbuki*) and the *Ulozhenie*, or Legal Code, of 1649, more than 95 percent of the printed titles were devotional, mostly prayer books, catechisms, psalters, and sermons.[7] Although our knowledge of the dimensions of reading and literacy in the seventeenth century is extremely limited, it is clear that a much wider range of literature was read than was printed. Such ancient methods of reproduction as hand copying and woodblock printing were widespread and thriving, and they accounted almost entirely for the circulation of fables, song sheets, religious poetry, a great many prayer books, and the entire corpus of Old Believer literature.[8] Printing was in practical terms an exclusive instrument of institutions of the official church and, to a limited degree, the state. All other voices, whether competing or complementary, had to resort to hand copying. A dawning secularization of printing, in other words, was simply not in evidence.

Still, printing was not without its place in Muscovite society. Certain selected titles, including corrected prayer books, psalters, and alphabet books, were published in very large print runs, running into tens and perhaps hundreds of thousands, far larger than what hand copying could produce. To the extent that these books circulated in Muscovite society—a subject that remains largely unexamined—they brought to life some of the most powerful capabilities of movable type, mostly in the service of a militantly reformist Orthodox church.

In the first half of the seventeenth century, to give one illustrious example, the endeavor to compose uniform and authorized editions of printed prayer books unleashed a long-simmering debate within the church over whether an authoritative and corrected text required a return to the Greek originals, as Patriarch Nikon maintained, or whether a proper Slavonic edition could be fashioned from the extant manuscript translations, as the Zealots of Faith insisted. This struggle involved far more than the question of editorial accuracy, as it brought to the surface all the crosscurrents within the church over the autonomy of the Russian church, the relationship with Byzantium, and the sanctity of traditional Slavonic forms of prayer. To both sides, the fate of the Russian church would be resolved around the formulation of the prayer books. When Nikon won, he was in a position to set the course for the new editions and, through them, for the exact language of worship. Nikon, in fact, was very energetic in printing thousands of copies of the new texts and circulating them to the monasteries and parishes, where they were read aloud. The presses of the Orthodox church thereby extended the debates concerning the correction of texts into a general popular controversy that soon precipitated a tumultuous, violent schism within the church. Thus, in this episode, the technological capacity of movable type to produce uniform editions contributed to turning the long-standing controversy over discrepancies in texts into a major struggle, and its ability to produce them in abundance became a powerful tool for the official church, which used it to force abrupt changes and so contributed to popular awareness of the changed texts and, inadvertently, galvanized resistance to them.[9]

By contrast, the government of Muscovy took rather little heed of printing. There is some evidence, to be sure, of an effort to circulate the *Ulozhenie* of 1649 among various segments of the population, but that was exceptional.[10] Most decrees were not printed at all, and, with few exceptions, the civil authorities saw little purpose in using movable type to communicate regularly with the population.

PETER'S REFORMS

Peter, of course, set about to change all of this, and on the advice of such trusted correspondents as Gottfried von Leibnitz, he embarked on an aggressive reorganization of printing in Russia.[11] During his travels in western Europe during 1698, for example, he hired several Dutch printers and merchants, including Jan von Thessing, to establish Russian presses in Amsterdam for publishing maps, charts, and books on technical subjects.[12] Although these initial efforts produced very few publications, they led to the enlistment of several established printers into the service of the Russian government, most notably Ilia Kopievskii, an elusive figure who worked for Peter in Amsterdam, Danzig, and Moscow before disappearing in 1709. Peter also hired two other printers of note: Fedor Polikarpov, a graduate of the Likud brothers' typographical school in Moscow, who directed the *pechatnyi dvor* through most of Peter's reign, and V. A. Kiprianov, who became Moscow's leading cartographer and book merchant during the reign.[13]

Peter's program called for more than talented individuals, however. As part of his administrative reforms, he founded several new institutional publishing houses, including the St. Petersburg Press in 1711, which soon became the leading organ of the government in the new capital; the senate presses in both Moscow and St. Petersburg in 1719; and a new naval academy press in 1721 to print schoolbooks and books on naval science. In addition, the old *pechatnyi dvor*, which at some point came to be called simply the "Moscow Press" (Moskovskaia tipografiia), gained several new printing presses and employees.[14]

Each of these new presses came into being directly because of Peter's orders, and all of the new institutional presses were intended primarily for governmental use. Certainly the church had easy access to the Moscow and St. Petersburg presses, but the demands of the state came first. Even the single new monastic press, established at the Alexander Nevksii Monastery outside St. Petersburg in 1719, came into being largely to serve as an organ of one of Peter's leading ideological supporters, Archbishop Feofan Prokopovich.[15]

Another aspect of this secularization in the service of the state was the introduction of the new civil orthography in 1707. Peter believed that the old orthography was too archaic to allow for an easy rendering of new technical or educational books. The publication of modern knowledge required something simpler, more latinized, and with fewer obscure vowels and notations. By law, therefore, all secular books were thenceforth to be set in the new type, while books of faith would continue to use the old orthography. Thus, type itself was introduced as a visible symbol of statism and, more specifically, of the separation between the government's publishing program and the church's.

In practice, however, matters were more muddled, since it took the publishing houses several years to acquire enough new printing presses and type fonts to complete the transition. Between 1707 and 1725, fully a third of the titles printed in the old orthography were secular books or laws and notices initiated by the state. Conversely, some of the books that came out in the new orthography were religious. As the governmental publishing houses acquired more presses, they gradually abandoned the old type, so that by the early 1720s the vast majority of governmental publications did employ the new orthography. The church, by contrast, had only limited access to the new materials, and its publications consequently did not undergo significant orthographic revision.[16] The point, however, is that a strict orthographic differentiation of secular and religious books took place only at the very end of Peter's reign. Thus, the secularizing effects of Peter's reform of the alphabet, if indeed there were any effects, could have appeared only after his death.

Paradoxically, the rigid state control probably limited printing's ability to act as an agent of secular or at least lay culture, since Peter denied access to any but the most highly placed individuals within the church and officialdom. Spontaneous expressions from Russian society simply had no place in this universe. Even Kiprianov, the only private publisher of the Petrine era, required a special privilege to operate his press, and even then he printed exclusively what the government ordered.

The formal lines of authority through which both new and old presses functioned further underscored the primacy of official business. In 1701, Peter placed all Russian presses, formerly directed rather loosely by the Department of Printing (*Prikaz knigopechataniia*), under the newly revived Department of Monasteries (*Monastyrskii prikaz*) and its chairman, Ivan Musin-Pushkin.[17] As a civil office, the Department of Monasteries brought all publishing, including monastic, directly under civil control, a control that continued after the Department of Monasteries was merged into the Holy Synod in 1722.[18]

Structuring and revitalizing the press in so centralized and hierarchical a manner suited Peter in numerous personal and political ways. It permitted him to play an intimate role in nearly every aspect of book printing. The increased printing capacity gave him the potential to issue as many copies of as many books as he chose. By making Musin-Pushkin directly and personally responsible for overseeing printing, moreover, Peter was ensuring that a loyal and trusted friend would be in charge, and through Musin-Pushkin he could exercise control over how each press functioned editorially.

Peter's personal involvement in publishing went well beyond consultation and ordering that new presses be established. He oversaw translations, contracted with printers, approved copy, and demanded periodic progress reports from publishing houses.[19] Typical of the intensity of Peter's involvement is the following letter, sent to Musin-Pushkin on January 4, 1709:

I received your letter with the books by Rimpler and Borgsdorf and the [new civil] alphabet.[20] But the imprints in these books came out poorly compared with previous ones, neither clearly nor fully formed; in this [matter] it is incumbent upon you to see to it . . . that they be published well. . . . Also, . . . the binding on those books [which you] recently sent is done hurriedly, not very cleanly. . . . Also, make sure that the geometry book and the other one by Borgsdorf are hurried along;[21] but with the Kirghorn drafts, I have not ordered them to hurry, but to engrave them carefully. Fifteen hundred or two thousand of the calendars arrived here. . . . Two thirds [of them] should appear in semiquire so that officers can enter their affairs for each day in them and so that people to whom they are sold [can] too (they will buy them willingly). I have ordered that they be sold in Moscow and throughout (other) cities.[22]

Two weeks later, on January 19, Peter sent another letter to Musin-Pushkin:

I am sending a book on Swedish military law that I have ordered published in octavo, but first it must be corrected. In some places it has been very poorly translated and in some places there is some very coarse speech. In addition, I am sending a history of Troy which also should be published (it is not necessary to reedit it).[23] . . . When the geometry book is completed publish 200 [copies] of it and, as I have directed, do not sell it, but send ten or fifteen [copies] here. Also, publish 300 or 400 of those architecture books,[24] as were sent out to Mister Gagarin and, as I have directed, do not sell them, but send ten or fifteen of them here.[25]

As this correspondence makes clear, every aspect of the operation, from the selection of books for publication to editing and distribution, came under the personal scrutiny of the tsar. It is difficult to imagine his being more involved short of operating the presses himself. His interest is even more impressive when we realize that, when he wrote the letters quoted above, Peter was in Voronezh to oversee the reconstruction of his fleet for the battle of Poltava.

Such direct participation, in addition to satisfying Peter's fancy to do everything himself, reflected his determination to use the press as a tool of reform and as a means of getting his message out in a manner that could reach any conceivable audience. In the seventeenth century, official publications had been limited to only the most important new laws, and print runs were rather low.[26] Thus, the communication of information from the government to the nation had normally depended on public announcements or on the circulation of hand-copied versions. Under Peter, however, hundreds of laws and notices came out in print runs that often ran well into the thousands. By the latter part of his reign, laws and notices were appearing at a rate that exceeded one printing a week. The government then disseminated them (or at least attempted to) at little or no cost, posted them in public places, and ordered the parish clergy and local officials to read them aloud. In theory, therefore, the entire population could read or hear official pronouncements about as often as they heard prayers.

To understand fully what it meant to Russian society to receive the word of the state in such a continuous fashion requires a better understanding of the actual communication of the laws and of popular culture than currently exists. In light of the haphazard education of the parish clergy and its lack of familiarity with the new orthography, it is not even certain, for example, that local priests were capable of transmitting the laws. But some points are clear enough. Peter had come up with a use of printing that, if properly executed, would obliterate the barriers between literacy and illiteracy and between the capital and the nation. In principle, everyone could now know the will of the tsar and the state, everyone could now see an official copy with the tsar's seal, and everyone could hear the tsar's words. One might plausibly hypothesize that Peter's new policy engendered in the populace a clearer vision of the connection between the (mostly disagreeable) changes that they were experiencing and the will of the tsar. At any rate, it most certainly brought the voice of the state to the provinces with an intensity that hitherto only the church had achieved. To that extent, it was a powerful instrument of secularization.

THE REPERTOIRE OF PETRINE BOOKS

Here, then, was Peter's design: The emperor would take over printing, expand it, and use it to circulate whatever useful information he wanted, to whomever he wanted, in whatever quantities he wanted, and on whatever terms he chose. As a result, Peter's will simply dominated the output of the presses. Between 1708 and January 1725, official pronouncements accounted for approximately 60 percent of all published titles (see table 1.1).[27] The tremendous print runs of many of these pronouncements suggest that they accounted for an even higher percentage of the total volume of printed material.

As emperor, Peter could, and often did, order that the government disseminate publications either to a particular audience or throughout the society. Circulating the word of the state was intended as more than a simple informational service, however, for it soon came to serve

TABLE 1.1
Subject Composition of Russian-Language Publications,
1700–January 1725

Subject	Number of Publications	Percentage of All Publications
Laws, manifestoes, and regulations	581	44
Official information and notices	192	14.6
Religion	308	23.5
Military affairs (excluding laws and regulations)	104	7.9
Calendars	24	1.8
Vedomosti	24	1.8
Alphabet, grammar, and language	22	1.7
History and geography	33	1.5
Technology and science	14	1.1
Secular philosophy	7	0.5
Belles-lettres	3	0.2
Total	1,312	99.9

SOURCES: Derived from data in Bykova and Gurevich, *Opisanie izdanii napechatannykh kirillitsei*, *Opisanie izdanii grazhdanskoi pechati*, and *Opisanie izdanii napechatannykh pri Petre I*; and Zernova, *Svodnyi katalog kirillovskoi pechati*.

an unmistakable ideological function as well. Peter was hardly the first Russian ruler to see the importance of explaining the virtue and necessity of obedience in the face of unpleasant changes, but the expression and distribution of that message did change quite dramatically in his reign.

Most significant, of course, was the change in the ideology itself. Peter was now the emperor, instead of simply the tsar, as well as the first servant of the state. Obedience, therefore, took on a more statist and hence a more secular cast, not an easy notion for people who were raised believing in the "holy tsar."[28] Obviously, the broad circulation of laws and public notices gave the new basis of authority some immediate and concrete meaning, but the laws and regulations could hardly legitimate themselves. Such legitimation had to come from other, more traditional and respected sources of authority, such as icons, panegyrics, propaganda, theological tracts, and sermons, all of which depended on wide circulation to be effective.

Official propaganda in Peter's time emphasized both the majesty of Peter and the greatness of the state, in particular its military greatness. The glory of military victory appeared in various media during Peter's reign: public spectacles, numerous displays of fireworks, sermons, prayers, special medallions, triumphal marches, etc. Nearly all of it was reflected in print, occasionally—according to fragmentary sources—in very large print runs. Fifty-five descriptions of fireworks, for example, were published in Peter's reign, most of them with elaborate copper engravings which depicted the scene and the event being celebrated for those who could not read.[29] Peter acknowledged a personal penchant for such celebrations, his explanation being that they accustomed people to the sounds and sights of guns and artillery.[30] But no one could miss the fact that fireworks displays and fireworks literature nearly always celebrated the state or the imperial family.

Military victories and treaties were extolled in print in other ways as well. The Treaty of Nystadt, for example, went through several printings in 1721 alone, and in 1722 Peter commissioned his famous official history of the Northern War and ordered a print run of 20,000.[31]

These celebrations of victory implicitly demonstrated that the manifest glory of the state bore witness to the rightness of obedience to it, and this implicit message was then made explicit in the many sermons, theological tracts, prayers of thanks to victory, and pictures from iconographic engravings that Peter had published.[32] Certainly not all of these publications received extravagant print runs; figures vary from a few dozen for prayers of thanksgiving for victory to over 22,000 copies for Archbishop Feofan Prokopovich's famous tract of political legitimation, *The Right of the Monarch's Will*.[33] Nevertheless, the reign as a whole saw the publication of about seventy religious titles that celebrated some aspect of imperial greatness and many of which spoke of a path to grace that required obedience to the authority of the emperor and, through him, the state.

Respect for authority also was a prominent theme in the closest thing to a mass-circulation volume which Petrine Russia offered: the alphabet books, of which there were at least four St. Petersburg editions, with a total print run that exceeded 3,000, and eighteen Moscow printings between 1700 and 1725, with a collective print run of about 150,000 copies.[34] But these are more appropriately referred to as pamphlets than books. The longest of them ran to only nineteen pages, only eleven of which had words on them, all in very large type. They usually were unbound and were sold for only three kopeks. Their primary function was to teach the new orthography and arabic numerals by listing side by side the old and the new forms. But in order to illustrate the letters, they used a mnemonic device that gave short phrases after each letter which, as Max Okenfuss has pointed out, expressed in simple and clear language the virtues of faith, piety, obedience, and respect for the tsar.[35]

Obedience and loyalty, of course, were the least that Peter demanded from his subjects. From those groups and individuals with aspirations to power or high position he demanded a good deal more: tireless and technically up-to-date service; adaptation to European customs and institutions; and a willingness to accept education. In his usual less-than-delicate manner, Peter inundated these favored groups with a flood of publications—newspapers; technical and training manuals; textbooks on law, history, grammar, and foreign languages for secondary schools; and primers—which he expected them to read and understand.[36]

Peter's idea of a newspaper, the periodical *Vedomosti* (1702–27),[37] was more a perpetual celebration of governmental authority and military glory than a newspaper in any modern sense, since it contained little more than carefully selected and edited official documents, such as announcements of the arrival and departure of merchant ships and trading delegations, recent commercial agreements between Russia and its neighbors, and news of foreign affairs and wars in particular.[38] Peter envisioned that *Vedomosti* would be an organ of information on the current events about which his newly educated servitors ought to be apprised. Thus, official notices would be sent "from various states and cities to the . . . Department of Foreign Affairs and other departments, from [them] . . . to the Department of Publishing and then . . . these bulletins [would be published] in the press . . . and [Russia would] sell them to the world at an appropriate price."[39] He hoped in this way to circulate details "of wars and other matters which would be suitable for notification to the people of Muscovy and surrounding states."[40] To ensure a steady flow of foreign information into Russia, moreover, Peter assigned several translators from the College of Foreign Affairs to work full-time as translators for *Vedomosti*.[41]

Vedomosti also offered narratives of recent events that demonstrated the military might of the Petrine system. News of victories in the wars against Sweden and Turkey and general praise of the Russian army appeared with great regularity, but news of losses or of ineffectiveness in the army did not. The onset of the Bulavin revolt was not reported, for example, but the suppression of it was.[42]

While the intended readership of *Vedomosti* was not clear, certain facts about its printing and circulation can be determined. It was printed an average of thirty-five times a year in its first five years, with average print runs of between 2,000 and 4,000 copies.[43] Whether all these early issues were actually sold is unclear, but Peter's ignorance of and disinterest in even the most elementary marketing techniques, such as selling subscriptions or setting low prices, suggest that he had no concept of what the appropriate size of an edition would be.[44] Evidence from later years suggests that the actual readership was quite a bit smaller than Peter's initial expectations. Between 1708 and 1712, an average of only fourteen issues per year was published; between 1713 and 1717, seven per year; and in 1718, only one issue appeared.[45] Print runs dropped as well to a few hundred copies per issue in the middle years of Peter's reign and to less than a hundred at its end.[46] What few sales figures are available, for the periods from 1708 to 1709 and from 1711 to 1713, confirm both the modest size of the readership and its gradual decline.[47]

Some issues, to be sure, sold well over half of the copies printed, but several others sold much less. In absolute terms also, sales figures varied a great deal. In 1709, for example, issue no. 8 had a print run of 150 and sold 23 copies, yet issue no. 11 in the same year was printed in 2,500 copies and sold 1,328. The variable, in that year, seems to have been the contents: the best-selling editions of *Vedomosti* in 1709 wrote at length about the victory at Poltava, while the others had no news of consequence. Peter, however, wasn't interested in popular or market definitions of news, and in spite of occasional big sellers, the percentage of copies sold declined steadily from 62 percent in 1708 to 39 percent in 1712 (table 1.2). On a number of occasions, Peter ordered that unsold copies of *Vedomosti* be distributed gratis, but over time even this circulation diminished. After a number of years, consequently, thousands of unused copies of *Vedomosti* had accumulated.

These figures present a clear, if rather bleak, picture. Print runs declined sharply, but sales declined even more sharply, aside from the two anomalous issues printed in 1709 (see note to table 1.2). Thus, one is drawn to the conclusion that not many people shared Peter's sense of what was newsworthy. Not until print runs had fallen to 100 copies per issue around 1720 was some stability reached. At that level, the frequency with which *Vedomosti* appeared was able to make something of a comeback, reaching nearly forty issues a year in the early 1720s.

Even at forty issues a year, however, the circulation of Peter's newspaper was meager by comparison to the European press of his day. In England, for example, nine newspapers, each of which came out between two and six times a week, accounted for sales of about 44,000

TABLE 1.2
Printings and Distributions of *Vedomosti*, 1708–12

	Total Printed	Average Print Run	Average Sold	Average Given Away	Average Total Distributed
1708	6,098	407	254 (62%)	101 (25%)	355 (87%)
1709ᵃ	10,501	875	504 (58%)	223 (25%)	727 (83%)
1711	3,329	471	267 (57%)	26 (6%)	293 (63%)
1712	1,844	205	80 (39%)	17 (8%)	97 (47%)

SOURCE: *Vedomost: vremeni Petra velikogo*, pp. 79–84.

ᵃ The unusually large figures for 1709 derive entirely from the two special issues describing the victories at Poltava. Each of these had print runs of nearly 3,000, over half of which were sold. Discounting these issues because of the unique circumstances involved, one arrives at figures which resemble the norm much more closely: total printed, 4,475; average print run, 447; average sold, 240 (54%); average given away, 177 (40%); average total distributed, 417 (94%).

copies a week in 1704.[48] The difference between that and *Vedomosti*'s 100 copies a week speaks eloquently of the ineffectiveness of *Vedomosti* as a news organ or as an instrument of cultural reform and, by implication, of the limitations of Peter's command-based approach to publishing.

When Peter made more of an effort to target his printing to a particular clientele, however, his record looks a bit better. Thus, his technical books were printed mostly for a military or scholastic audience, an objective which is reflected both in the books' contents and in their relatively modest print runs. The contents of the technical books were largely military: general signals, military and naval science, military fortifications, and mathematics, virtually all of which was translated or adapted from foreign sources. With the exception of field manuals, which were given extensive print runs and distributed at no cost, these books tended to come out in print runs of a few hundred to a thousand. In other words, they closely approximated the size of the populations to which they were directed.[49]

Similar circumstances marked the printing of school texts. Mostly translated, they had moderate print runs and were sold through the few existing institutional book shops to students, and only infrequently to the general public. Most of these books taught specific skills— geometry, algebra, grammar, and the like. But some, such as Pufendorf's *Introduction to European History*, which was used in courses in the Naval Academy, or Quintius Curtius's *Life of Alexander the*

Great, taught students about the traditions of the European world in which they were now expected to function and presented heroic examples which they were supposed to emulate.[50]

Even more explicit attempts to create modern citizens came from the primers, of which *Iunosti chestnoe zertsalo* (A Mirror of Honor for Youth) was by far the most vigorous. This book, which came out four times during Peter's reign with total print runs of about 2,000 copies, has received a great deal of attention recently from scholars who see it as an important pedagogical or socializing text for students in the state-run primary schools and technical academies. Although only thirty-one pages long, it included a complete copy of the basic Petrine alphabet book, a set of specific rules of proper behavior and etiquette, such as showing respect for one's elders and not spitting in public, and lessons teaching humility before the tsar and the different forms of behavior appropriate to gentry and servants.[51]

Books such as these were intended to ease the transition from the old world of holy tsar, *zemskii sobor*, and the *Domostroi* to the new world of the emperor, table of ranks, and civic virtue, or at least to give it a wider meaning. Of course, the old world, as several scholars have recently demonstrated, was already on its way out well before Peter's accession, but the changes in everyday life, in behavior, and in technical training were nevertheless startling and, from the serving men's point of view, abrupt. All these new acculturating books, therefore, appeared as agents of change rather than as reinforcements of tradition. Similarly, the state's ceaseless bombardment of its servitors with new information, from the laws to technical manuals, was, in volume alone, something entirely new. Little wonder, then, that Peter put a high premium on the ability to read, without which a servitor could not hope to keep afloat in the sea of paper.

None of these books was intended as an alternative or successor to the Orthodox religion, however. Despite his dislike of traditional ceremonies and his infamous mockeries of the church hierarchy, such as the Most Drunken Synod; despite the highly visible symbols of statism and this-worldly affairs, such as the Neptune Society and Peter's donning military uniforms rather than sacred vestments; and despite the aggressive campaign to introduce the civil orthography, Peter was a believer who profoundly and quite openly looked to the church for support. Church officials like Feofan Prokopovich provided important sources of legitimation, and they had to be permitted to spread the word of God as well as the word of the state. Peter also depended upon the church to provide him with a ready-made communication and distribution network as well as press workers (graduates of the

Likud brothers' typographical school) and to continue to act de facto as the empire's most effective and extensive school system. But Peter also recognized that the church's primary obligation was to minister to the laity.[52]

Not surprisingly, therefore, religious, mostly devotional, publishing remained the single most important facet of printed culture during Peter's reign. Church books comprised almost a quarter of all published titles (see table 1.1) and over 40 percent of all books. These percentages do represent a sharp decline from the near monopoly which church books enjoyed in the seventeenth century, but that comparison is misleading, since far more religious titles came out under Peter—about twelve a year—than at any time in the seventeenth century.[53] Many nominally secular titles, moreover, such as grammars, alphabet books, and calendars contained such items as lists of saint's days, moral lessons on piety and faith, and daily or weekly devotional prayers.

In addition, devotional works often had large print runs, especially those books published in monastic presses or the Moscow Press. Books of Hours, Books of Months, and psalters regularly came out in print runs of 2,000 to 15,000. Special prayers, such as those for blessing newly built churches, came out in runs of over 10,000, and a book of lessons and sermons for priests' children came out in a print run of 17,000 copies.[54] Consequently, at the level of production, religious literature thrived under Peter.

THE CIRCULATION OF BOOKS

But what about at the level of dissemination and reading? Prerevolutionary scholars such as Pekarskii and Gavrilov tended to draw rather deprecatory conclusions concerning the circulation of Petrine books, but contemporary Soviet specialists see things differently.[55] Luppov argues, for example, that Peter did succeed in circulating secular books, despite numerous financial and organizational problems, in part because he was prepared to give thousands of volumes away, but more fundamentally because his new secular books corresponded to the needs and interests of his literate nonclerical subjects.[56]

> As we already know, the seventeenth-century book received wide circulation among various groups of the Russian population. What, then, was new in this regard in the eighteenth century? . . . The basic feature of the Petrine era in comparison with previous periods is connected with the fact that the secular books, of which

31

there were few even in the second half of the seventeenth century, had an especially wide circulation. Another feature of the Petrine era consisted of the fact that in that period the number of lay book owners significantly increased.[57]

To support this position, Luppov and several other Soviet scholars have produced and synthesized a wide array of numerical and qualitative evidence which appears to show an extensive circulation network, relatively high sales for certain secular books, and a broad-based popular receptivity to these new books.[58] But their interpretation of the numerical sources, which they concede are riddled with gaps, unexplained discrepancies, and questionable bookkeeping methods, is highly problematic. Too often these difficulties have been disregarded or have been resolved only through employing several broad and often dubious assumptions.

Beyond the numbers, however, there are questions concerning the process of distribution. Luppov believes that secular books found their way to readers from all social groups and throughout the empire. But the evidence for this position is quite thin; much of it is episodic, coming from occasional references in letters and petitions. As a consequence, we cannot completely rely on him for information about the mediating steps from printing to reading or what one might call the infrastructure of publishing.

What, then, were the best sellers of the Petrine era? Unfortunately, reliable sales figures for the Petrine era (or for the entire eighteenth century, for that matter) are difficult to come by. The major publishing houses occasionally put together inventories of stocks on hand, and by comparing what remained with original print runs—when such figures are available—scholars have come up with what might be termed "stock depletion figures." But what do such figures mean? Certainly, they cannot be taken as sales indices, since too many volumes were distributed at no cost to captive markets, or left the presses in the form of wages or through losses by flood, fire, or disappearance. Still less do such numbers reflect reading per se. Even if a certain percentage of the depletion is accounted for by delivery to individual readers, there is no basis for assuming that recipients necessarily read or had an interest in what they received. Demand or popularity, after all, were insignificant factors in Peter's equation, and a market for leisure books, of which there were very few, had not yet developed. In short, with the exception of those few titles that sold on the open market or those for which a clear captive market existed, the depletion figures simply tell us the rates at which books left the publishing houses.

To a limited extent, printshop ledger sheets can be used to give an indication of income and expenses—an approximate guide to sales volume. Depletion and sales figures provide upper limits for the distribution of specific titles, from which some suggestive patterns emerge; and the number of printings of a given title, especially where print runs are known, may say something about whether or not that title was being circulated.

Some of the numerical evidence, fortunately, follows so consistent a pattern that certain conclusions are inescapable. It is clear, for example, that printing under Peter cost the government a great deal more money than it earned. Between 1714 and 1726, the St. Petersburg Press spent about 4,000 rubles a year in direct printing costs alone and sold only about 1,300 rubles worth of books annually.[59] Even after they juggled their figures to include subsidies to the press and took into account the value of books sent to government offices for which they never received payment and books given to press workers in lieu of cash wages, officials of the press still came up short. As a result, the press was often without sufficient cash to pay its bills.[60] Similar problems apparently befell most of the other strictly governmental publishing houses as well.

The Moscow Press's experience, however, was more muddled. In 1726, Fedor Polikarpov conducted an audit of that press's receipts for nearly the entire duration of Peter's reign (1683–1724) and came to the startling conclusion that it should have been operating at a profit of about 2,700 rubles a year![61] Yet other documents told a different story. Between 1721 and 1724, for example, the Moscow Press spent over 40,000 rubles on books whose earnings came to less than half that amount. It had been so chronically short of cash that it needed a substantial subsidy from the Department of Monasteries to stay afloat and, even with this subsidy, reported operating losses for several years.[62] Stocks on hand, moreover, were accumulating at a very rapid rate. One inventory shows that the press was storing books in its warehouse that had a gross retail value of 60,000 rubles in 1726.[63]

Financial shortfalls, of course, do not ipso facto reflect poor sales, inadequate dissemination, or disinterest in books. Unpaid bills, some of which were very large and were years overdue, accounted for some of them, as did Peter's habit of ordering that certain publications be given large print runs and no-cost circulation.[64] This practice simultaneously drove up expenses and held down revenues, since subsidies from Peter's private accounts fell far short of covering expenses and prospective buyers would hardly have paid for a title that could be had at no cost.[65]

The heavy hand of the tsar may also have had a beneficial effect on revenue, since servitors, students, and institutions were in no position to refuse an imperial order or recommendation to purchase books. But Peter's persuasiveness clearly had its limits. Gross proceeds from sales did not keep pace with the burgeoning output of books, and they may not even have sustained themselves on an absolute scale, since, according to one set of documents, the Moscow Press earned about 7,000 rubles a year between 1702 and 1715, but only about 4,000 rubles a year between 1721 and 1726.[66] Some of that decline undoubtedly resulted from Moscow's loss of business to the St. Petersburg Press. But the St. Petersburg Press's earnings from all sources averaged just under 2,000 rubles a year.[67] The two presses, which collectively accounted for over 90 percent of all titles printed in the early 1720s, therefore had a lower combined annual income (6,000 rubles) in the early 1720s than the earned income from Moscow Press alone (6,300 rubles) in 1702.[68] If inflation were factored in, moreover, the decline would look even steeper. None of this, to say the least, corresponds very well to Luppov's image of a dramatic expansion in the size and social base of reading.

Equally telling in this context is the continued strength of the Moscow Press vis-à-vis St. Petersburg, in spite of the larger number of titles printed by the St. Petersburg Press in the 1720s. Moscow, of course, was bigger and more centrally located than St. Petersburg, and its book-selling network was older and better developed. But the Moscow Press also was the main organ for religious publications, a fact that raises the possibility that the more traditional religious publications sold better than the statist ones.

Pursuing this hypothesis, of course, requires looking at the circulation of specific titles, a difficult assignment for the Petrine period. Over the last century, several inventories listing either sales or stock depletions of Petrine books have appeared in print.[69] Unfortunately, however, they are littered with arithmetic discrepancies between print runs, rates of sales, and rates of depletion. To give just a few examples: One inventory shows *Geography; or, A Short Description of the Earth* selling 448 copies between 1715 and 1718, but another set of documents shows it appearing in two Petrine editions whose print runs totalled only 272 copies, and a third source lists 163 copies remaining in stock in 1722! Similarly, the *History of the Destruction of Jerusalem* is shown as having a single print run of 232 copies in 1716; yet 308 copies had apparently been sold by 1718—and sixteen copies remained in stock in 1722.[70]

Many of these problems presumably arose from accounting mistakes

34

made at the time of recording and are beyond the reach of the scholar to resolve. The most one can do, therefore, is to list recorded sales and depletions as accurately as possible—which has been done in tables 1.3 and 1.4—and then determine what, if anything, they indicate.

These two lists shed light on a number of issues. First, they show just how narrow a range of publications received even a moderate circulation in St. Petersburg. These, after all, were the top sellers from the St. Petersburg Press during those years, yet only nine titles were distributed in more than a thousand copies (and it is unlikely that all of those were sales). All of the secular titles, moreover, with the exception of calendars, the *History of the Destruction of Troy*, and the *History of the Destruction of Jerusalem*, were directed to specific and largely captive audiences. The rest were intended either for the use of specific categories of servitors or as part of school curricula.

Equally noteworthy is the fact that these figures fail to reveal a clear secularist or modernist trend.[71] Rather, what they suggest is the appearance of a narrowly statist utilitarianism, focusing upon laws and regulations, intermingling with devotional and educational books as the primary fare of St. Petersburg's readership. But can any of this be called new or cited as evidence of the success of Peter's policies? The printing and even the reading of laws of major importance, after all, were not new to the eighteenth century; as Luppov has shown, officers and lay notables had bought and read the *Ulozhenie* of 1649 already in the middle of the seventeenth century. Even *Aesop's Fables*, although not in print in seventeenth-century Russia, nevertheless was known to Russians before 1700 from foreign editions and hand-copied versions which could be found in various libraries and repositories.[72]

Evidence from the Moscow Press, although less extensive, represents an even stronger thread of continuity with pre-Petrine traditions. Moscow did a better job of bookselling than St. Petersburg, as the income figures demonstrate, and its success apparently was based heavily on devotional and educational literature. A fragment of a sales sheet of 1710 from the Moscow Press Bookshop indicates that only five "secular" books, all of which were part of a formal curriculum, had sold at all, and among these, only the alphabet books (2,289 copies sold) sold more than eighteen copies.[73]

A more complete listing, covering the two-year period from mid-1714 to mid-1716, shows a similar pattern (table 1.5). Only alphabet books, calendars, and school psalters sold well. Of the books with moderate sales, devotional works predominated. Other titles, consisting largely of schoolbooks intended for secondary education, hardly sold at all.

TABLE 1.3
Sales in St. Petersburg Press Book Shop,
1715–March 1718

Title or Type of Publication	Date of Publication	Number Sold	Approximate Sales per Year
Calendars and Books of Month	Annual	2,471	760
Vedomosti	Periodic	1,500	461
"Manifesto on the Disinheritance of Alexei Petrovich"	1718	1,329	1,329
Alphabet books	1714, 1715, 1717	1,280	393
Military articles	Mid-1715	1,121	373
Military charter (*ustav*)	Mid-1716	913	456
Book of Military Exercises, Ceremonies, and Obligations	Mid-1715	500	165
"Manifesto Specifying the Salaries and Levies for Government Workers"	1715	460	141
Geography; or, A Short Description of the Earth	Mid-1715	448	150
Prayers and services		352	108
Books of Hours		318	97
Mirror of Honor for Youth	1717	311	248
History of the Destruction of Jerusalem	Mid-1716	308	154
"Manifesto Forbidding the Making of Promises"	1715	308	94
Apothegmata	1716	242	107
A Book of Weights and Measures	1714	215	66
Catechism of Feofan Prokopovich	Mid-1717	140	140

SOURCES: Pekarskii, *Nauka i literatura* 2:689–94; Luppov, *Kniga . . . v pervoi chetverti*, pp. 135–39.

TABLE 1.4
Stock Depletions at St. Petersburg Press, 1713–22

Title or Type of Publication	Date of Publication	Approximate Total Print Run	Number Distributed	Annual Depletion Rate
Calendars	Annually[a]	10,700	10,400	927
Military charter	1714-21	10,860	8,000	888
Alphabet books	1714, 1715, 1717, 1719	3,300	2,700	300
Naval charter	1720-22	2,600	2,500	833
General Signals (for soldiers)	1714-20	3,500	1,700	188
Mirror of Honor for Youth	1717, 1719	1,900	1,550	258
Book of Hours for students	1716, 1717	1,270	1,200	171
Ecclesiastic regulations	1721	1,200	1,065	533
Spiritual alphabet	1717, 1719	1,200	1,000	166
Catechism of Feofan Prokopovich	1717, 1722	1,213	587	98
Vocabulary books	1718, 1720	800	565	113
Aesop's Fables	1713, 1717	At least 599	At least 538	55
Synopsis[b]	1718	600	475	94
Pufendorf, Introduction to European History	1718	600	400	80
History of the Destruction of Troy	1717	600	325	55
Books of Weights and Measures	1714	1,000	300	33
History of the Destruction of Jerusalem	1716	232	216	30
School psalters	1716	1,200	200	28

SOURCES: Derived from data in sources shown in table 1.1 and in Pekarskii, *Nauka i literatura* 2:683–89; Gavrilov, *Ocherki istorii*, appendix 1; and Brailovskii, "Polikarpov-Orlov," pp. 6-12.

NOTE: For a similar table, see Luppov, *Kniga ... v pervoi chetverti*, pp. 143–44. Luppov's table, however, is less inclusive and suffers from mathematical errors.

[a] Eleven printings.

[b] No further information about this title is given in the sources.

TABLE 1.5
Sales of Publications from Moscow Press, 1714–16

Type or Title of Publication	Retail Price	Number Sold
Alphabet books	3 k.	13,364
Calendars	10 k.	2,041
School psalters	50 k.	1,714
Prologue for the year	4 r. 50 k.	197
Works of Ephraim the Syrian	70 k.	143
Deliberation on the Image of God and Its Reflection in Man	—	143
Weekly prayers	70 k.	131
School grammar (bukvar')	20 k.	89
Aesop's Fables	30 k.	38
Geometry	1 r.	34
Quintus Curtius, Life of Alexander of Macedonia	1 r. 20 k.	32
Examples of How to Write Compliments	50 k.	32
Sobornik	3 r. 50 k.	33
History of the Destruction of Troy	70 k.	30
Apothegmata	40 k.	23
Lexicon	—	23

SOURCE: Luppov, Kniga . . . v pervoi chetverti, pp. 131–33.

These figures, to be sure, are not comprehensive, since the total income from all books listed in this inventory amounted only to about 3,000 rubles over two years, at a time when the press's income ranged between 4,000 and 10,000 rubles a year. There is a huge discrepancy, moreover, between the sales shown here and the print runs given in printed catalogues, especially for religious books. It is possible, therefore, that books directed toward parish priests or schools simply bypassed the bookshop and circulated through a church-organized network.[74] But whatever the total figures were, prayer books clearly predominated.

Sales and bookshop depletions do not tell the whole story, especially since the records are so fragmentary. In addition, one must make an accounting of those publications whose entire print runs were given over directly to Peter or to an arm of the government. For those volumes, of course, the connection between demand and reading on the one hand and dissemination on the other is problematic, but at least these figures give an indication of what was, and was not, successfully dispersed.

What is learned from these figures is that the government freely spent money for large print runs of some important manifestoes or panegyric publications, but its success in circulating them outside St. Petersburg was fairly limited.[75] A 1727 inventory, for example, listed twelve St. Petersburg publications of the 1720s, with print runs totaling 26,913 volumes (an average of 2,443 per title), which Peter gave over to the Synod to circulate at no cost. Twenty-five thousand, or 94 percent, of the copies had been dispersed by 1729. A similar inventory taken in 1727 listed five gratis titles for Moscow with print runs totaling 45,290, or 9,058 per title, yet of these, only 8,378, or 18 percent, were dispersed. To give some examples: The St. Petersburg Press printed 2,350 Russian-language copies of the *Manifesto on the Disinheritance of Grand Prince Alexei Petrovich*, and it disseminated 1,950 of them. At the same time, the Moscow Press printed 11,000 copies but dispersed only half of them. St. Petersburg dispersed its entire run of 7,800 copies of the "Oath to the New Rule of Succession"; Moscow, by contrast, printed 28,000 copies but dispersed only 828. St. Petersburg disseminated all 5,100 of its copies of Prokopovich's *Right of the Monarch's Will*, but Moscow printed almost 17,000 copies (in 1726) and dispersed fewer than 3,000.[76]

These figures perhaps salvage some credibility for the notion that St. Petersburg's readership was more receptive to Peter's books and hence less traditional than Moscow's. Given the high concentration of servitors in the capital, that would hardly be surprising. But in the end, the preponderance of the evidence on circulation and reading argues for the view that for St. Petersburg and Moscow alike, traditional and religious works remained comparatively attractive. For the rest of the nation, religious works continued to predominate even more completely, since, other than the laws and notices which people had to listen to at least occasionally, only prayer books, alphabet books, and calendars were distributed in sufficient quantities to have much of a chance of reaching into the provinces in any significant numbers. In fact, once one left the major cities, hand copying was very likely to be more prevalent than printed books of any sort.

In the last analysis, therefore, the history of Peter's reshaping of the press is a classic demonstration of the strengths and limitations of an aggressive, governmentally controlled, instrumental publishing system. With relative ease, Peter was able to gather the necessary physical means to improve printing and was able to print more or less what

he wanted and as much as he wanted. To some extent, he even succeeded in exposing his subjects to his output. He certainly made the
voice of the state a more immediate presence than it had been before.
But with the exception of a relatively small group of students and
servitors, Russian society seems to have assimilated very little of it.
Both the quantity and the character of book-buying in 1725 was, as
best as can be determined, not radically different from what it had
been in 1702.

Peter's failure, if one can call it that, certainly involved matters
unrelated to printing, such as the lack of success of his primary schools
and low literacy. But explanations of a general social nature miss a
crucial point: the command basis of Petrine dissemination was ill-
equipped to respond to demand or to create a readership. Bookshops
were as rare in most of the empire in 1725 as they had ever been, and
provincial peddlers hardly ever carried secular printed books. One
cannot say how many people actually did read in Petrine Russia or
what they would have liked the presses to publish, but the thriving
trade in manuscripts and woodblock prints suggests that book printing
was not responding to the existing type or level of demand.[77] Thus,
Peter failed completely to establish a basis for mutual communication
between publishers and readers, and secular printing, although far
more widespread and visible than before, was dependent largely on
the tsar's will and massive subsidies to keep going. It is no wonder,
then, that immediately after Peter died in 1725, his entire publishing
network nearly ground to a halt.

TWO

The Church and the Academy

IN SPITE of the impressive annual increases in the number of books being published, the last years of Peter's reign witnessed a growing determination on the part of Russian officialdom to reverse the chronic losses that had put printing deeply in the red. The St. Petersburg Press, for example, moved its bookshop out of the press's building and into the main trading quarters (*gostinnyi dvor*), and it contracted with local traders and hawkers to sell books on the street.[1] The Synod, attracted by V. V. Kiprianov's assurances that he could run a profitable publishing operation, seriously weighed his offer to lease the Moscow Press for twenty years at a thousand rubles per year.[2] In the end, however, the Synod declined the offer, and none of the measures which it did undertake had any noticeable impact on income or losses. Thus, when the first extensive audits were taken in 1726 and 1727, the presses were deeply in debt and saddled with huge stocks of unsold books.[3]

With Peter the Great now dead, Russia's government came into the hands of a succession of weak and even illiterate rulers, none of whom had the power, the vision, or the inclination to defend printing's virtues against its manifestly burdensome costs. Consequently, when confronted with the evidence of runaway budgets, they forced publishing to submit to an extensive consolidation, which by 1728 had almost completely dismantled the Petrine publishing edifice.

The reorganization began on July 15, 1726, when Catherine I forbade the publication of any new book without her direct approval.[4] Shortly thereafter, the Supreme Privy Council sent a strongly worded note to the Synod suggesting that, since church presses were operating at a large deficit, all religious printing should be confined to the Moscow Press, with the other presses to be sold or sent to Moscow.[5] This suggestion was ignored by the Synod, which refused to close the St. Petersburg and monastic presses on its own initiative. On October 16, 1727, however, Peter II took the matter out of their hands by commanding that henceforth only two of the existing publishing houses— one in Moscow for church books and one in St. Petersburg at the

Senate for the publication of laws and official notices—could continue publishing.[6]

By the terms of this *ukaz*, the Naval Academy Press, the civil branch of the Moscow Press, most of the monastic presses, the Kiprianov Press, and the St. Petersburg Press were closed at least for a time. To be sure, some of these presses had already become largely inactive since Peter's death, but by legislating out of existence the major part of the publishing network, Peter II essentially brought the Petrine publishing system to an end.

The immediate consequence was a precipitous decline in publishing output, from about fifty books a year in the early 1720s to only about twenty a year in the late 1720s.[7] Nominally, this drop resulted from the determination of the government to bring the costs of printing under control. Implicitly, though, it involved a major retreat from the policy of using the printed word as a major instrument of government, since whole categories of books that Peter had fostered in order to teach his servitors how to work and behave nearly disappeared from publishers' lists for a couple of decades. During this time, the government became so selective in publishing that it even cut back on the printing and circulating of laws.

Left to its own devices, the autocracy might very well have let publishing dwindle to almost nothing. However, while the government was determined to curtail its own use of the press, it was not averse to letting peripheral branches of officialdom take over the reins of institutional publishing, albeit with severely reduced financial resources. Thus, in the next few years, primary responsibility for printed communications in Russia passed from the emperor to the Holy Synod and to the newly formed Imperial Academy of Sciences.

Formally, of course, the government was surrendering very little, since these organizations were part of the structure of government, but practically, both the Synod and the Academy achieved substantial autonomy. In 1727, Peter rescinded his predecessor's order of the previous year compelling all publications to have prior approval from her before going to press. Laws and notices, if they were to be published at all, were now to be handled by the Senate Press. Other favorites of the Petrine era simply went by the boards as Russia's rulers left the editorial direction of publishing more or less alone. Governmental departments were instructed to deal directly with the Senate Press or the Academy if they wanted to publish something, rather than involve the tsar, and at times it appeared that the autocracy's sole concern was to keep costs down. Church presses were instructed not to incur new debts, even when that restriction obliged the Synod to curtail several planned publications. The Academy of Sciences similarly received too small an annual allotment, about 30,000 rubles for all its activities, to allow for more than a modest subsidy for the Academy Press.[8]

Although it may have appeared as a simple fiscal and administrative reorganization at the time, the transfer of day-to-day responsibilities to the two leading organs of religion and secular learning had important long-range implications for Russian printing and, more generally, for Russian literate culture, since over time the two publishing houses evolved into separate and even competing organs of ideas and information. The physical plants, editorial direction, and networks of distribution became separate, and even the orthographies that were employed were now clearly different, since, as a result of the edict of 1727, the church retained all the type fonts in the old orthography, and the secular presses used only the new. The respective hierarchies grew increasingly conscious of their particular missions and protective of their own domains, and the entire period witnessed a competition to preside over the development of Russian literate culture. Within the Academy, a bitter and often demoralizing struggle raged for several decades among various groups over the relative value of pure science, material culture, and vernacular language. An equally acrimonious battle pitted the Academy as an institutional defender of the autonomy of a lay and secular literate culture against the Synod, which insisted upon the primacy of faith and the religious hierarchy in all cultural spheres.

The parties to these debates carried on their struggle in several different arenas, but in almost every instance one of the biggest prizes over which they fought was the right to control or have easy access to printing. The course of the disputes had important influence on the evolution of Russian printing, and it affected the resolution of such basic issues as censorship, editorial policy, and the right to disseminate books. Printing, in turn, became the vehicle by which the victors could preside over the future course of literate culture. This struggle, then, was no sideshow; rather, its outcome would determine who would inherit the moral and intellectual mantle of Peter the Great.

From the outset, the Academy and the Synod sought support both within and outside the government, but the Senate had made it clear that all publishing had to get by on diminished funds from the government. Clearly, officialdom had far less interest in the outcome of the competition than did the participants. Gradually, therefore, Russian publishers had to turn their focus away from the government and toward civil society as an alternative source of moral and financial support. This substitution of the resources of civil society for the resources of the state—to turn Gerschenkron's formula for industrialization on its head—had marked, if quite distinct, long-term consequences for religious and nonreligious publishing. In the 1730s and 1740s, however, the Academy Press proved to be much more flexible and ultimately more effective than the Synod Press in addressing the interests of Russia's educated elite.

THE ACADEMY OF SCIENCES PRESS

The Academy of Sciences had been one of the last great achievements of Peter's reign. Peter had been visibly impressed by the learned academies that he had seen on his two trips to the West, and by the middle of his reign he broached the possibility of opening a Russian academy with such notable figures as Leibnitz and the Russian diplomat-historian, V. N. Tatishchev. Both of his learned correspondents argued against establishing an academy before Russia had developed an educational system that would be able to provide it with suitable candidates. In Tatishchev's metaphor, it would be like building the trough before there was any water. Peter, however, was confident that once he had built the trough he could channel a river that would some day run into it.[9] He also believed that an academy, even one staffed by foreigners, would give Russians something to strive for and would bring Russia closer to the world of European scholarship and letters.

Serious planning for the academy went on between 1717 and 1725, including the construction of a library, the creation of research facilities, and, most importantly, the recruitment of foreign scholars. There was no mention of a press in the initial plans, and when the Academy actually began operation in 1725, it issued its first publications, mostly announcements of public lectures, through the old St. Petersburg Press.[10] As other civil presses became less and less active during 1725 and 1726, however, the Academy was left without an outlet. In 1726, therefore, the Academy received permission to order a type font from Holland and, under the terms of an edict of 1727, it began to publish under its own imprimatur.[11]

In the first few years of its activity, the Academy Press was little more than the successor to the reorganized, i.e., secularized, St. Petersburg Press, whose work essentially had come to a halt by the beginning of 1727. Most of its letters, materials, and press workers came from the St. Petersburg Press, as did its profile of publication, which, because of its small budget, included very few titles—mostly calendars, public notices, and other official news.[12] Within a decade, however, the Academy of Sciences Press had blossomed into the most important secular publishing house in Russia, as it became the outlet for everything but the most narrowly official civil and religious publications. Between 1727 and 1755, the Academy of Sciences Press printed about half of all new books and over three-quarters of all books that came from secular publishing houses.[13]

The flowering of the Academy Press was, for the most part, a product of the emergence of the Academy itself as the leading institution of elite secular culture in Russia: as the Academy prospered, its press prospered. But the connection between the two was neither simple nor automatic. It depended, first of all, on a new editorial policy that the press adopted in the late 1720s, which, for the first time in Russian publishing, allowed selected groups and individuals to publish what they wished. Gradually, an array of groups took advantage of the Academy Press's accessibility by publishing an ever-expanding repertoire of books, including more scientific, historical, and literary titles than had ever made their way into print before.

Not surprisingly, the initial beneficiaries of this open-door policy were the Academy's own scientists in residence. Foreign scholars had been recruited to St. Petersburg, largely from Halle and Berlin, with the promise that they would have facilities for research and for publishing their findings. In return, they grudgingly agreed to conduct university classes and to train the first generation of lay Russian scholars. All of these activities required books and a press, and the scientists at the Academy simply took it for granted that they would be allowed to employ the Academy Press as they saw fit.

No other group, of course, had ever been so presumptuous as to assume that it had an a priori right to publish in Russia. Yet this expectation apparently conformed with the understanding of the Academy chancellery, which placed relatively few obstacles in the way of scientific publishing. In spite of quarrels over the relevance of pure science versus teaching and arts and crafts, and in spite of accusations concerning the misuse of funds, scientific research and publishing went on. In order to publish a monograph, a scientist had simply to submit it to the Academic Conference, which presided over all of the Academy's scholarly activities. If the conference approved of the work—and such approval usually was forthcoming—the monograph went directly to the press with instructions to publish. At that point, the press notified the chancellery, which then had to grant final approval for publication. Strained relations between the conference and the chancellery often delayed publication or subjected the work to extensive "clarification," but most research did eventually come out.[14] Unfortunately, most of this scientific activity went on unseen by St. Petersburg society, which, rather than recognizing that the scientists had broken new ground in opening Russia's presses to new elements of society, came to regard the Academy as a foreign enclave that catered more to the whims of its own scientists than to the needs of the host country.

The problem was that most of the Academy's business was conducted in languages that few Russians understood; and when something did happen to appear in Russian, most laymen were intimidated by and resentful of the unfamiliar jargon. But what could the Academy do? Peter had wanted a genuine European scientific academy, and there simply were no Russian scientists around in 1725. From the beginning, therefore, the Academy depended almost entirely on foreigners. Three-quarters of its members between 1725 and 1742 (thirty-seven out of fifty) were German-speaking.[15] Most of the administrators and many of the clerks also were native Germans, and for the sake of convenience the Academy's internal business was conducted in German, and until 1773 the Academic Conference kept its minutes in either German or Latin.

The languages of scholarship and pedagogy were equally incomprehensible to the lay readership. Academicians, naturally enough, sought their public not among the local educated groups but among the international community of scientists, whose common languages were Latin and German.[16] Even the Academy's university lectures were conducted in Latin, a common practice in German universities of that era. The original corps of students at the Academy, most of whom had come from abroad with the professors, presumably were untroubled by this practice. But the use of Latin in these lectures necessarily limited their accessibility among Russians to graduates of an ecclesiastical academy.[17]

All of these circumstances conspired to set the Academy off from the rest of educated society in ways that were quite visible to Russians in the capital. During the 1730s and 1740s, this separation allowed the early public misgivings to balloon into a full-fledged critique of an institution that appeared to be failing to carry out its responsibilities to educate Russian students and to disseminate knowledge to Russian society. In the minds of its enemies, the Academy of Sciences had become an expensive extravagance that Russia could no longer afford. In the words of Christopher Manstein, a German who served in the Russian military at this time:

The only fruits borne by this institution, at a huge expense . . . are that the Russians now have a calendar based on the St. Petersburg Meridian, that they can read newspapers in their own language, and that several German scholars invited to St. Petersburg know enough mathematics and philosophy to earn 600 to 800 rubles a year. . . . The Academy is not so organized as to enable Russia to receive from it even the smallest benefit, because its members are not predominantly engaged in the study of languages, moral sciences, civil law, history, or practical geometry— the only sciences from which Russia could benefit.[18]

Thanks to the support of powerful figures at court, the Academy weathered these early storms, and by midcentury it took on a more visible and highly acclaimed role within Russian intellectual life. But even in those early years, much of Manstein's criticism was less than fair. Certainly there was no shortage of individuals who, like the Orientalist Gottlieb Bayer, absolutely disdained learning Russian or teaching Russian students.[19] Eduard Winter has further argued convincingly that the scientists who came from Halle were, on the whole, mediocrities who adopted a posture of superiority toward Russia in order to obscure their own shortcomings as philosophical thinkers and researchers.[20]

But the chasm that separated the Academy from educated Russian society was hardly a product of willful and aloof personalities alone. The failure of the educational system to provide large numbers of qualified Russians and the necessity of publishing in the international language of science were circumstances that stood beyond the power of individuals to change. Some scientists, in fact, did make overtures to educated society during the 1730s, yet their efforts were greeted with skepticism and outright hostility.

Their dilemma is well illustrated by the experience of the Academy's first scholarly periodical, the *Commentarii Academiae Scientarium Imperialis Petropolitinae* (or *Academic Commentaries*). Begun in 1728, the *Academic Commentaries* served for several decades as the Academy's primary outlet for the publication of scholarly monographs, largely in the natural sciences.[21] Its early issues included essays by Joseph Delisle, Gerhard Friedrich Müller, Georg Bilfinger, Leonhard Euler, and other prominent foreign scientists at the Academy. It came out at least once a year in print runs that ranged from 150 to 600 and, as its title indicates, exclusively in Latin. Most copies went abroad

47

to European scholars and scientific organizations, and almost none went on public sale in Russia.

The Academic Conference had intended to print simultaneous Russian translations of each issue, but this experiment was short-lived. When a translation of a portion of the first issue appeared, several people bought it and some tried to read it. But according to its editor, Müller, "No one was willing to commend the book, they could not understand what they read, and they blamed their lack of comprehension on the obscure terminology and the poor quality of the translation. The upshot of this was that the publication [in Russian] was not continued."[22] The problem, in this case, was not a lack of good will but an intellectual dissonance between the Academy's pursuit of science and St. Petersburg society's search for practical wisdom. Yet several members of the Academy did persevere in trying to spread learning to the educated Russian public. Some, including Müller, Johann Gmelin, and August Schlözer, published systematic historical and anthropological studies of Russia and opened up Siberia to scientific investigation.[23]

The academicians also were responsible for sustaining what was left of the tradition of informational journalism during the second quarter of the eighteenth century. *Vedomosti* had finally expired early in 1727, and for several months St. Petersburg was without a regular source of official news. At the end of the year, the Academy chancellery decided to fill the void by printing a successor newspaper, the *St. Petersburg News (St. Petersburgskie vedomosti)*, which came out without interruption in both a Russian and a German edition from then until 1917. Throughout the eighteenth century, it appeared twice a week, with print runs ranging from 300 copies early in the century to 2,000 copies at the end. It was much longer than its predecessor, containing four to eight pages in addition to supplements which appeared several times a year.[24]

For the first several decades during which the *St. Petersburg News* appeared, its editorship fell to various leading figures from the Academy: Müller (1728 to 1735) and Müller's aide, Johann Bröme (1735 to 1748), and, after 1748, Mikhail Lomonosov. In spite of its being composed by academicians rather than statesmen, its tone and contents remained official: notices, announcements, laws, news of wars, and the like. Journalistic commentary as such still was impermissible. Occasional translations from western newspapers did appear, but these consisted largely of speeches of foreign monarchs or discussions of foreign customs.[25] The newspaper regularly included commercial notices and advertising, and in the 1730s and 1740s it even printed an occasional poem. But these did little to alter the substantially official nature of the newspaper.[26]

Even this modest reportage was sometimes too venturesome for the authorities, however, and in late 1742 the Senate complained to the Academy that the newspaper contained many unfair and inaccurate articles. The Academy was ordered thenceforth to submit each issue of the newspaper to the Senate Press prior to its being sold publicly.[27] In 1751, a similar complaint was filed by the Empress Elizabeth herself, and the Academy was forbidden to publish articles that referred to any member of the imperial family without gaining the prior permission of the empress.[28]

Minor as they were, these brushes with officialdom bear comment because they demonstrate one important consequence of the transfer of civil publishing out of central governmental hands. Such complaints had been inconceivable or at most had been in-house matters in Peter's time because government and publishing were indivisible. Now, however, the Senate was forced to address the oversight of publishing as an external problem. Eventually, the need to define a new relationship between the government and the press became so acute that it led to the initiation of a full-fledged censorship. In the short run, however, the Senate's interest in monitoring the Academy Press essentially ended with its review of the newspaper. No other informational publications of the Academy received such official scrutiny, and even the *St. Petersburg News* usually came out without undue interference.

The Academy also was able to print completely on its own a periodical that came much closer to general-interest journalism than the newspaper did. This was the *Monthly Historical, Genealogical, and Geographical Notes to Vedomosti (Notes)*, which appeared monthly between 1728 and 1742.[29] The *Notes* were conceived by Müller as a vehicle for the publication of articles on a wide variety of topics and of commentary on some of the articles that appeared in the *St. Petersburg News* itself. Like the *News*, it appeared simultaneously in Russian and German. After the debacle with the Russian volume of the *Commentarii*, the *Notes* became the only Russian-language organ for many members of the Academy of Sciences. Mindful of the skepticism and limited attention of Russian readers, it focused less on hard sciences and scholarship—although these were present—than on the propagation of useful and amusing information, including articles on farming, hygiene, anatomy, and simple mathematics, as well as on "popular scientific" matters such as news of recent expeditions and archeological findings and descriptions of Siberian tribes. Occasionally, poetry and literary criticism also appeared in it.[30] The *Notes*, then, represented a major endeavor on the part of a small group of academicians to reach a lay Russian audience on mutually acceptable territory.[31] It was, in fact, the first such concession to public interest made by anyone in the history of Russian printing.

THE CORPS OF TRANSLATORS

Whatever its shortcomings, then, the community of foreign scholars proved to be more sensitive to public interest than Russian officialdom had been. Over time, this modest concern for discovering what people wanted to read grew into something approaching a self-conscious mission to shape and preside over the making of a lay, vernacular, educated culture, largely by means of translation. This endeavor brought several full-time translators into the employ of the Academy, virtually all of whom were native Russians. By 1735, their numbers had grown large enough to form a group, the so-called Russian Conference, which began to fashion its own ideas about what should be translated and why.

The Russian Conference represented a first modest gathering of lay Russian intellectuals in a collective and professional setting. Although it never achieved the cohesiveness or self-consciousness of the *kruzhki* of later times, its participants did engage in secular intellectual activity and they did get paid for it.[32] They took seriously their role as the appointed vehicle for making western literature available to Russian readers, a mission for which they engaged in furious, if inconclusive, debates concerning grammar, style, and the literary vernacular. During the mid-1730s, their translations comprised the heart of the Academy's publications list.

Several noted translators were members of the Russian Conference, including Vasilii Adodurov, Stepan Krasheninnikov, Semen Protasov, and Aleksei Protasov.[33] Its most important member, however, was its secretary, Vasilii Trediakovskii, who during the 1730s and 1740s became the leading figure in the evolution of a literate secular culture in Russia. He translated more artistic literature than anyone else in the group did, he was instrumental in standardizing the grammar of vernacular Russian, and he was a central figure in the debates on literary style and vernacular language.

In some ways, therefore, Trediakovskii could be called Russia's first modern man of letters.[34] Born to a priestly family in Astrakhan in 1703, he came as a layman to study in Moscow's Slavonic Academy in 1723, and by 1727 he had already written an elegy to Peter the Great.[35] In 1726, Trediakovskii received permission from the Synod to study abroad, and he spent the next four years as a student at The Hague and in Paris. While he was in Paris, he attended lectures at the Sorbonne and continued to write poetry, both in Russian and in French.

Upon his return to Russia in 1730, Trediakovskii asked the Academy Press to publish his translation of Paul Tallemant's romantic fantasy, *Le voyage à l'isle d'amour de Lycidas*. The Academy consented and included in the volume several poems written by Trediakovskii himself while he was in Paris.[36] The publication of this novel, in itself of little moment, nevertheless established several significant precedents for secular publishing. It was the first piece of fiction of any kind published in Russia since the second edition of *Aesop's Fables* had appeared in 1717; it was the first completely unsolicited and unmandated work to be accepted for publication by a civil press in Russia; and it was the first work to be financed by a private patron, in this case the Russian ambassador to France, Prince Boris Kurakin.

All of these precedents simultaneously reflected the breadth and the limits of the Academy's new-found willingness to open its presses to private interests. On the one hand, Trediakovskii's translation was not in itself part of any institutional publishing agenda and it therefore served as an announcement to educated society that it was now appropriate to make claims on the press. On the other hand, Trediakovskii's claims were those of an "insider" and drew support from high court circles, and it was by no means clear that all such claims would get a similarly sympathetic hearing.

In the aftermath of his translation of Tallemant, Trediakovskii became something of a celebrity. Although his work was welcomed by some, other people were apparently shocked that such a work could appear. In Trediakovskii's own words:

> The various judgments of it corresponded to the variety of individuals, their professions and their tastes. Court personages were satisfied in full with it. Among those belonging to the clergy were those who were well disposed toward me; but there were others who criticized me as they had criticized Ovid in the past for his excellent book where he deliberated on the art of love; they say that I am perverting Russia's youth.[37]

This salaciousness apparently came to the attention of Empress Anne, whose fondness for ribald entertainment was already notorious, and in 1732 Trediakovskii became the official court translator of Italian operas into Russian. Anne had recently brought an opera troupe from Italy to perform at the court in St. Petersburg. Since few people at the court understood Italian, Anne instructed the Academy to have Trediakovskii translate the librettos into Russian.[38] Between 1733 and the middle of 1735, Trediakovskii translated and published the librettos of thirty-eight Italian operas. Because of the depressed state of publishing in the mid-1730s, these translations accounted for approximately half of all titles published in that two-and-one-half-year period. They also represented the largest single infusion of western literature, no matter how light, into Russian culture up to that time. Since the translations were intended only for the amusement of the court, however, print runs were held down to just 100 copies per opera. Consequently, as instruments of cultural dissemination or of westernization, these librettos had little if any impact on literate Russians outside the court.

Upon the convening of the Russian Conference in 1735, Trediakovskii gave up the pleasantries of the opera and focused instead on the weightier philosophical matters which often preoccupied the self-conscious translators of the 1730s. During the next few years, he devoted particular attention to developing a proper grammar and style for modern written Russian and to enumerating the moral and cultural obligations of translators.

There is no need to recount here Trediakovskii's well-known disagreements with Lomonosov and with Antioch Kantemir on the proper form of versification in Russian, the proper meter, and the like.[39] But the technical aspects of Trediakovskii's positions reflected some interesting assumptions about the social responsibility of writers and about the craft of translation. Trediakovskii rejected both the use of Church Slavonic as the basis for a literary Russian and the assimilation of foreign words into the Russian language. Vernacular Russian was rich enough to provide a modern grammar and vocabulary, and, if it were standardized and developed, it would be capable of expressing modern ideas in Russian. Stylistically, however, Russia's literary and poetic expression could benefit from a synthesis of Slavonic and Romance forms and rhymes. Such a synthesis, he argued, required the translator to develop an intimacy with foreign literature and to acquire practical experience in translation. Translations functioned as literary laboratories in which one could try out various modes of expression that could provide Russia, as a nation that lacked its own classical secular literary tradition, with a literary language. The translator therefore acted as both the creator and the protector of language by ensuring that new forms and styles would be rendered without destroying native Russian.

In a speech delivered at the opening of the Russian Conference in 1735, Trediakovskii maintained that the translator had the additional obligation of acting as the medium for transmitting European culture and knowledge to Russian society.[40] Curiously, Trediakovskii said nothing about the translator's responsibilities for differentiating good or useful ideas from bad ones, but he did argue that the translator was obliged to express these ideas in ways that were familiar to Russians or that used existing Russian literary roots. Trediakovskii here seemed to be suggesting a dichotomy between the content of ideas and the forms in which they were expressed, and although Russia could and should absorb the former totally, the latter constituted the essence of culture and, for that reason, native tradition had to remain preeminent.

Given his preoccupation with form, it is ironic to witness Trediakovskii's lack of success in putting his principles into practice. His "slavicisms" were so stiff and artificial that even he found it hard to use them, and later translators more or less ignored them and continued to employ foreign words and constructions at will.[41] Nevertheless, his image of the translator as a defender of the language and protector of the national culture is important as perhaps the first expression of a unique and important role for the lay man of letters in Russia. For the purposes of this study, moreover, it is noteworthy that he identified that social role with communications, cultural transference, and dissemination to a reading public, rather than with the creation of new ideas.

Trediakovskii, of course, was not especially interested in discussing the importance of the printing press to his own thoughts or to Russian culture more generally, but many of his ideas bring to mind those aspects of Renaissance humanist scholarship that, as Eisenstein notes, did indeed lend themselves to an appreciation by contemporaries of the contribution of movable type. Formalizing a grammar and developing a vernacular style were important not as abstract or scholastic problems, but because they had consequences for the nation and for society. Since literate Russians would be influenced by their exposure to the new culture, the possibilities for widespread dissemination infused these discussions with great meaning for the participants. However, it was not merely the presence of movable type in Russia that mattered here, but its accessibility through the Academy of Sciences Press. It had not been the translators who labored at the Synod or at the College of Foreign Affairs, after all, who worried about a new literary vernacular but those who drew their pay from the one institution in Russian society that could lay claim to presiding over the future of the vernacular language and lay literary culture and that had a stake in the outcome. Thus, in this instance, the institutional context was as critical to determining the role of printing as was the technology of movable type itself.

Printing played an equally significant, if unacknowledged, role in the discussions of the translator's social obligations. Movable type provided the means for guaranteeing the dissemination of translations whose texts were absolutely identical to each other and to the letter of the master copy. It thereby gave the translator the possibility of carving out a socially meaningful role through dissemination and of maintaining editorial control over the language used in each copy that went out.

By conflating the issues of vernacular language and cultural dissemination, therefore, Trediakovskii followed well-trod paths of Renaissance culture. But certain of his activities within the Russian Conference appear to have been oddly unmindful of the power of print. Trediakovskii seemed uninterested, for example, in the ideological role which translators might play in acting as the import agents for selecting which ideas filtered into Russia. For him, form and style were transcendent. More perplexingly, he expressed only an intermittent interest in circulating his own works widely. The entire discussion of grammar and style, for example, took place almost entirely in camera, and when the Russian Conference did manage to get samples of the new forms into print through translations and grammars, it failed to disseminate them very aggressively. It almost seems as if the influence to which they aspired related more to the nation as a cultural whole than to particular readers or even the reading public in general.

Nevertheless, the corps of translators remained the most active publishing group at the Academy. After the flight of foreign scholars had run its course by the mid-1740s, translations accounted for well over half of all new books that came out in the natural sciences, technology, history, philosophy, literature, and military science. Much of this upswing came from the demands of instructional curricula and the patronage of the empress, but, increasingly, translations were being generated by the translators themselves. This spontaneous activity was a reflection of the growing assertiveness of translators within the Academy, both intellectually and financially. Translators wanted to bring their favorite works into print, and they were finding it relatively easy to do so. They discovered, moreover, that the definition of success in the Academy Press was an economic one, and that with greater success came greater remuneration.

In theory, Academy translators had always received at least modest salaries, between 100 and 200 rubles a year in the 1730s.[42] Because of the Academy's perennial cash shortage, however, compensation often came in the form of clothing, grain, or books rather than in cash.[43] To turn these goods into money, a translator had to sell them on the street, not a very attractive arrangement, to say the least. Several things happened in the 1740s to change this state of affairs. First, the Academy Press, which had been operating at a loss, decided to search for a means to increase its income. At about the same time, translators within the Academy began to demand better salaries and more hard cash. Since the government was no longer willing to provide additional subsidies, the Academy was forced to look to private sources of funds, either through patronage or on the open market.

Patronage had been coming more or less regularly to the Academy from the empresses in the 1730s and 1740s, most often for odes, fireworks literature, and other panegyric works. Anne also had paid for the librettos and a few works of history, and Elizabeth underwrote the publication of a number of stories.[44] Elizabeth's largesse had also enabled Jacob Stählin, a professor of rhetoric and poetry at the Academy, to publish sixteen odes and panegyrics in the 1740s, with print runs that ranged from 500 to 1,200 copies, and in 1747 Elizabeth underwrote the publication of an old but hitherto unprinted translation of Fénelon's *Adventures of Telemachus*.[45] But the 1740s also saw a substantial growth in private patronage from prominent court figures, including Boris Kurakin, Mikhail Vorontsov, and Kirill Razumovskii.[46] In addition, some translators arranged to publish their own works by paying the entire cost of a print run themselves.

Equally important in this regard was the Academy's new commercial consciousness. During the second quarter of the eighteenth century, the Academy seemed determined to improve income by selling more books. Johann Schumacher, curator of the Academy's library, scoured western Europe for years in search of a respected business manager for the bookshop before settling on Gottlieb Clanner of Leipzig.[47] More to the point, the Academy conducted a series of informal studies in the 1740s and 1750s for the purpose of learning how to improve book sales.[48]

In April 1743, for example, Andrei Nartov, director of the Academy chancellery, and Sergei Volchkov, secretary of the Academy, submitted a report on how best to sell Academy publications. They began by pointing out that the Academy had accumulated enormous backlists which were worth thousands of rubles and that, among these, the non-Russian publications had clearly been poor investments since native Russians did not buy them. It might be possible to deplete the stocks of these books by selling them in regions and neighborhoods where Germans and Baltic peoples resided, but in the long run the Academy would be better off financially if it ceased to publish in German as well as in Latin. Instead, they argued, the Academy should concentrate on Russian-language books and should make contact with high officials, merchants, schools, and churches to remind them of their responsibilities to buy books and to find out what sorts of books interested them.

Nartov and Volchkov placed special emphasis on the merchants, who, they believed, would willingly buy moral-educational, historical, and other "useful" books.[49] In order to understand this report, we must recognize that Nartov and Volchkov had no particular grounds for speaking so hopefully about Russian merchants. Nartov, at least, was motivated rather by a deep hostility toward the influence of science, foreigners, and foreign languages at the Academy. He had long ago concluded that the Academy should place more emphasis on disseminating practical skills and practical books that would be of interest to Russians, rather than the arcane science that was of interest only to the scientists themselves. Having recently succeeded in ridding the Academy of many of its foreign scholars, Nartov quite naturally wanted to extend his victory to the activities of the press.

But politics was not the only issue here. Other reports from the 1730s and 1740s, while less hostile to Latin and German, nevertheless agreed that the Academy had to do a better job of making its wares known in the major cities, in the provinces, and abroad, and of learning and responding to what the Russian public wanted to read.[50] In fact, the Academy had already begun to place notices of impending publications in the *St. Petersburg News*, to circulate catalogues of books in print, and to disseminate selected backlists to provincial officials.[51] But these were just the very first steps in establishing a line of communication with the reading public.

Most of the other reports, it should be noted, were extremely general. They usually followed Nartov's example of projecting personal impressions and interests onto all of literate society. But the Academy Press, eager to have a core of best sellers, was prepared to take their recommendations to heart. In this situation, translators, because they provided the Academy with ready access to popular literature, found themselves in a position of some influence.

Translators soon came to realize that the Academy's sales consciousness afforded them a degree of leverage with which to demand higher salaries, bonuses, and more hard cash.[52] Thus, in August 1747, Volchkov, who had contributed several translations over the years, sought a raise in pay by insisting to the Academy chancellery that his translations had been popular and financial successes for the Academy and that some of that success should be passed on to the translator. He maintained that his translation of *The Life of Marcus Aurelius* had sold 1,800 copies, Gracian's *The Courtier*, 1,000 copies, and Florinus's *Economy*, 1,200 copies.[53] Yet he was earning less money from these books than other translators who had not provided the Academy with such good service. The Academy agreed with Volchkov's general proposition, acknowledging that his translation of *Aesop's Fables* had earned over 1,254 rubles and his translation of Morvan de Bellegarde's *The Upbringing of Children*, over 174 rubles. In addition, his just-released translation of Curas's *Introduction to General History* was expected to sell well.[54] Volchkov got his raise.

A few other translators of the 1740s received similar treatment, and soon all manner of people were submitting material to the Academy. Academy employees began to work on translations in their spare time, and in at least two instances independent (*vol'nye*) translators were given fifty rubles each for the rights to their unsolicited manuscripts.[55]

By 1750, the Academy had brought together a staff of perhaps half a dozen commercially conscious translators whose opinions on the usefulness and salability of a given manuscript were given serious attention. Thus, in 1745, the chancellery ruled that if a paid translator felt that a given translating assignment was not generally useful he could bring the matter before the Academic Conference.[56] More importantly, a translator who had proven his ability to produce profitable translations was likely to convince the Academy to accede to his judgment on what should be published. The translators therefore served as a medium of demand through which the reading public (or at least that portion of it which had access to Academy books) could, for the first time, influence the overall profile of publications.

The Academy Press's receptivity to literary translations also made the press into a haven for the handful of young intellectually minded servitors who were beginning to emerge from the service academies in the 1740s.[57] Virtually all Russian writers of the middle of the eighteenth century got their start in publishing as translators. For them, translating became something of a rite of passage that allowed initial entree to the press, after which it became relatively easy for them to have their own literary works printed. Thus, Trediakovskii and Lomonosov published volumes of their poetry only after completing this kind of "apprenticeship" given over to translating; and, after making his name as a translator, Alexander Sumarokov was able to publish three of his plays, *Khorev* (1747), *Oreston* (1751), and a reworking of *Hamlet* (1748).[58]

The change from translator to published author, unfortunately, usually was an expensive one for the writer. Sumarokov, for example, was obliged to foot the entire bill for printing his works (at least until 1763, when Catherine II became his patron), since his plays did not sell very well. Yet he was more fortunate than most. Few people could gain entree to the Academy and even fewer had the resources to publish at their own expense. Thus, several original stories as well as the traditional fables and stories, the so-called literature of the masses, remained in manuscript at this time.

It is premature, therefore, to speak of a profession of letters in Russia in the 1750s. Still less was the Academy of Sciences Press turning Nevskii Prospekt into a Russian Grub Street, since the number of money-making translations, after all, was still quite small. But the Academy's recognition that it could use translations to introduce Russia to western culture and to develop a literary language, on the one hand, and to earn money by responding to popular interests and tastes, on the other, was certainly a giant step toward the discovery of the public.

The Repertoire of Books, 1725–55

The public, in turn, was beginning to discover publishing in a variety of ways. For graduates of elite secondary schools, education led to reading, and reading led with relative ease into translating or writing, both of which, in turn, could lead to publishing. This affinity between the press and the elite public was just emerging in the 1740s. Indeed, not until the expansion of secondary education in the middle of the century did intellectual interests actually take control of the press. Nevertheless, the effects of the new lay intellectual interests on the overall profile of books could already be seen in the second quarter of the century. As table 2.1 indicates, secular printing took on a more humanistic character between 1725 and 1755: humanistic titles accounted for about half of all books in the civil orthography and slightly more than a quarter of all books. This becomes especially clear in table 2.2, comparing the composition of books published in this period with the composition of those published in the Petrine era, when informational and military works had played a much larger role.

However, the symmetry between academic intellectual life and the repertoire of published books had its limits. Some matters that were prominent within the Academy had rather faint resonance in print. For example, even when the occasional translations are included, the percentage of scientific books printed in Russian (less than 3 percent of all books and a little more than 4 percent of all books in the civil

TABLE 2.1
Subject Composition of Titles Published, 1725–55

Subject	Number of Titles Published	Percentage of All Titles Published	Percentage of Titles Published in Civil Orthography (N = 553)
Laws, manifestoes, and regulations	103	11	19
Official information and notices	68	7	12
Religion	382[a]	41	1
Military affairs (excluding laws and regulations)	21	2	4
Calendars	42	4	8
Journals	47[b]	5	8
Alphabet, grammar, and language	14	2	2
History and geography	47	5	8
Technology	25	3	4
Science and mathematics	24	3	4
Secular philosophy	20	2	4
Belles-lettres	71	8	13
Odes	64	7	12
Total	928	100	99

SOURCES: See note 7, chapter 2.

[a] Of these, 375 were in the old orthography, 7 in the new orthography.

[b] Each year that a journal was published has been counted as a separate title. For example, *St. Peterburgskie vedomosti* was published annually beginning in 1727 and has thus been counted as 28 titles (1727–55).

orthography), was completely unrepresentative of the prominence of science within the Academy. The controversies over grammar and literary styles took place almost entirely in camera, as fewer Russian grammars came into print in the 1750s than in the 1720s. Alphabet books certainly continued to appear with great frequency and large print runs. Between 1726 and 1755 the Moscow Press alone produced twenty-two printings with a total print run of nearly 370,000 copies.

TABLE 2.2
Subject Composition of Russian-Language Titles Published,
1700–1725 and 1725–55

| | Percentage of Titles Published in: | |
Subject	1700–1725 (N = 731)	1725–55 (N = 825)
Official information and notices	26	8
Religion	42	46
Military affairs	14	3
Calendars	3	5
Journals	3	6
Alphabet, grammar, and language	3	2
History and geography	5	6
Technology and science	2	6
Secular philosophy	1	2
Belles-lettres	1	16
Total	100	100

SOURCES: See note 7, chapter 2. See also Luppov, *Kniga . . . v poslepetrovskoe vremia*, p. 57, for a similar calculation.

But nearly all of the alphabet books that were printed in those years taught only the old orthography, as the instruction of literacy reverted largely to the church. Not until the 1780s, in fact, did alphabet books that taught the civil orthography return to print in significant numbers. Thus, the Academy's debates over language, style, and the vernacular had very little contact with the teaching of basic literacy.[59] Even the scientific interest in the exploration of the ethnography and geography of the Russian Empire, a heated and often politically tinged issue in the Academy, rarely was manifested in print.

The overall profile of books, conversely, continued to reflect the influence of institutional interests outside of the Academy. The great majority of the Senate Press's seventy-five books, for example, were informational or legal,[60] and many Academy publications that were produced on behalf of other governmental offices had a narrowly official character.[61] Informational and technical books thus continued to be more numerous than humanistic ones, and if individual laws and notices were included, the scales would tip even more heavily in favor of officialdom.[62] Equally revealing is the high representation of traditional books of faith, which not only remained the largest single category of books in the second quarter of the eighteenth century, but comprised an even higher proportion after Peter (46 percent) than during his reign (42 percent). These figures suggest that there were still severe limitations on the Academy Press's ability to claim the attention of Russia's readers.

A comparison of print runs and modes of distribution makes those limits stand out even more sharply. Most of the Academy's new books, whether translated or original, had print runs of 1,000 copies or less, and literary, philosophical, and scientific books rarely exceeded print runs of 600. Among the Academy's publications, only the very best sellers, such as textbooks directed to captive audiences, received print runs of 1,500 or more, and within this restricted group only primers and calendars, whose print runs approached 10,000 by the mid-1750s, had much hope of reaching a wide national audience.

By contrast, the word of officialdom—laws, notices, and informational books—regularly came out in print runs numbering in the thousands of copies. However reduced the number of titles was from Peter's time, the government still produced a much larger total volume of material than the intellectual interests around the Academy could hope to achieve. In addition, it had at its disposal the administrative network of the state, including the churches, to distribute its publications or to have them read them aloud.

The Synod could also rely upon massive printings and institutional distribution more easily than the Academy. The figures on print runs that Luppov and others have uncovered indicate that the Synod did regularly print service books, church primers, sermons, and psalters, in editions that ranged from 1,200 to 17,000 or more.[63] Archival records from the Moscow Press show further that saints' lives, the Gospels, liturgical song books, and the New Testament had regular reprintings that ranged from 1,200 to 7,200 copies per print run.[64] Most of these, too, had a guaranteed reading audience among the clergy and, as the spoken word, among the laity. Thus, if any individuals at the Academy had any hope of competing with the more established voices of the church and state for the eyes and ears of the Russian people, that hope soon foundered on the unequal competition. Despite the Academy's sensitivity to popular interest, it probably failed to carve out much of a readership outside of the elite public in St. Petersburg. For the wider circles of readers, the main sources of ideas and information remained the government and the church.

THE SYNOD PRESS

The Synod, of course, was aware of its nationwide audience and, in the face of what it perceived to be the Academy's ungodly challenge, it developed a variety of strategies to sustain the faithful and condemn the voices of modern thought. The restricted resources granted to it after the dismantling of the Petrine printing system initially limited the Synod to a simple consolidation of its authority over religious books and publishers by centralizing editorial responsibilities. Its immediate goals appear to have been, first, to effect strict fiscal accountability and, then, to impose a complete uniformity of the Word. Thus, for the years between 1727 and 1740, the Synod ruled religious publishing with an iron hand. Most deeply affected by this policy were the monastic presses, which since 1722 had come under increased pressure to bring their publications into line with those of the Moscow Press. For the monasteries, submission to central authority was the only alternative to a strict reading of the edict of 1727, which would have forced them to close entirely. Thus, the church presses in Kiev, Chernigov, and the Alexander Nevskii monastery continued to publish in the 1720s and 1730s, but they now operated under new constraints.[65] In August 1726, for example, the Caves Monastery in Kiev was forbidden to print any books that had not already been printed by the St. Petersburg or Moscow Synod Press.[66] In October 1735, the Synod allowed the Caves Monastery to continue printing Books of Months only on the condition that it cease to include in them such extraneous matters as weather predictions and advice on when to build houses and when to have children.[67]

The Moscow Press also came under strict synodal control in these years. Rigid accounting rules obliged press directors to get prior permission for all individual expenses over twenty rubles and to prepare monthly debit and credit sheets.[68] In addition, all new publications required the prior approval of the Synod chancellery. Such fiscal and editorial conservatism had only modest practical consequences, however. To be sure, the output of the Moscow Press declined between 1726 and 1740, to about eight books a year, or about half of its output of the previous several years. But much of this decline was a result of the elimination of secular books from its repertoire after 1726, rather than from any major disinvestment in religious publishing. Print runs remained high, and these publications apparently continued to circulate reasonably well.[69] Furthermore, many prayer books could be used year after year, so that, over time, the absolute number of printed prayer books in circulation must have been very great. By contrast, the handful of massively printed secular publications, such as calendars and laws, were highly perishable, and most of those which could be reused, such as the Petrine primers and alphabet books, were not reissued after the late 1720s.

In fact, the Synod maintained and even strengthened its commitment to publishing prayer books in those years. What it sacrificed, on the whole, was panegyrics. Prayers and homilies to the tsar and to military victory, although still read aloud at public spectacles and in the churches of the court, were far less likely to get into print or to receive large printings in the 1730s and the 1740s than they had been a decade or two earlier. The Synod largely conceded this entire endeavor to laymen and lay presses, which between 1725 and 1755 printed over thirty odes and panegyrics.

Implicitly, then, the Synod was extricating itself from affairs of state and devoting its presses to a reemphasis of faith. In this context, one might well wonder whether the separation of the printed language into a religious orthography and a civil one had the effect of sharpening popular perceptions of a separation between sacred and secular knowledge. In Peter's time, the changeover from the old to the new orthography had been confused and incomplete. During the period between 1727 and 1755, however, the Synod printed all but seven of its books in the old orthography, and the Senate and the Academy of Sciences employed only the new. Catechisms and prayer books, moreover, used Church Slavonic rather than vernacular Russian. Anyone, regardless of ability to read, would now be able to recognize the difference between sacred and secular books either from the sound of the language or from the appearance of the printed page.

One might speculate that the differences, if they were generally perceived, probably gave the Synod an advantage over the civil presses. Religious books, after all, looked and sounded much as they had for at least three generations. Their typeface also resembled the script used in hand-copied texts, almost all of which continued to follow the old orthography. Civil press books, by contrast, looked new and sounded new. Since most alphabet books of this era taught the old orthography rather than the new, readers—especially those who were barely literate—were likely to find the text and appearance of church books to be much more accessible than Academy or Senate publications. To the extent that people equated "new" with "alien" and "old" with "familiar," they likely would have been inclined to see one affinity between church books and tradition and another between civil books and change and external authority.

Without plunging further into popular culture, it is impossible to say with any confidence whether such perceptions were widespread in Russia at this time. At any rate, if they were common, they likely were confused by the Synod's decision to publish some of its books— although not books of worship—in the new orthography after 1755.

By then, of course, a half-century of reeducation through primers and government-sponsored secondary education had largely succeeded in familiarizing the better-educated groups in society with the new orthography, and the Synod felt a need to keep in step. The roots of this compulsion to compete for the attention of educated society on an equal footing can be seen as early as 1740, when the Synod undertook a complete modernization of its publishing facilities. Despite its continued preeminence in reaching a relatively popular audience, the Synod remodeled with thoroughness: new presses, new type fonts, more books, and lower prices. According to published catalogues, between 1741 and 1755 the Synod printed 276 titles, a threefold increase over the previous fifteen years.[70]

At the same time, it granted the Moscow Press greater flexibility in running printing operations, in order to publish books more quickly, and it began to sell its publications with a new aggressiveness.[71] One searches in vain for documentation that would explain the reasoning behind this abrupt change of course, but some of the features of the new printing policy conformed rather well with the Synod's general policy of imposing exclusivity on religious institutions at this time, related particularly to the reorganization of the parish clergy and the growing opposition to science and secularism. In his recent study of eighteenth-century parish priests, Gregory Freeze has demonstrated how synodal policy in the 1730s and 1740s was well on the way to turning the parish clergy into a closed hereditary caste. Parish priests in principle now had to attend primary-school classes and sometimes more advanced seminary classes, and they had to be able to read and write. All of these requirements tended to differentiate and even isolate parish priests from other groups in the countryside. In addition, the Synod redoubled its efforts in the 1740s to reserve the local churches for worship only and to impose a sense of decorum and solemnity upon the tone of church services. In particular, the Synod wanted churches to cease being scenes of general social gathering, celebration, and beer-drinking, and it expected parish priests to take the lead in setting a tone for church activity that reflected a strict segregation of sacred and secular.[72]

Most of these changes, Freeze makes clear, had little, if any, effect upon a laity that was mostly unaware of the church's intentions and unmindful of its new demands. Much of the parish clergy, however, did recognize the extent to which their relationship to the laity had changed. Literacy and reading opened cultural realms that few parishioners could experience, and the strict separation of the church from everyday social and commercial intercourse contributed to the isolation of the priest from village life.

Whether or not the Synod saw the cultural separation of the clergy as desirable, its approach to printing in these years clearly had the effect of reinforcing separatism, primarily through granting priests a much greater but more exclusive access to books. A church edict of July 1742, for example, ordered the Moscow Press to print 17,000 primers with catechisms for distribution only to candidates for the priesthood.[73] At the same time, the church made the Bible (including both the Old and the New Testament) more accessible to seminarians by ordering new but limited printings in 1739 and 1751.[74]

In spite of the appearance of manuscript Uniate and Old Believer Bibles, Russian Orthodoxy had never approved of broad circulation of the Word. To be sure, there had been, since the late seventeenth century, regular reprintings of the New Testament and, even more frequently, of the Gospels.[75] But seventy-five years had elapsed since the last official Orthodox Bibles that included the Old Testament had been printed in 1663, and in the interim many copies had worn out or had been destroyed.[76] The Synodal chancellery, however, had no wish to make the Word generally available to the laity. Thus, the Bibles were distributed to a select and closed public. They came out in Slavonic rather than in vernacular Russian, and apparently had modest print runs (the 1739 edition, for example, had a print run of 139 copies).

These Bibles tended to remain within the hierarchy and the ecclesiastic academies. Thus, even parish priests were unlikely to have owned or to have read a printed Bible except, perhaps, when they were in the seminary. But even though the Synod did not entrust its parish clergy with Bibles, it did send them other books, since literacy had given the priests, or rather it gave the Synod through them, new tools with which to enforce the church's will. The Synod, accordingly, began in the 1740s to send out printed instructions to priests covering all aspects of pastoral responsibilities, including large numbers of sermons and prayer services which parish priests were supposed to use as guides in conducting worship and in giving moral instruction.

Not all of the church's books could be closed to the laity, of course, but the Synod was determined to keep tight control over what appeared on the open market. First manifested in the prohibition of 1735 against the long-standing practice of including advice on practical subjects in Books of Months and almanacs, this policy eventually influenced every decision involving religious printing in the post-Petrine era. At one point, the Synod even refused to do business with the hawkers and petty merchants who had been selling religious books for decades in the trading quarter near Spasskii Bridge in Moscow.[77] In their stead, the church opened up its own shop by the bridge and lowered retail prices in order to maintain more control of its own markets.[78]

There were apparently several causes for this separatism and anti-secularism, but one important consideration was the Synod's conviction that the Academy Press was exercising a pernicious influence on Russian society. From the Academy's inception, and especially after the death of Feofan Prokopovich in 1736, the church expressed alarm over activities at the press and demanded the right of prior approval over the publishing and sale of all Academy books.[79] Feofan's successors in the Synod were confirmed opponents of the Academy who sermonized often against the evils of science.[80] The Synod opposed the publication of scientific monographs, especially the *Academic Commentaries* (many seminarians, after all, had studied Latin and could therefore read them). It resisted the republication of the works of Pufendorf, it attempted to put a halt to the new literary translations coming out of the Academy, and it frequently interceded with the Senate to attempt to halt the publication or sale of potentially dangerous books, whether written at home or abroad.[81] Even Trediakovskii ran into trouble when the Synod opposed and was ultimately able to postpone the publication of his translation of Rollin's *Ancient History*.[82]

The Academy's bookshop, the *knizhnaia palata*, also felt the Synod's criticism. In 1739, for example, the Synod alleged that the Academy had been selling imported books on religious and moral themes without first receiving the Synod's approval.[83] This activity violated the church's monopoly over works of faith, and the Academy was obliged to take the offending books off the shelves.

The government also maintained an interest in what sort of books were being imported. In 1738, for example, Empress Anne forbade the importation from Lvov into the Russian Ukraine of Polish calendars that made some objectionable references to astronomy.[84] In 1743 the Senate went so far as to forbid the importation of books published abroad in the Russian language, since a Russian-language press had been operating in Halle and was sending books into Russia.[85] This must have been a recurring problem, because an edict of 1750 again forbade the practice.[86] This latter law went even further, in that, for a brief period, it forbade importation of *any* book that mentioned the name of any "formerly well-known personage" in the Academy of Sciences. The Academy brought the sweeping wording of the law to the attention of the empress, who modified it to read that only works of former Academy members that had previously been published in Russia could not be imported.[87] These incursions, however, focused on very specific concerns that affected only a small part of the Academy's publishing and bookselling activities. Certainly they did not add up to a coherent campaign by officialdom to have a controlling hand in the Academy's activities. The Synod, by contrast, did want control, and in the early and middle 1740s it made repeated and partially successful appeals to the Senate in an effort to gain broad powers over secular presses.[88]

Officials at the Academy, of course, disliked the Synod's intrusiveness because it upset publishing plans and deprived the Academy of full control over its own press. Almost invariably, the Senate was put in the middle, forced to conduct halfhearted investigations at the Synod's behest and to mediate between the two parties. New legislation was thus required to establish lines of authority that would delineate clearly what the Academy could do and what the Synod could demand. To a certain degree, such a resolution emerged in 1747, when the Senate issued the "Academic Regulations," which revised and updated Peter the Great's original Academy charter.

The regulations went into great detail on the structure and functions of the Academy, including the number of employees, their responsibilities, and their salaries. In general, however, they granted the Academy chancellery a great deal of autonomy.[89] Nowhere, however, did they explicitly discuss censorship, and the fact that they omitted any reference to senatorial or synodal responsibilities in overseeing Academy of Sciences books left the Academy chancellery to infer that it could exercise an autonomous authority of oversight and approval of Academy Press books. In the wake of the new regulations, therefore, the Acdemy set up its own censors, or "correctors," and it proceeded to treat editorial control almost entirely as an in-house matter.

This inference, which drew practical support from the Senate, marked a victory for the Academy. The Synod remained the direct overseer of all books of faith, of course, but it could exercise only informal influence over secular books that had no religious content. Although the Synod could and did continue to hector the Senate about dangerous books, D. V. Tiulichev has shown convincingly that its persuasive power was greatly diminished, and between 1747 and the mid-1790s far more books were published over the Synod's objection than were banned.[90] For its part, the Academy was careful to procure prior permission whenever one of its books contained prayers or fragments of prayers. But as a general rule, the Academy steered clear, whenever possible, of including prayers in its books, a practice that both diminished the friction between the Synod and the Academy and further accentuated the differentiation between secular and religious books.

Thus, by the early 1750s the separation of church, governmental, and academic publishing that had begun in the 1720s was largely complete, and each was now free to develop on its own without undue interference from the other. At this point, the presses complemented each other rather well: the church propagated the faith; the state circulated laws and notices; and the Academy took responsibility for developing lay culture, secular secondary education, science, and entertainment. Each, moreover, had carved out clear, if overlapping, domains in literate society: the government's readership was centered in its officials; the church's primary readership was the clergy; and the Academy's readership came from students and from within the small cosmopolitan educated society.

But it must be reiterated that all of these readerships were still small. Hampered as it was by economic backwardness, a seemingly low literacy rate, and geographic and institutional centralization, Russian printing remained terribly primitive. Indeed, the combined efforts of church, state, and Academy produced fewer than 900 titles between 1725 and 1754 (see table 2.3). As late as 1750, the annual publication figures remained lower than those of the last decade of Peter the Great's reign and far below those of other European states. Books remained expensive, hard to obtain, and rare for much of Russian society, and

TABLE 2.3
Books Published in Five-Year Intervals, 1725–54

	Number of Books Published	Annual Average	Annual Average of Books in Civil Orthography	Annual Average of Books in Old Orthography
1725–29	87	17.4	9.4	8.0
1730–34	127	25.4	20.4	5.0
1735–39	107	21.4	17.8	3.6
1740–44	223	44.6	22.6	22.0
1745–49	177	35.4	17.0	18.4
1750–54	175	35.0	18.8	16.2
Total	896	29.9	17.7	12.2

SOURCES: See note 7, chapter 2.

as a consequence the older forms of communication continued to prosper.

It is also noteworthy that church and state were able to combine printing and their institutional networks to speak to the illiterate masses in ways that the Academy, which lacked a nationwide network, could not begin to emulate. The significance of the Academy of Sciences Press, therefore, lay not in any immediate broad social or secularizing impact, but in what its inner development augured for the future. Seen in this light, the modest achievements of the Academy become significant, even remarkable. After 175 years in which Russian printing limped along with few markets, little if any means of responding to popular interest, and only occasional contributions to intellectual innovation, the Academy of Sciences in the course of three decades had made advances in all of these areas, albeit on a very small scale. Popular demand and the wishes of outside individuals now were acceptable, even desirable, considerations both for determining some of what the press was prepared to publish and for deciding how it proposed to distribute its books to Russian readers. All of this, needless to say, was light-years away from how Russian presses behaved during Peter the Great's rule. Furthermore, the Academy's combination of intellectual and economic sensitivity became a precedent for the rapid expansion of institutional publishing which took place in the context of the dramatic rise of elite secondary education in the 1750s and 1760s.

THREE

Schools and Publishers

IF THE SECOND QUARTER of the eighteenth century witnessed a flirtation between lay intellectual life and Russian printing, the third quarter marked a veritable betrothal. Indeed, the years between 1755 and 1775 saw the emergence of a generation of culturally minded youth, the young "literati" as they sometimes are called, who undertook to construct an intellectual life that would conform to their acquired interests and tastes.[1]

Scholars have long agreed that the middle of the eighteenth century marked a change in Russian intellectual life, but, with some exceptions, they have not been very clear about what, in fact, was different.[2] Certainly there were more writers of importance in the 1760s than in the 1730s and 1740s, but the numbers still remained quite small. There does not seem to have been a great deal of change in their professional or social stature. Most literati continued to be drawn from an elite consisting mainly of the well-educated gentry, and, as David Ransel and others have shown, virtually all of them continued to place greater stock in their careers in state service than in literary affairs.[3]

Scholars of the history of ideas have written a great deal about the world views of the men of the 1760s but not very much concerning what made them different from their predecessors. Disagreements unquestionably arose among the young literati and between them and their forebears, but these disagreements, most scholars concede, did not involve fundamental changes in world views or ideologies. And although the current debates over the relative impacts of German natural law and French rationalism and the "early" vs. the "late" Enlightenment on Russian letters has clarified understanding of what these literati were thinking about, neither side posits a major change occurring between the 1740s and 1770s.[4]

Yet the fact remains that the intellectual world of the 1760s and 1770s looked very different from the world of the 1740s. But if ideas, politics, mentalities, and professional activity had not changed very much, what was new? The answer, it seems to me, must begin with numbers: There simply were many more laymen—both gentry and nongentry—coming out of secondary school and engaging in intellectual activity in the 1760s than there had ever been before.[5] That they were not, strictly speaking, professional writers is true enough, but the mere fact that they dedicated much of their time to intellectual pursuits is a change in itself.

The particular forms which this intellectual interest took are certainly well known in the literature: new journals, clubs, masonic lodges, translating and publishing societies, reading circles, and even private secondary schools. Irrespective of motivation or ideology, this activity marked a major quantitative leap in cosmopolitan intellectual life. Equally important is the fact that the intellectual institutions, social and professional roles, and modes of communication which the generation of the 1760s created survived largely intact as the essential foundation of Russian intellectual life, at least until the middle of the nineteenth century. Thus, above all else, the literati of the 1760s were institution builders upon whom much of the future course of intellectual history came to rest.

Approaching intellectual innovation from an institutional perspective introduces several historical subjects, some of which have little to do with movable type. As numerous scholars have noted, the system of humanistic and general secondary education that came into being in midcentury imbued the service gentry with an outlook of humanitarianism, modernism, and moral duty. It also encouraged the educated elites to familiarize themselves with the accumulation of ideas and information that European civilization represented. When the educated youth of the 1750s and 1760s attempted to reify their moral vision through social activity, however, their experiences had everything to do with movable type. Indeed, between 1755 and 1775, students, teachers, and recent graduates simply took over most of the institutional publishing houses and used them as staging grounds from which they could reach the nation as a whole and around which they could construct a congenial intellectual life for themselves.

Needless to say, this invasion had a dramatic impact upon printing. In less than twenty years the number of books and journals published per annum rose from about 50 to over 190, the majority of which came in one way or another from the needs and interests of the circles at the secondary schools (table 3.1). Topically, the transformation in editorial direction led to a marked rise in the proportion of literary and other general interest books. They comprised over 50 percent of all published titles during this period, while the proportion of religious books declined to just over 20 percent (table 3.2). As in the second quarter of the century, this decline was less a reflection of church inactivity—the Synod in fact produced more books per year in the

TABLE 3.1
Russian-Language Books Published in Five-Year Intervals, 1756-75

	Number of Books Published	Annual Average	Number in Civil Orthography	Number in Old Orthography	Annual Average of Books in Civil Orthography	Annual Average of Books in Old Orthography
1756–60	262	52.4	193 (73.7%)	69 (26.3%)	38.6	13.8
1761–65	805	161.0	631 (78.4%)	174 (21.6%)	126.2	34.8
1766–70	767	153.4	701 (91.4%)	66 (8.6%)	140.2	13.2
1771–75	958	191.6	897 (93.6%)	61 (6.4%)	179.4	12.2
Total	2,792	139.6	2,422 (86.7%)	370 (13.3%)	121.1	18.5

SOURCES: See note 7, chapter 2.

1760s than it ever had before—than it was a manifestation of the sheer magnitude of the new wave of general interest in publishing.

The inner dynamics of publishing also underwent significant changes as the Academy of Sciences Press's pursuit of ideas, entertainment, and income set the standard for other institutional presses, which thereby came to link themselves more closely with lay educated society and less with government and the Orthodox church. As a result, humanistic, literary, and so-called useful books began to play a more substantial role in Russian literate culture.

EDUCATIONAL REFORMS

All of these changes, although important in themselves, must be understood primarily as a consequence of the reforms in education which took place in midcentury. One of the more visible drawbacks of the new imperial service system had been the relative ineffectiveness of the organs of secular education. The state primary schools were virtual failures; military schooling reached few people, to whom it gave proficiency in only a narrow range of technical subjects; and the Academy of Sciences gymnasium and university classes attracted very few Russians in their first decades, and only a relative handful of these graduated.[6] Study abroad, it now appears, was more common than was once thought, but access to it nevertheless was highly restricted.[7] Thus, in 1750 Russian society still depended very heavily on ecclesiastic academies and church schools to provide a majority of its educated people. This state of affairs changed measurably in the middle of the

TABLE 3.2
Subject Composition of Russian-Language Titles Published, 1756–75

Subject	Number of Titles Published	Percentage of all Titles Published	Percentage of Titles Published in Civil Orthography (N = 2,422)
Laws, manifestoes, and regulations	123	4	5
Official information and notices	321	11	13
Religion	547	20	7
Military affairs (excluding laws and regulations)	50	2	2
Calendars	95	3	4
Journals	111	4	5
Alphabet, grammar, and language	63	2	3
History and geography	270	10	11
Technology	53	2	2
Science and mathematics	101	4	4
Secular philosophy	318	11	13
Belles-lettres	482	17	20
Odes	258	9	11
Total	2,792	99	100

SOURCES: See note 7, chapter 2.

century as new schools opened, previously existing ones expanded their enrollments, and a higher percentage of enrolled students graduated. Many schools, moreover, rewrote their curricula to teach a wider array of subjects than they had previously.

To some degree, this improvement was the result of the reorganization of old institutions rather than the creation of new ones. The Academy of Sciences gymnasium and university classes, for example, underwent only modest curricular and instructional changes in the 1750s and 1760s, but the number of students in attendance—and the number of Russian students in particular—rose markedly. Between 1751 and 1765, 590 students attended the gymnasium, of whom about

85 percent were Russian.[8] During the same period, about a hundred students, the majority of whom were Russian, attended the Academy's university classes. Similarly, the religious academies and seminaries were marked more by numerical growth than by consistent curricular changes. Enrollment figures vary enormously from source to source, but there is general agreement that Russia's seminaries had between 5,000 and 6,000 students annually by the mid-1760s and that the numbers rose sharply in the next twenty years.[9]

In elite military education, however, the changes were multifaceted. Military academies, of course, dated back to Peter's day, but their curricula were narrowly technical in scope. In 1732, however, a new academy, the Gentry Infantry Cadet Corps, opened in St. Petersburg, and its curriculum was intended not only to train the sons of the less affluent members of the gentry for careers in the army but also to prepare them to be civilized and cultured citizens.[10]

Until the 1750s the Infantry Cadet academy produced relatively few graduates, although some of these, including Alexander Sumarokov and Mikhail Kheraskov, went on to play important roles in the development of Russian literature. In the early 1750s, however, the Infantry Corps expanded its enrollment, and shortly thereafter two more academies opened in the capital, the Naval Cadet Corps (1752) and the Artillery and Engineering Corps (1758).[11] The numbers of students attending these academies varied from year to year, but the figures ranged from 50 to 200 cadets per school.[12] Thus, between 1755 and the mid-1770s the cadet academies had produced perhaps 2,000 to 4,000 graduates.

In addition to the corps, the network of four-year military garrison schools and hospital schools which were scattered throughout the empire grew substantially in the 1750s and 1760s. These schools provided primary education to lower officers and common soldiers. Their curricula were entirely utilitarian (reading, arithmetic, use of field manuals), but they brought literacy to more soldiers than had ever before received it.[13]

Such a numerical growth unquestionably enriched Russian intellectual life, but educational reform went further both by creating new categories of schools and reforming curricula. The first and most important step in this respect was taken in 1755: the founding of Moscow University, the first genuine university to open in Russia and the first secular institution of higher education of any sort to open in Moscow.[14] Moscow University also opened two boarding schools in the city, one for sons of the gentry and one for sons of the *raznochintsy*, and in 1758 it opened a gymnasium in Kazan.[15] In its first twenty years the

74

university itself graduated over 300 students.[16] Attendance at the Moscow gymnasia was much higher; generally between 200 and 500 students were enrolled at any one time.[17] (No matriculation figures are available for the gymnasium in Kazan.)

Formal schooling also became available to gentry girls with the opening of Ivan Betskoi's Smolnyi Institute in 1764.[18] Smolnyi, of course, was not a training ground for future servitors, since women were not allowed to serve in the ranks. Nevertheless, it did provide a general education to some noblewomen in Russia who could then take part in the cultured world of the educated gentry.

The great majority of students at all these schools, regardless of their level, were Russian-speaking, and most of them either completed their courses or came close to completing them.[19] One need only recall the paucity of Russian students during the early years of the Academy of Sciences' gymnasium to see what an accomplishment this was.

Several factors contributed to the success of the university gymnasium and the Cadet Corps in attracting and keeping students, but the most important was the growing acceptance of formal education by the upper and middle gentry. To get ahead in service, to improve one's status, and to be a truly cultured adult, the gentry came to believe, required a civil and largely humanistic education. In Raeff's words, "it was believed that unless a Russian acquired a smattering of everything that the West had to offer, he could not be considered educated or even civilized."[20]

The very wealthy could arrange for private instruction at home with a tutor, but such tutors were expensive and often they promised much more than they delivered, as satirists and memoirists of those years have made vividly clear. Formal education, by contrast, was less expensive, often more rigorous, and linked more directly to a career in service. Enrollment in the cadet academies counted as years in military service and, after 1758, so did attendance at the university gymnasia. Thus, education came to satisfy both social ideals and service status.

Within a very short time, the accumulation of newly cultured students began to have a marked effect on the educated elite in Russia. Their concentration in the cities or in military regiments made them highly visible and contributed to their self-consciousness. After several years there came to exist what might be termed a critical mass of several thousand educated people, many of whom were more or less permanently ensconced in an urban and increasingly cosmopolitan environment. They often worked together and shared common interests and tastes, and from their midst there emerged a collective consciousness of being the *obshchestvo*—the educated Russian public whose values, tastes, and interests were to set the tone for the rest of society. To a large extent, their shared characteristics revolved around reading and writing. Thus, the secondary-school graduates of the 1750s and 1760s provided a market, such as it was, for Russian elite culture, and, more importantly, they played a decisive role in determining what books institutional presses published. In short, the graduates of these academies, along with their families and friends, composed a clearly defined and self-conscious urban reading public—a social context, as it were, for the Russian Enlightenment.

This new phenomenon was also partly due to the revised curricula, which came to emphasize a cultural rather than technical education and to lay particular stress upon modern or classical languages, history, mathematics, and moral philosophy.[21] Some of the academies also taught astronomy, physics, political philosophy, and law. In the process of familiarizing this generation of service gentry with general European culture and modern languages, the secondary schools provided a set of moral ideals, assimilation of which became the threshold for entry into civilized society.[22] Putting these ideals into practice, moreover, necessitated reaching outside of their own milieu through printed communications to reach the students of the military garrison schools, hospital schools, and seminaries, whose graduates provided a potential readership for the books that the elite students wished to publish. To be sure, these wider circles of readers never really coalesced into a public. Even though there were many times more graduates from these schools than from the elite academies, they were geographically more scattered, less visible, and culturally and socially more heterogeneous than was educated society. Whether or not most of them even read books outside of school is unclear. In the short run, then, their contact with printing might have been limited to their need as students, soldiers, or priests. In the long run, however, they constituted a literate presence in the provinces of which publishers were aware and whom they attempted to reach. Thus, they became an important basis for an attempt to extend the printed culture of the educated groups in the major cities to the nation as a whole.

All of this, perhaps, followed inevitably from the marriage of humanistic education to the demands of state service, but the persistent prominence of printing in scholastic settings is nevertheless striking. Between 1752 and 1774 eight new institutional presses were opened in Russia, four of them at elite schools—the Naval Corps (1752), Moscow University (1756), the Infantry Corps (1757), and the Artillery and Engineering Corps (1765). In the period between 1755 and 1775 these scholastic presses, along with the Academy of Sciences

Press, dominated Russian publishing, accounting for about three-quarters of all published books (tables 3.3 and 3.4).[23]

In many ways, this aggregate category reflects a certain commonality of experience that distinguished the scholastic presses from the governmental and church ones. Begun with narrowly conceived educational mandates and modest budgets, the scholastic presses came to seek out private donors, patrons, and even a popular market. The pursuit of outside support broadened their editorial activities and resulted in repertoires of books that greatly exceeded the limits of their initial charters. Individual characteristics and problems did manifest themselves, however, and these had critical influence over the ultimate direction which publishing took. The histories of the individual presses therefore require some discussion.

THE SCHOLASTIC PUBLISHING HOUSES

The first new publishing house, the Naval Corps Press, opened its doors early in 1753. For the first years, its publications were limited

TABLE 3.3

Number of Russian-Language Titles Published by Individual Presses, 1756–75

	Number Published
Moscow Presses	
Moscow University	685
Synod	351
Senate	52
Total	1,088
St. Petersburg Presses	
Academy of Sciences	969
Infantry Corps	258
Naval Corps	140
Artillery Corps	25
Military College	57
Synod	105
Senate	124
Other	26
Total	1,704

SOURCE: Based on data in *Svodnyi katalog* and Zernova, *Svodnyi katalog kirillovskoi pechati*.

77

TABLE 3.4
Number and Percentage of Russian-Language Books Titles Published,
1756–75, by Category of Press

Category of Press	Number	Percentage
Scholastic	2,075	74
Governmental	259	9
Church	458	16
Total	2,792	99

SOURCE: Based on data in *Svodnyi katalog and Zernova, Svodnyi katalog kirillovskoi pechati.*

to serving the needs of its cadets and of the navy in general, which meant technical, informational, or narrowly educational books.[24] In 1763 the press's manager complained that the corps was wasting the talents of its employees by not utilizing the press more fully.[25] With a meager annual budget of 1,800 rubles, the Naval Corps Press had been able to produce only twelve titles in its first ten years. In order to take fuller advantage of the print shop's capacity, the manager requested that he be allowed to accept private orders for publication and that the press be permitted to print books of a more general nature than it heretofore had. This request was quickly granted by the Admiralty College and approved by the Senate, and by the end of the year the Naval Corps Press began accepting private orders.

The other major cadet publishing house of this time, the Infantry Corps Press, achieved a similar status, although by a less circuitous route. Opened with a small budget in 1758, the Infantry Corps Press was mandated to publish "books in the Russian language for the education of lower officers and cadets at the corps . . . specifically arithmetic, geometry and general history . . . and for special military ceremonies . . ."[26] Rather early on, however, it began to accept outside manuscripts, and it even published on its own account certain books, such as translated Italian opera librettos, which fell outside the official mandate.

The fact that the managers of the Naval and Infantry Corps presses showed interest in accepting noninstitutional support demonstrates that they assumed, first, that private manuscripts and money would be forthcoming from St. Petersburg society and, second, that they could attract it to their publishing houses.

These possibilities were further enhanced by the relative editorial autonomy enjoyed by both presses. The Naval Corps Press, for example, was obliged to gain approval only from its own academic overseer, Count Andrei Poletika. For the Infantry Corps Press, an affiliation with the Academy of Sciences Press led to a slightly more cumbersome system, in which a committee of five professors representing the Academy and the corps reviewed all publications, but only for the purpose of eliminating illegal or blatantly offensive material.[27] Although this editorial committee did insist upon some excisions and textual modifications, it rarely imposed outright bans. Thus, by the early 1760s the way was cleared for the cadet publishing houses to solicit manuscripts and patronage and to base their repertoires on the demands of whatever public made itself known. Almost overnight the presses blossomed into very active literary centers.[28] The Naval Corps Press's output grew from one book a year in its first decade to ten a year in its second, and between 1758 and 1775 the Infantry Corps Press printed 258 Russian-language books, an average of fourteen a year.[29] For both presses, the ability to accept privately financed books seems to have made the major difference. Several individuals and even some institutions, notably the Synod and the imperial court, began to patronize the Infantry Corps Press regularly in the 1760s.[30] The evidence for the Naval Corps Press is less specific, but it too seems to point to the importance of outside funds.[31]

But who would provide these funds? Governmental institutions subsidized publications that were of use to them, but these were not usually general-interest or literary books. Local merchants and patrons, for their part, had developed a satisfactory relationship with the Academy of Sciences Press, whose commitment to profitability and intellectual achievement was by now well established. It appears that most of the money came from within the cadet milieu itself—students, teachers, and recent graduates of the corps, whose motives were not to make money but simply to bring their own works or the works of their friends into print. Private financing was thus merely a means by which cadets and officers could gain access to the press and thereby transform their own cultural interests from private and personal affairs into public ones.

At first glance, these interests, as manifested in published books, were remarkably eclectic, spanning diverse topics, genre, continents, centuries, and languages. Books for use in courses included texts on history, geography, medicine, and foreign languages as well as on military and naval science. The cadet presses also produced a wide range of general-interest books, including some of the earliest Russian translations of Voltaire (including *Zadig* [1765] and *The History of the Crusades* [1772]), Christian Gellert (*The Life of the Swedish Countess*

79

G. [1766–68]), and Molière (*The Sicilian* [1776] and *Amphitryon* [1761]), as well as numerous other lesser-known moralistic stories and romances.[32]

No Russian publishing house before this time, not even the Academy of Sciences Press, had produced so many general-interest titles, yet without minimizing the significance of cadet publishing, one nevertheless must comment on what was missing from it. Excepting occasional poetry or panegyrics by Sergei Domashnev, Ippolit Bogdanovich, and Iakov Kozel'skii, cadet presses printed precious little original literature. Even among the relatively numerous literary translations, there were noteworthy absences. Other than Voltaire's dramas and Diderot's comedy, *The Illegitimate Son*,[33] the cadet presses published almost nothing from the French Encyclopedists. Their commitment to moralistic literature rarely extended beyond works whose morals could be told through rather light tales of adventure and romance. Natural sciences and serious philosophical tracts, whether modern or ancient, were largely ignored, and classical literature and history—the type of books that had been popular for half a century or more—were barely in evidence. Thus, although the cadet books conformed in some ways to Raeff's characterization of the cosmopolitan nature of educated society in the 1760s, the "smattering of everything that the West had to offer" was in other ways rather exclusive.

Precisely why the cadets accepted some current trends and ignored others is difficult to determine; the usual explanations for editorial selectivity—censorship, profit, and ideology—seem not to be very important in this case. Censorship was a marginal and episodic affair and, in any event, it was not the authorities who imposed these limits but the cadets themselves. The pursuit of income focused on private subsidies and patronage much more than on sales on the open market, and there is no evidence that anyone associated with cadet publishing held views that might somehow have called for the exclusion of original literature, classics, philosophy, and science.

This selectivity does seem to have a certain affinity with the cadet corps curricula, however, which offered courses in history, moral upbringing, and, above all, modern languages, but not in classical languages or literature, rhetoric, natural sciences, or political philosophy.[34] This curricular structure had a direct and obvious bearing on the textbooks which the corps printed—mainly grammars, history books, and moral-educational books. The majority of general-interest books, however, were submitted and financed by private individuals, yet these too did not wander very far from the limits defined by the curricula, except in the direction of translated light fiction.[35]

Upon closer examination, what seems to have been at work here was a certain correspondence between the limits of the curricula of the corps and the limits in the literary outlooks and ambitions of the corps's intellectual circles. The largest group of contributors consisted of rather obscure cadets or officers (usually recent graduates of the corps) who had composed translations of typical romances or moralistic tales from French, German, or English and who, with their own funds or with the funds of a friend, wished to publish them.[36] Most of them, like Peter Pastiukhov and Alexander Shablykin, produced perhaps a couple of lightweight translations at some stage in careers which otherwise were given over to service. A few students, such as Alexander Khrapovitskii and Peter Svistunov, continued to publish translations for several years, but even they did not become important literary figures. These students apparently saw translating less as a serious intellectual endeavor or pursuit of moral influence than as a literary exercise that served as a rite of passage into the world of educated society.

Such was not the case, however, for the teachers at the cadet corps, who comprised the second category of the press's authors. Among these were some better-known individuals, including Iakov Kozel'skii, Luka Sichkarev, and Sergei Nakoval'nin, all of whom had received some higher education before coming to teach at the corps.[37] Sichkarev, for example, had attended university classes at the Academy of Sciences prior to his arrival at the Infantry Academy in 1762.

In his classic study of *raznochintsy* intellectuals in the eighteenth century, M. M. Shtrange has argued that these teachers composed a discrete, nongentry cadet corps intelligentsia who possessed a certain collective identity and manifested distinct intellectual ambitions.[38] Although subsequent scholarship has shown this argument to be both overdrawn and anachronistic, Shtrange does have a point in characterizing the teachers as a distinct group, at least if publishing is any index. In the service of their students, many of them authored or translated textbooks, moral-educational works, history books, and, less frequently, plays and odes. After several years of scholastic publishing, some of the cadet corps teachers, most notably Kozel'skii, developed into leading pedagogical and literary figures. Yet, with few exceptions, these loftier endeavors took place outside of the confines of cadet publishing. While Kozel'skii was teaching at the Artillery and Engineering Corps, for example, he translated eight dramas and history texts for the Infantry Press Corps, but his more serious translations, such as K. F. von Moser's *The Gentleman and the Servant*, bore the imprimatur of the Academy of Sciences Press.[39] Similarly, Sichkarev translated a light English work called *The Merry Philosopher* for the Infantry Corps Press in 1766, but after leaving the corps in 1768, he went on to translate several Greek sermons and a book by the seventeenth-century Pietist, Johann Arndt, called *Studies in Christianity*, for the Moscow University and Academy of Sciences presses.[40]

Thus, these teachers apparently perceived certain cultural limits to cadet publishing and translating, defined by the curricula, that precluded using the scholastic presses as organs of serious thought or original literature. By the early 1770s this identity was so well established that many experienced translators and their patrons forsook the cadet presses in favor of the intellectually more ambitious and potentially more lucrative ventures which had begun at the Academy of Sciences Press. As a result of this modest flight, the managers of the cadet presses began to comment in the 1770s on their inability to procure new translations and patronage, a fact which led cadet publishing into a decline from which it emerged only in the mid-1780s.

The cadet presses, then, never operated at the intellectual forefront of St. Petersburg society, but they did bring something new and important to Russian publishing. Never before had educated Russians with few, if any, intellectual ambitions moved so easily from the classroom to translating and publishing. These were amateurs in every way: they were young, unpaid, active for only a short time, and ultimately of little importance in the history of ideas.[41] Their eagerness to translate and publish books which were interesting and entertaining to themselves provided Russia with hundreds of newly published titles.

Unfortunately, few of these translators have left personal records of their student or poststudent years. Thus, we do not know whether they perceived translating and publishing as entirely personal acts or as brief attempts to reach out in some small way to the interests of the reading public. In one sense, the preparation and publication of manuscripts were, in themselves, expressions of public interest, since cadets and officers were readers as much as they were writers. One may assume, moreover, that whatever impressions they held of the reading public at large derived in great measure from what they and their friends wanted to read. But the preponderance of evidence points to at least some interest in readers beyond the immediate cadet milieu. In the 1760s, for example, both the Infantry and the Naval Corps opened public bookshops, and, although their proximity to the corps themselves suggests that these shops were most often frequented by cadets and officers, both of them were situated on major thoroughfares and were open to the general public. Both presses, moreover, published several catalogues of books for sale at their respective bookshops, and by the mid-1760s they were also printing advertisements for newly published books in the *St. Petersburg News*.[42]

Most cadet press titles were publicized regardless of whether or not they were privately financed, and in theory these books were available to everyone who could read.[43] In practice, however, it is unlikely that the public for cadet presses extended very broadly outside of St. Petersburg. No mention is made in the catalogues or in the newspaper notices of outlets in other cities or of arrangements to purchase by mail. Thus, although the cadet corps books may have been highly accessible in the capital, they could not have had a significant national audience. In the end, therefore, the role of the cadet presses in Russian educated life was a parochial one, limited both by the scope of their intellectual vision and by the geographic confines of their distribution network. As Kozel'skii and Sichkarev had recognized, the pursuit of loftier goals and the ambition of achieving moral influence required moving to the presses of the leading centers of knowledge at Moscow University and the Academy of Sciences.

Moscow University Press

The initial edict that established Moscow University, curiously, said nothing about a press but instead spoke of the need to provide the population around Moscow with more teachers and to put "lazy men" to work.[44] But from the outset, the first rector of Moscow University, Ivan Shuvalov, wanted to establish a university publishing house.[45] He purchased materials from the Moscow Synod Press, the Academy of Sciences Press, and foreign presses, and in March 1755 he received permission from the Senate to begin publishing books.[46]

After publishing only official notices, lectures, a few textbooks, and the *Moscow News (Moskovskie Vedomosti)* in its first few years, the Moscow University Press grew very quickly both in size and in scope. In 1760 it owned eleven printing presses and employed seventy-eight full-time workers.[47] By the mid-1760s it was printing close to 40 books a year, and between 1756 and 1775 it published nearly 700 Russian-language titles and well over 800 titles in all. The subject composition of its Russian-language publications during that period is shown in table 3.5.

Pedagogy, of course, had the most immediate influence on the press's output, since the university required up-to-date textbooks for its students, who often were obliged to purchase personal copies. In contrast to the Academy of Sciences, instruction at the university was conducted mostly in Russian, and students at the university's gymnasia could

TABLE 3.5
Subject Composition of Moscow University Press Russian-Language
Publications, 1756–75

Subject	Number	Percentage
Laws, manifestoes, and regulations	8	1
Official information and notices	167	19
Religion	70	8
Military affairs (excluding laws and regulations)	19	2
Journals	34	4
Alphabet, grammar, and language	50	6
History and geography	53	6
Technology	20	2
Science and mathematics	24	3
Secular philosophy	126	14
Belles-lettres	152	17
Odes	152	17
Total	875	99
Books in foreign languages	131	

SOURCES: Based on data in *Svodnyi katalog*; Mel'nikova, *Izdaniia napechatannye*; and N. N. Mel'nikova, *Izdaniia Moskovskogo universiteta, 1756–1779* (Moscow, 1955).
NOTE: Because of the Moscow fire of 1812, almost no print-run figures are available.

choose either a Russian or a Latin course of instruction. In addition, some professors, most notably Semen Desnitskii, objected to depending exclusively on foreign textbooks for their courses and insisted upon lecturing in Russian to provide some balance.[48] Thus, after a few years, the university's faculty began to translate many texts for their courses into Russian, or they wrote their own.[49] In this context, the breadth of the university's and gymnasia's curricula, which included law, medicine, political philosophy, modern languages, classical languages, astronomy, physics, and mathematics in itself elevated Moscow University Press above the cadet presses.

But pedagogy was only one influence on publishing at the university. In contrast to the cadet corps, Moscow University was obliged by statute to provide books for the whole population of Moscow rather than for just its own students.[50] The university administration, moreover, expected (in vain, as it turned out) that the press would turn a profit and provide revenue for the university at large. When initial operating expenses had created a deficit of 25,000 rubles by 1761, Shuvalov urged the press manager to publish books quickly, efficiently, and profitably, and when a series of minor problems delayed the publication of some potential big sellers, Shuvalov demanded that the work be completed forthwith.[51]

In keeping with this policy of generating income, the press advertised its books very actively by printing book notices in almost every issue of the *Moscow News*, in the back of many other Moscow University publications, and in separately printed catalogues. Between 1762 and 1775 the bookshop—which had been placed in the hands of two experienced German book dealers, Christian Wever and Christian Rüdiger—circulated at least nine catalogues of available titles.[52] It also sought to expand the market for its books by contacting potential agents in several provinces in the 1760s and 1770s and by arranging tentative contracts with them.[53]

But the pursuit of income does not account for either the range or the size of the university's publishing activity. Indeed, most of its books seem to have sold rather poorly. The press, after all, was the first secular publishing house in Moscow and had little practical experience or conventional wisdom by which to fashion a publishing repertoire that would be immediately popular with Moscow's readers. Nor did the press have the benefit of a patronage which could provide financial support and some measure of the interests of the public, at least not until the late 1760s.[54] At that time a few university administrators and employees, including Wever, Shuvalov, Kheraskov, and Vasilii Adodurov, began to subsidize the publication of certain books, but even then Moscow University benefited very little from patronage or other external sources of cash when compared with the other scholastic presses. How, then, was it able to pay for so many new books? Unfortunately, there appears to be no way of giving an informed answer to this question, but one can say that the catalyst for making Moscow University Press into a creative intellectual force came less from the open market than from the students and teachers of the university itself.

The single most important step in this regard came when the university appointed the poet and translator, Mikhail Kheraskov, to act as the university's censor and press overseer from 1757 to 1761. He was followed by another author and teacher, Anton Teil's, as overseer and by a professor of rhetoric, Anton Barsov, as censor.[55] Prior to 1757, Kheraskov's literary accomplishments had actually been quite modest, but upon arriving at the university he began to write and publish a great many odes and dramas. Within a year of his appointment he had translated and published a collection of Molière's plays and Alexander Pope's *Essay on Mankind*. By 1770 he had published twenty-six separate titles of his own work. His example encouraged a number of university professors, such as Nikolai Popovskii, Anton Barsov, and Johann Reichel, to write and publish their own works, both scholarly and literary, and to translate a great deal of European literature. Popovskii, for example, translated several other essays of Pope, and Reichel became the editor of a popular journal, *A Collection of the Best Works (Sobranie luchshikh sochinenii)*.

The decision to place administrative and editorial control over the press in the hands of prominent literati underscored the university's commitment to literary activity at a relatively high level. It enhanced the university's status as the centerpiece of Moscow's budding lay intellectual life by attracting educated people to the press, who then were encouraged to publish. Many of the earliest graduates of the university and its gymnasia, for example, decided to stay in the city and take advantage of the press to pursue their own interests rather than going off to serve in the capital. In the early 1760s a cluster of intelligent and ambitious young men, including such future luminaries as Nikolai Novikov, Ippolit Bogdanovich, and the FonVizin brothers, joined with their mentors at the university to create a lively intellectual atmosphere, much of which was built around publishing activities. The first fruits of their labors came almost immediately, in the form of a series of privately initiated literary and philosophical magazines.

Prior to the late 1750s, journalism in St. Petersburg had been limited to a biweekly newspaper, a scientific monograph series in Latin, and two vaguely general-interest monthlies, Müller's *Monthly Works (Ezhemesiachnye sochineniia*, 1755–64) and the *Notes* to the *St. Petersburg News*. Moscow had only one periodical, the biweekly *Moscow News* that began publication in 1756. Between 1760 and 1764, however, six new literary magazines were launched in Moscow, five of them published in Russian and one in French.[56] The magazines were printed entirely with private funds at the Moscow University Press and were produced by Kheraskov and the community of professors, students, and recent graduates who had gathered around him.[57]

None of these early private journals was a great literary or commercial success. All but one, *Useful Entertainment (Poleznoe uveselenie)*, folded after less than a year and most of the original contributions were quickly forgotten. Yet these journals provided Kheraskov's coterie with an important and largely unprecedented outlet for original and translated literature that, in Kheraskov's own words, allowed them "to defend virtue, to prosecute vice and to entertain society."[58] What is important here is not so much their actual impact on public morals—Kheraskov, in fact, gave the journals low marks for moral influence—but the fact that the university youth saw themselves as responsible instruments of both morality and entertainment who required print to establish a public voice. In contrast to the cadets, whose flirtation with publishing was usually quite brief, many of the Moscow University literati came to treat journalism, translating, and publishing as morally uplifting and lifelong endeavors, albeit ones that were expected only to complement lifelong careers in service.

Recent studies have shown that the particular moral vision that inspired this generation to embrace publishing, for all its civic piety, remained intensely personal and concerned with living the most moral life possible. Scholars have demonstrated that the literati assimilated their views from the German pietism taught to them by university instructors such as Reichel, Johann Schaden, and Philip Dilthey, many of whom had been trained by Christian Wolff and Justus Möser.[59] Yet without minimizing the heritage of German natural law in forming the world view of students at Moscow University, one is nevertheless struck by the fact that when they began to publish, the university students showed a preference for French drama and rationalism. Several of them, for example, participated in a project to translate and publish several articles from Diderot's *Encyclopédie*. This project had first been discussed by Kheraskov in the early 1760s, but it was only in 1767 that a three-volume selection of articles from the *Encyclopédie* came out as part of a joint project with the Academy of Sciences.[60]

The *Encyclopédie* project was just one aspect of the growing interest in the French Enlightenment, for Moscow's literati also translated the works of numerous contemporary French writers, including Voltaire, Rousseau, and d'Alembert, and those of older renowned dramatists such as Molière. Moralistic literature, by contrast, was quite sparsely represented. Christian Gellert, one of whose works had already appeared in an Infantry Cadet Press edition in 1766, did not have a Moscow University Press printing until 1773; Stephanie Genlis's books did not begin to appear at Moscow University until 1779; François Fénelon was published once in Moscow in 1766 but not again until 1778; and Johann Dusch's work did not have a Moscow edition until Novikov took over the press in 1779.[61] Indeed, until the late 1770s, the press's portfolio of moral-educational tracts consisted of a single 1759 translation of John Locke's *Some Thoughts concerning Education* (prepared not by a student but by a Professor Nikolai Popovskii), and several translations of Marmontel's light moralistic stories.[62]

Even more perplexing in this context is the unmistakable preference for the French language over German, since, according to some accounts, the competence of the French teachers at the gymnasia was often in doubt while the German teachers were regarded as on the whole more professional.[63] Whatever the reason, the university's translators turned far more frequently to French originals or even to French translations of books that were written in other languages than they did to German, English, Greek, or Latin originals. Popovskii's translation of Locke, for example, was based on a French edition. As table 3.6 shows, the period as a whole witnessed a preponderance of translations from French originals, in marked contrast to the first half of the century, during which German and Italian dominated.

It would be a mistake to conclude from this evidence that the students' pietism was illusory, but it does appear that the movement from classroom to printing press involved at least a partial shift from *Aufklärung* to *lumière*. Since printing was the agent that transformed intellectual deliberations from private acts with largely personal consequences into social ones with broader significance, this shift is quite important. It was the printed literature, after all, that the reading public saw and reflected upon rather than the private deliberations, and as a consequence educated society identified the literati with France, Voltaire, and the *Encyclopédie* rather than with Germany, Wolff, and Leibnitz.

This circumstance encapsulates many of the paradoxes and confusions which have made the intellectual strands of the Russian Enlightenment so difficult to disentangle. Students who were imbued with a vision of personal and civic virtue and with a heightened sense of

TABLE 3.6
Publication of Books Translated into Russian, 1756–75

Original Language[a]	Number	Percentage
French	402	52
German	175	23
Italian	54	7
Latin	54	7
English	36	5
Other	44	6

SOURCE: Based on data in *Svodnyi katalog*.

[a] If calculations were based not on the original language of the work but on the language from which the Russian translation was made, the proportion of French works would be even higher than is shown in this table.

patriotic duty, both of which drew inspiration from pietism, published mainly entertaining translations from French which exalted reason and skepticism and which cultivated frivolous tastes and attitudes ("Voltairianism") among the educated public which the literati found alien and, by the mid-1770s, mildly distressing.

In the short run, these paradoxes were barely perceptible. Everything was so new, especially in Moscow, that the mere capability of publishing large numbers of modern works relatively easily was, in itself, a marvel and a source of pleasure and optimism. In the late 1760s, however, the initial wave of activity began to wane as most of the members of Kheraskov's group left Moscow to serve on the new Legislative Commission in St. Petersburg. In 1770 Kheraskov himself left; by that time, the flight to St. Petersburg had thoroughly drained the university of students and teachers.[64] In the space of two years, the city of Moscow lost most of its leading writers and many other educated people, and then in 1771, it fell victim to an even worse calamity, the plague. This time thousands of people fled the city, including the city administration and the administration of the university. For the next two and one-half years, Moscow University Press operated at a greatly reduced rate, and it was sometimes difficult to keep it open at all.[65]

By 1774, the press had revived to a point where it was publishing more books than it had before the plague had broken out. But the intellectual luminaries, most of whom had remained in the capital, proved to be irreplaceable. As a consequence, the press relied mostly on accepted genres, proven authors, and textbooks until the very end of the 1770s, when many of the original student members of Kheraskov's group returned and revived Moscow's intellectual life.

In the mid-1770s, then, Moscow University Press experienced a decline that chronologically paralleled the ebbing productivity of the cadet presses. Although their respective declines were very different, they all dramatized the fragility of the economic and cultural basis of Russian publishing at the time and the instability of a success built entirely upon the creative energies of a small group of people. Indeed, after decades of steady growth, the only Russian publishing house with the ability to sustain an intellectual and institutional vitality was the Academy of Sciences Press, which seemed, in fact, to thrive when all other presses suffered.

THE ACADEMY OF SCIENCES PRESS

In the late 1750s the Academy of Sciences had eleven printing presses in operation, and by 1770 it had at least seventeen, an expansion which made it one of the larger publishing houses in Europe.[66] The press had quite clearly grown too large to continue to rely upon the Academy chancellery for day-to-day planning.[67] In the 1760s, therefore, the printers themselves took over control of the routine operations of the press from the Academy chancellery.[68] This arrangement permitted the Academy to retain a great deal of influence in deciding what would be published, especially since a representative of the chancellery was empowered to review every manuscript prior to publication.[69] Nevertheless, press operations became much more autonomous.

To be sure, throughout this period the Academy maintained its commitment to scholarship. It continued to publish a monograph series (now the *Novi Commentarii*), it sent scientific publications to academies abroad, and it went to some lengths to regain fiscal credit abroad so that it could continue to engage in an international exchange of scientific works. Emboldened by its new-found reputation, the Academy expanded its scholarship in these years to include Russian-language books for a domestic readership which, perhaps, would show a greater curiosity about such subjects than the previous generation had. Thus, between 1755 and 1775, the Academy published important historical works by Mikhail Lomonosov, Mikhail Shcherbatov, V. N. Tatishchev, and G. F. Müller. In addition, it printed significant topographical and ethnographic descriptions of the Russian empire by Müller, Peter Simon Pallas, Rychkov, and others.

But scholarship, for all its prestige, remained mostly unremunerative, and the Academy press, more than any other publishing house, sought hard cash and profitable translations. Between 1755 and 1765, the Academy employed sixteen full-time translators, and in 1766 it hired approximately a dozen more.[70] Most of the new translators were gymnasium students, former students, or young men whom the Academy had sent abroad for their education. All of them, significantly enough, were placed under the supervision of the best-selling translators of the 1740s and 1750s, Vasilii Lebedev and Sergei Volchkov.[71]

By the 1760s, full-time translators were earning salaries that ranged between 80 and 350 rubles a year. As an added incentive, the Academy began to pay certain proven translators by the page, allowing them to approximate or exceed what they could have earned in other branches of the service.[72] In addition, personal influence was used to generate new and potentially profitable translations. In the late 1750s such prominent figures as Lomonosov and Jacob Stählin suggested that the press should publish more translated books, and in 1761 the Academy chancellery ordered each member of the Academy and each professor of the Academy's university to send a list of books in his respective field that, if translated, would have a broad appeal to the reading public.[73]

All of this activity encouraged ever more people to submit unsolicited translations for publication and, they hoped, remuneration. Translators from other governmental offices, for example, presented the Academy with a steady stream of translations which they had prepared in their spare time.[74] Also, various employees of the Academy presented literary manuscripts that they, too, had prepared on their own time.[75]

The Academy press, however, beyond simply providing entertainment, was committed to maintaining its intellectual leadership, which obligated it to publish books even when profits were not in prospect. Thus, in 1768, when Catherine the Great decided to exploit some of the intellectual talent that had been assembled at the capital for the Legislative Commission in order to form a new group named the Society Striving for the Translation of Foreign Books (Sobranie staraiushcheesia o perevode inostrannykh knig), she used the Academy press as her primary medium rather than the Senate or cadet presses. Catherine's intellectual ambition in those years was virtually boundless. Through the Translation Society, she intended to put dozens of people to work translating important books, supporting them with an annual subsidy of 5,000 rubles from her own account. This combination of remuneration and intellectual stimulation attracted a broad spectrum of people. Semennikov compiled a partial list of forty-four people who took part in the Translation Society, some of whom were former university students and well-known writers, such as Iakov Kozel'skii, Grigorii Kozitskii, and Vasilii Ruban, but many others of whom were rather obscure figures—Academy translators, minor employees of the Academy, or simple guards officers who had gotten involved with Catherine's circle. In fact, the line which divided the society's translators from Academy translators and from the more informal literary circles at court was crossed so often that there was considerable confusion about the status of the Translation Society within the Academy. Some translators were drawing double salaries, and it was not always clear whether a book was being submitted to the press on behalf of the Academy or on behalf of the Translation Society.

In spite of these confusions, the Translation Society lasted until 1783, and during that time it was responsible for the publication of 112 separate translations, which ran to 174 volumes.[76] When it ceased publishing, moreover, it had completed an additional 29 translations for publication, and it had begun work on nearly 100 more.[77] In its day it was probably the leading Russian voice for the French Enlightenment, since it published over a dozen separate selections from the *Encyclopédie*, along with individual works by Corneille, Mably, Montesquieu (including *The Spirit of the Laws*), Voltaire (*Candide*), and Rousseau. Once again, however, German natural law made little appearance. Of the leading moralists, only Christian Gellert was represented, and he only by comedies and romances. Reason, adventure, and romance were the order of the day, whether it be French drama, the classical literature of Cicero and Homer, or English novels such as Fielding's *Joseph Andrews* and *Amelia* and Swift's *Gulliver's Travels*. Of course, since the empress paid the translators' salaries—and because she was, after all, the empress—she wielded enormous editorial influence over the society's choice of manuscripts. But her translators seem not to have expressed dissatisfaction with her choices.

The experience of the Translation Society revealed Catherine at her best as patroness of the arts, but it also showed her at her parsimonious worst. Although generous with salaries, the empress was reluctant to bear the costs of printing. The Academy paid for paper, ink, printing costs, distribution fees, and the wages of press workers. Since the print runs of most of the Translation Society's early publications were high—normally 1,200 copies per book—this amounted to quite an expensive undertaking.

Obviously it would have been imprudent, to say the least, for the Academy to have demanded that Catherine pay for all expenses related to the publishing of her society's books. But the Academy clearly was concerned. In March 1770 the Academy chancellery complained to Catherine that the publications of the Translation Society had generated little income and had proven to be very poor sellers. It requested either that it be given more control over what was translated or that the Translation Society bear some of the costs.[78] These suggestions went unheeded, and in April 1771 the Academy found itself still underwriting in toto the Translation Society's publications.[79]

In April 1772 the Academy tried again. In return for being relieved of the costs of publication, the Academy offered to hand over all but 2 percent of the income earned from the sale of the Translation Society's books in the Academy's bookshop.[80] Apparently, this approach drew a more favorable response; after mid-1772 a few of the society's titles appeared "at the cost of Her Majesty's private offices." Still, this method of financing paid for fewer than half of the society's books, and the Academy's problem of large and unprofitable cash outlays remained unsolved. The Academy, therefore, adopted several new approaches. It decided, first, to order smaller print runs, closer to the level of demand. After 1772 the Translation Society's titles' print runs mostly ranged between 300 and 600. This change reduced material costs, but it had little effect on the cost of labor, most of which went into setting type. Unless the society's books sold better, producing them would still be unprofitable.

In an effort to address the marketing problem, the Academy arranged contracts with various merchants to sell the society's books both in St. Petersburg and in the provinces. The most important such arrangement involved a St. Petersburg bookseller, Matvei Nikiforov, who agreed to sell the books for a 10 percent commission or a fee not to exceed 300 rubles annually. Two other merchants, Mikhail Fomin and Mikhail Tiulpin, agreed to sell the books on consignment from Nikiforov.[81] This second solution was promising, but it did not guarantee the Academy against losses. In fact, if the merchants could not find additional buyers, the Academy actually would have increased its debt, because the contracts guaranteed a minimum fee to the consignees. Thus, the Academy turned to educated society in pursuit of patrons who would underwrite publication of the Translation Society's books.

The irony of seeking patronage for the empress—the erstwhile patroness—could not have been lost on officials in the Academy. Still, the campaign met with a good deal of success, and by 1775 about half of the Translation Society's titles were being financed privately. A few merchants and wealthy gentry pledged support; in some instances, the Academy insisted that the translators themselves pay the publication costs. But by far the most interesting episode in the search for financiers took place in 1773, when the Translation Society and the Academy of Sciences entered into an agreement with a group calling itself the Society Striving for Publishing Books (Obshchestvo staraiushcheesia o napechatanii knig).[82]

Very little is known about the origins of this new society or about its participants. Some historians have plausibly argued from the similarity of the names that the Publishing Society came into existence at Catherine's behest in order to support the Translation Society, but all that is known for sure is the identity of the Publishing Society's founders, Nikolai Novikov and a St. Petersburg bookseller, Karl Müller.

The sources do not indicate when Novikov and Müller actually formed the Publishing Society. The first reference to it in Academy sources came on January 30, 1773, when the title page of Kheraskov's tragedy, *Borislav*, indicated that it was published by Novikov "at the expense of his society."[83] A letter published at approximately the same time in Novikov's journal, *The Painter (Zhivopisets)*, made reference to the Publishing Society by inquiring why it published mainly translations and why its books were so expensive in the provinces.[84] This letter, signed by "the lovers of wisdom from Yaroslavl," implies that the Publishing Society had been active for some time. It is widely believed, however, that the letter actually was written by Catherine in order to draw attention to the Publishing Society.[85]

Cognizant of the problems that the Translation Society had experienced, and armed with little capital, Novikov and Müller embarked on an active marketing campaign for their books. Advertisements were printed in the *St. Petersburg News* and in the back of some books published by the Academy. As an added inducement, Novikov offered discounts for multivolume or advance purchases.[86] Evidently, these measures were not especially successful, because the Publishing Society proved unable to meet its financial obligations to the Academy; as late as 1784 Novikov had an unpaid debt to the Academy from those years of over 839 rubles.[87]

The Academy, to be sure, did not make Novikov's job very easy. The press had spent so much money on publishing the works of the Translation Society that it had begun to experience cash shortages. To alleviate this problem, it instituted the requirement that all patrons of privately submitted manuscripts pay half the publication costs in advance.[88] In effect, Novikov and others had to make large payments before they received any income from sales. This requirement was more than the Publishing Society's apparently limited resources could bear, and by the end of 1774 the Publishing Society had ceased to exist. During its two-year life, it had underwritten the costs of eighteen books.[89] About half of them were Translation Society books, and most of the rest were original works by contemporary Russian writers.

The Academy's position in this matter is understandable. By virtue of the awkward circumstances, the Translation Society was costing the Academy more money than it could afford, and these uncontrollable losses necessitated other avenues of compensation. By choosing such a rigid fiscal policy, however, the Academy inhibited private individuals from expanding their contacts with its press. Novikov, for example, severely curtailed his publishing after 1774, resuming in earnest only after moving to Moscow in 1779. The Academy, in turn, was left to pay most of the printing bills of the Translation Society for another nine years.

In spite of this troublesome financial experience, the Publishing Society marked another milestone for Russian publishing. For the first time in Russia, individuals had come together on the periphery of a scholastic institution to create a separate publishing society that exercised a high degree of autonomy over manuscript procurement, fund raising, and editorial decisions. In this way, representatives of the literati were gaining more control over publishing, and, if they proved solvent, the Academy was prepared to let them do so.

NOVIKOV AND THE LITERARY MAGAZINES

It bears noting that the movement of editorial control into the hands of an independent society was predicated on the union of intellectual (Novikov) and commercial (Müller) interests with which scholastic printing was now quite familiar. Müller was a German-born merchant with experience in the book trade. Little is known about his role in the Publishing Society or his motives for getting involved, but he was on good terms with Novikov and his St. Petersburg friends, and in all probability he provided the group with whatever economic expertise it had.

Novikov, on the other hand, had had little commercial experience. Gentry-born, he had received his education at Moscow University and had served for a number of years in the Izmailovskii Regiment and then on the Legislative Commission. Although he was not unmindful of the economic realities of publishing, his interests lay in ideas and moral persuasion rather than in profits. He had had some minor connection with the private journals of the early sixties, but his serious entry into publishing took place after he moved to the capital in 1765. In 1766 he published books with both the Academy of Sciences Press and the Infantry Cadet Press, and by 1773 he had subsidized the printing of twelve titles, mostly his own translations.[90] By all accounts, though, Novikov's visibility in St. Petersburg's intellectual life was linked less with his early publishing ventures than with his role as secretary of the Legislative Commission and his prominence in reviving journalism in the capital during the so-called era of the satirical journals of 1769 to 1774.

General-interest journalism, it will be recalled, had relatively deep roots in St. Petersburg society, going back to the *Monthly Notes* of the late 1720s. Through the 1750s and early 1760s, this tradition continued at a modest level, relying primarily on the community of scholars and translators at the Academy of Sciences. In 1755 the Academy began to print a new journal, the previously mentioned *Monthly Works*, under the editorship of G. F. Müller. During its ten years in print, this journal published a mixture of literary, informational, moralistic, and scientific works by such authors as Lomonosov, Shuvalov, Kheraskov, and Trediakovskii. Although its print runs ranged

95

up to 2,000 copies per issue, most sources indicate a sales level closer to 700 copies per issue, still a respectable figure for St. Petersburg at that time.[91]

In 1759 St. Petersburg saw the birth—and death—of its own first private journals, of the sort that appeared shortly thereafter in Moscow: the Academy's *Dililgent Bee (Trudoliubivaia pchela)* and the Infantry Cadet Corps's *Holiday Time (Prazdnoe vremia)*. Relatively little is known about the financial or literary contributors to these journals, since the articles, essays, and translations were unsigned, but most specialists believe that each of them was essentially a one-man operation: the first being run by Sumarokov and the second by a teacher at the Infantry Corps, P. Pastiukhov, who apparently filled its pages largely with his own translations.[92]

The private journals lasted less than a year, however, and with the closing of *Monthly Works* in 1764, popular journalism lapsed in St. Petersburg until the empress and her literary friends and Novikov and other former students of Moscow University joined hands to revive it. Thus, the opening of the first satirical journals in 1769 marked a major renewal which pointed up once again the important creative spark which the Moscow generation of the 1760s provided.

So much has been written about the literary and polemical content of these journals that reviewing it here would serve little purpose. Suffice it to say that between 1769 and 1774 sixteen magazines were published in the capital, and about half of them were satirical.[93] Virtually all of them were organized and financed either by the court or by the literati themselves, and, like the books of the Publishing Society, they were editorially semiautonomous. The total number of participants in these journals ran into the dozens and included Novikov, Kheraskov, Ruban, Emin, the FonVizins, Bogdanovich, Chulkov, Sumarokov, and many other products of Moscow University or the Academy of Sciences. As with the Translation and Publishing societies, however, the leading organizers were Catherine, through her secretary Grigorii Kozitskii, and Novikov. Novikov edited four journals during this period: *The Drone (Truten'), The Painter (Zhivopisets), The Hair Net (Koshelek)*, and *The Ancient Russian Library (Drevniaia rossiiskaia vivliofika)*, the first three of which were satirical weeklies. Kozitskii edited one, *Bits of This and That (I te i se)*.

Most of the satirical journals were popular and financial failures. Their print runs ranged from 300 to 800 copies per issue, but their sales were a good deal lower. The majority closed after just a few issues. Novikov's *Drone*, however, survived for two years and sold out its first year's run, which it reprinted, with the combined sales of the printings averaging about 1,200 copies per issue.[94] Similarly, his *Ancient Russian Library* stayed in print for three years (1773–75).[95]

Despite their lack of popular success, the satirical journals became important stages on which the literati could display foreign satire, especially translations from Addison's *Spectator Papers*, as well as satire on Russian reality. Authors posed ludicrous situations or described imaginary places in order to gently criticize government, the empress, rural tradition, and educated society. Beyond simply entertaining, this mockery had its serious side. Denis FonVizin, for one, saw it as a means of criticizing aspects of Russian political life and of suggesting improvements in the character of Russian rulership. Novikov used satire as a congenial genre for discussing the virtues of national pride and Russian culture and for deliberating on the role of educated people in shaping that culture through disseminating good books.

In an issue of *The Painter*, for example, Novikov wrote an article on publishing and bookselling, entitled "News from Millionaia," in which he said that, in the past, few interesting and useful books had been published in Russia.[96] Now, many good books were being translated into Russian, but Russia's readers still preferred to read exciting, romantic novels.

> Who in France would believe it if we were to say that *Tales of Magic (Contes de fée)* was more widely sold than the works of Racine? But in Russia, *1001 Nights* has sold much better than the works of Sumarokov. And would not a London bookseller be horrified if he heard that here sometimes 200 copies of a published book would not be sold in ten years? Oh, the times! Oh, the customs! Be brave, Russian writers! Soon your works will be sold widely.[97]

Novikov seems to have been making two points here. First, he wanted readers to have books of a higher quality than the romantic and historical tales that the scholastic presses were printing in abundance. His attack on *1001 Nights* was especially pointed, since the Moscow University Press had recently put a multivolume edition of those stories through a second printing.[98] Its popularity, moreover, was so great that the press had already published translations of such modern imitations as Thomas Gueuellette's *1001 Hours* and *1001 Quarter Hours*.[99]

Secondly, as an alternative to such frivolity, Novikov was recommending publishing and disseminating the works of Russian writers. Clearly, he did not oppose translations, as some of his comments in this article and his support of the Translation Society attest. But he was concerned that the proliferation of translations and, presumably, the remunerative lure of becoming a translator were inhibiting the creative will of native authors and hampering the attempts of these authors to reach Russian readers.

The *Painter* article was not the first place in which Novikov had expressed these sentiments. In *A Dictionary of Russian Writers*, which he published in 1772, Novikov presented biographical information for about 300 Russian writers.[100] Most of the writers included in this *Dictionary* were still alive in the 1770s, and there is a general consensus that Novikov's intention was to promote their works.

Novikov was disturbed by the effect that the untempered adoption of foreign culture and customs was having on Russian educated society. Thus, his *Ancient Russian Library* printed numerous historical documents that he had gleaned from various state archives with the assistance of Empress Catherine, G. F. Müller, and Mikhail Shcherbatov. In its first volume (1773), Novikov averred that he was publishing the journal in order to show Russian readers the richness of their heritage and customs and the needlessness of copying French fashions.[101] In that same year Novikov republished a 1627 topographical guide to Muscovy, *Ancient Russian Geography (Drevniaia rossiiskaia idrografiia)*, in order to demonstrate the antiquity of Russia's tradition of secular learning.

Despite his close friendship with Karl Müller, Novikov invested far more energy in his potential moral and intellectual influence than in financial concerns. Most of the Russian writers whose works he sponsored were not very popular among the broad reading public, nor did his historical publications sell well. *The Ancient Russian Library*, for example, even with a 1,000-ruble contribution from the Empress, lost a great deal of money. Clearly, projects such as these would have been quickly abandoned by a more commercially conscious person.

Yet the experiences of those years did teach Novikov something of the economic realities of publishing. Semennikov has shown, for example, that Novikov earned a healthy profit from sales of *The Drone*.[102] One of the articles from *The Painter*, moreover, reveals a certain hardheaded realism concerning the economics of publishing. In this essay, Novikov was answering the letter, mentioned above, in which the "lovers of wisdom from Yaroslavl" had inquired about the objectives of the Publishing Society and had complained that in the provinces only rich men could afford to buy the society's books. In his response, Novikov feigned ignorance of the policy or membership of the Publishing Society but praised its activities, anyway. The society realized that writers and publishers should not be averse to making commercial arrangements with merchants. Books were indeed expensive, but this problem he blamed on the large number of middlemen with whom one had to deal to get books into the provinces.[103] Only when writers agreed to involve themselves in the task of distribution would their books be read by people other than the rich.

Novikov's response presents the clearest picture of his vision of publishing, and it suggests the ambivalent feelings of many leading literati. Clearly mindful of finances and middlemen, Novikov nevertheless expressed no interest in making money. Rather, his only concern was how to get the most books to the greatest number of people at the lowest possible price. Those who should benefit were writers and readers, not merchants.

Much of what Novikov was saying reflected the state of Russian publishing in the 1770s. On one hand, scholastic presses did at times allow income to dictate publishing policy, they were often more receptive to publishing translated potboilers than more serious original work, and they did place financial barriers in the way of native authors, most of whom had to pay to publish their own works.[104] In terms of marketing and distribution, the Academy of Sciences Press had been active in seeking provincial markets precisely during the era of the satirical journals, and among the publications which the Academy made available to provincial outlets and buyers were the books of the Publishing Society.[105] Thus, Novikov's worries were to a degree justified.

On the other hand, Novikov's connection with the Academy press, the satirical journals, and the Publishing Society had elevated him to a level of prominence equaled only by Catherine herself, with whom he was able to cooperate journalistically and financially throughout the 1770s. For a few years this cooperation had brought together most of the leading figures of lay intellectual life in Russia, and even years later, after Novikov and Catherine had parted company intellectually, the vestiges of these activities could still be seen. When Novikov began publishing in Moscow, for example, he published several Translation Society books.

But St. Petersburg society could not sustain this spirit of cooperation. By the mid-1770s, writers began to grow disenchanted with the empress, to drift away from the endeavors she was sponsoring, and even to move away from the capital altogether. This dispersal had many facets to it, but one factor which perhaps has been overlooked is the extent to which the literati had outgrown the simple structure upon which Russian intellectual life and, in particular, Russian publishing still rested. After two decades in which secondary and higher education continued to produce intellectually minded people, maintaining the literary elite in one city and in one extended publishing network was simply unwieldy.

The evidence suggests, moreover, that although the Academy press was quite willing to pay literati (or anyone else) cash for translations that would sell well, most writers had to go it alone when they wanted to publish something serious. More notables, to be sure, were patronizing the arts in the 1760s than ever before. Academy sources indicate that major patrons of the period included Baron A. G. Stroganov, Lieutenant General Trusov, Prince Bestuzhev-Riumin, Ivan Betskoi, and Nikita Panin.[106] But these men preferred to pay for honorific and panegyric publications (odes, celebratory fireworks literature, and the like) or, as in the case of Panin, works in foreign languages. None of these men gave any money to the Academy of Sciences Press for the publication of serious Russian literature, and, after the new financing rules went into effect at the press, even such support as they had given substantially ebbed.

Nor did serious writers receive much help from the St. Petersburg merchantry. After 1774, for example, Karl Müller was reluctant to spend money on publishing books, Matvei Nikiforov and his associates did not go beyond distributing the Translation Society's books, and of the Academy's own booksellers, only Johann Weitbrecht ever underwrote an Academy edition of a book.[107] Of course, the Academy booksellers were in a somewhat different position than the others, since they had the option of convincing the Academy press to publish a book out of its own funds.[108] But in those instances their arguments were based on a book's potential profitability rather than on its intellectual merit.

Thus, it is not surprising that prominent writers of the 1760s and early 1770s found themselves running up large publishing debts which they were unable to pay back. Novikov, for example, was more than 800 rubles in debt by the mid-1770s; Sumarokov was almost 700 rubles in debt prior to coming under Catherine's wing; and by 1766 Emin found that he could not pay for his already published four-volume reworking of Rousseau's *La Nouveau Héloïse*, entitled *Pis'ma Ernesta i Doravy*.[109]

Most writers, then, received financial support only when they composed translations. The distribution of available capital and the tastes of the reading public simply made any other course infeasible. This one-sidedness had an obvious impact on the ratio of translated to original literature that was published. Translations accounted for slightly more than a quarter of all published titles, over a third of all titles in the civil orthography, and over half of general-interest books. For literature, the translation figures were even higher. Not including odes, over 70 percent of all literature and poetry was translated work, and in some genres the figure was even higher. For example, Vasilii Sipovskii, who studied the eighteenth-century Russian novel in painstaking detail, found that, until 1763, Russia produced no original novels, and between 1763 and 1775 only twelve original Russian novels were published.[110] During the same period, Russian presses published 123 translated novels.[111]

Comparison with other European countries shows how meager this output was. In England, for example, Ian Watt has estimated that between 1740 and 1770 there were at least twenty new novels a year, and by 1770 the number approached forty.[112] Admittedly, England produced more novels than any other country in the eighteenth century. Nevertheless, the comparison indicates that the gap between Russian and western literary productivity was still quite large.

Thus, the rise of general-interest scholastic publishing led to several unforeseen complications for Novikov and his generation that reflected a disequilibrium between the intellectual aspirations of the literati and the organization of publishing. Increasingly, the literary elite were becoming uncomfortable with the synthesis of entertainment and moral persuasion that the Academy had developed in the 1740s and that they themselves had accepted in the late 1750s, and they resented devoting so much of their time to the former at the expense of the latter. When Novikov criticized the publication of books for profit which pandered to the lowest common denominator of taste among the reading public, he was implicitly calling for a different arrangement than the one that had reigned for thirty years. Similarly, his criticism of indiscriminate translating was a marked break with the enthusiasm with which Trediakovskii had greeted virtually any general-interest translating forty years earlier. Both Novikov and Trediakovskii supported translating as a source of cultural enrichment, but whereas Trediakovskii saw translating as perhaps the most exalted responsibility of intellectuals, Novikov was more skeptical. To the extent that translating threatened to turn Russian letters into a mere mirror image of France, it was deleterious to native traditions, culture, and especially to capable Russian writers.

One cannot help but marvel in all of this at how quickly intellectual life had changed in Russia. An elite that a generation earlier was prepared to bring almost any sort of general-interest literature into print was now finding that the success of their own endeavors was giving them pause. Novikov and his friends appear to have been curiously unmindful of the dilemma they themselves were responsible for, by overseeing the circulation of books from the French Enlightenment and popular literature that, to a certain degree, misrepresented their own positions to the reading public. But Novikov's apprehension over the fate of Russian writers was a legitimate concern, and his efforts to provide them with a forum that was intellectually less ambiguous and that involved less personal risk financially were only the first steps in redressing the imbalance between the burgeoning ambitions of writers and the still limited financial means of educated society and the printing network to support them. One alternative to these financial restraints was the private journalism of the 1760s and 1770s, in which the financial burden of publishing a possibly unprofitable volume was borne by several people. But journalism was only a partial palliative for the continued economic limitations of institutional publishing.

Clearly, in the absence of a major rise in popular demand for Russian originals, the institutional presses were not going to bear the cost. Nor were patrons willing to take up the slack, especially given the inflexibility of the Academy. The only solution, then, was to find a way of allowing the representatives of society—writers, patrons, printers, and even merchants—to gain even greater control over publishing, so that they would not be so dependent upon the presses' ability to balance their books. In this context, private publishing suddenly made very good sense in the 1770s, and in the last quarter of the eighteenth century the government finally gave way to economic realities and relinquished its monopoly over publishing in Russia.

FOUR

The Emergence of Private Publishing

IN THE MIDST of all the changes which had touched eighteenth-century Russian publishing, the government's monopoly over the presses had remained constant. For most of the century this monopoly had been a helpful, sometimes stabilizing, and even creative force. Institutional control had provided presses with material support, editorial mandates, ready-made markets, and a haven in which energetic and intellectually talented people could engage in public expression. Given the country's lack of a well-developed and articulated public demand, institutional advocacy gave direction and definition to Russian publishing. The government's monopoly also had proven itself to be flexible editorially and financially in allowing access and a degree of autonomy to a variety of groups and institutions that represented a broad spectrum of economic and intellectual interests.

But by the 1770s Russian publishing had, in most respects, outgrown the government's guiding and nurturing authority. The most visible manifestation of these growing pains in the early years of the decade was the conflict between the increasing number of people who wanted to publish freely and the financial reluctance of the institutional presses to let them do so. Economic problems had become sufficiently vexing that long-time patrons and writers, such as Stroganov and Novikov, had reduced their publishing activity rather than pay printing costs in advance. This situation had not created any crisis, since the institutional publishing houses remained open to new literature, and in fact they were printing record numbers of books. But it did create a problem both for the presses that continued to run in the red and for the literati who had to search rather hard for adequate remuneration.

Previously, when confronted with the fiscal difficulties of printing, the Senate had adopted a policy of retrenchment, which led ultimately to a readiness to accept private capital and initiative. In this instance, however, retrenchment was virtually impossible, in part because many of the books that spilled the most red ink were being published at the behest of the empress, but also because there remained a tremendous demand to use the press. Thus, the most practical solution that lay open was to allow still greater private investment in printing and thereby reduce the financial obligations of the government. After jealously guarding its monopoly for so long, however, the government quite naturally was unwilling to give it up easily. As late as 1768, for example, the Senate refused to act on a petition by Count Alexander Stroganov for permission to open a Russian-language press and reading library at his home in St. Petersburg.[1]

However, when a typesetter from the Academy of Sciences, Johann Friedrich Hartung, petitioned the Senate with a similar request in 1771, he received a more sympathetic hearing. In his petition Hartung emphasized that as a native of Germany—he had come from Munich in the 1760s—he wished only to serve the foreign community in St. Petersburg by publishing books in Latin and in German. Technically, therefore, he was not seeking an exception to the government's monopoly on printing Russian books, and the Senate agreed to grant his petition on the condition that he not publish books in the Russian language, public notices, religious books, or any restricted or offensive material.[2] Thus, on March 1, 1771, Hartung became the first acknowledged private publisher in Russia since the demise of Kiprianov's press in 1708, an accomplishment which has earned this otherwise unremarkable figure a permanent place in the annals of Russian publishing.[3]

Hartung's press, of course, had no direct impact on Russian-language printing or on the Russian reading public.[4] But the privilege granted him did set a visible precedent, and in July 1776 Johann Weitbrecht and Johann Schnoor, both German-born printers with several years of experience in Russian institutional publishing and bookselling, applied for and received permission to print Russian books.[5] Weitbrecht and Schnoor worked together until 1782, when each set up his own publishing house. Their success encouraged others to follow suit, and between 1780 and 1783 the Senate granted three additional privileges to private Russian presses.[6]

At about the same time, the privatization of printing was also furthered when several institutional presses that had been in financial trouble were rented out to individuals, upon whom few editorial or financial restrictions were imposed. Once again, Schnoor broke new ground when, in 1773, he leased the press of the Artillery and Engineering Corps. After he joined Weitbrecht in 1776, Schnoor transferred his lease to two other German printers, Christian Klein and Bernhard Hecke, who operated the press until Klein's death in 1784.

Leasing agreements such as these soon became common, largely because of their manifest advantages over both institutional and private printing. They allowed the lessee to go into business without having to purchase expensive machinery, recruit and train workers, or find a suitable location. They also freed him from having to petition for a privilege from the Senate. For the leasing institution, rentals provided a welcome end to financial entanglements and losses without losing editorial control over publications that it wished to sponsor. Thus, in May 1778 a Lapland merchant, Otto Gustav Meier, leased the Moscow Senate Press, and in 1780 a Dutch printer, Friedrich Hippius, took over his contract.[7] In March 1779, Moscow University leased its press for ten years to Novikov.

The "Free Press" Law of 1783

Between 1776 and January 1783 presses that were owned or rented by private individuals in Moscow and St. Petersburg printed over a quarter of all Russian-language books, and this at a time when publishing was burgeoning. But the transformation to a private printing system received its most important stimulus when, on January 15, 1783, Catherine the Great issued an edict that granted private individuals the right to own and operate a private printing press (*vol'naia tipografiia*) without having to receive a special privilege from the government.[8]

In one stroke, this law eliminated the major restraint on the growth of private publishing houses in Russia. Following upon it, private interests moved with remarkable speed to take over printed communications. Between 1776 and 1801, thirty-three individuals or partnerships opened private presses in Moscow and St. Petersburg, and another five rented institutional ones. Collectively they published over two-thirds of all Russian books in the last quarter of the century and nearly four-fifths of them between the proclamation of 1783 and the onset of censorship in 1795. To appreciate the full significance of these figures, we must realize that nearly 8,000 titles were produced in Russia in the last quarter of the century—over three times what had been produced in the previous two centuries. By the mid-1780s, Russia's presses were printing about 400 Russian-language books and journals a year, with a peak of nearly 500 titles in 1788 (see table 4.1).

Clearly, the press law of 1783 was an act of considerable consequence, and it raises several obvious questions. Why, first of all, were the Senate and Catherine so willing to surrender the state's monopoly over printing so easily and apparently with little forethought? At the very least, one would suspect that Catherine's cameralist views on government and society would have led her to want to maintain an active presence in directing the nation's primary means of public com-

TABLE 4.1

Russian-Language Books Published in Five-Year Intervals, 1776–1800

	Number of Books Published	Annual Average	Number in Civil Orthography	Number in Old Orthography
1776–80	1,198	240	1,087	111
1781–85	1,315	263	1,220	95
1786–90	1,936	387	1,852	84
1791–95	1,865	373	1,761	104
1796–1800	1,531	306	1,422	109
Total	7,845	314	7,342	503

SOURCE: Based on data in *Svodnyi katalog* and in Zernova, *Svodnyi katalog kirillovskoi pechati.*

munications. Conversely, who within Russian society was so willing to devote their energy and wealth to an enterprise like publishing that was difficult to organize and was unlikely, based on past experience, to yield great profits? Finally, one needs to explore how the transfer of publishing into private hands affected both the development of intellectual life and the relationship between printing and Russian society as a whole.

Scholars have long been aware of the advent of private printing in the 1780s, and some have recognized it as a phenomenon of some significance. Too frequently, however, their discussions have amounted to little more than hagiographic discussions of Nikolai Novikov. Kliuchevskii, for example, has dubbed the 1780s "the Novikov decade," and other scholars have also given great attention to Novikov's career while all but ignoring everyone else's.[9]

Novikov, to be sure, did more than any other single individual to advance the publication of books and to establish networks for their distribution. In his prime in the mid-1780s, he was responsible for publishing over a third of all Russian-language books, and he may have sold an even larger share. Nevertheless, Novikov did not act alone. Many other people also found their way into publishing, and some lasted longer than he did. Collectively, they put out more books in the 1780s than Novikov did, and even after Novikov had all but ceased to publish in 1789, private presses as a whole remained active and managed to fill much of the gap left by his inactivity, at least until most of them succumbed to the highly restrictive press laws of 1795 and 1796. Surely, therefore, the advent of private printing and its importance for Russian society involved more than the vision of one very great man.

Recent Soviet scholarship, fortunately, has begun to consider the development of private printing in a more general context, and to a limited degree it has begun to address the questions of motives and interests in explaining the new law on free printing presses. One view, for example, has it that demands by publishers and writers in the 1770s and 1780s in essence forced the empress to enact the 1783 law. According to this argument, the exodus of literati to Moscow in the late 1770s and their disaffection from the Academy and the cadet presses reflected their displeasure with a publishing system that bound them to an empress whose policies they felt had become increasingly repressive. Some scholars also have pointed to the ebbing fortunes of the Panin party, to which several literati were attached, as a motivation for moving to Moscow to establish a separate literary life. What was at stake here, then, was a political struggle for freedom of the press.[10] Thus, Novikov's leasing of Moscow University Press is seen as a political and even defiant act.

This hypothesis contains a number of weaknesses in both logic and evidence. It seems unlikely, first of all, that disaffected and out-of-favor literati could gain access to the empress or that she would feel compelled to listen and ultimately give way to them. Even more inconsistent is the insistence that once Catherine had granted "freedom of the press," she began to move against the liberal opposition and later against the press itself. Why would a ruler grant a concession to a perceived opposition if she intended to become more, rather than less, repressive?

At no point have the defenders of this argument been able to demonstrate either that literati had, in fact, suffered from an absence of press freedom before 1783 or that any among them felt that they had suffered. Moreover, even if writers had expressed such feelings privately, it does not necessarily follow that they had any interest in owning printing presses. Most of the original petitioners for private publishing consisted, after all, not of literati but of artisans and merchants. The literati became involved in printing only later, and then in rather small numbers.

Thus, the question remains: Why did Catherine enact the law of 1783? Conclusive evidence, unfortunately, is not available. No known documents survive which address the issue or suggest extensive deliberations at court. Still, the circumstances of publishing at the time imply that economic expediency rather than politics was the most significant consideration.

Far from yielding to pressure, Catherine and the Senate apparently acted with a free hand and with little thought for potentially detrimental consequences. Once Weitbrecht and Schnoor had broken the ice, the government made only perfunctory checks of petitions for private presses and granted them with little objection. The Senate evinced little interest in press rentals, which appear to have been arranged without prior Senatorial approval. Similarly, no dissonant voices were heard to oppose the 1783 law from within the government. Thus, rather than being born of struggle, the advent of private printing was remarkably uncontroversial.

This lack of controversy is consistent with the prevailing Western view that the political climate of the 1780s was characterized more by a persistent loyalty to Catherine than by overt opposition. Writers, in particular, were materially supportive of and supported by her, and whatever disenchantment they expressed with her policies, they showed little interest in oppositional politics. The advent of private printing therefore seemed to pose no serious political or ideological threat for the government. Once it became obvious that a large number of people were prepared to bear the expense of publishing privately, and after the experiences of the 1770s and early 1780s showed that private publishers were harmless, there was little reason to stand in their way. Officialdom, after all, had long since surrendered editorial direction of scholastic publishing to educated society, and that act had had few negative repercussions. To surrender physical control would simply complete the process, with the important added benefit that the institutional presses would be freed from the tortuous and financially draining commitments to unpopular books which had soured their relations with the literati and with the empress. Catherine herself knew these financial traps all too well from her experience with the ill-starred Translation Society, and if someone else were willing to bear the risks and provide some support for the literati, that was all to the good. In this regard, it may be more than coincidence that Catherine ended her subsidy to the Translation Society in 1783, in spite of the fact that several dozen manuscripts had not yet been printed.[11] She probably viewed private publishing primarily as a means of disencumbrance. But what can one say about the motives of the publishers themselves?

In a recent article, V. A. Zapadov has suggested that the issue of freedom of the press had ceased to be an urgent matter for writers after the government decided to grant the first printing privileges in the late 1770s. Writers and publishers, however, wanted to be able to

produce books without submitting everything to the time-consuming
and stifling censorship apparatus of the Academy, the university, and
the cadet corps. The real struggle, therefore, involved the cause of
freedom of speech.[12]

On Zapadov's behalf, it should be acknowledged that during the
1780s and early 1790s private publishing was editorially simpler and
freer of governmental involvement than scholastic publishing had been.
Institutional oversight was loosely defined and, as shall be seen, infrequently enforced. But otherwise, there is little basis for accepting
Zapadov's point of view. Scholastic publishing could be time-consuming, but the problem usually was less the censorship process, of which
few people seriously complained, than the more mundane organizational difficulties involving the cumbersome and perhaps overly expensive process of securing in-house approval at two or three levels.
Waiting for it often required several adjustments of publication sched-
ules, print runs, and publication notices, during which time it was
necessary to pay the salaries of a large full-time printing staff. This
inefficiency was less visible to writers, however, than to the printers
and booksellers at the scholastic presses, and it was from their ranks
that the first private publishers came. Weitbrecht, for example, had
been the manager of the Academy of Sciences' foreign-language bookstore, and his partner, Schnoor, had managed the Artillery and Engineering Corps Press. If anyone had gained a clear view of the problems and prospects of institutional publishing in Russia, it would have
been they. Perhaps they believed that they could do the same job more
cheaply and efficiently and even make some money. But was the prospect of making money the primary motive for most of the private
publishers, and if so, did their expectations prove to be realistic?

THE PRIVATE PUBLISHERS: A COLLECTIVE PORTRAIT

To answer these questions requires exploring the lives and experiences
of the publishers themselves in some detail. Few of them left personal
statements of their hopes and intentions, but thanks largely to the
recent extensive archival research of I. F. Martynov, T. I. Kondakova,
and other contemporary Soviet bibliographers, we now know a good
deal about their backgrounds.[13]

By far the largest group to enter into publishing in the last quarter
of the eighteenth century consisted of the aforementioned merchants
and artisans who had had experience in some aspect of printing or
bookselling; fully three-quarters of all private publishers came from
their ranks. Most of them were non-Russian, mostly German speakers,

who either were born abroad or were born and raised in the neighborhoods of Moscow or St. Petersburg populated by foreigners.[14]
Several of them, including most of the pioneers of the 1770s, had
already been active in Russian publishing for a number of years before
procuring a private press. Weitbrecht, for example, had begun selling
books in St. Petersburg in the early 1760s. Christian Klein had worked
as an Academy typesetter since the 1750s, and Christian Rüdiger had
been an employee of the Moscow University Press bookshop since the
late 1760s. An equal number, however, seem to have arrived just prior
to entering into Russian publishing. Friedrich Brunkow, for example,
arrived in St. Petersburg in 1790 and began to publish shortly thereafter.

Regardless of when they arrived, virtually all of the foreign-born
publishers became engaged in one or more aspects of printed communication when they started to work in Russia, and, more importantly, most of them remained engaged in printing-related occupations
for many years. Typically, they started working as typesetters for an
institutional press or as bookbinders. Several of them also worked as
booksellers, either to supplement their artisanal trade or as a profession
in itself. Still others, such as Weitbrecht and Klein, actually managed
institutional presses for some years before they began to work at
presses of their own.[15]

One would expect from this commitment to the printing trades that
these publishers had received some training and experience in their
chosen profession in their native lands. In general, however, there is
little available information on these men that would shed light on their
pasts. A few have left a trail, most prominently Bernhard Breitkopf,
who had come to St. Petersburg in the early 1780s to oversee the
Russian trade of one of the oldest and most distinguished publishing
and bookselling firms in Leipzig, the Breitkopf family firm. The Breit-
kopfs had been doing business in Russia since Peter the Great's day,
and they had sent hundreds of books to institutional buyers and occasionally to private book collectors. Because of the ever-expanding
nature of the Russian trade, Breitkopf's father decided to send Bernhard to St. Petersburg to open a permanent Russian office for taking
orders and, soon afterward, for publishing.[16]

But Breitkopf was the exception. Most of the foreign-born publishers
appear to have been tradesmen of little note back home. Many were
rather young when they arrived in Russia, and one suspects they came
to Russia in order to seek opportunities for work and business in
trades whose guilds may have been difficult to enter in their native
lands. From such a perspective, Russian publishing, even with all its

drawbacks, may have looked rather attractive. Here was a visibly expanding and undeveloped trade and market to which they had relatively open access. After serving an apprenticeship of sorts at an institutional press or small business in a related trade, they moved willingly and easily into private business.

Similar observations pertain to the tradesmen and merchants of Russian origin who entered into private publishing. To give a few examples: Emelian Vil'kovskii had been an assistant at the Academy of Sciences bookshop in St. Petersburg since 1775, and he worked there until the Academy fired him in 1784, at which time he started his own press.[17] Fedor Galchenkov, with whom Vil'kovskii formed a partnership in the 1780s, had been a salaried translator and proofreader for the Academy of Sciences Press. Matvei Ovchinnikov had been a bookseller before opening his own press, as had several other publishers.[18] Again, one presumes that these tradesmen looked to publishing as an occupation and as a means of earning a profit. But, as with the foreign-born publishers, a lack of evidence precludes arguing this position definitively.

In addition to the artisans and merchants, there existed a small but aggressive corps of literati or "intellectual" publishers, whose backgrounds and motivations were very different. Most of its members came from the gentry, and most had had a considerable degree of education.[19] Novikov, Ivan Lopukhin, and most of the members of their publishing group had attended Moscow University or its gymnasium, and Peter Bogdanovich had gone to a gymnasium in Leipzig.

As a rule, these men also had careers in state service in the capital: Novikov had been in the Izmailovskii regiment, Reshetnikov had been a brigadier in the army, and Bogdanovich had been a lieutenant. It comes as no surprise, therefore, that many of the intellectual publishers knew one another and that they often frequented each other's company. Lopukhin worked closely with Novikov at Moscow University (during Novikov's second tour there) and had been a member of his Masonic lodge. Ivan Rakhmaninov had been an active journalist for several years, and he had begun his intellectual life as a translator for Novikov's journal, *Morning Light*.[20] Ivan Krylov and his associates—Ivan Dmitrevskii, Alexander Klushin, and the famous actor, Peter Plavil'shchikov—began as assistants to Rakhmaninov. When their own publishing enterprise faltered in the mid-1790s, they sold it to Plavil'shchikov's brother, Vasilii, who operated it under various auspices for many years.[21] Krylov, of course, went on to be one of the most prominent and popular writers of the early nineteenth century. Less is known about Bogdanovich's contacts with other intellectual publishers, but his experience as an academic translator, editor of a journal (*Akademicheskaia izvestiia*) in 1779, and his closeness to Sergei Domashnev, the president of the Academy of Sciences, brought him into contact with many writers.[22]

Social and occupational differences thus set the two groups of private publishers from each other quite sharply. But how meaningful were these differences for their experiences when they entered private publishing? Upon examination, it does appear that the differences did have their effects but with a number of qualifications.

The intellectual publishers did not have a monopoly on contacts with writers. Weitbrecht, Schnoor, Rüdiger, and Christopher Claudia, because of long-standing associations with either the Academy of Sciences or Moscow University, had extensive dealings with writers. Ovchinnikov, Galchenkov, Vil'kovskii, and Vasilii Okorokov also seem to have worked with literati. In addition, the publishers had dealings among themselves that frequently crossed social lines. Bogdanovich, for example, financed books in the presses of Vil'kovskii, Galchenkov, Weitbrecht, and Schnoor.[23] Reshetnikov published some books in Lopukhin's press, and the Ponomarevs published books in a variety of presses. Moreover, several publishers owned or managed bookstores, which gave them extensive relationships with other publishers. All of these experiences indicate certain commonalities that publishing imposed upon its practitioners.

Yet in the end, the practical distinctions between trade publishers and intellectual publishers outweighed the similarities. Firms managed by experienced printers lasted an average of eight and one-half years (slightly longer if they were managed by native Russians) and printed about eight books a year, whereas those run by intellectual publishers lasted an average of only five years but printed seventeen books a year. Firms run by experienced publishers thus operated at a modest and steady level, but intellectual publishers tended to print more books during their comparatively short tenures.[24]

Not surprisingly, these bursts of intense activity often left intellectual publishers exhausted and bankrupt. The records of the Senate, the Synod, and the Academy of Sciences show many cases of intellectual publishers who entered the fray with enthusiasm and soon amassed large and unpayable debts. Bogdanovich, for example, had to sell his press because of his indebtedness to the Academy of Sciences. Ultimately, the Senate decided to banish him to his father's estate in Poltava rather than see him go further into debt. This decision created its own problems, as Bogdanovich sent numerous petitions and protests to the provincial authorities, complaining that he had been treated worse

112

than Socrates and demanding that he be allowed to return to St. Petersburg or Moscow. This impassioned correspondence not withstanding, Bogdanovich remained in Poltava.[25]

Experienced publishers, to be sure, were not immune from financial difficulties. Ovchinnikov found after a few years that he had overextended himself by operating both a press and a bookstore. In the end, he went deeply into debt to the Academy of Sciences Press and struggled in vain to reestablish his solvency.[26] Similarly, Brunkow's Russian-language press lasted only five years, during which time it produced a mere twenty titles. Weitbrecht, Galchenkov, and Vil'kovskii had similar, if less dire, problems. But in contrast to the intellectuals, experienced printers generally found ways to forestall bankruptcy for several years at least. Even when individual enterprises closed, moreover, experienced publishers usually managed to remain active. Weitbrecht, for example, went from the Academy bookshop to his own bookshop to his partnership with Schnoor. In 1781 he and Schnoor went their separate ways, each opening his own private press. Schnoor continued to publish privately into the nineteenth century, while in 1784 Weitbrecht, apparently after some private lobbying, received a commission to operate a press for the use of Catherine's private offices and the College of Foreign Affairs.[27] This press, known as the Imperial Press, functioned, for all practical purposes, as Weitbrecht's private publishing house until his death in 1803. One can trace similar career patterns for Rüdiger, Claudia, Vil'kovskii, Galchenkov, Hippius, Okorokov, Otto Meier, and Andrei Reshetnikov.[28] Intellectual publishers, by contrast, usually tried publishing once and then abandoned the enterprise. Only two intellectuals, Novikov and Plavil'shchikov, persevered beyond one switch.[29]

Experienced publishers, in addition, were more likely to combine publishing with other aspects of the printing trade than were intellectual publishers. Kondakova and Martynov have noted the frequency with which bookbinders and booksellers entered into printing.[30] For most of the experienced publishers, these activities were complementary features of a complex trade which permitted them to impose a great deal of control over their businesses and commercial networks. Thus, Weitbrecht maintained a large book trade during his entire publishing career and, on a more modest scale, so did Breitkopf, Vil'kovskii, Ovchinnikov, and several others. But only Novikov, Bogdanovich, and Plavil'shchikov among intellectual publishers ever stooped to engage in the book trade, and two of these sold only their own publications.[31] It is clear, therefore, that experienced publishers were more likely to look upon printing as long-term businesses or careers

113

than were intellectual publishers, most of whom continued to treat it as an extension of their literary avocations. Thus, of the thirteen eighteenth-century private publishers who continued to function in the nineteenth century, twelve were experienced printers and the other was the writer, Vasilii Plavil'shchikov, who was the son of a merchant.[32]

To be able to stay in business for a decade or more, private publishers had to have a sharp eye for profit, since Russia's market for books still fell far short of the big businesses that had grown up in France and Germany. Because entry into this market was, by definition, a risk, commercially-minded publishers sought ways of reducing risks and securing reliable buyers. Press leasing, for example, was a relatively safe method of entering into private publishing, since, in return for paying a fixed annual rental fee that ranged between 500 and 4,500 rubles, a printer took control of the entire publishing and bookselling operation of a given governmental institution. The contract required only that the printer continue to pay the wages of the press's employees, maintain the equipment in good working order, and print those works of an informational or educational nature that legislative mandate required of the press. For most institutional presses, these obligations were not especially burdensome, and the mandated publications usually went to a predetermined and often captive readership. The printer thus avoided the expenses of buying materials and recruiting employees, and he received full compensation for all titles printed for institutional purposes. For the Russian market, these contracts offered a reasonable opportunity to earn money. Eight eighteenth-century publishers did sign rental agreements, and all but one of them—Novikov— was an experienced publisher.

Another financially attractive arrangement involved entering into a contract with an institution to gain the exclusive right to publish everything that the institution wanted to have printed. These contracts were highly remunerative for the publisher, who bore almost no risks and received a guaranteed income. Thus, when Catherine the Great founded the Commission for Establishing Public Schools in 1782 and granted it the right to contract for textbooks and primers, experienced publishers avidly bid for the contracts.

The School Commission is well known to students of public education in Russia for its efforts to establish a network of primary schools throughout the empire. It has been praised by later commentators as diverse as Pavel Miliukov, who called it "progressive," and Dmitrii Tolstoi, who said that its underlying ideas were "so sound that they outdistanced not only their own time but ours as well."[33] In essence, its program, embodied in the Statute on Public Schools, envisioned the establishment of a three-tiered primary school system throughout the empire, reaching even into the rural areas of remote provinces. The curriculum that its inspirer, the Serbian pedagogue Fedor Jankovic de Mirjevo, composed concentrated on basic knowledge—reading, arithmetic, history, and geography—and on moral behavior and etiquette. The system achieved only modest success; few schools actually opened and attendance in them was often no better than that in the primary schools of Peter's time. During Catherine's reign, no more than 20,000 students attended the public schools at any one time. With the formation of the Ministry of Education in 1803, the School Commission went out of business.[34]

Despite these shortcomings, the commission was a very active disseminator of elementary textbooks, most of which it procured through exclusive contracts with private publishers. The terms of these contracts varied, but they all seem to have assured the printer a good profit. One contract, for example, required the commission to pay the printer a fee of three rubles for each 1,000 signatures (*listy*), regardless of format, for books with print runs of up to 1,000 copies. For books with higher print runs, the fee per signature rose.[35] Since the commission's printings often ran into the tens of thousands—the total run of Jankovic's primer, for example, has been estimated at 100,000— the publisher's income was quite substantial.[36] In addition, the publisher could bill the commission directly for all costs incurred while printing its books. The commission, indeed, not only underwrote all costs, including the salaries, but it also paid an additional unit cost for each copy of a published book.

The School Commission was evidently prepared to spend a lot of money to have these books published.[37] Between 1784 and 1800 it spent about 14,000 rubles a year for books and maps, of which over 12,000 rubles went directly to private printers. (The remainder went to the Synod Press in St. Petersburg.[38]) These funds, moreover, paid for a relatively small number of titles (forty-four in seventeen years) with very large print runs (an average of 7,300 copies per title). The large print runs kept expenses low by minimizing the investment in printing presses and the cost of typesetting, and at the same time they made large sales possible. Thus, a printer could invest less money initially in presses and salaries, since he could run off a great many copies of a printed sheet on one press, and he could ensure against long periods of inactivity per press.

The promise of such high gross proceeds with a guaranteed income was a great attraction to commercially-minded St. Petersburg pub-

lishers, and whenever the commission was dissatisfied with one publisher, several others rushed in to take his place. Yet, among all those
who submitted bids, none was from the literati.

These bids provide a rare glimpse into the economic conditions of
publishing in the 1780s and 1790s, and they cast light on the assumptions and expectations of the commercially minded publishers.[39]
There are some variations, of course, and individual printers may have
submitted unrealistically low estimates in order to receive a contract,
but, for the most part, the bids are relatively consistent with each
other. The documents show that publishing in Russia was still an
expensive proposition. A printing press cost between 250 and 400
rubles, the average being slightly under 300 rubles, and a full set of
civil-orthography type cost about the same. The cost of other materials
was between 200 and 300 rubles per press, bringing the total initial
investment to between 750 and 1,100 rubles per press—a considerable
sum, about equal to the annual salary of a high-ranking state servitor.
In comparison, a Frenchman of the same era could pick up a small
press and type for the equivalent of a journeyman printer's wages for
a few months.

Salaries comprised another major expense. The highest salary, from
200 to 350 rubles a year, went to the manager, but a print shop also
required an editor or proofreader, a typesetter, a press operator, an
inkman, and between four and seven assistants for each printing press
in operation. Total annual salaries ranged between 700 and 1,400
rubles per press. Thus, before a single book appeared, a printer with
a moderate printing operation could expect to make an initial investment of between 1,450 and 2,800 rubles. Larger operations, obviously,
cost a good deal more.

Once publishing began, a printer had to purchase disposable supplies—paper, ink, binding, thread, and the like. The cost of each of
these items declined considerably during the eighteenth century, but
over the course of years these expenses nevertheless mounted up. The
cost of paper, which varied enormously by quality and by supplier,
was generally between one ruble seventy kopeks and six rubles per
ream.[40] Normally, a ream of average quality white paper, the most
popular variety, cost between two and three rubles.

To give these figures perspective, assume that a 200-page book,
published in octavo (sixteen sides per signature), had a print run of
600 copies. That would have been a typical edition of an average-
length book of the day. Each copy would have consisted of twelve
and one-half signatures, and the total edition would have required
7,500 signatures, or about fifteen and one-half reams. At two to three

rubles a ream, paper costs for this average edition would have been between thirty-one and forty-seven rubles. For a 200-page book with a quarto format, or 400 octavo book pages, paper costs would have doubled.

Ink and thread cost between fifteen and thirty-five rubles per book. Binding, an option on most books, usually was done by a special binding shop, which added ten kopeks or more to the cost of a book, depending on the quality of the materials.[41] In toto, therefore, disposable items could add between 50 and 110 rubles to the cost of an "average" edition. Finally, a publisher had to pay for repair and replacement of machinery, rent, and postage, all of which very easily could have mounted to several hundred rubles a year.

On the basis of these figures, it appears that a small to moderate printing firm owning one press and publishing about ten books a year could have expected to spend between 2,300 and 4,400 rubles in its first year, and between 1,600 and 3,600 rubles in each succeeding year. Those were very large sums of money for a country in which a high state servitor earned only 1,200 rubles a year, and a merchant with 10,000 rubles in capital ranked in the first tax guild of that estate.[42]

In order to make a profit on the open market, therefore, a publisher of this magnitude would have had to be a commercial genius. Most books of 200 pages cost between thirty-five and seventy kopeks each at retail, yielding a maximal income for an average publisher of between 2,100 and 4,200 rubles a year. If a publisher sold his books exclusively at retail, he would have had to sell at least 85 percent of his stock to meet his annual expenses. Considering the cost of capital investment, he would have been obliged to sell virtually all his books for several years before he went into the black.

Most publishers, of course, fell far short of selling out all their stock, and even when they did, a certain percentage of the proceeds had to go to booksellers, peddlers, or advance purchasers at discount prices. The few big-selling and high-profit volumes, such as calendars, almanacs, and text books, usually fell under privileges held by the Academy of Sciences. Thus, it is not surprising that commercial publishers sought out guaranteed contracts and markets. But not everyone could obtain a fat contract. Most of the experienced private publishers, in fact, lived or died on the open market, where making money was a good deal more problematic. In order to survive, they had to adopt the familiar strategies of seeking patronage and subventions or of publishing only books with large or dependable markets.

By contrast, when the enterprises of the intellectual publishers are viewed from an economic perspective, one can see just how naive their proprietors were. Krylov and Associates, for example, compiled an initial fund of 2,000 rubles, with which the company expected to buy all the necessary materials and pay salaries. Once it started to publish, it assumed that income from sales would pay all operating expenses and still leave a surplus to give to charity. Predictably, the proprietors ran out of cash very quickly and sold the press.[43]

After the mid-1770s, private financiers drifted away from the scholastic presses and toward smaller presses, whose cash flow problems were somewhat less acute. This change brought substantial capital to private presses in the 1780s and 1790s, in which both intellectual and experienced printers shared. Bogdanovich, for example, received orders from the bookseller Ivan Glazunov, and he also printed catalogues for a number of other booksellers with whom he did business.[44] Novikov, Plavil'shchikov, and Ivan Sytin also printed books for other people. But the great majority of private orders went to experienced publishers.[45] Perhaps a third of Reshetnikov's titles came from private orders, and Schnoor, Claudia, Friedrich Meier, Otto Meier, Breitkopf, Hecke, Ovchinnikov, Vil'kovskii, and Isaac Zederban frequently accepted outside orders.[46]

Even more significant than the search for private capital was the dependence by experienced publishers on books or genres that had proven popular in the past and that therefore involved the fewest risks. Friedrich Meier, for example, published mainly love stories by popular writers. He did print a translation of Goethe's *Sorrows of Young Werther*, but only after receiving advance payment for it from the bookseller Timofei Polezhaev.[47] Zederban, another experienced publisher, printed tales, romances, popular histories, and medical handbooks. Most of the others issued similar sorts of books, rather than good literature (whether translated or original), long novels, or serious philosophy.

Experienced publishers did prove venturesome in one area, though. They warmly embraced the apparently burgeoning market for the popular adventure stories and romances that collectively came to be called *lubochnaia literatura* in the nineteenth century. The earliest volumes of this kind appeared in the 1780s and 1790s. Loosely bound, they contained large print and engraved illustrations. They often ran to 300 or 400 pages, quite long for the Russian reader, but their simple subject matter and language and their decidedly lowbrow style had broad popular appeal. All of them were brought out by experienced publishers.[48] An example of the type was the notorious *Prikliucheniia aglinskogo* [sic] *Milorda Georga* (*Adventures of the English Lord*

George), which was first published in 1782 and had six more printings before the end of the century and dozens more in the next century.

Milord George was not the only source of titillation. Since at least the 1760s, Swiss merchants, among others, had been sending quantities of bawdy literature to major booksellers in Moscow and St. Petersburg for distribution to the wealthy and educated public who could read French and German and could afford the high retail price.[49] As we have already seen, Russian translations of some of this literature had been available since the 1750s.[50] But by the mid-1780s, Russian translations or imitations were pouring forth, mostly from privately run presses. They included *The Tales of Wilhelm, The Paris Horseman, The Story of the Adventure of Prince Eck-Marine, The Story of Eliza, Written by a Friend*, and dozens of others.[51]

The contents of this early "Grub Street" literature in Russia has not received much attention from scholars. The stories could be as short as twenty pages but generally were more than a hundred pages. Illustrations were quite common, but several of the adventures and romances had few or none. In this respect, the literature seems to have had no organic connection to the traditional *lubki*, from which the name *lubochnaia* was derived. In the *lubki*, which remained popular throughout this period, the pictures were central. As Klepikov has remarked, *lubki* in the late eighteenth century still consisted mostly of one or two folio sheets with elaborate pictures of fairy tales whose meaning could be discerned without recourse to the line or two of text that usually appeared at the foot of the picture.[52] It is doubtful that *lubki* and the "Grub Street" literature appealed to the same audience. *Lubki* were true street or village fare, pasted on walls by hawkers and street vendors, accessible to anyone regardless of literacy, residence, gender, or social standing. Almost nothing is known about their print runs—although single sheets printed from wood blocks technically could be reproduced in great quantities—or about their prices, but all the evidence points to their being cheaply and haphazardly produced and very low in price. By contrast, "Grub Street" literature was part of a literate and printed culture that presupposed leisure and active reading. One had to sit down and read these novels or at least listen to them being read aloud. Moreover, even the cheapest of them, ten to twenty kopeks for some, was more expensive than any of the *lubki*, and several of the lengthier or multivolume adventures ran to more than a ruble.

Still, there is no question but that these novels were intended for the lowest common denominator of literate public amusement. Their cheap printings, their covers with suggestive or heroic graphics, their exotic or alluring titles (often with no mention of uplifting lessons or morals on the title page), and their indifference as to the author, whose name either appeared incidentally or not at all, clearly emphasized the point that an amusing or exciting story was contained in the pages. Indeed, their popularity may have arisen largely from the attractiveness of the titles, especially those that mentioned adventures, maidens, or the appellations of otherwise anonymous or mysterious European nobility such as "lord," "contessa," or "viscount." Publishers, at any rate, clearly perceived that titles such as these, rather than authors' names, would attract the widest attention. Whether their audience was "democratic," as convention has it, or simply large is not at all clear, but the fact that these books came out in such frequency indicates that the market for them was very wide indeed.

All of this information leaves no doubt that romances and adventures were translated and published primarily to make money, and, predictably, the vast majority of them came from the experienced private publishers. Some intellectual publishers, such as Bogdanovich, printed occasional adventures, and Novikov, in his prime, printed quite a few. But the literati, as a rule, were dismayed by the growing popularity of such books, and they looked with disillusionment upon a public that reduced reading to mere entertainment rather than using it for the loftier purpose of inculcating respect for Russian culture and individual moral improvement.[53]

Intellectual publishers, moreover, were reluctant to surrender editorial control in exchange for monetary gain. Such a posture is hardly surprising, but the consequences of this high-mindedness were economically painful for the literati. Without recourse to secure contracts or captive markets, most of them simply were unequipped to keep their enterprises afloat in the rock-filled waters of Russian publishing. Thus, those publishers who, like Bogdanovich, felt that their individual presses were striking a blow for independent speech or who, like Novikov, believed that they were emancipating the literati from dependence on governmental support must have been bitterly disappointed. But it would be uncharitable and misleading to dismiss intellectual publishing because of individual economic naiveté and failure. Its importance was real and long-lasting because of its collective impact on educated society in bringing into print hundreds of books that would not otherwise have appeared.

The literati were prepared to be quite bold when it came to publishing works that interested and amused them. Bogdanovich, for example, printed six books that he had written himself and twelve others that he had translated. In addition, he brought into print original compositions by Denis FonVizin and Fedor Emin.[54] Rakhmaninov, whose St. Petersburg press published only seventeen titles, produced four translations from Voltaire's writings, two original works by Radishchev, and three literary-philosophical (and poorly selling) journals. Similar personal literary and philosophical influences affected the presses of Lopukhin, Sytin, and Krylov.

This willingness to use the presses as organs for personal statements regardless of the size of the audience allowed the more serious writers to continue to have a public voice and look to the press as a vehicle for carrying on their dialogues over important issues. In the process it permitted those elements of the educated public that truly cared about what the literati discussed, but were too small to provide support for their publications, to participate in these dialogues.

Equally important was the collective impact that the totality of private publishers, especially the intellectual ones, had on literary life. No single publisher could provide a secure anchor for an intellectual life that was struggling to function outside of governmental institutions, but private publishing as a whole did, because even though many presses went bankrupt, there were others to take their place. During the 1780s and early 1790s many writers and translators abandoned the leading scholastic presses in order to pursue ideas or to make money at the leading private ones, to such an extent that by the mid-1780s the chancellery of the Academy of Sciences was expressing concern over the flight of printers, translators, patrons, and writers to the private presses.[55] The Academy Press's output had declined from an average of fifty titles a year in the 1770s to about thirty-five in the 1780s. To shore up its position, the Academy granted raises of 20 percent to all press workers. When largesse failed, the Academy tried veiled threats, warning employees that they had to abide by the contracts that they had signed with the Academy.[56] Finally, however, the Academy came to address its press's decline as an essentially economic problem. In order to make its publishing operations more efficient, it abandoned its long-standing policy of sending two-thirds to three-quarters of print runs into storage. The tens of thousands of volumes that had accumulated in the Academy's book depository were offered to booksellers at large discounts.[57] To ensure that these backlogs came to an end, the Academy decided to announce the publication of books before they were sent to press, so that it could ascertain the approximate level of demand for a given title.

The Academy also became more flexible in its payment of royalties for publishable manuscripts. A small number of writers, who formerly had to pay the Academy to publish their manuscripts, now received from fifty to a few hundred rubles for the rights to their works. Ippolit Bogdanovich, for example, received 700 rubles and 100 free copies for the rights to his *Collection of Russian Proverbs*.[58]

These various measures met with a certain degree of success. Inventories were reduced somewhat, and a few writers renewed their associations with the Academy Press. Most of St. Petersburg's literary and philosophical journals published in the 1780s continued to emanate from the Academy. But none of these measures succeeded in fully reversing the movement of writers away from institutional associations and away from St. Petersburg. Increasingly, the Academy Press, the mainstay of Russian literary-philosophical publishing for half a century, took on the configuration of a more narrowly defined educational press, issuing a higher percentage of textbooks, scholarly works, and informational publications. It printed only a few popular literary and historical works and even fewer original works, at least until the closing of most private presses as a result of the severe censorship laws of the mid-1790s drove some writers back to the Academy.

The experience of the Academy of Sciences demonstrates how a diversified and decentralized publishing system could encourage a corresponding change in the overall structure of Russian intellectual life. Surely the flowering of private publishers in the 1780s allowed a much more open access to print for writers and would-be writers, and this gradual realignment of writers with independent publishers in turn contributed to bringing intellectual life to a point where it could sustain itself outside of—if not necessarily in opposition to—the government. And perhaps this partial economic and institutional independence also played an emancipating role in the evolution of the literati's political and philosophical stance. To be sure, one would be hard pressed to suggest that there was a direct line of development from the advent of private intellectual publishing in the 1780s to the rise of an intelligentsia in the 1840s. But the activities of the literati and the publishers of the second half of the eighteenth century collectively fashioned around printing a set of increasingly self-sustaining intellectual institutions upon which the intelligentsia could rely when they finally did declare their political independence in the nineteenth century.

Novikov

It is in this context of reconstituting intellectual life to become more independently directed and self-sustaining that Novikov looms so large. For generations, scholars have been discussing the precise place of

Novikov in the history of Russian letters. Yet despite all the hagiography about him, there is no consensus over what he was trying to do or where his significance lay. The most persistent image, associated with such Soviet specialists as G. P. Makogonenko and A. V. Zapadov, is that of a champion of enlightenment, reason, and progress. To Makogonenko, Novikov's significance was symbolized by his move to Moscow, where his publishing activities became the beachhead of an emerging progressive, quasi-liberal gentry opposition that led directly from him through Radishchev to the Decembrists.[59]

The picture of Novikov as an oppositionist ideologue armed with a printing press has held sway for quite a long time. But a number of dissenting scholars, from M. N. Longinov in the nineteenth century to Gareth Jones, Marc Raeff, and others more recently, have shown convincingly that Novikov's pursuit of individual moral virtue took on an increasingly pietistic, nativist, mystical, and religious character in the 1780s, hardly the stuff of which quasi-liberal oppositionists were made.[60] This view, based on a close study of the personal interests of Novikov and his friends and on the contents of his philosophical journals, has provided a much-needed corrective to the unduly political and teleological tendencies of the older argument. But it puts far too much emphasis upon Novikov's private philosophical world. Novikov's main activity in the 1780s was, after all, publishing, since he wrote very little at that time, and it was the publishing that made him so important to his peers and his society. Before we can pass judgment on his significance, therefore, we need to retrace his career as a publisher and assess how well it corresponded to his personal moral world.

After the demise of the Publishing Society in 1774, Novikov curtailed his publishing endeavors sharply, financing only fourteen books during the late 1770s in the Academy of Sciences Press, the Infantry Corps Press, and the private press of Weitbrecht and Schnoor.[61] The hardships of publishing on his own also moved Novikov to engage other individuals in his enterprises. At various times in the late 1770s, two booksellers, Christian Torno and Karl Müller, and a typesetter named Mitropol'skii partially subsidized the publication of several of Novikov's books.[62] Still, during these five years, Novikov did edit four largely moralistic journals, including the successful *Morning Light (Utrennii svet)* from 1777 to 1780.[63]

But journalism was not enough for someone with Novikov's boundless energy, especially since he had resigned from his military post. Thus, while still in St. Petersburg, he began to have some affiliation with the activities of the Free Russian Conference of Moscow University. This conference had begun in 1771 with the goal of improving the Russian language by compiling accurate dictionaries and grammars.[64] Unlike its predecessors at the Academy of Sciences, the conference eschewed translation in favor of the republication of old Russian books and stories. It produced only one major work, however: Peter Alekseev's *Church Dictionary*, a book that resembled a primer for the reading of old religious books more than a dictionary.[65]

Novikov's role in the conference is difficult to assess. Notations on the title pages of two of his publications dated in 1776—*A History of the Scythians* by Andrei Lyzov and *A History of the Unjust Incarceration of the Innocent Boyar Artemon Sergeevich Matveev*—indicate that Novikov had prepared them as a member of the Free Russian Conference.[66] But otherwise he seems to have played no role in the conference at all.

At about the same time, Novikov took on a much more important commitment in the form of a growing involvement in the affairs of Russian Freemasonry, which culminated in 1775 when he decided to form his own lodge of "Martinists."[67] Novikov devoted himself very deeply to the organization and ideology of French Masonry. The journal *Morning Light*, for example, was overtly pietistic and masonic in tone, and the charity schools which it was intended to subsidize reflected the spirit of Christian civic piety which typified the Freemasons. His involvement in Freemasonry also took him to Moscow in 1778 to see Kheraskov, who had recently become the rector of Moscow University, on a matter involving their respective lodges.[68] During this meeting Kheraskov suggested that Novikov move back to Moscow and assume the direction of the Moscow University Press.[69] Novikov agreed, and in April 1779 the two parties signed a ten-year rental agreement. In return for use of the press, Novikov agreed to pay a rental fee of 4,500 rubles a year, to meet the university's publishing and salary obligations, and to continue to publish the *Moscow News*. Novikov also assumed responsibility for managing the university's bookstore.[70] By 1779, rental agreements, as we have seen, had become fairly common, but the leasing of such a large publishing house was unprecedented. The Moscow University Press was by then the largest press in the empire, both in physical size and in volume of activity, and it offered Novikov tremendous opportunities to influence the hearts and minds of Russia's readers.

As soon as he took control of the Moscow University Press, Novikov began to enlist the aid of old friends, students, and local Masonic figures, the most important of whom was the German teacher, Johann Schwartz. Schwartz had come from Berlin to Moscow in 1776, and between 1779 and his death in 1784 he taught seminars in German

rhetoric and linguistics at the university and directed individual translation projects.[71] A Martinist himself—his main inspirations were the
mystical works of Jacob Böhme and Louis Saint-Martin—Schwartz
was a dynamic figure who profoundly influenced Moscow's corps of
intellectuals, including Novikov, during the early 1780s.

In 1781 Schwartz and Novikov established the Friendly Learning
Society (*Druzheskoe uchenoe obshchestvo*) at the university. Its members were drawn from the Conference of University Pupils (*Sobranie
universitetskikh pitomtsev*), a group of students who were studying
philosophy under Schwartz's tutelage. The stated goal of the Friendly
Learning Society was to publish books that would assist parents in
the proper upbringing of their children. Like so many of its predecessors, however, the society could not have exerted much influence
on public morality, since its members translated only a handful of
moralistic books and two masonic journals, the *Moscow Monthly
Periodical* (*Moskovskoe ezhemesiachnoe izdanie*, 1781) and *Evening
Glow* (*Vecherniaia zaria*, 1782). The growing eccentricity of their
Rosicrucianism may well have cut them off from educated society to
a greater degree than their poorly selling journals could overcome.[72]

When Schwartz died in 1784, Novikov, as the unquestioned leader
of Moscow's intellectual life, drew the circle of Martinists and philosophy students closer to the press. As a consequence, he also took
them well outside of their personal moral world by engaging them
actively as authors and translators of scores of literary manuscripts.
Indeed, largely through the energy of this corps of writers, Moscow
University Press became the most active publishing house in the empire,
issuing about seventy Russian-language titles a year (ninety-five a year
in all languages) in the early 1780s.[73]

Not satisfied with this impressive output, Novikov chose to broaden
his publishing operation even further. In 1783, one of the young Masons, Ivan Lopukhin, founded a press which became a leading masonic
organ for Novikov over the next few years. And in 1785, Novikov
started his own printing firm, the Typographical Company, that published over 300 volumes in its seven years of existence.

As overseer of three publishing houses, Novikov presided over the
flow of huge quantities of money. He paid salaries to perhaps 200
employees, and he made editorial decisions concerning dozens of new
or newly translated manuscripts every year. By one count, Novikov
brought out the works of ninety different Russian authors in the 1780s.[74]

Obviously a publishing operation of this magnitude and with so
many claims upon it could not be sustained on the basis of one man's
vision or without considerable economic skill. Novikov had developed

a sensitivity to financial problems as early as the 1773 articles in *The Painter* and especially in his relations with the Academy of Sciences Press and the Translation Society, and he put this experience to good use in his work in Moscow. He could raise large amounts of cash when he needed it, and he understood the necessity of publishing certain books simply as moneymakers. Andrei Bolotov, for example, recounts a conversation in which he and Novikov laid plans for producing a popular and profitable journal, the *Magazine of Economics (Ekonomicheskii magazin)*, which Bolotov maintained made him both wealthier and famous.[75] Most scholars agree, moreover, that the popular romances and adventures which Novikov published in spite of his distaste for them were concessions to the need for cash.[76]

Novikov also was unmatched among intellectual publishers in his attention to the details of marketing and dissemination. An exchange of letters from the years 1779–80, in which Novikov was attempting to settle accounts with several booksellers who were distributing his St. Petersburg publications, shows an intimate knowledge of contracts, the number of books each one had, the cash value of those books, and alternate means of payment.[77] He built up Moscow University Press's provincial network to include seventeen regular outlets and about thirty occasional ones. In addition, booksellers and publishers in Moscow and St. Petersburg sold his publications either on commission or in exchange for his selling books that they had printed.[78] He offered generous discounts to booksellers (30 percent) and to advance subscribers (5 percent to 20 percent), and he did his best to bring out his publications at the lowest possible prices.[79] And he conducted a far-flung trade through the mail to readers in all corners of the empire.[80]

In light of these activities, Karamzin's comment that Novikov "traded in books as a rich Dutch or English merchant trades in products of all countries: that is, with sense, with integrity, with foresighted imagination," seems to contain some truth.[81] His activities certainly did not exhibit the financial naiveté and incompetence of other intellectual publishers. Yet when Novikov's publishing is studied more closely, it is clear that profitability was not the point at all. Profits, in fact, were so much less important than disseminating good works and supporting good writers that his business ultimately drowned in red ink, because of policies that may have made moral sense but that ensured that he would lose money.

In the years when Novikov managed only the Moscow University Press, his expenses were limited to the 4,500 rubles rental fee and the labor costs and printing expenses. The university owned about fifteen printing presses, making salary expenses 15,000 to 20,000 rubles a year.[82] Printing costs are more difficult to assess. Existing catalogues show the number of books published per year, their length, and their format, but they tell nothing about print runs or paper quality. If one uses a conservative estimate of 600 copies as an average print run and assumes that Novikov normally printed on medium quality white paper, an average edition would have cost about 120 rubles to produce. Over a year, approximate printing costs would then have come to a minimum of 11,300 rubles, but Novikov's actual costs undoubtedly were much higher than this. Inventories of Novikov's stocks taken in 1787 and 1792 reveal that he had on hand several thousand copies of many titles and that bookshops around the empire had dozens more. In addition, certain periodical publications, such as the literary journals and the biweekly *Moscow News*, most certainly cost hundreds or thousands of rubles each to produce. In all probability, therefore, printing costs were at least double the minimum figure. Thus, a very approximate estimate would put Novikov's basic annual expenses for Moscow University Press at between 35,000 and 50,000 rubles. Other expenses, including the costs of operating the bookshop, postage for sending books to provincial outlets, and the like, probably added a few thousand rubles a year more.

One expense that cannot be estimated at all was the honoraria and salaries that Novikov paid to his writers, editors, and translators, since salary and commission lists, if they ever existed, have not survived. During Novikov's tenure at the university press, his translators produced considerably more manuscripts than had the translators for the Translation Society, to whom Catherine had paid 5,000 rubles a year in the 1770s. Novikov, moreover, was renowned for his generosity with his publishing associates. In his efforts to convince Bolotov to edit the *Magazine of Economics*, for example, he offered to double what Bolotov was earning as an editor and contributor to the *Village Resident (Sel'skoi zhitel')*.[83] And according to the bookseller Kol'chugin, Novikov offered unusually high discounts to his book dealers. Thus, Novikov's largesse with employees and associates very likely cost him thousands of rubles a year.

Upon what resources could Novikov draw to pay these expenses? His testimony before the police in 1792 (after his arrest for allegedly inducing someone to convert to the Old Belief, ultimately leading to his imprisonment) indicated that the university itself, whose demand for textbooks, informational works, and public notices was continuous, was the largest and most consistent source of revenue.[84] In addition, Moscow University Press accepted printing orders from other govern-

127

mental and scholastic institutions. Novikov did not specify the percentage of the press's publications that fell into that category, but a review
of titles suggests that about a third represented such institutional orders.

Private patrons composed a second major source of income. Since
Novikov abandoned the practice of identifying patrons on his title
pages, it is impossible to determine the extent of private patronage,
but his testimony of 1792 acknowledged that such patronage existed.[85]
Other income came from book sales, subscriptions to books and journals, and occasional grants from wealthy admirers like Peter Tatishchev and, according to Novikov, the empress.[86] Also, governmental
offices and some individuals paid to have announcements and articles
printed in the *Moscow News*.

Once the Typographical Company started publishing, Novikov received a new influx of capital as the initial fourteen members of the
company contributed about 60,000 rubles in cash, Novikov and his
brother gave 80,000 rubles worth of books, and a wealthy Siberian
manufacturer, Grigorii Pokhodiashin, gave 50,000 rubles.[87] The cash
fund of 110,000 rubles should have sufficed for initial expenses and
for reserves, but Novikov was in constant need of more money. In
March 1789, he prevailed upon Pokhodiashin to sell his paper factory
for half a million rubles in order to keep Novikov afloat.[88]

When, in spite of these measures, Novikov still ran short of funds,
he was not averse to borrowing money or postponing debts. But his
most ambitious effort was to organize a new patronage society in
1782, called "Novikov and Company." During the next three years,
115 titles—60 percent of the Moscow University Press's Russian-language titles—carried the imprimatur of this group. Unfortunately,
nothing is known about its origins, membership, or financial means,
although one can presume that it resembled the Publishing Society of
the 1770s and that Novikov used it to provide subsidies for important
but unprofitable books. Its members, one would assume, included
people who had participated in the Friendly Learning Society and
related groups and others, like Tatishchev, who had rendered him
financial support in the past. But these people could not have supplied
Novikov with much capital, since most of them were drawing their
own salaries or honoraria from him. Still, somewhere from his extended network of clients and friends came enough money to publish
115 books.

To assign precise ruble values to these various sources of income
simply lies beyond the evidence, but it does appear that sales on the
open market (the presumed basis of profit or public influence) ran a
poor third to captive sales and philanthropic contributions. As far as

gross proceeds are concerned, in the 1792 interrogation the governor of Moscow, Prozorovskii, estimated that Novikov had earned
about 40,000 rubles a year during the 1780s. In response, Novikov
did not specify his actual earnings, but he did say that 40,000 rubles
was considerably below his average annual gross income. Some years,
he claimed, brought in as much as 80,000 rubles.[89] However, he did
not indicate whether he was referring to the 1780s as a whole or just
to the years in which he was operating three separate publishing houses.
In any case, one should exercise a good deal of skepticism toward
those figures, since Novikov's command of his records and inventories,
which were chaotically scattered in several different locations, was not
exact. Moreover, the Moscow University Press earned only about
45,000 rubles a year between 1806 and 1812 and just over 70,000
rubles a year between 1814 and 1825.[90] By that time, the publishing
business in general had begun a new boom, and the Moscow University Press was publishing about 130 titles a year, or about one-third
more than all of Novikov's presses averaged in the 1780s. Thus, Prozorovskii's figure of 40,000 rubles seems more plausible than Novikov's own.

Even if Novikov's optimistic assessment is accepted, his financial
situation was nevertheless bleak. If the figure of 80,000 rubles is reflective of the years between 1779 and 1785, Moscow University Press
may have met its expenses and perhaps earned a slight profit. But once
the Lopukhin press and the Typographical Company entered the picture, expenses must have far outstripped income. Between the two
new presses, Novikov published 350 titles—450 volumes—in seven
years. Gaps in the evidence preclude making a precise list of the expenses for these publications, but sixty-four volumes a year with
printings that must have averaged well over 600 copies per volume
would have cost, at the very least, 15,000 rubles a year in printing
expenses alone.[91] In addition, inventories taken in 1792 and 1794
revealed that Novikov owned twenty-one printing presses. It is unlikely
that he had full staffs for each of his presses, but even fifteen active
presses would have required spending between 15,000 and 20,000
rubles a year in salaries. Add to that figure all the other costs of owning
a print shop and the result is a conservative estimate of between 30,000
and 50,000 rubles a year in expenses. Finally, Novikov had purchased
equipment worth almost 41,000 rubles.[92]

During the Typographical Company's heyday, Moscow University
Press printed only about fifty titles a year, thereby cutting costs by
perhaps 5,000 to 10,000 rubles. Nevertheless, in order to have broken
even between 1783 and 1789, Novikov would have had to earn at

least 100,000 rubles a year, and, even by his own estimate, earnings in his best years did not approach that figure.

On the basis of these very approximate calculations, Novikov must have lost between 20,000 and 60,000 rubles a year after 1784, and on the eve of his arrest in 1792, he found that he had amassed enormous debts which he was unable to meet. Even after most of his books were sold at auctions in the 1790s and early 1800s, Novikov still could not liquidate his debts, and he ended his life (he died in 1818) in obscurity and poverty.

To lay the blame for these crushing losses entirely at Novikov's feet would be too harsh. As has been seen, publishing in Russia entailed a great deal of risk for all concerned, and it is unlikely that anyone could have profitably managed so sprawling an enterprise as Novikov's. Political events also adversely affected his ability to find new financial support or to maintain his national network. A nationwide raid on bookshops by the church and police officials in 1787 virtually shut down the book trade for four months (see chapter 8). This raid was directed largely at Novikov's books, and as a result Novikov became something of a pariah after the bookshops reopened later in the year. Personal publishing began to wane, and his relations with Moscow University cooled. By 1789, it was clear that former associates were becoming reluctant to submit manuscripts or contribute money and that the empress had instructed the university to look elsewhere for a lessee of its premises.

In these circumstances, Novikov's position became very difficult, and without Pokhodiashin's financial help, he could not have continued publishing until 1792. But these first acts of censorship, however disruptive they may have been, did not cause Novikov's financial problems. Sooner or later, the annual losses would have caught up with him when the well of benefactions finally ran dry. The fundamental basis for his bankruptcy, then, was his philosophical predisposition, which sacrificed profits to the main tasks of cultural and moral influence that Novikov had spelled out in the 1773 article on the book trade in *The Painter*.

Writers, he had argued, ought to involve themselves in the mechanics of publishing and bookselling in order to deliver more good books to more readers. The beneficiaries were to have been writers and readers rather than the middlemen. Publishing was therefore not a business but a social service and a philanthropic activity. Novikov, then, was carrying through his promises of a decade earlier in following a calling which, above and beyond the specific repertoire of books published and any ideological messages contained therein, defined itself as fulfilling the demands of a benevolent Christian civic piety.

Christian philanthropy, in fact, seems to be the unifying theme of all his work. Gareth Jones has shown that it was the guiding principle behind the publication of *Morning Light*, which, during its first year and a half of sales and circulation, brought in sufficient income from subscriptions to help subsidize Novikov's two boarding schools, St. Catherine's and St. Anne's.[93] Surely, a prosperous Dutch or English merchant would have plowed those profits back into the business. Novikov continued to draw proceeds out of publishing even when his losses were mounting up. Thus, in 1787, he spent some of his earnings as well as 50,000 rubles from Pokhodiashin, to buy food to ease the Moscow famine of that year.[94]

The manner in which Novikov pursued higher sales also corresponded to his mission of philanthropy. By employing a strategy that depended upon low prices, generous discounts, high print runs, and active and expanding trading networks, Novikov was all but guaranteeing that his margin of profit would be small or nonexistent. Similarly, his generosity with writers and translators may have allowed him to corner the market on Moscow's literary manuscripts, but his refusal to be selective ensured that he would lose a lot of money.

Novikov, it appears, was willing to face that problem. Notwithstanding his misgivings over the deleterious influence of Voltairianism, his urgent defenses of Russian writers and native traditions, and his growing commitment to Rosicrucianism, it was the determination to publish virtually anything of value that came his way that made Novikov's publishing enterprises so significant.[95] His publishing repertoire does not reveal a clear philosophical tendency but rather a general affinity for the topical composition of all books published in Russia at that time and a representation of virtually every strain of thought that had affected Russia's educated public since the 1750s.

The figures in table 4.2 show that Novikov's books tended more toward artistic literature and moral-philosphical tracts than to works of faith. Certainly, Novikov published more moralistic literature, including translations of Wieland, Gellert, Dusch, and Genlis, as well as some original moral tales by Fedor Emin, than did his predecessors at the Moscow University Press. Some of the plays and stories he published did contain mystical or masonic themes, and for a secular press the percentage of religious books was actually quite high, although these included more of the "classics of Protestant Pietism and Western Mysticism," as Raeff has called them, than the traditional prayer books of Russian Orthodoxy.[96] But none of this differed rad-

TABLE 4.2
Subject Composition of Novikov's Publications, 1779–92

Subject	Number	Percentage
Official information and notices	0	0
Other information	10	1
Religion	203	21
Calendars	90	9
Journals	25	3
Alphabet, grammar, and language	25	3
History and geography	93	10
Technology	35	4
Science and mathematics	40	4
Secular philosophy	127	13
Belles-lettres	290	30
Odes	35	4
Total	973	102

SOURCE: Mel'nikova, *Izdaniia napechatannye*, pp. 177–284, and Semennikov, *Knigoizdatel'skaia deiatel'nost'*, pp. 59–66.

ically from what had been common in Russian publishing overall for more than a decade.[97]

As a publisher, Novikov was a herald of the French Enlightenment in Russia. He printed several selections from the *Encyclopédie*, including several left in abeyance by the demise of the Translation Society, and over a dozen works of Voltaire. He also carried on the Translation Society's work in printing English novels, including Fielding's *Tom Jones* and Goldsmith's *The Vicar of Wakefield*, as well as a large number of frivolous romances. It may be true, as most specialists maintain, that Novikov published some of these merely to make enough money to support his less popular books.[98] But most of these books bore the imprimatur of the Typographical Company or Novikov and Company, an indication that they emanated from Novikov's circle of associates rather than as concessions to institutional obligations. From the public's viewpoint, therefore, they bore his stamp of approval.[99]

In spite of Novikov's personal philosophy and his publishing of several mystical books, therefore, few contemporaries saw his activities as a threat or as a challenge to existing ideas. Archbishop Platon of Moscow saw little reason to be concerned by Novikov's membership in the Masons, and Catherine herself showed little interest in the Masons, at least until the mid-1780s.[100] Surely, if there had been a threat or simply a general public discussion of Novikov's books, Catherine would have gotten wind of it, since there were many Masons in the ranks of state service.[101] But what sort of threat could there be when some of Novikov's closest associates in the lodges, such as Kheraskov, far from considering themselves to be critics of the *philosophes*, continued to translate leading Enlightenment thinkers and essayers from the *Encyclopédie* into Russian?

This is not to suggest that Novikov had no interest in using his editorship as a stage for telling readers what was important. He wrote very little himself in the 1780s; more than for other private printers, publishing was his means of disseminating his own ideas, mediated through other people's works, to the reading public. In addition to the moralistic, religious, and masonic books, he prefaced quite a number of books and journals with short notations which made clear his personal endorsement of the volume in question, and in other ways he encouraged many other projects.[102] But these particular interests were so fully subordinated to the larger goal of providing Russia with good books that none but the best-informed readers could have discerned the ideological presence of the publisher.

Thus, Novikov's significance for Russian letters rests squarely on his energy as an active and eclectic publisher. Within the history of printing he can be seen as the first of the noted Russian publishers and booksellers, including Alexander Smirdin, Adolf Pliushar, and Nikolai Rubakin, who became major nineteenth-century cultural figures by devoting their lives and their fortunes to the furtherance of Russian letters. Novikov's contribution to his own time was even greater than theirs, however, because he combined his support with intellectual vision and leadership and active journalistic work. But his greater stature also derives from the fact that his enterprise was so visible and central to the shaping of an intellectual tradition in private publishing. Having established its overall viability outside of the protection of scholastic institutions, Russian publishing opened the way for reconstituting intellectual life as an entity separate from the state. To be sure, private publishing had not brought Russian writers to the brink of becoming a free-floating intelligentsia, but these writers now were faced with establishing one relationship with state service and a separate one either with a high-minded literary life or with hack writing and translating in the service of commercial publishing, neither of which could be seen as an extension of state service. Most of them were able to straddle this division for some time, a posture that was made necessary by the culture's inability to support a large literary profession. But increasingly, the two endeavors were seen as separate, if compatible, activities, and as a result of private publishing, a steady trickle of educated people found that they could pursue and even preferred the life of letters to the life of service.

Of course, such a choice was not necessarily a happy turn of events for literati such as Novikov who now realized that the mere creation or control of media was no guarantee of extensive moral influence. They had to accept the fact that the synthesis of service, entertainment, and public virtue, upon which their activities as literati were premised, was rapidly becoming a thing of the past. From a historical perspective, all of this was an inevitable consequence of the coming of age of Russian intellectual life. But for Novikov and many of his friends, publishing left not so much a feeling of maturity as a bittersweet sense of lost innocence and optimism.

FIVE

Publishing in the Provinces

IN TERMS of its intellectual and social consequences, there is no doubt that the appearance of private publishing in Moscow and St. Petersburg represented the single most important change in Russian publishing in the second half of the eighteenth century. But the breakup of the central government's monopoly over publishing had a less visible but still noteworthy geographic dimension, in the form of the opening of about twenty-five provincial presses during the last quarter of the century. These presses were mostly local enterprises with small outputs, limited press runs, and even more limited circulations. Provincial publishing produced less than 5 percent of all the books published during the period, and some presses printed no books at all. But the mere presence of provincial presses was an indication of something new which, to a certain degree, involved the decentralization of printing in Russia, and a few of these presses developed into quite lively places. More importantly, the advent of provincial publishing paralleled a modest intellectual awakening that was taking place in a number of provincial towns. Thus, the obvious question arises of whether the two phenomena were at all interrelated and, if so, whether the availability of printing affected the quality of local intellectual life.

Scholars have long recognized that the burgeoning literary life of Catherinian Moscow and St. Petersburg began at some point to radiate into the provinces. Traditionally, this process has been said to have its roots in the 1762 edict of Peter III which freed the gentry from compulsory service. Thus, in a classic account of eighteenth-century provincial society, N. D. Chechulin argued that, in the wake of the law of 1762,

> The gentry quickly took advantage of the freedom granted them; at once all the roads from St. Petersburg and Moscow were covered with gentry who left service and hurried home. And in this way there appeared in the provinces—in all corners of Russia— people who were not yet elderly ... who had absorbed the life of St. Petersburg and had become accustomed to it.[1]

Not only did these people bring with them the life of the capital, but

> in most instances they still were vivacious, still energetic, imbued
> with knowledge . . . with the growing striving to move forward,
> with a quest for improvement. These people, having . . . the fruits
> of education and the profits of knowledge . . . saw that they had
> to make a very fundamental impact on the simple, uneducated,
> isolated village society.[2]

As intellectual life began to change, books became an increasingly
important part of life in provincial circles:

> People appeared on provincial estates who were educated, by
> contemporary standards; who were great lovers of books; who
> collected libraries. . . . Their favorite reading was Rollin's *History*—in Trediakovskii's translation, *Marquis G****, *Gil Blas*,
> some classics . . . and others. . . . These people often found great
> pleasure in scholarly and important conversations.[3]

Chechulin's characterization has in many ways formed the basis of
our subsequent understanding of provincial intellectual life and, more
specifically, of provincial publishing. Leading Soviet scholars have
continued to look upon the unfolding of provincial literary life primarily as an extension of the more cosmopolitan Enlightenment in
Moscow and St. Petersburg. V. P. Semennikov, for example, described
the evolution of provincial printing as a phenomenon that followed
on the heels of the penetration of literary tastes and new schools from
St. Petersburg and Moscow into provincial capitals. He placed great
emphasis on the presence of celebrated literati or their friends in a
provincial capital, and his standard of success seemed to be the extent
of their participation in the provincial scene.[4]

More recently, A. V. Blium has written several studies of provincial
publishing and literary tastes, most of which follow Chechulin and
Semennikov in seeing provincial publishing as an outgrowth of bureaucratic and literary activities in the capital. In discussing provincial
printing, for example, Blium identifies those points at which provincial
publishing took on the literary character of the major cities as the
peaks of provincial achievement and significance.[5]

Blium, however, has also investigated other aspects of provincial
culture, some of which suggest important modifications to the accepted
view. His study of provincial reading habits, for one, distinguishes
between the literature and literary tastes of the educated gentry, on
the one hand, and the literature of the masses, on the other. Such a
distinction is well known, if poorly developed, in Soviet studies of

popular culture, but studies of printing have largely ignored the possible influence of popular culture on the activities of local presses. Blium believes that a democratic literate culture of sorts did exist in the provinces in the mid-eighteenth century and that its representatives did not take their lead from the literati in the major cities. This indigenous literate element, he maintains, was visible and was important to overall provincial culture. Unlike such scholars as P. N. Berkov, however, Blium seems to doubt that these two cultures had much to do with each other, at least in the provinces. Unfortunately, he never explores the possibility that provincial printing could have acted to bring the two cultures into contact. But if provincial printing somehow did engage these indigenous elements, one might expect that local or "democratic" groups would have tried to direct these presses to meet their own needs, just as groups in the capital had been doing.[6] One must look for such points of contact and perhaps recast the significance of provincial publishing to take local concerns into account.

In addition to raising the matter of local interests and influences, Blium has presented an implicit but valuable modification of Chechulin's timetables. Rather than placing emphasis on the 1760s, Blium looks more to the 1770s and 1780s as the time when the life of the major cities began to influence local literary activity.[7] This revised chronology largely corresponds to the direction that a great deal of other scholarship on the educated gentry has taken in recent years. Many specialists now seriously doubt that any massive migration homeward followed the proclamation of the new law of 1762, since the demands of income, status, and social consciousness made retirement to a more pastoral life rather unattractive to those ambitious educated gentry of whom Chechulin spoke. Without some incentives to attract them to the provinces, most gentry with lively minds would have remained in the major cities.[8] Virtually all of the activities to which Chechulin makes reference, moreover, took place in the last twenty years of the eighteenth century. Chechulin's own account describes the provinces entering a period of decay in those years, marked by frivolity and licentiousness rather than serious intellectual aspirations, but with little happening in the 1760s and rather a lot taking place a decade or two later, Chechulin's chronology appears suspect.[9]

When one looks specifically at provincial printing, as both Blium and Semennikov have done, one sees little evidence of any "Enlightenment" in provincial towns or, for that matter, any significant change at all prior to the 1780s. The only active publishers of Russian-language or Church Slavonic books outside of Moscow and St. Petersburg were the church presses, located exclusively in the Ukraine, at the Kiev

Academy and at seminaries in Chernigov and Lvov, and these presses had never been very active. Between 1743 and 1785 the Chernigov monastic press published seventy-four titles, and the press at the Kiev Academy was about as productive.[10] The vast majority of these books consisted of traditional prayer books, catechisms, and sermons, and most were printed in the old orthography or in Church Slavonic. Thus, although some monastic books did find a provincial lay market, it was the clergy that found them most accessible, and even then their circulation was limited mostly to the Ukraine.[11]

During the early years of Catherine's reign, some secular presses did make their way into the provinces but with very little consequence. In the 1760s, for example, two new provincial presses opened, one in Astrakhan and the other in the fortress of St. Elizabeth in Kremenchug, both of which printed primarily official communications and public notices—i.e., works that were not intended for general circulation.[12] The sole exception came in 1765 with the publication in Kremenchug of a translation of *Le café*, a comic drama written by the court playwright of Louis XV, Jean-Baptiste Rousseau.[13] Between 1765 and 1784 two more presses appeared in the provinces, one at a seminary in Kharkov and another at the Jesuit academy in Polotsk. During that twenty-year period no new secular presses appeared, and only one even came under consideration. The press in question had been requested in 1778 by Jacob Sievers, the governor of Novgorod, Pskov, and Tver, who wanted an official printing press to help administer his domain.[14] The Senate denied his request, however, on the ground that an operation of that sort would be too expensive.

Thus, through the early 1780s provincial printing remained, for all practical purposes, the preserve of the Ukrainian monastic presses, and the rest of provincial Russia remained entirely dependent on Moscow and St. Petersburg for its books, a circumstance which placed the provincial readership at the mercy of an archaic and often barely extant distribution network and book trade, and which often left readers with little recourse but hand copying.[15]

This situation finally began to change in 1784, when presses opened in Kaluga and Yaroslavl. Between then and 1801, twenty-six Russian-language presses employing the civil orthography appeared in twenty-three provinces.[16] Three developments seem to have been most responsible for this growth. The first, of course, was the edict of 1783 that enabled private individuals to open presses. Only nine of the new provincial presses were in private hands, however—in Tambov, Tobolsk, Yaroslavl, Kostroma, Riga, and the villages of Kazinka, Klintsy, and Ruzaevka—and for most of these, private ownership was comparatively short-lived.[17] Thus, the advent of private publishing was a far less consequential event in the provinces than in the major cities.

A more important stimulus to provincial publishing came with the reorganization of provincial governments initiated in 1775. Over a period of several years, beginning in the late 1770s, the new provincial governments attracted thousands of servitors to the provinces and placed at their disposal larger clerical staffs and annual budgets and more material resources than had ever been available to Russian provincial administration. In about a dozen administrative centers, these resources came to include a printing press, as part of a program to allow provincial administrations to print official communications, as Sievers had suggested in 1778. Most of these presses were located, as one would expect, in the more heavily populated provinces or those that had become major regional admininstrative centers. But occasionally, smaller provincial towns, such as Perm, received printing presses. Conversely, several large and important areas, such as Tver and Glukhov, did not. In the end, the determining factor was less the size and importance of the town than the articulation of a need for publishing by a provincial official and his ability to persuade local notables to pay about 1,000 rubles for a press and at least 500 more rubles per year in salaries.[18]

The last general circumstance from which provicial publishing benefited was the organization of local gentry corporate activity, most often around philanthropic societies, that followed more or less from the 1785 charter to the nobility. Most commonly, local commissions of public welfare, whose existence was mandated by the 1775 reforms but which were staffed by the local gentry independently of the Table of Ranks, procured the presses, ostensibly to issue notices of local importance. In this way, printing presses came to Kaluga, Smolensk, Kharkov, Ekaterinoslav, and Kursk.

One other provincial civil press, the so-called campaign press of Prince Gregory Potemkin, fits none of these categories. Potemkin had taken a press from the Military College in St. Petersburg in August 1787 to use when he led Catherine and Emperor Joseph II of Austria on their travels through southern Russia. This press was supposed to be used for printing laws and official notices that the empress wished to issue while in transit. But after Catherine's return to the capital, Potemkin, who remained in the south to pursue the latest Turkish war, kept the press with him, and between 1789 and 1793 books printed in Kremenchug, Elisavetgrad, Iassy, and Bendery all contained the notation "from the campaign press."[19]

During the military campaign, Potemkin expanded the press's rep-

139

ertoire to include works of various genres, most of which had in common their lavish praise of Potemkin's military achievements. These books included a collection of prayers composed by Archbishop Amvrosii of Novorossiia that asked for continued military victories, and some odes to Potemkin himself that Peter Karabanov had written.[20] The campaign press also printed two religious tracts and it reprinted the 1757 Russian translation of Pope's *Essay on Man*.[21] There is evidence that it even printed works in French, Latin, and Greek.[22] When the Turkish war ended, Potemkin, before departing the south, gave the press to the Ekaterinoslav Office of Public Charity, which used it modestly for the next several years.

Besides the secular presses, two new religious presses appeared in Russia during the 1780s, an Old Believer press in the village of Klintsy and a civil-orthography press at the Kiev Academy.[23] Neither of these presses constituted entirely new printing endeavors; the Old Believers had been carrying on a sporadic underground publishing operation for several years, and the Kiev Academy had been publishing prayer books and texts in the old orthography and in Church Slavonic for many years. Each of them nevertheless represented a noteworthy change. For the Klintsy Old Believers, the 1783 law meant recognition of the press's right to exist, if not of the sect's liturgical doctrines, and a temporary end to official censure. Such an aboveground existence allowed the Old Believers to conduct a more active publishing campaign and to disseminate their books more openly. For the Kiev Academy, the new civil press facilitated printed communication with the laity, and it allowed the academy to expand its printing of nonreligious texts, including grammars, dictionaries, and even a medical handbook.[24]

During the last quarter of the eighteenth century, this array of new and preexisting provincial presses produced 267 Russian-language books, about 240 of which appeared in the last sixteen years of the century. The high point came in the first half of the 1790s, when provincial presses as a whole averaged about 26 books a year. However, as can be surmised from these figures, the most active provincial presses printed no more than three or four books a year, and most produced even less. Very little is known about their print runs, but the runs that are known usually were below 300 copies.[25]

Provincial publishing thus produced only a small fraction of what was available in print in Russia during these years, and very little of what it did produce managed to make its way to Moscow and St. Petersburg, since the avenues of dissemination to those cities were even more primitive than those going in the opposite direction. It was virtually impossible, therefore, for provincial books in general, let alone the publications of a single press, to have an impact upon the literary mainstream of Russian society in the 1780s and 1790s. Educated society even in the provinces probably had a difficult time gaining access to provincially published books and identifying the repertoire of books from local presses. Still, the overall scope of provincial publications is an important general indication of whether the provinces simply followed the lead of the major cities or whether local influences manifested themselves. Relevant figures are presented in table 5.1

A comparison of these figures with those of all books printed in the last quarter of the eighteenth century reveals that, in general terms, the subject composition of provincially published titles approximately corresponded to that of all titles published in the period. The only noteworthy differences were the relatively small percentages of religious, philosophical, and historical works in the provinces and the presence of regional studies. Otherwise, artistic literature, although slightly less dominant than in the major cities, continued to be the most important single category of books, with religious volumes and official notices following behind.[26] This parallel extended to the area of translation, where, Blium has calculated, 43 percent of all provincial books were translations, compared to 45 percent for all books.[27]

TABLE 5.1
Subject Composition of Provincial Press Publications, 1775–1800

Subject	Number	Percentage
Official information and notices	37	14
Religion[a]	27	10
Journals	5	2
Alphabet, grammar, and language	21	8
History, geography, and secular philosophy	27	10
Technology and science	21	8
Belles-lettres	93	35
Odes	25	9
Regional affairs	11	4
Total	267	100

SOURCE: Based on data in *Svodnyi katalog* and in Semennikov, "Bibliograficheskii spisok."

[a] Including both Orthodox and Old Believer.

141

These similarities seem to confirm Chechulin's and Semennikov's suggestions that provincial publishing represented in the main an outward extension of the literary life of the major cities. Even in a closer examination of the major categories of books, the parallel continues to hold true, albeit with certain subtle variations. Provincial artistic literature, for example, followed the trends set in the major cities but in a lighter and more derivative tone, consisting mostly of operas, love stories, and adventure tales. To be sure, a couple of Derzhavin's original works appeared for the first time in the provinces, as did a certain amount of locally inspired literature, some of which has drawn occasional attention from literary historians. But more often, provincial presses issued familiar works, such as Beaumarchais's *The Barber of Seville*, and books in familiar genres, such as the volume of moral fables translated from German and printed in Kaluga in 1785.

The quality of moral and philosophical titles, though varying greatly from province to province, also was largely derivative of the less than lofty standards established by the cadet presses in the major cities. Provincial presses tended to reproduce the better known moral-educational tracts by Stephanie de Genlis and the gently moralistic stories of Christian Gellert, but not the works of the *philosophes*.[28] There were some exceptions, such as in Tambov, where Gavril Derzhavin, the conservative poet, published a condensed translation of Helvétius's *De l'esprit*.[29] But in general, provincial publishers left the *philosophes* alone. The provinces, then, were not developing their own literary or philosophical traditions with their presses.

But to conclude from this that Chechulin was correct in pronouncing provincial publishing to be nothing more than a pale reflection of literary trends from Moscow and St. Petersburg—a periphery of the periphery, as it were—would be unwarranted, since some varieties of books quite vividly reflected local participation. Among them were compendia of historical and geographical descriptions and peculiarities of the local region or town, collections of local fables, the works of local poets or novelists, sermons by local clerics, and odes written in honor of an event of local or regional significance. When all of these titles are considered, they turn out to compose a much larger mass than the rather small number of narrowly defined regional studies would lead one to suspect.

Local initiative also appears in the handful of provincial journals that appeared in the late 1780s and early 1790s. At first glance, provincial journalism in the eighteenth century would appear to be little more than a curiosity, since the total of five provincial journals amounted to less than 2 percent of all provincial titles and only about 5 percent of all journals printed in Russia during the last quarter of the eighteenth century.[30] These journals have not attracted much attention in histories of Russian journalism or literature, since they published few original writers and almost no memorable works. Their circulations were limited at best, and their tenures were characteristically brief. They do deserve attention, however, for their significance in local intellectual life.

During 1788, for example, Tambov had an informational weekly, the *Tambov Herald (Tambovskii vestnik* or *Tambovskiia izvestiia)*, which, despite its brief existence and apparently poor sales, had a stimulating effect upon local literary life. Over the course of a year, forty-nine folio issues of the newspaper came out, and according to Derzhavin, who was its inspiration, editor, and overseer, it managed to keep the local citizenry informed of events of local importance, food prices, and new regulations and laws.[31] Although no one was willing to carry on with the newspaper after the first year, it succeeded in attracting interest in the local press, which then managed to keep active for several years, while other local ventures that Derzhavin had championed, including a local school and theater, rapidly deteriorated after his departure.

In the two other towns with local journals, the effects on local literary life were similar. In Yaroslavl, Vasilii Sankovskii, a veteran of the literary circles of Moscow in the 1760s and the editor of one of the earliest so-called private journals, *Good Intentions (Dobroe namerenie)*, gathered a small literary circle around himself.[32] Sankovskii had come to Yaroslavl in the 1760s, and in the mid-1780s he was serving as the secretary of the local Office of Public Welfare. After Yaroslavl procured an institutional press in 1784, he prevailed upon it to organize a local magazine, *The Solitary Wise Man of Gotham (Uedinennyi poshekhonets)*. This magazine attracted a great deal of new interest and activity that permitted Sankovskii to enlist a large number of local gentry and clergy to write for the journal. In addition, he received some essays from his old friends from Moscow, including Vasilii Ruban and Vasilii Petrov.[33] The end result was a journal that combined the style of the early literary magazines of Moscow with articles that had a distinctly local flavor. One issue, for example, celebrated the opening of a new foundling home by printing the texts of the speeches given to commemorate the event as well as some poetry that had been composed to mark the occasion.[34]

This journal succeeded, then, in taking the model of the literary magazine from the cosmopolitan literati and modifying it to reflect the world of Yaroslavl's educated elite. In the process, it allowed local

143

groups, who were the chief (perhaps the only) beneficiaries, to absorb the more advanced and universalistic literary vision of the major cities without surrendering local identity. Such a synthesis provided an important, if fragile and short-lived, institutional basis for linking provincial intellectual life with the major cities in a rudimentary nationwide cultural network. Nevertheless, the magazine failed to achieve a large local following outside of the immediate coterie that produced it, and after a year of poor sales, it was reorganized and rechristened the *Monthly Works Published in Yaroslavl (Ezhemesiachnoe sochinenie izdavaemoe v Iaroslavle)*. That, too, was short-lived; it closed within a few months.

The only provincial journals that attracted even a modest popular following were the magazines published in the Siberian town of Tobolsk, *Irtysh* (1790–91) and the *Scholar's Library (Biblioteka uchenaia*, 1793–94). They, too, included a blending of reprintings from older journals and local literature, mostly poetry, and again the literary merits of the journals were, by general agreement, negligible. But, entirely through the efforts of local people, these two journals developed a wide subscription network, ranging between 100 and 186 subscribers spread throughout most of Siberia and much of European Russia.[35]

Tobolsk, to be sure, had developed an unusually active cultural life prior to the appearance of *Irtysh*, including a local seminary, a primary school, and a literary circle with several local poets, such as P. P. Sumarokov.[36] Some of the local merchantry and administrators, moreover, had worked for a number of years to enhance the town's position as a provincial intellectual center. But the journals effectively transformed this endeavor from a project of interest only to the town to one that made Tobolsk the acknowledged center of Siberian literary life. To a considerable degree, *Irtysh* and the *Scholar's Library* fostered a regional awareness among educated groups by becoming the literary organ of Siberia, both as the conduit of cosmopolitan culture to the region and as the voice of Siberian lay culture to itself and to the rest of the empire, including Moscow, St. Petersburg, and Kiev.[37]

To a limited degree, therefore, the Tobolsk magazines succeeded in creating a dialogue between center and periphery and in communicating with a national audience. Provincial journals thus had a considerable short-term impact locally and regionally that greatly exceeded their small number and their modest financial and artistic achievements. Such roles as they did play ultimately revolved around the journals as public institutions much more than around their literary imaginations. This fact suggests further that the proper place to seek the social significance of provincial publishing as a whole is not in its literary repertoire but in its social role as an organizer of intellectual life. Lay provincial presses uniformly depended upon local funds and the participation of a socially heterogeneous mix of local people. Those presses that failed to inspire local support generally closed after a few years or, as happened in several cases (Tula, Saratov, Viatka, Simbirsk, and Astrakhan), they printed nothing at all until the nineteenth century.[38] The successful presses, conversely, managed to ingratiate themselves with one or more local groups, stir up a certain degree of local enthusiasm and activity, and thereby transform themselves into centers of lay cultural life.

Two of the local successes were directed by well-educated gentry, Nikita Sumarokov in Kostroma, whose press operated from 1793 to 1796, and Nikolai Struiskii, in the village of Ruzaevka, who published from 1792 to 1796.[39] Neither of these men was especially active as a publisher, each printing only about two books a year for a few years in the early 1790s, but each of them had lived in the locale for a long time and each attempted to use his press to promote local interest. Sumarokov published mostly volumes on local affairs or books written or collected by other local residents, such as a speech by a local seminary teacher, Iakov Arsen'ev, celebrating the end of the war with the Ottoman Empire, a locally produced medical handbook, and a local tract on celebrating Lent.[40] Struiskii, on the other hand, printed only works that he had composed himself.[41] This prolific man wrote plays, moralistic stories, elegies, odes, and letters, most of which he immediately published. Those works that he could not publish personally he sent to leading presses in Moscow and St. Petersburg for publication.[42] Whether anyone paid attention to his eccentric output is not known, but Struiskii did go so far as to place announcements in the newspapers informing readers of impending volumes. In one such notice, he even apologized to his public for typographical errors that had marred one of his previous publications.[43]

Three of the other local presses also belonged to long-time residents, but in these instances they were merchants: Dmitrii Rukavishnikov in the Old Believer village of Klintsy, Peter Kotel'nikov in Kaluga (1793–96), and Vasilii Kornil'ev in Tobolsk (1789–94). In contrast to the gentry publishers, Kornil'ev and Kotel'nikov had some familiarity with the book business, the former as the owner of a paper factory and the latter as a bookseller.[44] They also had contacts with local literary groups and allowed the presses under their control to print a wide range of locally generated general-interest publications, such as the two literary magazines in Tobolsk. In addition, in 1792 Kornil'ev published something of a "Who's Who" of western Siberia, entitled *A Short Index of the Former Military Governors . . . of Tobolsk and All the Other Cities of Siberia,* as well as some essays by local teachers.[45]

The other merchant, Rukavishnikov, handled his press much differently. As the single printing press in Old Believer hands within the Russian Empire (and one of only two Old Believer presses anywhere), the Klintsy press fulfilled an important public role for a large and geographically diverse population. Often during the eighteenth century, members of the Klintsy community had been obliged to devote a great deal of energy to the hand copying of sacred texts, a job at which they excelled. With Rukavishnikov's press, however, this changed. Between 1783 and 1787, although he was constantly under the scrutiny of the Synod, Rukavishnikov managed to put out and circulate a steady stream of Old Believer tracts.[46] Exactly how many books he printed in those years is not known, but he appears to have been quite active.[47] Even after the government, in 1788, forbade Rukavishnikov to publish any further, two other Old Believer merchants succeeded in operating the press clandestinely for several years.[48]

Another press that was under the authority of local interests, the Voronezh province administration press, founded in 1798, deserves special mention because of its singular success in embracing not only the literature of the major cities and local flavor but also some fairly sophisticated local intellectual pursuits.[49] The dominant figure in directing the Voronezh press was Efimii (or Evgenii) Bolkhovitinov, a teacher at the local seminary and later a theologian of some prominence. Bolkhovitinov was born into a clercial family in Voronezh in 1767. His education began at the Voronezh Seminary, but in 1786 he went to the Slavonic Academy in Moscow. While in Moscow, he attended lectures at the university, and apparently he had some contact with Novikov's circle.[50] Upon returning to Voronezh at the end of 1788, Bolkhovitinov took up duties as a teacher in the seminary. At this point, he gathered around himself a study group that included seminarians, province administrators, and local gentry. For several years this coterie read and discussed books on serious philosophical, political, and scientific matters. Several of its members became prominent educators or religious leaders many years later. Bolkhovitinov himself became an important professor in the Kiev Academy and the Metropolitan of Kiev under Alexander I.[51]

It is not clear why, after several years, Bolkhovitinov's group decided to obtain a printing press, but whatever the reason, the books that it produced reflected the intellectual depth and the combination of cosmopolitan and local interests that had moved Bolkhovitinov to form the group in the first place. Other than the official and informational works that the province administration mandated, most titles concentrated upon serious literature and theology. Between 1798 and 1800, Bolkhovitinov published seventeen books, including a translation of Caspar Van Baerle's seventeenth-century *Poem of Noah's Ark*; several books by Bolkhovitinov, including a history of Voronezh, a book on Russian Orthodoxy, and a set of church songs; a collection of literary works by Russian authors, including Kheraskov, Derzhavin, and Lomonosov; and an original play that was performed at the local theater.[52]

No other provincial press achieved quite this level of serious-minded local support, yet, despite its intellectual singularity, the Voronezh press did share two significant characteristics with the five other locally controlled presses. First, all were organized by long-time residents rather than by newly arrived servitors or retiring gentry, and all were financed with money raised locally. Second, and more important, all of them eschewed the needs of officialdom and any hope for financial gain—there was not much money to be made, after all, from the sale of two to five titles a year—in favor of satisfying local aspirations and concerns. Moreover, all of them, except for the eccentric Struiskii, drew enthusiastic local intellectual support from a socially more heterogeneous amalgam of people in the provincial town than the elite literary presses of the major cities could. In no instance, however, was this support sufficiently large to sustain the press financially for more than a few years. The limited local markets could not provide a viable income to these presses, and, with few exceptions, the local notables could not patronize publishing except at a very modest rate.

A rather different pattern emerges from the activities of a group of publishers who had no roots in the local town but who had come into the provinces after having spent several years in the major cities—that is, those who most closely resembled the transplanted cosmopolitans upon whom Chechulin, Semennikov, and Blium have placed so much importance. The majority of them had come to the provinces to serve in the upper echelons of the reformed administrations, several had gone through the elite system of secondary education, and they had participated in the intellectual life of the major cities. Their lives and careers were thus rooted in the major cities, and their patience with the slower and less stimulating pace of life in a provincial town tended to be of short duration, as did their residence in the provinces.

Most of these publishers quite naturally had a fondness for the literary world that they had left behind, and they usually attempted to use the local presses to recreate some of that literary life. Often they had access to some institutional funds to apply to publishing, and they used these funds to reprint previously translated literary and philosophical works. Generally lacking in an abiding concern for local tastes, they printed what amused them, and when they left, their presses either closed or settled into a routine of printing mundane informational works. Far from being the pinnacle of provincial literary culture, therefore, these presses represented the least imaginative and culturally the most isolated of all the local presses. Nevertheless, a few of their directors did make an effort to embrace local literate groups, if not to learn from them then at least to introduce them to the higher culture and civilization that the capital could offer. Sometimes this effort met with considerable success in ways that resonated locally for years after the individual in question had departed.

The outstanding example of a cosmopolitan publisher with this type of local following was Gavril Derzhavin, who had come to Tambov as governor in 1785. Prior to that time, he had made a considerable reputation as an administrator, having served in various capacities in the military and civil bureaucracy since the late 1760s. At the same time, he had been a leading figure among the young intellectuals who were reinvigorating intellectual life in St. Petersburg. He had written a great deal of drama and poetry and had participated in several of the literary journals of the 1770s and early 1780s. He was, in short, a prototypical member of the literati of the late eighteenth century.

Derzhavin took his service responsibilities extremely seriously. After he had been in Tambov for only a few weeks, he expressed disgust at the low level of local talent and, in particular, at the abysmal ignorance of the law that typified the local servitors.[53] He further decried the virtual absence of an intellectual life: no circles, no publishers, and no books. To remedy the last of these deficiencies, he arranged for the provincial government to become an outlet for Novikov's publications. He then turned to Novikov with a more ambitious request: to start a publishing house in Tambov.[54] What came of this request is not known, but soon afterward, in November 1787, Johann Schneider, a master printer, opened a press in Tambov under Derzhavin's supervision.[55]

The first and only volume that Schneider printed was an edition of Derzhavin's speech in celebration of the opening of a local theater and school.[56] Shortly thereafter, Andrei Nilov, a former brigadier in the army who had recently come to Tambov, apparently at Derzhavin's urging, took over the press and ran it until the new press laws forced its closure in 1796.

By all accounts, Derzhavin dominated the Tambov Press until he returned to St. Petersburg in 1789.[57] Thanks to his energy, a number of returning officers, local gentry, local clergy, and local merchantry were able to participate in the Tambov publishing circle.[58] Even more remarkable was that several local gentry women were engaged as translators for the press.[59]

All these features conform to the most optimistic image of provincial intellectual life, albeit within a somewhat altered timetable. The participation of a wide circle of local residents, including women, suggests that books, literature, and ideas had taken root in the province very firmly indeed.

In a few other provinces where administrators established literary groups, although the specific circumstances differed, the overall course of events was similar. In Yaroslavl, for example, Governor Mel'gunov successfully organized a masonic lodge and a literary group, with the cooperation of a number of other people, most of whom had accompanied him from the capital. Many of them worked with Sankovskii's circle at the press.[60] Vice-Admiral N. S. Mordvinov attracted Semen Selivanovskii, a publisher from Moscow, Vasilii Petrov, a poet, and Prokhor Suvorov, a professor of mathematics at the School of Navigation, to come to Nikolaev and run a press.[61] Like Derzhavin, this group gathered around itself a circle of local people, who produced eighteen books between 1798 and 1800, almost all of which, according to A. G. Cross, "were written, compiled, or translated by people working in Nikolaev or nearby towns."[62]

Semennikov has written of similar groups that sprang up in Nizhnii Novgorod, Kaluga, and Kostroma.[63] But these were not as successful in attracting local interest as Derzhavin and Mordvinov were, and none of them survived for very long.

This intermingling of local energies and national culture also characterized the handful of publishers who came to the provinces not to establish roots nor to continue service careers but to escape from governmental harrassment in the major cities. Three of them, Selivanovskii, Ivan Sytin, and M. P. Ponomarev, had lost their private presses in 1796, and rather than give up printing entirely, they withdrew to the provinces to continue their careers as managers, lessees, or employees of administrative presses.[64] A fourth refugee, Ivan Rakhmaninov, had abandoned publishing in St. Petersburg in 1791, both for personal reasons and because of the notoriety that his friendship with Radishchev had attracted. He returned to his estate in the village of Kazinka in Tambov province, where he resumed publishing. He published a few titles there, but because of his associations he was watched extremely closely, and in 1794, on the pretext of a technical violation of the law, the police forced him to cease publishing.[65]

The other three refugee publishers managed to survive the difficult years of censorship during Paul's reign, thanks largely to the protection of local sponsors, and at the beginning of the nineteenth century, each of them left the provinces and returned either to Moscow or St. Petersburg to resume publishing. In the cases of Ponomarev and Selivanovskii, this meant a return to the most popular forms of literature and general-interest books. Sytin, however, never managed to revive fully the literary character of his earlier enterprise and instead turned increasingly to bookselling and operating a private library, tasks that he performed with considerable success.

The diverse backgrounds, goals and experiences of the provincial publishers, as well as the vast distances that separated them from each other, mitigate against any single overarching conclusion about their activities. Certainly, several of them enriched the intellectual lives of the provincial towns and villages in which they worked, yet their effects on the local literate populations were mixed at best. Even when local residents were engaged, literary and philosophical publications do not appear to have sold very well among them, and when the populace was not engaged, the local impact of the press was virtually nil regardless of what was published.

This impact was further circumscribed by the fact that few of the presses survived intact through the troubled years of Paul I's reign and the first years of the nineteeth century. Even the presses that had established roots in their communities, such as the Old Believer press in Klintsy and the literary presses in Voronezh, Nikolaev, and Yaroslavl, either closed down or declined drastically early in the nineteenth century. In 1807 most of those remaining were reorganized as a result of an influx of funds from the central government. After that time, most of them remained open, but they tended not to be very active. By far the most active provincial press of the nineteenth century, that at the University of Kazan, did not even exist in the eighteenth century. It would be a mistake, then, to make too much of this experience or to see in provincial publishing the beginning of a major geographic extension or pluralization of cosmopolitan culture. Rather, its importance lay in whatever roles the presses played in generating intellectual activity in their respective locales.

In the end, the combination of censorship, a failure even by local groups to take popular demand into account (except perhaps in Tobolsk), and the apparently limited population to which local presses could appeal severely curtailed the publishing activities and aspirations of local cultural figures. The simple fact was that provincial readers could not rely upon local presses for their books, and even in 1800 they remained heavily dependent on Moscow and St. Petersburg. The fate of provincial intellectual life, therefore, rested less on the activities of local publishers and servitors than on the ability of urban and local merchants to bring books from the outside.

SIX

The Russian Book Trade

IN TRACING the evolution of Russian publishing in the eighteenth century, we have seen the increasing urgency that all but the most eccentric or official publishers felt about discovering and communicating with a public or a readership. Those institutional publishers who earned their money from doing business for the government could rely upon administrative networks, schools, and churches to distribute books. Since 1726, however, a growing number of institutional, religious, and private presses had more and more turned to the market, or at least to private financing, to disseminate their books and ward off chronic debt. Discovering and supplying the market, however, required a viable book trade that could deliver the books and through which readers in the major cities and in the provinces could articulate demand.

The book-distribution network that Peter the Great had left was, if anything, even cruder, less responsive, and less stable than the publishing system. For the rest of the century, therefore, publishers faced a continuing and often frustrating challenge of creating a distribution system or, when it was feasible, contracting with other people who wanted to set one up on their own. This process, restrained for most of the century by the financial problems and limited output of the publishing houses, finally gained a certain stability and momentum during Catherine's reign.

As this system unfolded, it began to develop a character of its own and to make its own demands on publishers, whose response often shaped the activities of the presses and even came to determine which presses survived and which failed. The book trade also became an important influence in determining whether the scholastic and private presses developed a credible voice to rival church and state outside of elite cosmopolitan society.

THE BOOK TRADE AFTER PETER THE GREAT

As Luppov has shown, the book market had already begun in the fifteen years after the death of Peter the Great to establish a rudimentary commercial network that made use of caravans, hawkers, merchants, and colporteurs. According to Luppov, these changes were associated primarily with the Academy of Sciences' repertoire of new secular books that more closely corresponded to the needs and interests of readers than did the older works of religion and officialdom.[1] The evidence, however, suggests that although some individuals unquestionably did work hard to establish a viable book trade through the Academy's bookstore in the 1730s, and although they did substantially increase the Academy's income from publishing, the Academy's commercial system remained small, primitive, quite unstable, and in almost all respects less effective than the network that the Synod had established.

The Orthodox Church had operated a bookshop in Moscow at the old *pechatnyi dvor* since the middle of the seventeenth century. For quite some time it had also arranged with local merchants to sell books at the merchants' quarters, on Spasskii Bridge, and at other sites, and it relied upon rural caravans and colporteurs to carry prayer books into the countryside. In the late 1730s, the Synod took steps to centralize bookselling in Moscow, first establishing controls over hawking near the Spasskii Gate of the Kremlin and then, in 1742, opening a synodal bookshop near the bridge (see chapter 2).[2] It also began to consolidate its authority over the sale of books from other church presses and to receive compensation in cash for almost all books distributed to other church establishments.[3]

In addition to all of this, Luppov's recent explorations in the archives has uncovered fresh evidence of new and expanded contacts between the Synod and urban merchants in Moscow, St. Petersburg, and other towns during the late 1730s.[4] In 1738, for example, one Moscow merchant, Ivan Andreianov, bought over 800 rubles worth of books from the Synod press to sell at fairs in Moscow and elsewhere.[5] Income from these sources, however, averaged only 5,100 rubles a year in the 1730s, and, as Luppov points out, in spite of a more or less steady growth in income over the course of the decade, from 3,100 rubles in 1732 to 7,200 in 1740, the average for the decade was no higher than the average achieved between 1702 and 1715.[6] However, the press was providing somewhat fewer books in the 1730s than it had been earlier, and, in contrast to the Petrine years, all of its books in the 1730s were essentially religious.[7] Individual religious titles, in other words, were bringing in more income than they had during Peter's reign, a fact which indicates that the Synod press in Moscow was doing a more effective job of selling religious books through its expanded network in the late 1730s than it had done when selling a mixture of religious and official ones a generation earlier. With the annual output of religious books more than doubling in the late 1740s and 1750s, moreover, the Synod's income must have grown as well.

In contrast to this relatively broad reach, the Academy's early book-trading network in the 1730s and 1740s appeared very fragile. In its first years it sold books from a makeshift office in the building from which public notices and *Vedomosti* had been distributed.[8] In 1728 the Academy opened a regular book-selling office, the *knizhnaia palata*, that oversaw the activities of the book depository (*knizhnyi magazin*) and a bookshop (*knizhnaia lavka*). A year later the *knizhnaia palata* received permission to sell books at the Synod's bookshop.[9] In addition, it made provisional arrangements with V. V. Kiprianov and a bookbinder named Voitchev to sell Academy publications in Moscow on commission.[10] All of these arrangements reflected the Academy's aggressive approach to bookselling, but none brought the Academy the national market that it sought. The contacts with Moscow continued only sporadically through the 1730s and essentially came to a halt in 1739. Relations with provincial colportage and regional markets were even more haphazard and depended almost entirely on the good will of peddlers for the sale mostly of calendars.[11]

The Academy's problems in this regard were manifest. Its books were expensive, its own resources were limited, and it was unable or unwilling to advance credit to peddlers. The peddlers, perpetually short of cash, were not in a position to venture their own capital on behalf of an institution whose books addressed no known provincial demand. From their perspective, it made far more sense to spend their limited resources on alphabet books, prayer books and teaching psalters from the Synod, for which a reliable national market already existed, than to risk their money on the obscure Academy books. Peddlers, consequently, were willing to take only the calendars, for which there was a large and apparently unsatisfied national market.

Unable to employ colportage as its link with the provincial market, the Academy began compiling lists of its recent publications and sending them to the province administrations.[12] But this endeavor had little success, and it soon ended. It thus became clear that if the Academy were going to sell its books, it had to create a market of its own, and the most likely place to do that was in St. Petersburg itself.

In the first couple of years of its existence, the Academy bookshop was ill-equipped to sell books; its sales were small (506 rubles in 1729), and its contacts within the city were minimal. To improve its visibility, in December 1728 the *knizhnaia palata* placed its first announcement of recent publications in the *St. Petersburg News*, including a historical calendar which contained, among other things, "curious descriptions of the land of Kamchatka."[13]

Eager to establish a better sales record, the Academy went through several bookshop managers in the 1720s. Ultimately, the director of the Academy's library, Johann Schumacher, after an extensive correspondence with various German book dealers and scholars, hired Gottlieb Clanner, a book dealer from Leipzig, to manage the *knizhnaia palata*. During his tenure of almost nine years at the Academy (1730–38), Clanner made enormous progress in improving the St. Petersburg market, in reopening trade with foreign book dealers, and in raising the revenues of the bookshop.[14]

In Clanner's first year, the receipts from book sales grew to over 6,000 rubles, and during the next four years they averaged more than 5,300 rubles.[15] Not enough is known about bookkeeping procedures at the *knizhnaia palata* to determine whether or not the bookshop was making a profit, but it is clear that Clanner was selling fewer than half of the books he received at the shop. By 1739 the bookshop had accumulated a backlog of 59,000 rubles worth of books. This came to a backlog of about 6,500 rubles a year, or 1,200 rubles more than average income.[16]

Still, Clanner did increase revenues, an accomplishment of no mean proportion at the time. He did so in part through wider nationwide calendar sales and marginal improvements in the Moscow trade, but his main achievements were in the capital. He regularly placed notices of newly published books in the *St. Petersburg News*; he issued the first periodic catalogues of books for sale; and he agreed to allow a few local peddlers to sell books on commission at the bridges, from stalls in the merchant quarters, and in the foreign neighborhoods.[17] All of this created a citywide network that made Academy books readily available, albeit at high prices, to likely readers. It was this network that provided the initial readership for the Academy's list of literary and historical translations that proved to be popular and profitable in the 1740s.

But these markets remained very tenuous, and Clanner's successor, a man named Preissler (or Preisser), almost drove the bookshop into the ground.[18] Contacts with Moscow's dealers were dropped, money started to disappear, and in 1742 income had fallen to 2,900 rubles.[19] At one point, Preissler was even imprisoned for committing "disorderly acts" and on suspicion of embezzlement.[20] As late as June 1750, complaints were still being received at the Academy chancellery that the records were not yet in order and that there were no accurate inventories.[21] Finally, in August 1750, Preissler was replaced by Stepan

Zboromirskii, who stayed on as manager of the bookshop for several years.[22]

The Academy did have two other markets in these years that Preissler did not entirely destroy. As the sole outlet for foreign-language publications, the Academy was in a good position to develop an international trade based on its own scientific publications and to become the leading Russian outlet for books printed abroad. Accordingly, Clanner and other Academy officials devoted a great deal of attention to negotiating with foreign book dealers, to whom various Russian institutions owed long-standing debts, in order to reestablish commercial contact. Much of the initial activity revolved around stocking the Academy's library or the private libraries of the members of the Academy, but some of it was public.

The earliest of these contacts were initiated in the late 1720s by book dealers in Amsterdam and Leipzig who were interested in setting up bookshops in St. Petersburg or in selling their books through the Academy.[23] Prior to Clanner's arrival, the Academy had rejected these overtures, but it did agree to send its own books abroad.[24] By 1731 a limited trade in Academy books had begun in Amsterdam, Leipzig, and perhaps in Hamburg.[25] The publications in which foreign dealers showed most interest were scientific monographs, especially issues of *Commentarii*, but some interest was expressed in stocking portraits and seals printed at the Academy.

Clanner's arrival brought renewed efforts at selling foreign publications in Russia. Clanner contacted book dealers in Holland and Germany to get lists of recently published books, and in 1732 books published abroad went on sale.[26] However, this trade soon ran into obstacles. It seems that Clanner had imported a few books which had already been published by the German-language press at the Academy of Sciences. Such undercutting of domestic publishing, however inadvertent, drew severe criticism from the president of the Academy, L. L. Blumentrost, and from the Senate, which deemed the incident serious enough to warrant edicts in 1734 and 1750 barring the practice.[27]

In 1736 Clanner made a trip to Holland and Germany in order to try once again to arrange for the purchase of foreign publications.[28] But he did not succeed in ironing out all the difficulties, and by the mid-1740s the Academy's foreign book trade had declined to the point where virtually the only books coming into Russia were those that had been ordered directly for libraries.[29] Finally, out of utter frustration, in May 1747 the Academy instructed Preissler to end all accounts with foreign book dealers as equitably and quietly as possible.[30]

This outcome did not sit well with the members of the Academy, and in November 1747 the new president of the Academy, Kirill Razumovskii, suggested that perhaps trade could be reestablished if people who were fluent in foreign languages, especially French, went abroad to draw up lists of books that might be worth selling in Russia.[31] This plan drew considerable support, and in 1748 Johann Taubert, who was planning a trip abroad anyway, was recruited for the job.[32] In addition, a Swiss book dealer, Franz Hirt, was hired by the Academy to help reestablish links with foreign book dealers.[33]

Taubert was abroad for over two years, and in that time he worked out agreements with book dealers in Paris, Amsterdam, London, and Leipzig, contingent upon an equitable settlement of all current financial disputes.[34] These agreements effectively reopened the foreign book trade, and by the early 1750s books were flowing through the Academy to the foreign neighborhoods of St. Petersburg with some regularity.

Upon his return, Taubert set down his reflections on the book trade in a small report entitled "A Project for the Orderly Establishment of a Bookshop."[35] Such reports were not new, and Taubert's recommended little that had not been suggested before: balance the financial ledgers, find out what kinds of books people were interested in buying, and sell more books. However, Taubert's went further than the other reports in suggesting that the press and bookshop identify specific potential publics and the interests which those publics expressed.

He pointed out quite reasonably that the Russian-language publications were popular only in Russia and that foreign-language publications should go, by and large, for export. He argued, further, that foreign book dealers should be discouraged from sending books to Russia that either violated the law or elicited no interest from Russian readers. Specifically, he listed books on law and religion and prayer books as items that ought not be imported.

Taubert did not speculate about what kinds of books should be imported or who would buy them. Presumably, the import market would continue to come largely from members of the Academy and other foreign residents of the capital. But the new literary groups that were forming at the cadet corps and elsewhere may also have begun to purchase foreign literature at the Academy. Some writers were requesting books from friends abroad, and it is entirely possible that they directed similar requests to the Academy.[36]

Even with this newly emerging literary public, however, the Academy's book trade remained severely restricted as long as it was limited mostly to a single city. Luppov has recently uncovered archival evidence showing that the Academy's bookshop averaged only about

3,000 rubles in annual income between 1749 and 1752—fully 2,000 rubles a year less than it had in the early 1730s.[37] Over 15 percent of that amount, moreover, came from calendars, even though prices for calendars were ten kopeks or less, as compared to an average book price of close to a ruble.[38] For an institution that aspired to a balanced budget and a national audience among merchants, tradesmen, gentry, and students, this was far from acceptable.

THE EXPANSION OF THE MARKET

This situation improved in the second half of the century, as an extensive trade in secular books evolved thanks largely to the commercial sensitivity of merchants to the entreaties and demands of publishers, literary circles, and secondary-school students, and to the less clearly articulated demands of a more diffuse but growing readership.

The improvement began very simply in the late 1740s with an expansion from a one-city to a two-city trade. Rather than consigning its books to independent merchants, who had proven to be unreliable and prone to running up large debts, the Academy decided to run its own bookshop in Moscow. The Academy would then be able to put all of its publications on sale without worrying about the solvency or perceptions of merchants.[39] In August 1748, the Senate's Moscow office was asked to find a place in full public view, preferably near Spasskii Bridge, from which the Academy could run a bookshop.[40] The most appropriate site, not surprisingly, turned out to be Kiprianov's old store. However, Kiprianov, who had his own doubts about the Academy's solvency, insisted on a high sale price of 5,000 rubles or an annual rental of 500 rubles. The Academy was unwilling to pay that much money, and a lengthy negotiation ensued, during which time the Academy also searched unsuccessfully for an alternate site.[41] Finally, in March 1749, an agreement was reached with Kiprianov (the terms of which are not specified in the sources), and the Academy was able to open its own Moscow outlet.[42]

Since the market in Moscow had been neglected for so long, orders began pouring into the Academy at a great rate. Initially, these were blanket orders simply to fill up stocks, but soon the Moscow bookstore began to make specific requests to St. Petersburg, mainly for French and German grammars, copies of *1001 Nights*, and official documents such as the academic regulations.[43]

In the mid-1750s Jacob Stählin was asked to evaluate the book trade in Moscow and to make recommendations on how to improve it. Stählin confirmed that this market had been badly neglected and emphasized that any change in the way the book trade had been conducted would have been an improvement.[44] As part of his evaluation, Stählin compiled monthly debit and credit sheets for the Moscow bookstore for the years between 1750 and 1756.[45] He discovered that in this period the bookstore had earned 16,515 rubles in sales (see table 6.1) and had spent 16,296 rubles (including wages of 1,500 rubles). When some additional sources of income were added, proceeds rose to almost 20,000 rubles and, according to Stählin's figures, the net profit was 3,677 rubles.

Luppov has found some other records in the Academy's archives concerning the Moscow bookshop's initial sales during these years. For 1753, the only year in which total gross sales were given, Luppov's source shows an income of 1,956 rubles, or slightly more than the figure from Stählin's report, 1,893 rubles.[46] But the Academy records are far more revealing than Stählin's in documenting the extent to which this income reflected the diversification and secularization of Moscow's demand. The Moscow readers were buying not only religious books and calendars, but also a wide range of secular books. For example, they had spent 300 rubles a year for foreign-language books and for more than 100 copies each of particular titles in history, literature, and moral-educational books by such authors as Fénelon, Rollin, Aesop, Lomonosov, and Curas, in spite of the fact that these books cost 30 to 50 percent more in Moscow than in St. Petersburg.[47] This diversification took place, moreover, prior to the opening of Moscow University.

The point here is that the connection with Moscow finally succeeded

TABLE 6.1
Income from Book Sales at the Moscow Bookstore of the Academy of Sciences, 1750–56

	Total[a]	Monthly Average[a]
1750–March 1751	758 r. 64 k.	54 r. 19 k.
March–December 1751	2,805 r. 25 k.	280 r. 53 k.
1752	3,756 r. 82 k.	313 r. 07 k.
1753	1,893 r. 11 k.	157 r. 76 k.
1754	2,955 r. 48 k.	246 r. 29 k.
1755	2,755 r. 41 k.	229 r. 20 k.
January–July 1756	1,590 r. 15 k.	227 r. 16 k.

SOURCE: RO GPB, *fond* 871 (Stählin collection), no. 108, p. 2.
[a] r. = rubles, k. = kopeks.

both because the network had been regularized and because a market for leisure, secular books had evolved. The Academy could hardly have established a regular Moscow market without this diversification in reading habits. But the discovery of this diversity depended upon creating a stable distribution system that overcame the unwillingness of merchants to venture their own resources in uncharted markets.

Once it became clear that there now were two significant urban markets for secular books in Russia, merchants were more amenable to carrying them, and with the expansion and reforms in secondary education that took place in the 1750s and 1760s, a few of the new scholastic presses also made steady progress in arranging, first, an effective two-city trade and, then, a rudimentary national market. The first step in this proliferation was that each new publishing house opened its own public shop on the premises. Most also followed the Academy's example in publishing periodic catalogues of books for sale and in placing notices in the St. Petersburg or Moscow newspaper. From these catalogues it appears that the shops occasionally carried books of other presses as well. During his long tenure (1757–81) as an employee and then manager of Moscow University's bookshop, for example, Christian Wever arranged to sell books from several St. Petersburg scholastic presses in exchange for their selling some of his, and the Infantry Cadet Press arranged a similar trade with the Academy of Sciences.[48] But these arrangements stayed within established institutional lines and as a consequence did little to develop an extensive network. Without some means of giving independent merchants and small traders entry into the market, the book trade was not going to be able to go very far.

Bookselling was an easy business to enter, however, since a prospective dealer required little capital and faced none of the legal complications such as those that beset private publishing. As economic conditions permitted, therefore, a variety of individuals, most of them foreign-born, began to sell books either independently or as agents for one of the publishing houses. From the early 1750s until scholastic publishing reached its height in the early 1770s, the number of regular booksellers in Moscow and St. Petersburg grew from about six to about fifteen. At that point, bookselling underwent a dramatic upsurge that closely paralleled the expansion that was taking place at that time in private publishing.

The publishers, though, were not directly responsible for creating the book-trading network; indeed, publishers and booksellers often had different and even conflicting interests. In order to earn a living, booksellers had to be sensitive to the demands of readers as well as to the needs of publishers, as a result of which booksellers often exerted influences upon the publishers rather than vice versa. Those who published for the sake of making money were as beholden to demand as booksellers were, and they came to fashion their output largely on the basis of what booksellers told them. But many publishers in Russia had other matters on their minds besides profits. The literary-minded publishers were more inventive and original, but they also were prone to be less responsive to popular demand and hence less interesting to the book dealer and his customers. Thus, bookselling was more commercial and less likely to be affected by politics, ideology, and the vagaries of press laws than was publishing; and, whereas publishing had attracted men of disparate backgrounds—literati, merchants, artisans, administrators, and even military officers—bookselling drew mostly merchants and artisans.

The majority of these were foreign-born merchants who had come to Russia at an early age, endowed with little capital but equipped with backgrounds in either trade or commerce. Several, such as Breitkopf, Schnoor, Weitbrecht, and Rüdiger, are already familiar to us from their work at institutional bookstores and publishing houses in Russia or as managers of private presses.[49] Breitkopf, for example, had come to St. Petersburg to manage the Russian trade for his family's publishing and bookselling firm in Leipzig.[50]

Other foreign-born booksellers lacked formal connections with institutional publishers, but several of them had been subsidizing publishing in institutional presses for a number of years.[51] Karl Müller, for example, had been born in 1749 in Lübeck, the son of a bookbinder, but his father had moved to St. Petersburg a year later to take a job with the Academy Press.[52] Having grown up in the book business, Müller came to know several of the leading writers who had gathered around the Academy, and by the early 1770s he was supplying some of them with cash in order to be able to publish their books. He went on to run a successful private bookshop for several years. Christian Torno began as an independent bookbinder in St. Petersburg, selling a few books on the side from his workshop. Over time, bookselling took up more of his attention, and eventually it became his primary occupation.[53]

The Russian book dealers in Moscow and St. Petersburg were fewer in number than the foreign-born ones, but they too came mostly from trade and industry. Some, such as Ivan Kruglov and Ivan Nikiforov, began as little more than street traders who, over time, developed more or less permanent arrangements with the leading institutional publishers. Most, however, including Matvei Ovchinnikov, Ivan Zelennikov, Ivan Reshetnikov, and the members of the Ponomarev family, had first worked as typesetters and publishers, and several others, including Nikita Dmitriev, Nikita Vodop''ianov, and the aptly named Ivan Perepletchikov ("bookbinder"), had been bookbinders before turning to the book trade.[54] At least one bookseller, Nikita Kol'chugin, had begun as a typesetter at Novikov's Typographical Company.[55]

By the mid-1780s, bookselling had become sufficiently profitable to begin to attract wealthier merchants who lacked experience with books but who apparently saw a future in them. From their ranks came many early bookselling magnates, including the Glazunov family, Ivan Zaikin, Timofei Polezhaev, Ivan Zotov, and several others, most of whom entered the book trade at an early age and remained in it for the rest of their lives.[56]

Regardless of background, the majority of Russian-born booksellers came to register themselves in the first or second merchants' tax guilds in the 1780s and 1790s. Kol'chugin, for example, had been born into the peasantry, but he registered in the second guild in the early 1780s.[57] The major exceptions to this pattern were Novikov and Bogdanovich—members of the gentry who engaged in selling books. A member of the gentry could not by law register in a merchants' guild, but one may infer from their nonparticipation in the process of bookselling that the educated gentry, in general, considered selling, much more than printing, to be primarily a commercial and, therefore, socially inappropriate profession.[58]

Given the overall social homogeneity of both Russian and foreign-born booksellers, a dichotomy of intellectual versus commercial motivations would seem to have little relevance. G. I. Porshnev did claim to have discerned a distinction between "cultured" and "commercial" book dealers,[59] but these categories, while having some applicability to certain mid-nineteenth-century dealers, such as Adolf Pliushar or Alexander Smirdin, fail to provide much of an index for those of the eighteenth century. The choices made for each category seem to have been arbitrary, and in any case less than a fifth of all eighteenth-century book dealers appear on Porshnev's lists.

Recently, A. A. Zaitseva has posited a different but equally questionable line of demarcation by suggesting that competition for markets set native-born book dealers apart from foreign-born ones, at least in St. Petersburg. She argues that the foreign publishers often knew each other from common membership in a German bookbinders' workshop in St. Petersburg, they tended to cooperate among themselves against the Russian newcomers, and they were more likely to set dynastically controlled family firms with several bookshops.[60]

However, while competition was present in the book trade and did on occasion lead to unpleasantries and rivalries, such instances were quite out of the ordinary. Most of the time, bookselling was marked by a spirit of cooperation that crossed over ethnic and national boundaries. Booksellers often formed consortia to make joint orders from publishing houses in order to avail themselves of the discounts that publishers offered on large orders.[61] They also pooled their resources to subsidize the printing of a number of books whose print runs they would share proportionally.[62] Finally, some dealers printed joint catalogues or accepted catalogues of their competitors as appendices to books that they had financed with their own money.[63] In fact, despite the seemingly crowded market, few signs of cutthroat competition or mutual hostility have come to light.

With such high levels of cooperation and social uniformity, one might expect book merchants to have developed some collective organization or at least to have voiced collective demands to publishers or to the government. But the unusual nature of Russian commerce in general, in which professional or genuine guild organizations (as opposed to the loosely structured Russian guilds which had virtually no corporate function other than to demarcate levels of income and rates of taxation among merchants) rarely appeared, typified the book trade as well. Most of the foreign-born book dealers in Russia no doubt knew about guilds and their power to maintain profit margins by controlling entry into trade and access to markets, but they apparently did not attempt to employ similar methods in Russia. Consequently, they were obliged to carve out markets and promote sales on their own.

Booksellers who wanted to expand their sales and income employed one or more of several alternative strategies. For many, the first task involved a public announcement that they were in business and that they had certain titles for sale. Typically, the announcements appeared as newspaper advertisements that listed their place of business—usually in or near the merchants' quarters—along with the books for sale and their prices. Quite a number of the booksellers, in fact, are known to us only through these notices.[64] As booksellers grew more prosperous, some of them began to print periodic inexpensive and unbound lists of books in stock. For a long time, this practice had been limited to institutional booksellers with large stocks and sufficient capital to print catalogues, but in the last third of the century a growing number of independent booksellers printed catalogues, and by the end of the century there were over 200 such catalogues in print.[65]

In addition to announcing the availability of a given title, the catalogues indicated the size of a book dealer's collection, the number and locations of shops he owned, and the terms under which books could be bought, ordered, or sometimes borrowed. Using this information in conjunction with other evidence, such as the fragmentary surviving book orders placed by book dealers to the larger publishing houses, an estimate can be made of the number of large-volume book dealers who were active in Russia at any given time. By augmenting these documents with information gleaned from newspaper advertisements, archival references, and some secondary accounts, it is possible to draw a general picture of the level of bookselling activity in Russia during Catherine's reign. The number of booksellers in Moscow and St. Petersburg grew from about fifteen in the mid-1770s to about forty in the 1780s and well over fifty in the 1790s. By the end of the century, moreover, there were another fifty booksellers in the provinces.[66]

One can infer from the combination of limited capital, locations that indicate book stalls on the street or in the merchants' quarters, and sparse newspaper notices that many of these booksellers had a very modest trade. Some, to be sure, devoted a good deal of time to other pursuits, others received large quantities of a single title, either through auction or as repayment for a debt, and still others dealt primarily in wares other than books. But each of them had become sufficiently tied to the book trade to be identified as a bookseller in at least one source. As table 6.2 shows, moreover, among those bookshops whose volumes can be estimated, the proportions of large ones (carrying 500 titles or more) and medium-sized ones (between 100 and 500 titles) increased during this period.

These figures vividly demonstrate how much more resilient bookselling was than publishing. Predictably, the number and volume of booksellers rose sharply in the 1780s when publishing was in full flower. But even after the onset of censorship had cut the number of published books almost in half in the late 1790s, booksellers continued to prosper. Plavil'shchikov, Weitbrecht, Rüdiger, Brunkow, and Ovchinnikov, among others, sold books for a much longer period of time than they printed them.[67] Other prominent booksellers—Zaikin, Torno, Polezhaev, Sopikov, Müller, Nikiforov, and several others—sold books for several decades, and Kol'chugin and the Glazunov brothers started family firms which, in spite of periodic harassment, sold books over a period of several generations.[68]

All of these manifestations of success suggest that booksellers had an easier time making money in Catherinian Russia than did publishers, for whom profits and even survival were highly problematic. At

TABLE 6.2

Number of Bookstores by Size of Shelf Stocks of Russian-Language Titles, 1760–95

Number of Russian-Language Titles in Stock	Number of Bookstores for which Data Are Available[a]			
	1760	1775	1785	1795
2,000 or more	0	0	0	2
1,000–1,999	0	0	1	4
500–1,000	0	2	7	5
250–499	0	1	3	5
100–249	2	4	4	6
Less than 100	3	5	6	9
Total	5	12	21	31

SOURCES: Compiled from data in booksellers' catalogues, archives, newspapers, etc.

[a] Bookstores for which no data are available—but whose existence is attested to by newspaper advertisements, notices in the back of books, or governmental reports—were probably relatively small.

one level, this success reflects their ability to gauge readership demand accurately and to respond to it irrespective of what publishers may have wanted. But how did booksellers manage such a feat in the face of publishers' financial struggles?

THE ECONOMICS OF BOOKSELLING

Unfortunately, no complete bookseller's ledger sheets have survived, making a detailed study of the economics of the book trade impossible. But common sense would argue that booksellers largely avoided many of the costly capital investments in materials, salaries, equipment, and the like that proved to be so crippling to publishers. A bookseller's only fixed costs were rent, salaries for a small clerical staff, and the investment in a stock of books purchased from publishers at wholesale prices. Some dealers managed to eliminate this last expense by selling books on commission for a percentage of the retail price rather than buying them outright.

Still, bookselling was not a guaranteed success. One had to sell books at prices that were high enough to provide a reasonable net income yet not so high that the reading public could not afford them. In the first half of the century prices had been very high and the purchase of books had been beyond the means of all but the wealthiest readers. As production costs declined in the second half of the century, however, book prices fell significantly. Plays and short stories published in the 1780s cost as little as ten kopeks. But most books still cost between forty kopeks and a ruble, a high price even at the end of the eighteenth century. The dealer, moreover, had little or no control over the retail price, which was fixed by the publisher.

To compound the difficulties, publishing houses tried to shift some of their financial risks to booksellers by forcing them to accept books on highly unfavorable terms. In 1766, for example, the Academy of Sciences Press arranged to supply books to an Archangel merchant, A. I. Fomin, at a 10 percent discount, and calendars at a mere 1 percent discount.[69] The Academy was willing to pay the shipping costs, but it demanded that Fomin accept copies of all books published by the Academy, albeit in quantities of his own choosing. Fomin balked at this condition, reasoning that he might get stuck with unpopular titles. In the end, the Academy relented, and Fomin was allowed to select his own titles.

Had Fomin been doing a very large book trade, a 10 percent margin might have sufficed. But the reading public of the 1760s and 1770s, particularly in a locale such as Archangel, could not possibly have generated much business. Fomin's gross income for the first three years of his book trade came to just under 900 rubles.[70] A 10 percent margin would give him a net income of 90 rubles, or 30 rubles a year. After deducting his expenses, he probably lost money on the deal.

Fomin was fortunate in that he dealt in a wide variety of goods and could afford to run the bookshop mainly as a public service to bring literature to the relatively literate and sophisticated merchantry of the town. But what about someone who wanted to make books his primary commodity? How could he hope to survive financially, even in Moscow or St. Petersburg, on a 10 percent margin? In all probability, he could not. Thus, by extracting such high prices from its outlets and thereby limiting the profits of booksellers, the Academy of Sciences and other institutional publishers may have inhibited the entry of merchants into the book trade in the early years of Catherine's reign and, ironically, delayed the formation of the very distribution network that they wanted to create.

To be sure, the publishers themselves were in a difficult position. Production costs were high, yet the market could not bear high prices. To have given booksellers a bigger discount would have made it impossible to maintain any profit margin for themselves. A couple of examples should illustrate the problem.

In 1770 the Academy published a special four-language edition of

Catherine's *Instruction to the Legislative Commission (Nakaz)*.[71] This was the first complete edition of the *Nakaz* to appear in Russia; it contained several new chapters which had not been included in an earlier (1768) Senate Press edition. Publication in German, French, and Latin, as well as Russian, was intended to appeal to foreign audiences, to the vanity trade, and, of course, to those people who wanted to read it for its political and legal importance. The Academy prepared a large print run—3,600 copies—and to keep the costs down it used ordinary white paper and a simple binding. But even with such economies, the book's length—403 pages—and the need to set type in four languages drove up the total cost of printing the edition to 5,300 rubles.[72] To cover the high cost of production, the Academy set a retail price of two rubles, a 36 percent markup over the cost of printing each volume. Undoubtedly, the two-ruble price excluded from the market many people who might otherwise have bought the book. But was it high enough to give the Academy a decent profit?

Retail outlets, receiving their usual 10 percent discount, purchased copies of the *Nakaz* from the Academy for one ruble eighty kopeks each. Since each copy cost the Academy one ruble forty-seven kopeks to produce, it was left with a margin of thirty-three kopeks for each copy sold at an independent outlet. Perhaps if all the copies of the *Nakaz* had been sold, the gross income would have sufficed to cover expenses and leave a small profit. But the realities of the book market were otherwise. As late as 1783, the Academy had so many unsold copies of various editions of the *Nakaz* on hand that it offered to sell them at seventy kopeks each or sixty kopeks for bulk orders.[73] If the Academy had granted more generous discounts, of 20 or 30 percent, from the outset, it might have sold more copies, but then its margin would have dwindled to nearly nothing.[74] Yet, if the retail price had gone even higher, hardly anyone could have afforded it.

The four-language edition of the *Nakaz* was an unusually expensive volume, but with many of the more moderately priced titles the situation was as bad or worse. A volume of children's stories, for example, was published by the Academy Press in 1766 with a print run of 600 copies.[75] Since production costs were low—only 112 rubles—the Academy was able to set a retail price of either twenty or twenty-five kopeks (the sources disagree), for a margin of between 9 and 34 percent. At the lower price and with a 10 percent discount, the Academy would have realized a profit over production costs of 1.3 kopeks per copy. The higher price would have given it a profit of 6.3 kopeks, but in neither instance would the margin have left much money to cover incidental costs.

Economic problems such as these prevented any dramatic easing of the Academy's discount policy through the rest of the eighteenth century. To compensate, the Academy added enormous markups of those publications for which a captive audience existed or that were issued in response to an unusually high demand. Thus, a 2,500-copy edition of Lomonosov's widely used *Russian Grammar*, published in 1765, was marked up 250 percent over production costs, and a book of daily lessons for army officers, printed in 1777, was marked up 230 percent.[76] As printing became more efficient, the Academy managed to establish margins of 30 to 40 percent above production costs, and as demand grew, publishers felt somewhat less pressure to squeeze every kopek out of the bookseller. But the need to distribute certain official publications at cost, and the ever-present white elephants, such as the highbrow literature which the empress's Society for Translating Books foisted on the Academy Press during the 1770s, continued to prevent publishers from granting more generous discounts to booksellers.[77]

There is little question that, at some point, someone had to be willing to break this cycle if business were going to expand to meet the growing demand. But the Academy proved very reluctant to alter its system, except when it was dealing with former employees. Thus, after leaving the Academy, Weitbrecht was able to negotiate a unique verbal agreement in 1768 to sell a large volume of Academy Press books that the Academy sold him at a 33 percent discount.[78] Weitbrecht's arrangement was most unusual, however, and it was predicated on his proven ability to sell books. Martynov recounts that the Academy reaped sales totaling 17,000 rubles between 1768 and 1782 from this contract with Weitbrecht.[79] But no other dealers could expect this treatment, and in the early 1770s the best terms that the Academy could offer Russian dealers were 12 percent discounts for very large orders and 10 percent for regular orders.[80]

Not all prospective dealers passively accepted these terms, however, and when the Academy entered into negotiations with merchants from abroad or from the western, largely non-Russian provinces—whose businesses hardly depended on selling Academy books—it found itself in a more difficult bargaining position. Thus, in 1770, a major Riga publisher and bookseller, Johann Friedrich Hartknoch, rejected the usual 10 percent discount, as well as the requirement that he accept at least six copies of each book that the Academy published. Instead, he offered to sell the books on commission for a 25 percent share of the proceeds, and then only if he had the authority to select the titles and quantities that he wanted.[81] After initial resistance, the Academy acceded, and for the next several years Hartknoch sold about one thousand rubles worth of Academy books annually. Subsequent to Hartknoch's experience, a number of other non-Russian merchants entered into similar contracts.[82]

The Academy's flexibility did not extend to negotiations with the less experienced Russian booksellers. Discounts did rise, but only at a very slow pace. In 1784, for example, Russian book dealers received standard discounts of 14 percent on books and 3 percent on calendars.[83] By the early 1790s, the figure for books had reached 15 percent, and 18 percent for high-volume buyers.[84] Margins such as these allowed the larger dealers to earn a reasonable profit from Academy publications. But the smaller merchants could hardly have expected that the difference between income and investment on a 15 percent margin would have provided a very large profit.

Private publishers or other institutional publishers may have offered higher discounts to book dealers, but the available sources reveal very little information about their finances.[85] In testimony before the Moscow police in 1792, Kol'chugin reported that Novikov had offered discounts of 20 to 30 percent to five different booksellers. Such margins, if widespread, would have assured a healthy income to anyone who sold books for a living. But Kol'chugin intimated that Novikov's generosity was exceptional.[86]

If discounting arrangements were generally inflexible, what leverage did a book dealer have with publishers or with the public to increase income and profits? For popular books, merchants usually had the chance to place reorders or large advance orders, both of which became common in the 1790s as publishers grew sensitive to the necessity of accurately estimating the demand for a given volume before it went to press.[87] In some cases, increased or unexpectedly high interest expressed by booksellers would lead a publisher to produce an additional printing of a book that had recently appeared. Booksellers also made some progress in convincing publishers of the necessity of taking back books that were not selling well and of returning the money paid for them. The Academy had long been reluctant to take back books, since it already had more back volumes than it could handle. But continued resistance would have risked alienating the booksellers at a time when the Academy was struggling to remain competitive. It therefore agreed to the change.

In the long run, these changes allowed booksellers to mold their businesses to fit the demands of their buyers. The added flexibility gave merchants the edge that they needed to maintain a viable trade. Zaitseva has shown that several St. Petersburg book dealers moved their shops to the main merchants' quarters on Nevskii Prospekt in the 1790s, and some, such as Polezhaev, Zotov, the Glazunovs, Sopikov, and Zaikin, had to open two or three stores or to subcontract with other merchants to keep up with the added demand.[88] Success gave a handful of booksellers extra capital, occasionally running into tens of thousands of rubles, which they were able to use to give them additional flexibility and control over their trade. In particular, they began to exercise financial leverage over publishing by throwing their business to presses with best-selling books and by underwriting the entire cost of publishing titles that would sell well.[89] According to Martynov, Weitbrecht underwrote the publication of 250 books in his own press and in those of his friends between 1785 and 1803.[90] The Glazunovs, the most active financiers of their day who did not own their own press, paid for the publication of fifty separate titles between 1780 and 1800.[91] During the same period, Polezhaev and his assistant, Gerasim Zotov, financed forty-two volumes.[92] Vodop"-ianov, Müller, Wever, and several other prominent merchants followed suit. To ensure that their expenses would not get out of hand, a number of the booksellers supplied their own paper, arranged their own binding, and maintained control over distribution.[93]

By the early 1790s the approximately half-dozen booksellers and bookseller-publishers, including Novikov, Weitbrecht, the Glazunovs, Polezhaev, and Sopikov, who had developed into genuine commercial magnates were beginning to have substantial influence on what was published and what was sold. Their effective vertical integration of popular or literary publishing and bookselling allowed them to pay honoraria of several hundred rubles to prized authors and translators and to guarantee wide dissemination in Moscow and St. Petersburg. To a certain extent, therefore, bookselling entrepreneurs were taking the lead away from the scholastic presses in directing book culture, with the critical difference that directions now came increasingly from the market place, leading to the articulation of a demand that reflected a wider and quite different spectrum of interests than those of literati and students. The emergence of the bookseller, in other words, more often than not tended to put the most serious writers, or writings, at a financial disadvantage relative to the popularizers.

The larger dealers were more than willing to arrange highly lucrative private contracts, when they could, to compile entire libraries of important books for wealthy patrons. Weitbrecht was the most successful library builder; he received over 100,000 rubles from Catherine over a twenty-year period to buy books for the palace library, 14,000 rubles to put together I. N. Korsakov's library, and several thousand rubles more to assemble collections for other notables.[94]

Most booksellers, however, had to rely on less privileged circumstances to cultivate a market. To further their aims, they adopted various discount and subscription arrangements and placed regular advertisements in the newspapers. Sources do not reveal whether Russian booksellers compiled lists of regular buyers to whom they advertised directly through the mail—a common practice elsewhere in Europe—but it is clear that Russian booksellers attempted to establish regular clientele by converting their stocks into private circulating libraries. Such libraries had also become commonplace in western Europe rather early in the eighteenth century. In both England and France, for example, dozens of circulating libraries and reading clubs served those elements of the public that could not afford or chose not to buy books.[95] The borrowing terms were fairly uniform: For an annual subscription fee one could check out books either at an unlimited rate or up to a stipulated maximum. Alternatively, one could pay a borrowing fee that covered a shorter period of time or a smaller number of books. All subscribers received periodic notification of newly received titles.

These libraries held advantages for both readers and merchants. The readers saved money and learned of new books often before they were available for sale. The lists sent around by proprietors served as lists of suggested reading as well, thereby informing readers of the bookseller's opinions of the newly received books. Presumably, these services tended to broaden the social and economic base of the reading public. Certainly, this would have been the case in Russia, where books were expensive and the public for secular books was still in its early stages of development, and where other kinds of libraries, such as the institutional or monastic libraries, were generally closed to the public.

Circulating libraries also benefited the book merchants. A book that otherwise might have sat on the shelves and not brought in any income generated value by being borrowed. In addition, a circulating library, with its advance lists and long-term subscriptions, built up a regular group of clients for the book dealer and turned some of the shops into literary establishments.

There is some confusion over when the first reading library opened in Russia. Martynov claims that Weitbrecht opened one in St. Petersburg in 1770.[96] Another source says that a St. Petersburg book dealer named Sharov appended, to a 1771 catalogue, a notice informing the public of conditions for checking books out and for reading the *Moscow News* in the bookshop.[97] Still other sources identify the German-language libraries of academicians A. T. Guildenstadt and Johann Bacmeister as the first book lenders in the late 1770s.[98] What is clear is that, aside from Sharov, foreign book dealers serving mainly the French and German communities of Moscow and St. Petersburg operated all of the lending libraries at least until the late 1780s. In 1778, for example, François deMaret, the proprietor of a French-language bookshop in Moscow, opened a reading library with subscription rates of a ruble and a half per month or twelve rubles a year.[99] According to one historian, nearly all the other French-language bookshops followed suit and offered borrowing services.[100]

Some of the foreign libraries were quite large indeed. Johann Kaiser's library in St. Petersburg, for example, included about 2,000 volumes, of which 1,500 were in German, 322 were in French, and only 156 were in Russian. At the end of the century, I. G. Handslandt's library had 4,000 titles and 7,000 total volumes, again mostly in German and French.[101]

By the 1790s, though, private lending libraries had become a feature of educated Russian society as well, as five or six Russian dealers, beginning with Ovchinnikov in 1784, began to lend out some of their stock.[102] There was even a Russian lending library in the provinces, opened in the early 1790s at the Kaluga Office of Public Welfare by the local publisher and book dealer, Peter Kotel'nikov.[103] Membership fees were not low, however; at some Russian establishments the borrowing costs ran as high as two rubles a month.[104] Their clienteles, consequently, must have come from the more affluent segments of urban society.

THE INTERNATIONAL BOOK TRADE

It is also quite likely that the French and German reading libraries were drawing a growing portion of their own clientele from this affluent Russian public. During Catherine's reign, the influx of foreign teachers, technicians, and merchants into the capital increased, complemented by a growing interest on the part of educated Russians in learning about European culture. Popular fashion and secondary education's emphasis upon modern languages, moreover, ensured that a sizeable percentage of the educated public in the cities would want to read foreign-language books. Why, for example, should an educated person fully learned in French buy a Russian translation of Voltaire's *Candide* if it was available in the original? All of these factors contributed to a demand for foreign-language books that was sufficiently high to allow that branch of the book trade to expand substantially during Catherine's reign.

Supplying books for that market was no easy matter. Robert Darnton has shown that it took eighteen months between the time an order was sent from Russia to a dealer in Switzerland and the time the books actually arrived in Moscow.[105] Transportation and currency problems, moreover, conspired to raise the prices of these books astronomically.[106]

Yet the Russian market was apparently large and avid enough to compensate for the difficulties. Darnton has found that booksellers in Moscow and St. Petersburg ordered large quantities of French books from Switzerland in the 1770s, including "heavy doses of Voltaire and Rousseau" as well as a great deal of lighter and bawdier fare.[107] British export records to Russia show a more modest demand, but still a vigorous growth. Where the Russian trade had brought in only about nine pounds a year to British book dealers in the first half of the century, during the next thirty years the figure jumped to about eighty-five pounds a year.[108] Similar figures from Germany are unavailable, but there is ample evidence that a number of the leading Leipzig book dealers were engaged in an active Russian trade by the 1780s.[109]

Once these books arrived on Russian soil, they were brought to readers through a small but expanding network of dealers with contacts in western Europe. In the early 1760s Weitbrecht had overseen the flow of books from abroad, virtually alone, through his position as manager of the Academy's foreign-language bookshop. As an employee of the Academy, he ordered thousands of rubles of books from abroad to sell in the shop—e.g., 560 rubles for sixty-five copies of the *Encyclopédie* and for books by Fénelon, Buffon, and Newton.[110] Archival sources refer to his having printed large periodic catalogues of his holdings beginning in the mid-1760s.[111] Although none of these catalogues has survived, one can get a fair impression of Weitbrecht's energy from a passage in Andrei Bolotov's memoirs. Bolotov described being told of the Academy's Moscow bookshop. He went about to find the shop and, in his words, "my happiness was even greater when I found that shop because it had all the books I had seen in Königsberg and Prussia, every kind of French and German book, with and without binding."[112]

In the 1770s, Moscow's foreign-language book trade expanded to include in its network both Russian and foreign merchants.[113] Rüdiger and Wever, for example, stocked large quantities of foreign-language titles in Moscow University's bookshop from publishers in London, Paris, Leipzig, and several other European publishing centers.[114] A number of other outlets, such as the one opened in 1778 by the Frenchman deMaret and another opened in 1775 by an Englishman named Dodsley, dealt only in books published abroad.[115]

By the 1780s, merchants regularly advertised books just received from abroad in the *Moscow News*, and every major bookseller in Moscow carried a certain number of foreign titles to meet the apparently heavy demand.[116] The leading outlet, not surprisingly, was the Moscow University bookshop, which, according to one historian, ordered more books from abroad than any other single enterprise.[117] But on the whole, it was the foreign merchants who directed the import trade for books. In particular, the Gay brothers, François Courtener, Jacob Bieber, François Riss (or Ryss), and Joseph Saucet operated long-lasting and highly successful bookshops. Riss, for example, took over Novikov's network for ordering and distributing foreign books after the latter was arrested, and he subsequently became Moscow's leading book importer.[118]

One rarely reads of these foreign book dealers in memoirs or essays of the day, yet they must have played a major role in supplying the educated elites of Russia with reading matter. Unfortunately, rather little is known of their backgrounds and careers. Courtener, for one, was born in Strasbourg and came to Russia in 1782. He had had no experience in printing or in the book trade, and in fact his first business in Russia was a flower shop. Seeing a potential demand for foreign books, he began to supply them in his shop, selling mainly multivolume literary works, handyman books, presubscribed series, and stamps. A second Frenchman, Jean Gautier, had been born in St. Petersburg's foreign quarter. He moved to Moscow in the 1790s and went to work for Courtener, his first regular employment. In 1799 he opened his own shop, which dealt exclusively in imported books for many years.[119]

Other foreign book dealers took different roads to Russia and to their profession, but all came from the merchantry and all apparently were out to make money. Their greatest success in this regard came after the outbreak of the French Revolution in 1789. In theory, new laws progressively limited and later cut off the import of books from France. But at a time when official policy was becoming increasingly hostile to France, a steady immigration of French aristocrats and others who opposed the Jacobin direction of the revolution filled the foreign quarters of Moscow. Among these emigrés were several merchants who, upon coming to Russia, entered into the book trade to supply this newly created market. The presence of these new residents, who apparently read quite avidly, stimulated older inhabitants of the foreign quarters to engage in bookselling as well, and as a result, between

1790 and the end of the Napoleonic wars in 1815, the burgeoning French colony of Moscow spawned a long list of very active book merchants, including Jean Christian Horn, Dominique Bugnet, André Lemoine, and several others.[120]

In St. Petersburg, the sale of foreign books, though apparently less vigorous than in Moscow, continued to show some vitality. The Academy, the cadet corps, and some private printers published foreign-language books, and a number of merchants imported books from abroad. The Gay brothers had opened a shop in St. Petersburg in 1786, and Novikov's old confederate, Karl Müller, ordered heavily from France and Switzerland.[121] Zaitseva's research has found over twenty shops that either sold or lent foreign-language books in the late eighteenth century.[122] Some of these shops had book stocks running into the thousands, but most foreign-language book dealers of St. Petersburg were relatively minor traders who sold their wares from stalls and little shops in or near the *gostinnyi dvor*. Still, all these small merchants accounted for a significant aggregate business, whose presence on the main thoroughfares of the city, rather than in the foreign quarter, suggests a Russian-centered public.[123]

Beyond its effect on domestic intellectual life, the establishment of a vigorous trade in foreign books raised the hope that Russian publishers could find foreign markets for their own publications. Exports were probably impossible for the majority of smaller publishers, but for the larger institutional publishing houses, many of which printed books in foreign languages, the export market did prove to be a modest but reliable source of income.

The most significant non-Russian (if not exactly export) outlet was the Riga merchant, Johann Friedrich Hartknoch, whose firm had dealt on and off in Russian books for much of the century and who, in the 1770s and 1780s, regularly sold books from the Moscow University Press and the Typographical Company.[124] The Academy, meanwhile, had renewed and even expanded its contacts with outlets in Leipzig and Paris and, to a lesser degree, London, Amsterdam, Venice, and elsewhere.[125] In 1767, for example, Weitbrecht sent 2,400 rubles worth of books to Leipzig and 1,400 rubles worth to Breslau.[126]

Neither Moscow University's nor Novikov's records discuss their foreign trade to any great degree, and the catalogues do not mention foreign outlets other than Hartknoch. Moscow University continued to publish a large number of scholarly and technical titles in foreign languages, however. Since almost no market existed in Russia for these books, one can assume that at least a few of them made their way abroad. It is difficult to imagine, too, that Novikov did not use the university's foreign contacts to sell the Typographical Company's books. But no sources, not even Kol'chugin's detailed testimony of 1792, make mention of contacts with foreign outlets.

As for Academy titles, the majority of those exported continued to be scientific. Weitbrecht's 1767 shipments abroad, for example, included books on geography and natural science, maps, and portraits of the tsar.[127] The various series of scientific monographs printed by the Academy in Latin went largely to the non-Russian market. In 1783, one volume of the new *Actae* series, with a print run of 408 copies, was disseminated as follows: 23 copies went to members of the Academy; 6 were put on sale at the Academy's Russian bookstore; 96 were sold in the foreign-language bookshop; 28 were given as honorary copies to foreign scholars; 15 were kept; and 101 were used for the export trade.[128]

Russian-language and nonscientific books printed by the Academy still found little or no market outside Russia. In 1784, for example, the Academy circulated a stock list of old foreign-language titles that were in storage in very large quantities. These included ninety-six Latin, fifty German, and thirty French titles, published over a span of several years and largely unsold up to that time. Topically, they covered the entire range of the Academy's foreign-language publications. But foreign merchants, when ordering from this list, selected only scientific titles. Hartknoch, for example, accepted copies of works written by Euler, Epinus, Lomonosov, and other scientists but returned as unsellable copies of Rollin's *Ancient History* and several other literary and historical works.[129] Even the substantial discounts that the Academy offered on back orders failed to make general-interest titles more attractive to foreign merchants. Foreign merchants, moreover, all but ignored the Russian-language stock lists.

If readers in the West showed no interest in Russian-language books, what about the foreign colonies in Moscow and St. Petersburg? The impression one gets is that these colonies were generally insulated from Russian intellectual life and therefore had a limited interest in buying Russian books. But during the French Revolution, one merchant, Jean Christian Horn, tried to engage the French emigré community of Moscow in learning Russian and reading Russian books. Feeding on the general pessimism of the community and its outright revulsion toward Napoleon, Horn argued that the possibilities of returning to France in the near future were slim and that the royalists might as well accommodate themselves to their adopted home. This plea apparently met with some success, for Horn began to stock Russian language books regularly in his bookstore.[130]

Horn's experience, however, proved to be exceptional. Most of the bookshops in the foreign quarters declined to carry Russian-language books, or at least they listed none in their catalogues. Foreigners could, of course, buy books outside the foreign quarters, but their colonies, even in the late eighteenth century, were fairly self-contained, which suggests that such forays were not common.

At the end of the eighteenth century, therefore, Russia's relationship with the business of European letters, though more intimate, was still primarily one-sided: educated Russians eagerly absorbed European ideas, fashions, and books; but, notwithstanding a certain curiosity about Russian customs and a willingness to translate selected Russian writers, western and central Europeans continued to have rather little interest in buying Russian books.

THE PROVINCIAL MARKET

Until the end of the eighteenth century, therefore, the market for Russian books remained overwhelmingly domestic. Literary figures may have felt a certain sting of inferiority in their failure to establish a mutual dialogue with western thinkers or to establish a significant following abroad. But the domestic market was growing so rapidly that Karamzin, for one, was writing with excitement about people gathering in the streets of St. Petersburg and Moscow to read and discuss books. Surely it was the domestic public that mattered most and through whom the literati could fulfill their ambitions. The more critical issue for literati and booksellers, therefore, was not the audience abroad but the audience at home. They presumably knew what sort of market existed in the major cities, but the real challenge lay in making contact with the more diffuse but likely much larger number of provincial readers.

A variety of factors, including state service, education, poor communication, and a slow postal system, guaranteed that the heart of the book distribution system would remain in Moscow and St. Petersburg. But the provinces contained a potentially vast and largely unexplored market for secular books that, if it could be developed, could provide income for booksellers and audiences for authors and publishers. Thus, as the conditions of publishing improved, interest in reaching out to the provinces became more intense. Accordingly, in 1766, the Academy Press contacted potential outlets in the prov inces, offering to send books at its own expense to any willing agent. The response was mixed: evidently, few provinces were equipped to begin a regular book trade.[131] But at least one person was found in each province who was willing to place at least a few orders. In some of the provinces, the authorities ordered a local merchant to put up the cash and deliver the books. A few of these merchants, such as Fomin in Archangel, subsequently developed more or less regular arrangements with the Academy.[132] In Kiev and Nizhnii Novgorod, people who already referred to themselves as booksellers received the books.[133] In several other provinces, local governmental servitors took responsibility. Typical of these was Novgorod, where Governor Jacob Sievers acted as the local book agent.[134] In none of these provinces did the Academy's book trade begin to rival that of the two major cities, but taken as a whole, the entire provincial book trade added perhaps a few thousand rubles to the Academy's income.

At about the same time that the Academy was strengthening its provincial contacts, Moscow University Press also began to send books and other published material into the provinces. One report shows that between 1768 and 1776 Moscow University sent over 19,000 rubles worth of books to thirty-six separate locations.[135] The university earned only about 7,000 rubles (or less than 800 rubles a year) from the provincial market, but it did establish a more or less permanent link with several towns. By the 1780s Novikov, who put a great deal of energy into strengthening the provincial network, was able to list between ten and twenty regular provincial outlets where one could purchase Moscow University and Typographical Company books. One recent study has shown, moreover, that Novikov's books were sold at a large number of provincial shops that even his own catalogues did not list.[136] Novikov further offered to provide books to provincial readers anywhere in Russia directly through the mail.[137] Sources do not indicate how often Novikov actually filled orders by direct mail, but for publications that he sold on a subscription basis he used the mail quite heavily. Thus, between 1777 and 1780, he sent over 700 subscriptions to *Morning Light* to provincial readers.[138] Still, the network of provincial booksellers must have taken a larger share of the local trade than the direct mailing did, if for no other reason than that mailing books was very expensive.

By the late 1780s the provincial book trade had grown large enough to support several bookstores each in Nizhnii Novgorod, Kursk, Orel, Archangel, Kiev, and elsewhere, and some of these bookstores had several dozen titles in stock. Martynov has counted fifty-three provincial dealers in the Catherinian era selling books printed in Moscow and St. Petersburg, over two-thirds of whom were merchants.[139] One can judge the success of many of them by the facts that their names appeared year after year on order sheets and catalogues and that the proprietors of nearly all of these shops were referred to specifically as booksellers.

Thus, by the 1790s an extensive book trade network had linked secular publishers in the major cities and readers in the provincial towns in something of a national market. By that time, colporteurs presumably had long since agreed to peddle more than just calendars and primers, and as a consequence some secular books may very well have begun to filter into the countryside. Confirmation of sorts comes from Karamzin, who in his essay, "On the Book Trade and the Love of Reading in Russia," described his extensive discussions with booksellers who spoke of bringing literature to provincial fairs and of traders selling "learned goods" in the villages. From his observations, in fact, Karamzin was convinced that the countryside was aflame with a desire for exciting and pleasant novels.[140]

It is easy to believe that the relatively short, simple, unbound, and inexpensive popular romances and adventures that had captivated urban readers also found an audience in the provinces among those groups that could afford to read for leisure. Still, it is unlikely that the provincial book trade of the late eighteenth century allowed literary publishers to match the Synod or the state in attracting a wide provincial audience.

In spite of its national scope, the literary provincial market proved to be a financial disappointment. Publishing houses found that even in the best circumstances, most provincial dealers were able to sell only a very modest number of books. Not only did Moscow University earn very little money from its provincial sales between 1768 and 1776, but some towns for which the university had high hopes proved to be virtually barren. Orel, for example, sold none of the 173 rubles worth of books which it received, and Vyborg received 746 rubles worth of books but sold only 134 rubles worth. Even the relatively active provincial centers of the western provinces, in particular Smolensk and Glukhov, brought in only 500 and 1,100 rubles, respectively, and this was over a nine-year period.[141]

To a certain extent, presumably, these low sales rates reflected the inexperience of local agents, many of whom had to discover for themselves the level of local demand. But the evidence indicates that provincial sales remained low for years thereafter. In a follow-up study covering the years from 1777 to 1783, the Moscow University Press learned that its average annual earnings from the provinces had been below 1,000 rubles.[142] These figures are doubly telling in light of the fact that Moscow University had the largest and most active provincial network for secular books in the Russian empire. The Academy Press, by Martynov's count, had only ten provincial outlets in the 1780s, and no other press had more than five. Thus, it is not surprising that a Synod survey taken in 1787 found that most provincial bookshops had few books and that they usually had only a single copy of a given title. One rather typical bookseller in Kazan had eighty-seven titles on hand but only 118 total volumes, or about one and one-third copies per title.[143] Stock levels such as these suggest very modest expectations of the local market by booksellers.

Only a small minority of the books that were available reflected the literary tastes of the two major cities. Certainly, some shops in provincial towns had isolated copies of various works by Voltaire, Lomonosov, Fénelon, and Gellert, not to mention *Gil Blas* and the *Marquis G.*, but provincial booksellers more frequently purveyed educational and devotional books—grammars, catechisms, psalters, arithmetic books, and the like.[144] Equally revealing in this context is the relative absence of books that had come from private publishing houses other than the Typographical Company, which benefited from its unique affinity to the Moscow University Press. Only very occasionally did a book from a smaller private publisher appear in provincial towns, and these almost always came from the commercial and nonliterary publishers, such as Hippius, Ovchinnikov, and Otto Meier.[145]

If the initial discoveries of Moscow University's recent field expeditions are representative, moreover, leisure books had an even sparser representation in the countryside than in the provincial towns. Although their published findings to date can only be called preliminary, in every village in which these scholars uncovered books, the preponderance of volumes, regardless of their century of origin or of whether they were printed or hand copied, were concerned with prayers and devotions. After devotional works came alphabet books, both printed and hand copied and in both the old and new orthographies; folk tales; and sheet music. The moral and literary works of the major cities, on the other hand, were virtually unrepresented in the repertoire of village books.[146]

CONCLUSIONS

Thus, whatever its absolute dimensions, the secular book trade remained fundamentally an urban and largely cosmopolitan affair at the end of the eighteenth century, a fact which was not lost on the more perspicacious literati. Still, its growth in numerical terms during the second half of the century was impressive. It is difficult to assign precise numbers to this success, but for some dealers bookselling clearly involved considerable sums. Novikov's stocks ran into the hundreds of thousands of rubles when he was arrested in 1792. When Weitbrecht ultimately went bankrupt, he sold his books at auction for 100,000 rubles, a figure that represented a 60 percent discount from their retail value. I. P. Glazunov, the bookseller who purchased Weitbrecht's inventory, was doing an annual trade of his own at the time that ran well over 15,000 rubles in books and calendars.[147] Undoubtedly, most booksellers did not operate at so high a level, but there were many who made a satisfactory living at it.

Karamzin estimated that the overall trade in books in Moscow alone grew from ten thousand rubles a year in the 1770s to two hundred thousand a year by the end of the century. Numbers such as these tantalize the reader with their apparent precision. One is inclined to treat them seriously, moreover, because of Karamzin's closeness to Novikov's circle in the 1780s, his personal participation in editing journals, and his contacts with book dealers.[148]

Recent research suggests that Karamzin understated the figures for the 1770s and probably overstated it somewhat for the end of the century. Nevertheless, his estimates provide the only informed contemporary approximation of what the Moscow book trade was like at the turn of the century. Twenty shops doing an annual business of 200,000 rubles gave the average bookstore owner a gross income of 10,000 rubles a year. The big shops, of course, took the major share of the trade, and owners of the smaller shops must have fallen far below this average. Unfortunately, there is no way of estimating the median income, to determine how realistic these figures are, but if they are accepted with all the appropriate reservations, and if it is assumed that most Moscow booksellers received the usual 15 percent discount from publishers, net earnings would have come to 1,500 rubles a year per bookseller—a fairly respectable figure.

In St. Petersburg, presumably, the situation was much the same, although the slightly smaller number of book dealers and the considerably smaller population suggest that the book trade in St. Petersburg produced less income than in Moscow. As in Moscow, there is no way of determining with any precision the income of individual private merchants, but documents from a few institutional dealers give hints of the levels of income. A 1779 report on translations produced largely by Catherine's Translation Society at the Academy of Sciences Press listed titles published over a ten-year period.[149] During that time, income from the sale of these books had brought in 17,600 rubles. In that same decade, the Academy published a total of 530 titles, and the translations amounted to 18 percent of this total. If the revenue from other books was proportional to that from translations, total income during those years would have been slightly less than 100,000 rubles, or 10,000 rubles a year.

Academy officials believed that the works of the Translation Society were, on the whole, notoriously bad sellers. Certainly, they earned less money than did textbooks, primers, calendars, the *St. Petersburg News*, adventure stories, and popular romances, but they probably earned more money than many works in the natural sciences. Still, the Translation Society's books probably did not measure up to the average, leading one to infer that the Academy earned a good deal more than 10,000 rubles a year in the 1770s. The Academy's figures, moreover, were based in part on the wholesale prices which they charged booksellers; the income from the retail trade would naturally have been higher.

The Academy apparently earned much more income than this in the 1780s. To be sure, its total publishing output declined, and its share of the market declined even more. But a review of bookseller's orders from scattered years in the 1780s and 1790s reveals that several merchants placed annual orders of between 1,500 and 5,000 rubles each, and several others bought between 200 and 1,000 rubles worth of Academy publications annually.[150] A part of this business came as a result of the Academy's aggressive attempts to reduce its back stocks, but most of the orders were for recently published titles. Martynova and Martynov cite figures that show the Academy bookshop alone earning 40,500 rubles in book sales and 3,500 rubles in newspaper sales between August 1781 and April 1784, or nearly 15,000 rubles a year.[151]

Another leading supplier of secular books during this period was the Primary School Commission, established by Catherine in 1782.[152] Its method of distribution relied less on retail book sales than on direct delivery to schools, but it had probably the largest captive national market in Russia in the primary schools. As a public institution, the commission received substantial state subsidies that allowed it to sell its books at prices that often were below cost. But even at the discounted prices, the commission's annual average income from book sales was about 7,250 rubles in the 1790s.[153]

One can hardly draw sweeping conclusions about the volume of St. Petersburg book trade from such fragmentary data. But obviously, the total income from books sold in the 1780s and 1790s was much larger than that generated by the Academy and School Commission alone and therefore must have been several times what it had been a decade or two earlier.

Taken in concert with the institutional growth of the network of book distribution, these figures lead to some general characterizations of the Russian book trade of the second half of the eighteenth century. In sheer size, the system grew several times over during this period. In complexity, it had adopted many new practices and had moved toward a flexibility which was essential if the system were to continue to reach ever wider elements of the literate population. To be sure, critical problems of costs and distribution continued to plague the whole network, but even in these problem areas, the direction of change was positive.

One should not draw too sanguine a picture of the Russian book trade, however. Both in size and sophistication, it continued to lag seriously behind that of other European countries. A total of perhaps one hundred bookshops to accommodate a country with a population of about thirty million (excluding the newly added territories) pales when compared to England, France, or the German states. Even Ireland had more bookshops than Russia.[154] More to the point, Russia had developed only a very modest national audience for leisure books in general and hardly any audience outside of the major cities for serious books and journals. The secular book market, in short, could not yet rival the institutional networks of church, state, and public schools in gaining the attention of the Russian people.

The most persistent barriers to a broader dissemination of the printed word in Russia, the low level of literacy and the even lower level of active readership, stood essentially outside the capacity of the book trade to change. To the degree that booksellers could have influenced readership—through advertising, lists of suggested reading, reduced prices, and the like—they tried their best to do so. With all of its drawbacks, therefore, the Russian book trade had managed to evolve into a viable commercial system, and as a result, a communications network that gave readers and writers an institutional means of informing each other of their needs and wants was finally in place.

SEVEN

Book Sales and Reading

FROM EXPLORATION of the institutional side of Russian printing, it has become clear that most Russians did not read in the late eighteenth century, and most of those who did read probably read prayer books or narrowly utilitarian books rather than leisure books. Leisure reading, furthermore, was more likely to involve romances, adventures, or moral stories than serious or important works. The general shape of reading patterns, then, is already reasonably clear. But the actual numbers involved in these patterns—the relative popularity of particular books, authors, and genres, and the approximate numerical differences between utilitarian and leisure reading—are not. Exactly what did "popular" mean in the eighteenth century, and just how small was the readership for "Enlightenment" books?

SOURCES AND METHODS

Questions such as these suggest that more precise knowledge about book circulation needs to be acquired before final conclusions can be drawn about the role of printing in the eighteenth century. On one level, the analysis of publishing itself has already addressed the matter. There can be little argument at this point about the burgeoning number, variety, authors, publishers, and patrons of books during the eighteenth century, each of which reflected a general interest of one sort or another. But the interests of the literati, the church, and officialdom were not identical to popularity, and one therefore cannot deduce consumption of printed material merely from information on production. Certainly, as commercial activity gained importance, the relationship between interests and popularity became closer, but commerce hardly ruled supreme in determining repertoires even at the height of private publishing. Consequently, we need to turn our attention to sources that reflect circulation and public demand more directly.

Sales lists, of course, provide the best evidence for popularity, but explicit sales figures are a rarity for eighteenth-century Russia. Luppov, who has scoured the records of the Academy of Sciences more thoroughly than anyone else, has found that sales figures are largely unavailable after the 1730s, and none of the contemporary Soviet scholars who have studied books in the Catherinian period has come up with even fragmentary sales lists for the Academy. For other institutional publishers, private publishers, and booksellers, the situation is worse, since hardly any of their business records have survived, and those that have give general income figures rather than sales.

As an alternative to book sales figures, Luppov has managed to compute stock depletion figures for selected books from the 1730s and 1740s. These figures, it may be recalled, reflect the difference between print runs and subsequent inventories. Stock depletion presumably says something about dissemination, but it is far from foolproof as an index of demand. First of all, it can be computed for only a small minority of books, since print run figures are reasonably abundant only for the Academy and synod presses, and, somewhat less so, for some other scholastic presses, the Senate presses, and books published on contract for the Public School Commission. For most presses, print run figures are totally unavailable, and inventory lists are equally sparse. The Academy counted stocks only occasionally, and inventories of most other publishers survive only when they were the subjects of official reviews by the police, the Senate, or the Synod. In practice, then, stock depletions can be computed for a certain number of Academy Press books, some Public School Commission books, and little else.

Even with these figures on hand, moreover, there is still a basic problem in determining the relationship between stock depletion on the one hand and sales or distribution to readers on the other. Until the 1760s, most Academy books were sold by the press itself, a circumstance that allowed for simple inventory and accounting procedures. However, books were often removed from stock through loss and damage rather than sales, and, with the emergence of a more complex book trade during Catherine's reign, the depletion figure became only a vague approximation of sales.

Several weeks before sending a book to press, the Academy of Sciences published notices of the impending appearance of the book which invited both retail and wholesale customers to place orders. In normal practice, about a quarter of a print run went to the Academy's own bookshops and the remainder to its book depository. Book dealers could place orders either with the depository or, as appears more common, with the bookshop. This process usually worked well for the initial months or years after the publication of the book. After that time, however, the book depository often lost track of its holding and ceased printing notices of the book's availability. In succeeding years, when new readers might have revived interest in the book, the Academy would have to undertake a new inventory of back copies; or, as sometimes occurred, it reprinted the book only to discover that it had large stocks already on hand. In spite of reforms instituted in the 1780s, aimed at ending these inefficiencies, problems persisted, as a result of which there simply is no way to judge whether a poorly selling book printed in the 1760s or 1770s had no market or if the Academy and its outlets believed that it was unavailable. Conversely, high depletion figures tend to overstate sales, because they fail to take into account the number of copies that left the publishers but remained on booksellers' shelves. It should be evident, therefore, that stock depletion figures, although useful, provide only a very partial and highly problematic index to sales. There are, fortunately, several complementary, if less numerically exact, approaches to demand. In some cases, for example, print runs alone can be seen as reflections of general levels of distribution and reading. This was most obviously the case with those publishers who depended less on the open market than on private distribution networks, such as the publishers for the Public School Commission. Upon publishing a given work, the School Commission immediately began distributing the print runs within its captive market. Distribution continued unabated until supplies ran out, at which point the commission ordered a new printing if necessary.

The print runs of individual laws and public notices also reveal something about dissemination. These publications unquestionably circulated very widely, albeit at the discretion of officialdom. But their audience was as much a listening public as a readership, and, with some notable exceptions, there was no necessary affinity between physically receiving or being within earshot of a public announcement and demanding or reading it. Only in those instances where demand for a particular law was manifest can print runs and dissemination be considered as reflective of readership interest.

There also exist scattered sources that provide an accurate index of demand as mediated by booksellers' perceptions. The best of these are the surviving records of orders and reorders placed by book dealers with publishers, especially the Academy of Sciences Press. Recently, scholars have uncovered fragments of those records from the 1770s and 1780s, but the most abundant evidence of booksellers' demand comes from the years between 1789 and 1795, a period for which many of the Academy bookshop's records are available intact.[1] These documents shed considerable light on both initial and long-term interests in the Academy's publications. Book dealers developed their impressions of popularity from the buying patterns of their customers, most of whom came from the general public rather than from institutional or captive markets. When booksellers consistently ordered large quantities of a given title, therefore, it can be assumed that people were buying it. If reorders led to reprintings, it can be assumed that the existing print runs were exhausted. Conversely, when booksellers ordered a small quantity or ordered copies of a book only once, it can be concluded that demand for it was limited.

Similar, if less precise, conclusions emerge from analyzing the published catalogues of book dealers. The difficulties here lie in the inherent ambiguities of interpreting the catalogues' contents: A book's continued appearance in several catalogues year after year could reflect continuing popular demand, but it also could reflect poor sales and the failure of book dealers to rid themselves of the copies that they had initially ordered. A related problem derives from the ambiguous position of the institutional booksellers who produced most of the catalogues in the late eighteenth century. As salaried employees, the institutional dealers had limited control over the volumes in stock and less of a financial stake in maintaining an active turnover in inventory. As a consequence, the reappearance of a given title need not have reflected anything other than a bookseller's lack of interest in selling it or returning it to the institution's publishing house.

The catalogues of most private booksellers largely avoid these problems, since, if a book was not selling well, a private dealer could try to return it and get back his investment, at least from some publishers. In this way, independent merchants could keep their offerings reasonably up to date. But even their catalogues provide no information on the number of copies of a given book available for sale. Booksellers whose stocks also served as circulating libraries, moreover, would be inclined to keep extensive shelf lists without necessarily having more than one or two copies of any given book. Thus, even the very best catalogues cannot, by themselves, be seen as directly indicative of demand. The catalogues can be generally suggestive of booksellers' perceptions of popular interests, however, when they are read collectively. By analyzing the contents of the catalogues as an aggregate, the persistent presence or absence of certain publications can be a basis for inferences about whether or not the booksellers were ordering or reordering them. Consensus on a given book or category of books is presumably evidence of general popularity or unpopularity.

To a limited extent, one can draw similar inferences from the number of new editions or reprintings that a given work went through. When new editions of *Aesop's Fables* appeared every few years, for example, one can conclude with some confidence that the book was quite popular. But the publishing system remained too imperfect for this method to be wholly reliable. Because of the ambiguous copyright regulations, the flawed distribution system, or simple misunderstandings, two publishers could print virtually simultaneous editions of the same work without knowing of each other's enterprise. This duplication most commonly occurred when a Moscow publisher issued a book without having first determined whether an earlier St. Petersburg edition might still be available, or vice versa, but it has also been observed that institutional publishers occasionally reprinted their own books when they still had copies in stock. At times publishers even announced reeditions of books that, in reality, were merely old volumes with new title pages put on them apparently for the purpose of generating new interest in a work that previously had sold poorly. Consequently, one must be very wary of drawing firm conclusions when the only indication of demand comes from a single new edition, especially one issued in a city other than the one where the original edition was published.

Nevertheless, in many instances, reprintings or print run figures are the only available evidence. Print runs provide, at the very least, outer limits of sales, and these are meaningful figures when the printings are small or moderate. Many of the books of the Translation Society, for example, came out in such small editions (100 to 600 copies) that their dissemination was necessarily very limited. For periodical publications, such as journals or multivolume books sold by subscription, the progression of print run levels from issue to issue can be even more revealing. Few publishers were in a position to underwrite inflated printings month after month, and so their response to poor sales was generally to adjust their print runs downward or to close the journals altogether. In those instances when print runs stayed the same or rose, the logical inference would be that sales were brisk.

At best, this array of fragmentary sources can give only an impression of the relative demand for publications. But such an impression, even in its most general contours, can be quite revealing of the comparative popularity of different categories of books and even of different authors, and it can thereby suggest a great deal about the circulation of ideas in the eighteenth century.

UTILITARIAN PUBLICATIONS

In every part of Europe, the first genuine manifestation of broad public interest in the printed word centered not on books read for pleasure but on more narrowly instrumental publications, such as Bibles, religious and political pamphlets, almanacs, and catechisms. Because of their utility, their brevity, their relevance to daily prayer, or their simple and vivid prose, these publications appealed to broad circles of readers. Russia, as is well known, stood outside the world of political and religious ferment that gave most of these publications their topicality and large publics in the sixteenth and seventeenth centuries.[2] Pamphleteering, in fact, did not become widespread among Russians until well into the nineteenth century, except perhaps among the Old Believers. Other kinds of utilitarian publications, including calendars, teaching psalters, alphabet books, and primers, did nevertheless gain a surprisingly broad circulation in eighteenth-century Russia, for reasons that sometimes overlap with those that accounted for the popularity of pamphlets and almanacs in the West.

In all probability, the most widely circulated Russian publications in the eighteenth century were calendars and religious almanacs. Eighteenth-century calendars, of course, were not, technically speaking, books, but they included a great deal more information than simply the order of the days and months. Many of them ran to 200 pages in length, and some offered practical advice on a wide variety of subjects, including farming, family life, etiquette, prayer, humor, and the like. Some listed all the important religious holidays and festivals, with indications of the proper prayers to be recited at each occasion. Russian calendars, in short, resembled the popular European almanacs of the sixteenth and seventeenth centuries, without the latters' heavy dose of astrology.[3]

Since 1727 the Academy of Sciences Press had held a monopoly over the printing of secular calendars, and the Synod had authority over religious almanacs, and both of them realized from their own experiences and from the demands of street merchants that calendars were big sellers.[4] Print runs for them, in the twenty-five years that followed, fluctuated irregularly between 3,000 and 8,000 copies annually.[5] Whether most copies were sold is not known, but the absence of a consistent print run pattern suggests that the Academy had not yet determined the level of demand and consequently that actual sales fell somewhere between the two extremes.

From the 1750s onward, however, the publication of calendars began to increase very rapidly. Whereas only two kinds of Russian language calendars existed in the post-Petrine era, a religious calendar and a court calendar, in Catherine's time nine regularly printed calendars and numerous occasional ones were put on public sale. By the mid-1760s the Academy alone was printing a total of about 17,000 calendars a year.[6] By the mid-1770s that figure had risen to about 18,000, by the mid-1780s to about 25,000, and by the mid-1790s it had reached about 30,000. Over half of this last figure came from a single calendar that listed the holidays, astronomical information, zodiac signs, and the phases of the moon.[7] But by the 1780s other calendars were coming out in large print runs, among which were a calendar of history and geography that listed all the postal stations, roads, and tariff rates in the empire; a court calendar that discussed etiquette at court and listed all the important court days; and a number of religious calendars and almanacs that included the daily prayers.

The question is whether this outpouring of calendars in the 1780s and 1790s reflected public demand. Certainly not all copies of every calendar sold in any given year. Print runs for the *Historical Calendar* and the *Geographic Calendar* declined from about 1,000 copies a year each in the late 1760s to 500 copies a year a decade later.[8] Other calendars sprang up and, after a few unsuccessful years, disappeared.[9] On the whole, however, the evidence points to a very substantial and unsatisfied demand for calendars. One indication of a large demand comes from the steady rise in the aggregate print runs from year to year. In addition, a number of calendars went into second printings a month or six weeks after their original printings. But the most convincing evidence for the popularity of calendars comes from the orders sent to the Academy of Sciences book depository. Large-volume dealers, including Polezhaev, Sopikov, and the Glazunovs, placed regular annual orders of several thousand calendars each.[10] In addition, they often placed large reorders, at times requesting as many copies of ordinary calendars as the Academy had in stock.[11] Medium-sized and small book dealers also placed relatively large orders for calendars. Ovchinnikov, for example, ordered between 150 and 800 calendars annually in the 1780s.[12] Nearly half of the small or individual orders sent to the book depository, moreover, requested nothing more than calendars.[13] By the 1790s the Academy of Sciences found itself issuing three or four reprintings of the most popular calendars within a few weeks of the original printings just to accommodate the initial orders.[14] These facts leave little doubt that the Academy sold all or nearly all the major calendars that it could print. Whether other publishing houses, which printed some of the minor calendars, achieved similar success is not known, but it is difficult to believe that this vigorous demand would not have touched them as well.

Assuming, therefore, that Russians bought about 30,000 calendars a year in the 1790s, what does that figure indicate about the limits of the reading public under Catherine the Great? There is no question

of any other publication achieving sustained sales that even approached 30,000 copies a year in this period. For the 1790s, when
the population of "central Russia" numbered around 28 million, this
figure works out to about one calendar sold for every thousand people.[15]
This ratio of course cannot be applied to any specific groups or regions,
because of the imponderable character of distribution. As best as can
be determined, between 80 and 90 percent of the calendars went to
book dealers who were registered in Moscow and St. Petersburg, although these dealers could arrange to sell the calendars elsewhere,
either on their own or through colporteurs. It can be presumed that
some of the calendars found their way into the provinces and even
into the countryside, and also that the actual number of calendar
readers was considerably higher than the number of buyers, but there
is no reliable way of calculating a figure for either of these. Still, it is
likely that a disproportionately high number remained in Moscow and
St. Petersburg and that, consequently, the ratio was larger than 1:1,000
in the major cities and smaller elsewhere.

It would be difficult to draw any conclusions concerning the dissemination of new or secular ideas on the basis of calendar circulation
alone. Calendars and almanacs had been popular for quite a long time,
but they disseminated religious knowledge or catered to the mundane
needs of everyday life more than to those of enlightened secular culture.
Without knowing more about how people read calendars or whether
the intellectually more ambitious but less extensively printed versions,
such as the historical or geographic calendars, went to particular readerships, we really cannot go any further. But because of the calendars'
inherent obsolescence, few readers very likely depended upon them
for anything other than immediate information or amusement. Other
publications, by contrast, had smaller overall print runs, but their
utility continued over a longer period of time. Thus, it may be that
alphabet books, primers, and teaching psalters eventually reached more
broadly into Russian society than calendars did.

A good deal less is known about the publication of psalters after
1760 than before. They continued to come out with great frequency,
however, and there is no reason to believe that the Synod cut back
on print runs that, in the first half of the eighteenth century, had usually
ranged between 1,000 and 10,000. For primers and alphabet books
as well, printings were frequent and editions were often large. Okenfuss has found that

> probably more than 300,000 primers printed in Moscow were
> sold in the second half of the seventeenth century. In addition

numerous Ukrainian and Belorussian editions circulated in Muscovy. Almost 25,000 primers were printed in Lvov between 1662 and 1720 and they could be found throughout the western part of Muscovy. The Petrine civil primer was published nine times between 1710 and 1720: in the years after 1716 when education was being expanded rapidly, 1,200 copies appeared annually. At the end of the eighteenth century, when the Austrian-trained advisor Mirievo was building Russia's first national school system, his primer saw eight printings between 1782 and 1799: a total of 100,000 copies appeared.[16]

In other passages, he describes still other primers, including one by Metropolitan Platon, a widely published one by Catherine, and Feofan Prokopovich's Slavonic primer *Pervoe uchenie otrokom* (A Student's First Lesson), of which twenty-one editons were published between 1738 and 1798.[17] More recently, T. A. Afanas'eva has discovered that the various synodal presses were annually producing between 7,000 and 30,000 alphabet books in the old orthography from the mid-1730s until the late 1780s.[18]

What can be made of such numbers? Both Okenfuss and Afanas'eva quite plausibly infer from them that primers must have circulated very widely and that their function as the basic instrument for teaching literacy to Russian children made them highly influential vehicles for shaping the outlook of youth. After scanning the contents of different primers, moreover, Okenfuss concludes that they provided distinct and mutually incompatible models of childhood to those among the gentry, clergy, and *raznochintsy* who came into contact with them.

Okenfuss' conclusions appear to be fully consistent with the evidence he has produced. As he acknowledges, however, not very much is known about how these books actually circulated. Did specific groups of children use the primers intended for them, and if they did, did they assimilate the implicit moral lessons or did they merely learn reading and writing? For that matter, did alphabet books and primers even succeed generally in teaching children to read and write? Some alphabet books, for example, devoted a great deal of attention to the old and new alphabets and to letter formation, but they provided very little practice in reading words and sentences. Some of the more ambitious Catherinian primers, in contrast, seemed to make a leap from letter and syllable formation to complex ideas without spending much time on words and the structure of language.

A final problem with inferring social consequences from the contents of specific primers has to do with the ambiguities of dissemination.

For much of the century Prokopovich's primer was the most widely printed one, at least until Jankovic's primer started coming out in 1782. Can one really speak of a clear social differentiation of models of childhood when one primer dominated for so long? Can one be confident, moreover, that particular primers remained with discrete publics once they received their initial distribution? In contrast to calendars, after all, primers remained current, at least from the perspective of learning to read and write. Of course, the cheap methods used in reproducing primers, and especially the brief alphabet books, made them highly perishable and not likely to last for very long periods of time. Still, individual primers could have circulated for years, either by being passed from hand to hand or by recirculating in the second-hand book trade which colporteurs often conducted. If their primary attractiveness on the market lay in their utility in learning to read and write, the moral contents could have gotten lost or, conversely, competing moral visions could have reached the children in a single social group. To draw wide-ranging conclusions about culture and society from the contents of primers alone is therefore, at the very least, hasty.

Alphabet books and primers, nevertheless, did circulate in Russia in very large numbers, and, given their function and their accessibility, they probably represented the outer reaches of reading in the eighteenth century. They were just the beginning, moreover, of a significant outpouring of educational books that seemed to reflect, above all, a popular desire to learn to read and write and, to a lesser extent, interests in arithmetic and childrearing. The Public School Commission, mandated to serve the educational needs of primary school students, presided over the dissemination of much of this literature after 1782, a position that permitted it to transform the role of textbooks in Russian education. The average print run of its publications was about 7,500 copies, most of which went directly to students, and the number of copies of any given book often rose well above the average. A two-volume arithmetic primer, for example, entitled *Directions in Arithmetic*, went through five printings between 1783 and 1797, with a total print run of about 50,000 copies.[19] Similarly, *A Short Russian Grammar* by Evgenii Syreishchikov went through three printings between 1787 and 1796, with a print run totaling 25,000 copies.[20] Catherine's noted moral-educational tract, *On the Responsibilities of Man and Citizen*, went through six printings between 1783 and 1796, totaling at least 43,000 copies.[21]

Certainly these three titles outstripped most school books except alphabet books in print run and distribution, but their large numbers demonstrate the possibilities for general learning that were inherent in a policy that strived to supply each student with his own textbooks. The initial owners of the textbooks, upon leaving school, could have passed them on to other people, and if copies found their way into remote areas, they could have been passed on extensively—and perhaps recopied—from one generation to the next, or at least from one sibling to the next.

Since most of the widely circulated textbooks taught reading and writing, one would expect that they had a collective positive impact on the literacy rate. For Russia, documents such as parish records and wills that historians usually rely on in order to estimate literacy apparently are sparse for most of the eighteenth century and, with very few exceptions, unexplored. Thus, a quantified discussion of literacy rates is out of the question, but a variety of impressionistic evidence nevertheless suggests that textbooks may very well have expanded the numerical base of reading in Russia.

The sheer volume of their print runs, first of all, is impressive. Over the course of Catherine's reign alone, millions of printed volumes from the Synod, the Academy, and the School Commission came into circulation, and the records of the School Commission make it clear that school books were sent to the provinces in large numbers. Schools all over the empire requested and usually received the basic textbooks.[22] Archival sources even record instances when special printings of certain books were prepared for delivery to schools on various frontiers.[23] Books that taught language were likely to be hand copied once they got to the countryside.

There is a good deal of evidence to suggest, further, that basic texts, especially grammars, glossaries, alphabet books, and arithmetic books, were also circulating outside of the formal network created by the Primary School Commission. Undoubtedly, some of this demand came from students not served by any of the existing scholastic distribution systems, whether primary schools, garrison schools, or church academies. But sources indicate that much of the demand originated in the public market—i.e., from noninstitutional sources. The leading institutional bookshops always carried grammars and other language books in great abundance, reflecting the constant demand for these books from their own students. But private dealers also carried a broad selection of grammars, albeit in undetermined quantities. In the mid-1770s, for example, Karl Müller listed in his catalogue nearly every grammar printed in St. Petersburg in the previous five years, including the newest edition of Lomonosov's *Russian Grammar*, *An Abbreviated Russian Grammar*, and a number of books identified merely as Russian alphabet books.[24]

194

Other leading dealers, including Christian Torno and Christian Klein, did the same. In the 1780s and 1790s, as the choice of titles expanded, book dealers showed even more interest in language books than they had earlier. Schnoor, Ovchinnikov, Klosterman, Glazunov, Sopikov, and other important dealers advertised language books quite prominently in the various media. In 1787, for example, Ovchinnikov circulated a list of thirty-one newly received volumes, six of which were grammars or dictionaries.[25]

Booksellers' catalogues, unfortunately, are silent on the quantities of language books sold in each store, but their orders to the Academy in the 1790s make it clear that demand ran very high. In 1791, for example, Kol'chugin placed a sizable order from the Academy's stock list. Included in his requisition were ten copies of Lomonosov's *Russian Grammar*, twenty-five copies of an alphabet book, and thirty copies of the *Dictionary* of the Russian Academy. In that same year, Sopikov ordered 150 copies of an alphabet book; and Sokolov, Ivan Glazunov, and several other dealers ordered 100 copies each. A year later, Ivan Zaikin placed an order that included 350 copies of the same book.[26]

Such large orders indicate that the demand for basic language books outside of the school networks was quite substantial. The lack of actual sales figures prevents establishing with any precision how high demand actually went. Still, the numerous editions and the relatively high print runs leave little doubt that total demand approximated total supply. Lomonosov's *Russian Grammar*, originally published by the Academy of Sciences in 1755, went through seven Academy editions between 1755 and 1799, with print runs that ranged from 600 to 2,500.[27] His textbook on rhetoric also ran through seven printings in the second half of the century.[28] Nikolai Kurganov's workbook on writing Russian (*Pis'movnik*) went through six printings in Catherine's reign, at least one of which was financed for public sale by Timofei Polezhaev and Ivan Glazunov in 1790.[29] Moscow University and the Typographical Company printed nine editions of a book entitled *Abbreviated Rules of Russian Grammar* between 1773 and 1797.[30] The total print runs of this book are not known, but if they followed Novikov's normal practice, they probably ran fairly high.[31]

When one considers all the books on the Russian language that appeared in the last quarter of the eighteenth century, it becomes evident that the overall market for them was very large. In general, it seems plausible to conclude from this popularity that, in spite of the persistence of general illiteracy, there was a growing acceptance of the virtue and utility of learning to read and write among some segments of Russian society. Such an acceptance represented a victory for the autocracy, which had been trying since the Petrine era to convince servitors of the need to be literate and technically competent. Raeff, Freeze, and Shtrange, in their separate works, have shown that the generation of priests, *raznochintsy*, and gentry of the 1750s and 1760s was the first to accept an association between education and service. But that generation, depending as it did on elite schools, involved a very limited number of people. By the 1780s, it appears, the educational ethic had filtered down in a limited way to other elements of the population.

In contrast to this wide interest in reading Russian during Catherine's reign, the demand for foreign-language primers and grammars, although growing, remained relatively restricted. Francophilia, of course, had been characteristic of Russian educated society for the entirety of Catherine's reign, and so it is not surprising that thirty-three different French grammars, glossaries, alphabet books, lexicons, and conversation books came into print during that time. In addition, in the second half of the eighteenth century, Russian publishers printed six French dictionaries and a number of four-language lexicons that included sections in French. The print runs of Academy foreign-language grammars usually were between 1,000 and 1,800 copies per edition, and the Infantry Cadet Press ones ran between 300 and 800 copies. How well these grammars sold in the 1760s and 1770s is not clear; however, although several different grammars came out in the first half of Catherine's reign, only two of them went into second printings before 1780, an indication that demand was not taxing the available supply.

In the 1780s and 1790s, sales of French grammars proceeded more briskly. One that was printed by the Academy of Sciences and another printed by Moscow University each went through three printings in the course of fifteen years. Book dealers prominently advertised French grammars both in their catalogues and in the newspapers, and their orders for newly published French grammars were among the largest sent to the Academy. In 1790 and 1791, a number of the Academy's French grammars and alphabet books regularly elicited orders of ten to fifty copies each from the larger booksellers.[32] But in contrast to the demand for Russian primers and grammars, orders declined noticeably after a year or two. In any case, the total number of French primers and grammars in print was only a small fraction of the total number of Russian ones. Consequently, there is no question that reading in French remained far less widespread among the Russian public than reading in Russian was.

More problematic is the question of whether French or German was the more common second language of the educated public. Some scholars have suggested that German remained popular in the secondary academies during Catherine's reign, and the large number of books on the German language (twenty-eight) and German dictionaries (five) seems to confirm this. Once again, most print runs are not known, but fully six of the German grammars and conversation books went into multiple printings during Catherine's reign, led by Franz Holterhof's *German Grammar*, which had five Moscow University editions between 1770 and 1791.[33] This particular grammar may have gone primarily to the German classes at Moscow University's gymnasium, but a number of private publishers also printed German grammars, and, judging by book dealers' orders, the German grammars and word books published by the Academy of Sciences sold as well as or better than comparable French volumes. Ehrenreich Weissman's *German Lexicon*, for example, went through only two printings, but it consistently outsold Pierre Restaut's *General Principles of French Grammar* in the early 1790s.[34] To be sure, grammars were a good deal more sophisticated than lexicons, and a book on conversational French outsold both of them. But the overall patterns allow very little basis for distinguishing between the acceptance of French and the acceptance of German by well-educated Russians.

Other modern languages, it is clear, drew much less attention from eighteenth-century Russians. Guide books to the study of English, Italian, Greek, and Polish, although available, brought only intermittent demand from book dealers. Catalogues reveal that bookstores carried them only occasionally, and the number of reprintings was quite small. There were times, in fact, when Latin grammars outsold both English and Italian ones. Vasilii Lebedev's translation of *Compendium Grammaticae Latinae*, for example, went through seven editions between 1762 and 1792, with a total print run of about 12,000 copies. Most of these copies went directly to the Synod for use in the seminaries, but public demand, as evidenced by booksellers' orders, also ran rather high. Similarly, Christoph Cellarius' *Short Latin Grammar*, which went through three Moscow University and three Academy of Sciences editions during Catherine's reign, was the object of sustained demand for a number of years.[35]

In comparison to the interest in learning to read, the informal study of other basic subjects was more subdued. Arithmetic, home medicine, and other practical subjects did attract significant attention in the last third of the eighteenth century, but above all, it was the laws that sold best among these books. At least since Peter the Great had initiated the policy of extensive printing and circulation of new laws and public notices, institutional presses had produced selected laws in large quantities. The manifesto convoking the Legislative Commission of 1767, for example, came out in an initial print run of 20,000 copies, and subsequent editions, printed in Russian, German, Latin, and French, routinely came out in print runs between 2,000 and 10,000 copies each.[36] Other laws, of both greater and lesser importance, also had large print runs.

Mere printing, of course, did not indicate public interest, as the Petrine publishing experience made clear. But the public demand for laws and quasi-legislative notices was quite substantial. Luppov has shown that officers and notables of the seventeenth century already were buying significant quantities of the *Ulozhenie* of 1649.[37] Evidence from the middle of the eighteenth century also points to a continuing demand for laws, and by Catherine's reign, this demand had grown still larger.[38] The *Ulozhenie* of 1649 itself went through ten printings between 1759 and 1796 (eight by the Academy of Sciences and two by the Moscow Senate Press), and total print runs of the Academy's editions number approximately 8,500 copies.[39] There is no doubt that interest in the *Ulozhenie* rose substantially in the years during which the Legislative Commission was in session, but four of the editions, with a total print run of about 5,000 copies, came out between 1780 and 1796, over twenty years after the Commission had met. Demand, therefore, was unusually enduring.[40]

Catherine's major edicts, including the Instruction to the Legislative Commission, the province administration reform of 1775, charters to the towns, and the 1785 charter to the nobility—the last of which went through ten printings in fifteen years—drew significant and sustained interest among book dealers.[41] Important older legislative acts that continued to be the bases of current practice also gained a great deal of public attention. The Military Code of 1716, for example, which delineated the service responsibilities of officers, went through eleven printings between 1776 and 1796.[42] Most of these printings were moderate (1,000 copies or fewer per printing), and many copies went directly to the officer corps. But once again, bookstore orders from the early 1790s reveal an active public trade in it.

Public interest also extended to laws that did not necessarily play an important role in contemporary legislative practice. Collections of the major laws of the Petrine era and volumes of the early edicts of Catherine the Great exhibited high sales for several years. A volume of the laws enacted between 1714 and 1725, for example, went through seven widely sold printings between 1739 and 1799.[43] One could argue that part of the demand for laws came from a desire to curry favor with the empress or to show respect to her position as legislator. But the interest in Petrine edicts, many of which no longer had great relevance to contemporary legislation, suggests that other factors besides mere respect were involved.

One explanation for this interest lies in the exalted image of Peter's reign, which, by the middle of Catherine's II's reign, had reached nearly cult proportions. Both the government and the educated public saw Peter as the originator of the modern institutions in which they lived, and they admired those achievements greatly. Some clever writers capitalized on this admiration by collecting and publishing any written material that related to Peter's reign. The popularity of Golikov's two miltivolume collections, *The Acts of Peter the Great* and *Additions to the Acts of Peter the Great*, is one example of this celebration. Peter Krekshin's *A Short Description of the Glorious and Monumental Deeds of Peter the Great* had three printings between 1788 and 1794, and his *Tale of the Birth, Upbringing, and Crowning of Peter the Great* had two.[44]

But the cult of Peter the Great, as important as it had become, does not explain the interest in defunct or only marginally relevant laws among the reading public—e.g., the edicts of Catherine I and the legislation of several pre-Petrine tsars. Year after year book dealers ordered many copies of these laws, with no evidence of a sharply diminishing demand. Undoubtedly, practicality had some effect on sales. Laws, almost by definition, were of interest to particular groups such as state servitors, whose work required familiarity with the main points of the laws and with changes in legislation. The kinds of laws that sold well most consistently were those that discussed fundamental definitions of service, the basic functions of administration, and the privileges that accrued to those who served. Typically, the table of ranks, the province administration reforms, the military code, and the naval code sold much better than did less significant laws or laws that dealt with the conduct of commerce or the nature of taxation.

These laws also were useful in providing legislative signposts for the gentry's troubled deliberations over privilege and its role in Russian society. Equally relevant here is the possibility that interest in the rule of law and the role of law in society was transformed into a more general public concern among servitors over Catherine's goal of creating a Russian *rechtsstaat*. Whether the gentry respected the laws, tried to improve them, or looked to them for explicit answers to their questions about status and service remains unclear, but it is noteworthy that the last twenty years of the eighteenth century witnessed an increase in the number of practical guides to Russian law that were published and in the number of secondary-school courses in legal practice being taught.[45] Russian servitors may not have displayed much interest in the philosophy of law or legal principles, but they did strive to make practical sense of the laws, an endeavor that conformed with the wishes of the empress, who, in Richard Wortman's words,

> emphasized enlightenment and tried to instruct the nobility in the importance of the science of the law. With Catherine, a familiarity with the law began to be presented as part of the cultural equipment the nobleman was supposed to have, a necessary skill to dispatch his obligations to the state.[46]

This pursuit of necessary skills appears to have been rather shallow, however, for the sales of other utilitarian books were sharply lower than those of the laws. In the mid-1760s, for example, a home medical handbook written by Christian Peken came out in two editions, with print runs totaling 8,400 copies, for the use of students at the medical college. The first edition of 1,400 copies sold quickly, but most of the second edition was still in stock at the time of an inventory taken in 1784. From that time on, however, Peken's medical book sold very well, and in the 1790s two more printings came out, totaling 1,132 copies. In addition, a Moscow printing of unknown size came out in 1786, and an updated version, written by Peken's son, Matthew, and entitled *The New Home Medical Book*, came out of the Moscow University Press in 1796.[47]

These figures by themselves appear large, but they represent the summit of sales for "self-help" books. They pale, moreover, in comparison to the sales of such books elsewhere. For example, a leading Leipzig publisher of the time, Georg Goschen, asserted that an 800-page almanac entitled *Need and Help Book (Noth- und Helfsbüch)*, written by Rudolph Becker, went through eleven authorized and four pirate editions between 1787 and 1791. Goschen did not indicate the total number of sales in this period, but the initial printing ran to 30,000 copies, and subsequent printings presumably were also quite sizable. By 1811, he claimed a million copies of the *Need and Help Book* had sold throughout Germany.[48] By that assessment, Becker's book sold an average of 40,000 copies a year over a twenty-four-year period, a rate that was approximately sixty times that of Russia's best-selling laws. Even if one casts a certain skeptical eye toward such enormous figures, one still must concede that Germany stood well beyond what Russia was capable of in this period.[49]

Books were printed in Russia that were rather similar to Becker's. In the mid-1790s, for example, the Free Economic Society sponsored a competition in which it invited authors explicitly to compose original volumes that most closely resembled Becker's publication, and in 1798 and 1799 the society published the winning entry, the three-volume *Village Mirror (Derevenskoe zerkalo)*, whose total length ran to a little more than the 800 pages of the *Need and Help Book* (312, 296, and 200 pages).[50] The total circulation of the volumes is not known, but advance subscriptions to the first one ran to only 210 copies. For the succeeding two volumes, moreover, advance sales were made to only twenty-six and six subscribers, respectively.[51] With such a tepid reception, it is not surprising that the *Village Mirror* required no additional printings in the eighteenth century.

A comparison of this sort shows, more than anything else, that the definition of useful or general-information books differed markedly from country to country. The dividing line that separated books that appealed to a wide reading audience from those that appealed to a smaller and more elite one fell between practical publications that played a role in everyday life and more topical literary or informational books that functioned as leisure reading. Self-help books evidently fell on the popular side of the line in Germany, but not in Russia. But no Russian publication of any sort had a circulation that came at all close to the level of the *Need and Help Book*. Even the teaching psalters and alphabet books, most of which were quite short and inexpensive, never achieved 40,000 sales a year, and the lengthier grammars and textbooks of the Primary School Commission had print runs that totaled only a small fraction of that figure. All of these books, moreover, relied in large measure upon captive markets of schoolchildren to achieve their sales, whereas the self-help books sold almost entirely on the open market. Thus, Russia's most widely disseminated practical titles circulated far less extensively than comparable publications in Germany (or for that matter in England or France).

LEISURE BOOKS

When attention is shifted to leisure books, a similar situation emerges. By the 1730s, the wealthy and even the not so wealthy in most European societies had accepted leisure reading of novels, drama, and moral tracts, and Russia was no exception. Already during Peter's reign *Aesop's Fables* was popular, as were *The Meditations of Marcus Aurelius* and other works of the classical revival. These books served a social purpose in providing positive models of civic virtue for serving men to emulate. Wortman has suggested that servitors read Marcus Aurelius, for example, in search of "descriptions of civic virtue befitting a martial temperament" upon which to pattern their own lives.[52] But it should be borne in mind that these books were also entertaining—most of them, indeed, were rather light fare—and that even the most popular of them sold far fewer copies then comparable books did in the West.

In the second half of the eighteenth century the market for leisure books grew rapidly in Russia, and the number and variety of books in circulation were incomparably greater in the 1780s than they had been in the 1720s and 1730s. By the middle of Catherine's reign, the reading public had become large enough to provide an audience for nearly every kind of book for which a market existed in the West, and as a result the interval between a book's initial appearance in the West and its translation into Russian, which earlier had often run to forty or fifty years, was sharply reduced. The works of the leading *philosophes* appeared in Russia only ten or twenty years after their appearance in France, and by the 1780s the time had grown even shorter. Goethe's *The Sorrows of Young Werther* appeared in Russian only seven years after its appearance in German, and several of Wieland's works were translated into Russian just a few years after their appearance in German.[53]

This accelerated pace of translation reflects the ready-made universalism of the graduates of the elite schools, who endeavored to absorb and immediately disseminate examples of nearly every aspect of the European cultural tradition. Their eagerness presented some bizarre juxtapositions for the reading public, however, such as the major English novels of the early eighteenth century appearing at more or less the same time as the sentimentalist literature of Goethe and his generation. Equally odd was the publication of classical, Renaissance, Counter-Reformation, Enlightenment, and early romantic books all within one or two generations. Perhaps the most sensitive and intelligent readers could make sense of this onslaught, but less sophisticated readers very well could have become hopelessly confused by it.

Another source of confusion for readers was the anonymity of authors that was inherent in editorial and commercial practices. Most eighteenth-century booksellers followed the convention of advertising their books by title and genre rather than by author. An advertisement might even mention the translator without identifying the original author. These practices began to change only at the very end of the century, and not until the 1820s did most booksellers adopt bibliographic procedures that gave attention to authors. Thus, the question arises whether most eighteenth-century readers recognized favorite authors or whether they bought books by title or genre.

In this context, Karamzin's comments concerning the most popular books of his day provide an excellent starting point. In his essay on the book trade, Karamzin suggested that the leisure readership turned first to general categories of publications, specifically newspapers and romances. It was his view, however, that the public did pick and choose its favorite works and authors, including Fedor Emin's *Inconstant Fortune; or, The Adventures of Miramond* and Matvei Komarov's *The Unfortunate Nikanor; or, The Adventures of a Russian Nobleman*. Karamzin also maintained that the circulation of the *Moscow News* increased from 500 copies per issue in the 1770s to 4,000 in the 1780s and 6,000 in the 1790s.[54]

Scholars have tended to accept Karamzin's figures, although it is worth noting that no other evidence on the print runs or circulation of the *Moscow News* has ever come to light. For the *St. Petersburg News*, however, print runs tended to be rather modest, increasing from between 600 and 1,200 copies per issue in the 1760s and 1770s to between 2,300 and 2,800 by the end of the century.[55] Martynov has uncovered a document that showed the Academy of Sciences earning 3,500 rubles for newspaper subscriptions between 1781 and 1784, or about 1,200 rubles a year.[56] If figures such as these are representative of the outer reaches of interest, leisure reading must have been confined to a very limited proportion even of the reading population.

The numerous romances and stories that came out during Catherine's time collectively probably reached more readers than newspapers did. *The Adventures of the English Lord George* went through seven printings in the 1780s and 1790s. The first twelve volumes of a twenty-volume edition of *1001 Nights*—which to Novikov and his friends epitomized the low level of popular task—went through three complete and three partial editions during Catherine's reign, and, although records reveal neither the sizes of the print runs nor the number of books sold, booksellers placed large periodic orders for the series. The number of imitations, moreover, including *1001 Days, 1001 Quarter Hours*, and *1001 Stupidities*, attest to the commercial value attached to its name.

But *1001 Nights* was only one of numerous adventures and romances that sold well in Catherinian Russia. Abbé Prévost's famous *Adventures of Marquis G.*, the story of a man who traveled around the world, went through five partial editions between 1756 and 1793, with total print runs of about 4,000 copies.[57] Similarly, the historical tales of Alain Lesage, including the well-known *Campaigns of Gil Blas*, which went through seven editions between 1754 and 1800, with print runs of between 600 and 1,200, judging from booksellers' orders sold quite well.[58]

Adventure stories with Russian plots also sold well. Matvei Komarov, for example, wrote a story entitled *The Factual and True History of a Russian Swindler* (or some slight variation of this, depending on the edition) that came out seven times in various versions between 1779 and 1794. Stepan Kolosov's *The Life of a Certain Man (Zhizn' nekotorago muzha)* went through four editions between 1780 and 1791, and *The Unhappy Adventures of Vasilii Baranshchikov, a Burger of Nizhnii Novgorod, in America, Asia, and Europe,* by an anonymous author, came out in three editions between 1787 and 1793.[59]

The craze for romance, adventure, and exotica from abroad seems to have placed far more emphasis on the attractiveness of the title than upon the fame of the author. Still, there were some exceptional literary figures, such as Voltaire, whose name did bring widespread recognition. *Candide* sold nearly its entire print run of 1,200 copies between 1769 and 1779.[60] In the course of the 1780s an additional 1,300 copies of the work went on sale at the Academy bookshop, and another four editions came out of the Naval Academy Press.[61] Milton's *Paradise Lost* went through three printings between 1777 and 1796, and *Paradise Regained* also went through three.[62]

In general, however, Russian literary tastes were decidedly lowbrow. Important contemporary literary masterpieces, regardless of genre or title, were unlikely to sell very well if their authors lacked broad name recognition in Russia. The great English novelists of the first half of the eighteenth century, for example—Fielding, Richardson, Swift, and Defoe—first came to the attention of Russian readers in the late 1760s and 1770s, largely through the efforts of the Translation Society. But whereas their books enjoyed immediate and enormous commercial success all over Europe—to the point where they outsold French novels in France itself—they found no such reception in Russia. *Amelia, Joseph Andrews,* and *Jonathan Wilde* sold 300 or fewer copies each, at least until the 1780s, and the evidence indicates that their popularity increased only marginally after that.[63] Only Defoe's *Robinson Crusoe* managed to strike a responsive chord, going through four printings totaling about 3,000 copies during Catherine's reign.[64]

Other major works of European literature had similar modest sales. Galchenkov's translation of Goethe's *The Sorrows of Young Werther,* for example, went through three printings between 1781 and 1796, the first of which had a print run of 600 copies but sold only 125.[65] Not all book dealers carried the book, and bookshop orders from

1794, the year of the second printing, reveal only moderate interest from booksellers.

Even drama, an apparently popular and easily accessible genre, often had trouble selling well. Russian and Western plays were readily available not only in the literary magazines but also as separate publications, and, because of their brevity, unbound copies could be sold at relatively low cost (ten to thirty kopeks), a fact which made them attractive to booksellers. Bookshops, in fact, generally carried large stocks of plays, in particular the works of Wieland, Voltaire, Molière, Sumarokov, Karamzin, and Kheraskov. Even more significant, not only did the plays receive the usual kind of advance publicity, but several booksellers created special sections in their catalogues for drama, in which plays were listed by author rather than by title. Yet the popularity of the genre as a whole apparently did not carry over to all individual titles. To be sure, Voltaire's *Zadig, Candide*, and others went through several printings each in the eighteenth century, but only a few of Molière's plays, including *Amphitryon* and *George Dandin*, went through even a second printing. Others of his comedies, such as *The Bourgeois Gentleman* and *The Misanthrope*, had only single Russian-language editions in the eighteenth century.[66]

The market for Russian drama apparently was even sparser. Novikov's lamentation that he could not sell 200 copies of Sumarokov's plays in ten years is only one indication of the poor commercial value of Russian plays. The Academy had refused to print anything written by Sumarokov without receiving advance payment from Catherine, and in a financial statement prepared in the late 1760s, the Academy revealed that most of Sumarokov's plays had gone unsold.[67]

In the 1780s Novikov reprinted a large number of Russian plays and stories, including several by Sumarokov, but one must question whether he did so in response to public demand or whether he was trying once more to promote the works of his friends. Had there been any interest in most of these works, the public could have turned to the Academy of Sciences, which had a large and well-advertised stock of Russian drama from the initial printings.[68] But, with the exception of FonVizin's *The Minor*, which went through five editions from five separate publishers between 1783 and 1800, and Karamzin's *Poor Liza*, which went through four (including its initial publication in the *Moscow Journal*) in the 1790s, booksellers' orders reveal very little demand.[69] Novikov was perhaps republishing these plays in order to give them a second chance before the Russian public. His endeavor apparently included some mild chicanery that was intended, presumably, to present a more optimistic picture of popularity than was the case. The title pages of twenty-one of Novikov's editions of Russian plays bore the inscription "fourth edition," when in reality there had been only one prior edition for most of them.[70]

Russian writers could turn to the journals as alternative media through which the works of serious writers could be presented, together with some better known or less serious ones as a way of increasing circulation. In most instances, however, literary and philosophical journals sold as poorly as or worse than the least popular books. The highwater mark for journalism was reached early in Catherine's reign by Novikov's monthly journal of satire and commentary, *The Drone* (1769–70), which went through two printings of perhaps 2,000 copies per issue. For expressly moralistic journals, the highest figures were achieved by Novikov's *Morning Light* (1777–80), which reached about 800 subscribers in its first year. Otherwise, most of the several dozen literary and philosophical journals seem to have had very low print runs; they normally stayed in print a year or less, and they appeared on booksellers' stock lists only occasionally. Even if one takes the journals into account, therefore, total sales of original works probably did not exceed 1,500 copies for any but the most popular titles.

The only literature which appears to have sold uniformly well was moral fables and stories. The concern for personal morality cut across the otherwise rigid lines of educational curricula, and it seems to have cut across generational lines as well. *Aesop's Fables*, which had been popular in Peter the Great's day, maintained its popularity in the second half of the eighteenth century, going through five apparently sizable editions.[71] By all indices, demand was quite high, and in fact the book continued to be widely read well into the nineteenth century.

By the middle of Catherine's reign, this genre had grown to include several dozen other works, including such species as Giulio Croce's *The Italian Aesop*, which had three Russian printings between 1778 and 1782.[72] Well-known moralists of the period, including Stephanie Genlis, Christian Gellert, François Fénelon, Claude Lambert, and a number of imitators, flooded the Russian market with their books. One cannot begin to estimate the total sales of these books, but several pieces of information suggest that demand for them, though uneven, was generally high. Some authors, such as Fénelon and Jean François Marmontel, achieved notable success with their works. Marmontel's *Bélisaire*, for example, went through seven editions between 1768 and 1796; five of them were Academy editions, with print runs totaling over 4,000 copies, and they seem to have sold very well.[73] Similarly, Fénelon's *Adventures of Telemachus*, went through four editions between 1767 and 1797.[74]

Publishers of every sort printed large quantities of moralistic works, and booksellers usually carried large selections of them. Here again, title and genre were more important than author; most of the advertisements and title pages emphasized that they were stories, that they had a moral message, and that they had recently been translated from the French. The author's name, if it was mentioned at all, generally came last.

Such also seems to have been generally the case with moralistic tracts that focused specifically on aspects of childrearing. Some individual titles certainly sold quite well, including a book translated from German entitled *The Science of Living Happily* (four editions, three print runs of which totaled 3,300 copies), Ivan Betskoi's compendium of important translations on childrearing (six printings in the 1760s), a translation of Joachim Campe's multivolume *Small Library for Children* (four partial reprintings between 1783 and 1799), and several others. But the market also accommodated dozens of other titles on this theme, including a large number of Russian originals. A volume called *Friendly Advice for a Young Man Who Is Beginning to Live in the World* had six printings during Catherine's reign.[75] A handful of original moralistic stories, such as Fedor Emin's *Path to Salvation* and his *Moral-Educational Fables*, also managed to gain a certain prominence.[76] But these were exceptional. Most original moralistic works did not sell well. Even the works of Vasilii Levshin, which sold very well later on, did not have much of a public during the eighteenth century.[77]

Okenfuss has associated this outpouring of childrearing literature with Russia's "discovery of childhood," and the issue of whether these books transformed childrearing is treated in his study.[78] But for present purposes, it is relevant to the question of whether the publishers and literati were agents of secularization to note that the most popular kinds of books intended for moral upbringing were not childrearing tracts per se but Bible stories that were to be recited to children. A translation of Johann Hübner's *One Hundred and Four Sacred Stories from the Old and New Testaments*, for example, had eight printings between 1770 and 1800, and Father Benjamin's *Bible Stories for Children* had seven printings between 1774 and 1782.[79] There was, of course, nothing new or secular about the Bible, but these volumes represented the most extensive accounts of Bible stories ever printed in Russia and the first to be rendered in the vernacular. All were published by civil publishing houses and, although most copies went to the Primary School Commission, many were also put on public sale directly to the laity. Implicitly, therefore, they did represent a change in lay culture that allowed for a less mediated access to the Word for educated Russians and that allowed parents and tutors as well as priests to interpret the Word to their young charges.

A similar form of adaptation for children also characterized the most popular nonfiction leisure books. In history, for example, the most popular volumes included stories about Peter the Great, the newly published chronicles, adaptations from the chronicles, and historical stories. In one very widely published book, for example, the seventeenth-century monk, Innokentii, retold the history of Kievan and early Muscovite Russia in simple language based on a distillation of the chronicles, and between 1762 and 1798 five editions of his narrative appeared.[80] Popular volumes also came from such distillations or reworkings of the past as Aleksei Mankiev's *The Essence of Russian History*, which went through four editions between 1770 and 1800, two of which were financed by book dealers.[81] For the works of recognized historians, however, demand was significantly lower. Thus, the major histories of Tatishchev and Boltin, some of which are still read today, gained relatively little currency in their own century.[82] Only Shcherbatov, and perhaps Lomonosov, among the serious historians, sold well, and the former gained currency only in the 1780s and 1790s.[83]

Among non-Russian histories, classicism retained the preeminence in Catherinian Russia which it had held since Peter's day. The leading sellers were *The History of the Destruction of Jerusalem*, which went through nine printings totaling about 6,000 copies during Catherine's reign, and Guido delle Colonne's *History of the Destruction of Troy*, a big seller under Peter which went through six Catherinian editions.[84] *The Meditations of Marcus Aurelius* went through six post-Petrine printings of unknown size, three of these during Catherine's reign.[85] Other popular works of antiquity during Catherine's reign included the *Aeneid*, with five fragmentary editions, and three editions of a "reworking" of the *Aeneid* by Nikolai Osipov.[86] Other, more recently translated classical mythologies and histories, such as those published by Catherine's Translation Society, although printed in moderate editions (usually fewer then 1,000 copies each), in general failed to sell even as much as two-thirds of their initial print runs, and they rarely went into second printings.[87] The only prominent exception to this pattern was a 1772 translation of Ovid's *Metamorphoses*, which sold over 1,000 copies in the 1770s and went through two additional partial printings.[88]

The public was even less receptive to new or newly translated philosophical tracts, except for those that touched on childrearing. Cath-

erine and her coterie at the Translation Society had tried to present a
wide selection of philosophical titles from the more prominent representatives of classical and enlightenment thought to the Russian
reading public, but few philosophical works of the Translation Society
sold more than 400 copies in the first ten years of the society, and
many sold fewer than 200 copies. Leading European political and legal
philosophers of the Enlightenment—such as Hobbes, Locke, Hume,
Beccaria, and Montesquieu—either appeared in Russian in small single
editions or were not translated at all. The only Russian translation of
Hobbes, for example, was a single edition of his essay on citizenship,
and the market for the nonliterary works of the French *philosophes*
was little better.[89] To be sure, the major theoretical writings of Diderot,
d'Alembert, Hélvetius, Mably, d'Holbach, Condorcet, and others were
made available in one form or another during the eighteenth century,
but this remarkably topical and varied output contrasts vividly with
a very tepid reception on the open market. Montesquieu's *Spirit of
the Laws*, for example, came out in a single Russian-language edition
of 600 copies in 1775.[90] By the mid-1780s most of these copies were
still unsold, and even at a discounted price they drew only scant
attention from booksellers. Of course, these works were available in
French editions, and in all likelihood a considerable segment of educated society read them in the original. But even if most of the graduates of the secondary academies read the *philosophes* in the original,
a very large percentage of the reading public—i.e., those who could
not read French—remained untouched by them.

A revealing selectivity was employed in deciding which major philosophical works to publish. Locke's *Two Treatises on Government*
and *Essay concerning Human Understanding* were never translated
in the eighteenth century, but his essay *On the Upbringing of Children*
went through two printings. Similarly, only some of Rousseau's better-
known political essays were made available, and these sold much less
widely than did the sentimental *La Nouvelle Héloïse*, which went
through three partial editions between 1769 and 1792.[91] These patterns suggest that, in order to sell, books needed to be lively and
entertaining, regardless of their philosophical disposition. They had
to be readily comprehensible, and they had to set forth their points
of view either through fiction or in simple expository prose. The more
difficult a book was to understand, and the longer it was, the less
likely it would be to sell, regardless of the attractiveness of the title
or the fame of the author. Thus, Voltaire sold better than Diderot and
d'Alembert; Lesage sold better than Fielding or Richardson; Gellert

and Wieland outsold Dusch; and Emin, Bogdanovich, Karamzin, and FonVizin outsold Kozel'skii, Sumarokov, and Tatishchev.

These sales or circulation patterns also convey a clear general impression of the deeper concerns and interests of readers and of the relative popularity of the ideas of the Enlightenment. It can be inferred, for example, that readers had extensive practical concerns about the laws but quite limited interest in the principles or philosophy of law. They were more likely to be drawn to literature or general-interest nonfiction that presented easy and concrete examples or guides to personal behavior and fulfillment than they were either to abstract considerations of ontology and epistemology or to discussions of political virtue, civil society, or general social issues. They were eager to read descriptions of other times and other places, whether real or imaginary, but complex analyses of other societies, cultures, or politics left them cold. All of this points to a reading public with an overriding concern for aspects of everyday life, the ways in which other cultures lived and behaved, how they themselves should behave, and above all, how they should raise their children.

These concerns were characteristic of the eighteenth century, for in most respects the issues, as well as the search for answers in books rather than in spoken words, were markedly different from those of the previous century. In order to go beyond these generalities and to ascertain whether a more coherent and possibly transforming, if highly simplified, vision of the individual, of Russia, or of the world emerged from the milieu of popular books, however, one would have to devote far more attention to their specific content than is possible in a study such as this. But it is striking to see the extent to which new or newly translated books were obliged to coexist with preexisting patterns of popularity among the leisure reading public. Authors who had become popular in the late seventeenth century or during Peter's reign, such as Aesop or Marcus Aurelius, maintained their popularity during the reign of Catherine the Great. The entire corpus of lay or secular literature, moreover, existed alongside a sustained demand for devotional works, saints' lives, and Bible stories. It cannot be said with certainty whether these characteristics applied to a single undifferentiated reading public or whether there were separate publics for differing categories of books. But they do seem to add up to a coherent pattern of reading.

What seems to have been at work, first of all, was a simple reluctance on the part of the reading public in Catherine's time to venture beyond familiar books. One gets the sense, furthermore, of a strict division within leisure reading between, on the one hand, reading simply for pleasure, involving an indiscriminate attraction to romances and adventures, and on the other, nonfiction reading that, except for the more inquisitive intellectual groups, was highly selective, not at all venturesome, and narrowly instrumental. Readers, in other words, appear to have effectively sidestepped the literati's rush to assimilate all of European learning; instead, they relied for inspiration largely upon those few books that their parents and grandparents had read. If this was the case, then the anomalous manifest openness to new and unfamiliar books aimed at parents and tutors was a striking indication of just how profound the focus on childhood and childrearing was among educated groups. In the final analysis, therefore, the literary preferences of the reading public turned out to be far less encyclopedic than the "smattering of everything that European culture had to offer" that Raeff has described and, except for light literature, far more instrumental: the laws, heroic classics, and books for and about children. It is upon these books, consequently, that a social history of the Russian Enlightenment, the character of secularization among the educated laity and the common ground shared by the literati and the reading public, must be based.

EIGHT

Censorship

A BOOK that discusses the history of printing, especially one such as this that insists upon the primacy of the institutional context of printing, cannot be complete unless it addresses the question of censorship. But although one may admit the necessity of discussing eighteenth-century Russian censorship, one must also point out that it is one of the most thoroughly studied subjects in all of Russian history, and the basic facts are by now well known and fully digested. At the interpretive level, some disagreements persist concerning the motivation behind censorship and the severity of it, although there has been a certain narrowing of differences in recent years. Simply put, those scholars who believe that Catherine and the leading writers stood in separate camps conclude that censorship was omnipresent and getting worse, and those who see no such opposition or who maintain that antagonisms arose only late in Catherine's reign downplay censorship as an important historical force. But since this is not a study of politics, literary or otherwise, and since there have been no significant recent discoveries on eighteenth-century censorship, what new insights can this book possibly contribute to an understanding of the subject?

Without presuming to break new ground regarding the basic facts, this study nevertheless can add a new perspective by looking at censorship not as a problem of politics but as a problem of printing. Formally, censorship represented an expression, or implementation, of the right claimed by the authorities to intercede in publishing and book distribution. Above and beyond politics, the institutional relationship between government and printed communications underwent tremendous changes in the second half of the eighteenth century, and each of these changes required the traditional sources of censorship—the crown, the church, and the Senate—to redefine their responsibilities and concerns. At times these organs of authority failed to respond clearly to the shifting character of printing, with often confusing consequences. Never was this confusion more evident than in the years immediately following the advent of private publishing. Failure to anticipate how an independent publishing system might affect the capacity for censorship led to several episodes in which representatives of authority manifested confused and occasionally hysterical reactions over the appearance of certain books. To a large degree, therefore, the onset of a severe and systematic censorship in the 1790s can be seen as an unanticipated consequence of the failure to define the state's responsibilities in the 1780s.

CENSORSHIP AND INSTITUTIONAL PUBLISHING

During the reign of Peter the Great publishing was almost entirely an in-house activity, and, with the exception of the church administration's oversight of monastic presses, censorship as such did not exist, since books and presses did not function outside of officialdom. With the gradual removal of publishing from the halls of power under Peter's successors, however, the government defined an oversight process such that, although the tsar and the Senate were censors of last resort, review of books prior to publication became the private responsibilities of the leading publishing houses themselves. Thus, the Senate controlled the official presses, the Synod controlled all religious presses, and the Academy of Sciences controlled its own press.

In practice, the Synod was the most active overseer of printing during this time, since it felt constrained to struggle against the new secularisms contained in opera and science. The Synod had the exclusive right to approve the publication of books, or sections of books, that contained prayers or religious themes. This responsibility gave the Synod entree to the civil presses, which it exploited with some influence for the rest of the century. Outside of the church, however, the Synod could not physically prevent the publication of a book or seize a book that had contravened its monopoly on works of faith. To impose its will, the Synod required the intervention of the tsar, the Senate, or the police if its authority was not voluntarily accepted by a bookshop or civil publishing house, and, as has been seen, by the late 1740s the Synod could no longer assume that the Senate would consent to its demands.

The proliferation of scholastic presses in the 1750s and 1760s further complicated and restricted the Synod's position. There were now more publishing houses and far more secular books to keep track of, and the Synod's warnings about the harmful impact of some of these books usually fell on deaf ears. The new presses were subject only to self-censorship by a committee that included administrators and professors mostly from the institution itself but occasionally including a representative of the Academy of Sciences.

Involvement in the oversight process by the government or Synod was possible only in consultation with the censors, or "correctors" as they were called, at the request of one of the parties. Any time a religious subject was broached by a book that had been submitted to a scholastic press, as often occurred with primers and odes, the censorship committee was expected to consult the Synod beforehand, and, according to available records, it usually did so. But this acquiescence affected only a small minority of published books. If the Synod wanted to intercede with other books, it had to petition the executive authority of the relevant institution—e.g., the chancellery of the Academy of Sciences—that was empowered to grant final approval to publish. Since at every level the in-house authorities tended to accept the judgments of their own presses, the Synod's attempts to curtail or modify secular publications had a very limited impact. Thus, in two celebrated cases in the 1760s, the Synod complained about the supposedly irreligious and anti-Orthodox character of articles contained in two literary and general informational magazines, G. F. Müller's *Monthly Works* (*Ezhemesiachnye sochineniia*) and Sumarokov's *Diligent Bee (Trudobliubivaia pchela)*. The Synod demanded that the offending issues be confiscated, but the Academy's censors politely refused to take any action, and the Senate declined to become involved.[1]

It is important to recognize that no institution at this time, other than the Synod, attempted to keep apprised of books and presses. Neither the Senate nor the empress possessed any formal mechanism for reviewing books prior to their publication. To be sure, the Senate was mindful of the growing vitality and independence of print, and as a result it conducted three inquiries into Russia's presses during the 1770s (1773, 1775, and 1778).[2] But these reviews merely discussed the presses in general terms, and they made no recommendations other than to suggest that the Senate remain aware of what the presses were doing.[3]

Still, censorship never entirely disappeared, even in the most tolerant years of Catherine's reign. Absolutism was, after all, still in effect, and no one questioned the empress's right to ban a book. Given Catherine's cameralist political philosophy, her activist and interventionist approach to civil society in general, and her intense interest in the world of letters in particular, any abdication of her position as censor of last resort would have been inconceivable.

Thus, without having to search too far, episodes of censorship can indeed be found. In 1763, for example, Catherine's wariness of the atmosphere of intrigue and the series of palace revolts that had so typified court politics in previous decades led her to forbid the publication of works that mentioned the names of her immediate predecessors.[4] But the government had little enthusiasm for enforcing this regulation, and, according to most accounts, only imported books that violated the rule were subjected to effective censorship.[5] Political censorship of Russian books, in fact, almost disappeared in the 1760s. One of the very few cases occurred in 1764, when Catherine banned an ode to King Stanislaus Augustus written by Sumarokov.[6] The attention devoted by historians to this single case, in which no penalties were assessed, testifies to its uniqueness.

Even the personal displeasure of the empress rarely had a drastic effect on the press. In 1769, for example, the satirical journal *Miscellany (Smes')* published some translations that Catherine had found offensive. Yet her distaste led to nothing more than a slight rebuke.[7] In another and more celebrated affair, Catherine allegedly found Rousseau's *Emile* so shocking that, in 1763, she forbade its further importation into Russia—but she imposed only a partial ban on its being translated and published in Russia.[8] In a demonstration of the mildness of even this ban, the Moscow University Press continued to publish many of Rousseau's more radical works, including the *Discourse on the Origin of Inequality*, throughout the 1760s and 1770s.[9]

Given such evident reluctance on the part of the government to pursue a coherent policy of censorship or to create its own mechanism for overseeing the publication of books, where have Soviet scholars—who by now surely have uncovered every single case of censorship—found evidence to support their more draconian version of literary politics in the 1760s and 1770s? Traditionally, Soviet research has emphasized the dampening effect of informal or indirect sanctions. Some historians have argued, for example, that the insistence of the Academy of Sciences Press on receiving large advance payments before publishing the works of certain authors, including Sumarokov, Emin, and Kniazhnin, involved, at least in part, a desire to keep these authors out of print. Rather than openly denying them the right to publish, the Academy, and by extension the empress, adopted a policy that said nothing of censorship but that made publishing economically so difficult that the authors had their access to print effectively curtailed.[10] Another common contention is that Catherine refused to allow the publication of certain odes and plays that had been read publicly at court. According to this position, political considerations involving court politics and literary disagreements stood behind Catherine's decisions. Thus, a certain amount of original literature was forced to circulate entirely in manuscript because of Catherine's objections.

If taken at face value, these two arguments present a rather pessimistic view of political interference in literary life, to the point of making Catherine appear as a Janus-like figure with a public human-itarian and affirmative visage and an uglier and more repressive private one. Needless to say, most Soviet scholars have concluded that the behind-the-scenes oppression was the truer self. Were every point in this set of arguments beyond dispute, one perhaps would concede that the empress was something less than the champion of letters that she made herself out to be. But one would nevertheless have to conclude that none of this activity really amounted to a systematic policy of censorship, indirect or otherwise. The number of authors whose works were deprived of a reading audience was very small, and only a few more were delayed. Certainly, Soviet authors have not identified any significant individual authors who had failed to find a public voice. Thus, placing the handful of examples in the broader context of the ever-expanding opportunities to publish, it becomes clear that the evidence brought to bear by Catherine's severest critics does not amount to very much.

Moreover, those who suggest that the Academy's financial policy was politically inspired have failed to produce much evidence either that the Academic chancellery had political motives or that the empress incited the Academy into imposing stringent financial conditions. The circumstances of scholastic publishing at the time were such that eco-nomics was the overriding consideration, deriving primarily from the Academy's severe cash shortages. Far from having a political basis, these shortages derived from the press's openness to privately sub-mitted manuscripts, most of which sold quite poorly. Only after this policy was on the verge of producing financial ruin did the Academy become more contentious with authors. In virtually every case, whether it was Sumarokov's plays, Novikov's *Drone*, or Emin's essays, delays in publication and demands for minor editorial changes arose out of financial considerations, and in virtually every case the troublesome work eventually came into print.

The empress's role in all of this appears to have been benign as well. Her desire to expand the available translated literature through the Translation Society, however much it may have been motivated by an intention of controlling the burgeoning literary life, did provide salaries for several authors, and it greatly increased their access to print. One could say, in fact, that her very aggressive advocacy of publishing books that were of interest to the literati and hardly anyone else created, or at least exacerbated, the Academy Press's financial diffi-culties. When those difficulties threatened to have an adverse effect on the publication of original literature, moreover, she often came up

216

with the necessary funds, since she was a patron of such "opponents" as Novikov and Sumarokov.

These facts cast considerable doubt upon the presence or efficacy of informal and indirect censorship in the 1760s and 1770s. And indeed, the more recent literature on the subject has toned down the conspiratorialist argument considerably. D. V. Tiulichev's splendid article on the censorship of Academy of Sciences books, for example, has acknowledged the episodic character of censorship and the genuine tolerance toward the press that characterized the first half of Catherine's reign.[11] Similarly, V. A. Zapadov, although clinging to many of the old suspicions of Catherine's motives, has conceded that he could find very little evidence of a conflict between Catherine and the literati until the mid-1780s.[12]

The revisionist implications in these articles have received their fullest explication in K. A. Papmehl's book, *Freedom of Expression in Eighteenth-Century Russia*. Papmehl pictures Catherine as a true defender of and the leading voice of individual literary expression, who resorted to censorship only with the greatest reluctance, at least until the late 1780s. He maintains that Catherine genuinely perceived herself as an Enlightenment monarch and that her public pronouncements reflected her deepest sentiments. Censorship, or even keeping a systematic watch on the press, was anathema to her.[13]

Papmehl deserves a great deal of credit for posing an original and in many ways compelling argument. He does, however, misread Catherine to some extent by ignoring aspects of her rule that show the limits of her tolerence and her conservatism in social and economic affairs. Far from tolerating fundamental dissent, Catherine did move surely and swiftly when political and social order were threatened. This essential intolerance was reflected most clearly in her behavior toward the family parties at court, but it also manifested itself in many other ways. The fact that her sword was not turned against literature in the first part of her reign reflects not tolerance as much as the fact that writers and literary expression posed no serious threat. Thus, Catherine felt free to sponsor literature, convinced of its essential lack of oppositional force and feeling, perhaps, that advocacy was the best insurance against its becoming oppositional.

It was the perceived presence or absence of threat of one sort or another that ultimately determined the specific course of censorship during the second half of Catherine's reign. By the end of her reign in 1796, censorship had become severely oppressive; for some reason, between the late 1770s and the mid-1790s her policy underwent a drastic change. The usual explanations of this change have involved the Pugachev revolt, the French Revolution, hostility to the Freemasons, the articulation of progressive ideas among the literati, and the intensification of family political strife at court. All of these undoubtedly contributed to the onset of censorship to some degree, but none of them suffices to explain why Catherine came to feel threatened by the literati, most of whom she knew well and virtually all of whom remained quite tame. To understand why Catherine came to believe that publishing and writers were dangerous, we need to look more closely at the particular episodes of censorship and to inquire how the changing circumstances of printing in the 1780s may have influenced them.

During the first several years of private publishing neither the Senate nor the empress was cognizant of any intrinsic danger arising from a loss of authority. The Senate simply imposed certain minimal restrictions on each new publishing privilege and mandated that Moscow University, the Academy of Sciences, the police, or the Synod make sure that the press published nothing that was harmful or dangerous. The exact meaning of these directives was apparently left up to the institutions themselves, and, with the exception of the Synod's oversight of religious books, enforcement was lax.[14] Publishers apparently did not regularly submit their books for prior approval, and there is no evidence that the institutions of authority felt obliged to establish new organs to deal with the private presses. For all practical purposes, therefore, private publishing in the late 1770s and early 1780s functioned without any formal prior review.

The Senate's main concern in those years, in fact, was not dangerous publication but merely infringement of monopoly rights. In February 1780, for example, the Senate ordered the Infantry Cadet Press to stop violating the Academy's monopoly on calendars.[15] And in a somewhat more celebrated case, the Senate ordered Novikov to cease publishing textbooks over which the School Commission had a monopoly.[16] The Synod chancellery also was concerned with such infringements. In 1777 it complained that a Russian grammar published by Weitbrecht and Schnoor contained an unapproved catechism and prayer book. The Synod had granted permission to Weitbrecht and Schnoor to include the prayer book and catechism in a grammar that they had prepared for the use of schoolchildren in Novgorod, Tver, and Pskov. But the publishers made a minor modification in the catechism without first receiving the Synod's permission, and that led the Synod to demand that the entire print run be confiscated. The Senate concurred, and in August 1777 all the offending grammars were seized.[17] The Synod must have registered other such complaints, because in May

1780 the Senate acknowledged the Synod's concern over the publication of unauthorized religious material and ordered a search of all bookshops to remove any contraband of this sort.[18]

THE 1780s

Once the new law on private printing came into effect, however, publishing began to change more rapidly than the government had reckoned. Private printers and books now proliferated, but the law that had removed restrictions on the ownership of presses said little about censorship. The only stipulation in this regard was that the local police (*upravy blagochiniia*) should approve each book issued by private publishers prior to its going on sale, to ensure that none contained anything that went "against the laws of God and society."[19] By all accounts, however, the police took a lackadaisical approach to enforcement, and the law did not give any other institution besides the empress or the Senate the power to ban privately published books or to require their authors to make corrections in them. Thus, with each passing month, an ever-increasing volume of published books came out without any sort of prior review.

First to react to this newly unregulated world was the church. The Synod had grown wary of unrestricted printing, the independence of secular intellectual life, and the appearance of mystical and masonic fads within educated society. In the course of the 1780s, the church demanded numerous official press reviews, and somewhat later it began to seek a greater role in the oversight of the secular press.

The first serious threat to faith came not from the literati, however, but from the Old Believers. Throughout the eighteenth century the church had tried with mixed success to suppress Old Believer manuscripts and to check the spread of their influence. But when the Old Believers of Klintsy procured a printing press and then were able to publish with the sanction of the law, the possibilities for sacrilege became ominous. The church could not immediately stop the Klintsy press from publishing, although it was able to ban the sale of Old Believer books at provincial fairs. Only in August 1787, when the Synod received broad special powers to oversee the publication of books, did the Senate acquiesce to closing the Klintsy press (at least temporarily) and seizing all its books.[20]

Even at its moments of greatest influence, however, the Synod did not have the authority to conduct investigations without the approval of the Senate. For such activities, it needed the cooperation of the civil administration and the police. But although the laws had given the police a formal role in controlling the press, the police in most cities of the empire seemed oblivious to publishers and booksellers.

In Moscow, though, things were different. Private publishing was burgeoning there, hundreds of miles from the watchful eye of the central government, and since the enactment of the new law in 1783 the police chief of Moscow, Count Bruce, had been expressing his concerns about unregulated free expression. In 1784 he wrote a letter to Catherine stating his fears that illegal or offensive books might be published if there were not greateer controls over the press, and in response Catherine issued an edict that authorized Bruce to maintain a general watch over all Moscow publications.[21] In 1785 he forbade public performance of Nikolai Nikolev's play, *Sorena and Zamir*, on the ground that it was offensive to public morality.[22] On this occasion, Catherine countermanded his decision, and the play reopened, but in autumn of that year, Catherine informed Bruce and Archbishop Platon of Moscow that she had learned that some "strange and offensive books" were appearing in Moscow.[23] She ordered them to review all books published or for sale in the city and to prepare a list of the dangerous ones. In response, the Moscow authorities, under the direction of Bruce, Archbishop Platon, Archimandrite Moisei, Professors Anton Teil's and Anton Barsov, and an assistant police chief, Godein, undertook the first of several vigorous reviews of the state of publishing in Moscow.[24] In addition, the Synod prepared its own survey of all private publishers in Moscow and St. Petersburg.[25]

The review commission found very few titles that were in any way suspect. Indeed, Archbishop Platon, clearly embarrassed by his participation in the endeavor, informed Catherine that only six books contained ideas that went contrary to the teachings of the church and six others were of questionable virtue, leading him to recommend minor revisions in their texts.[26] As to mystical and masonic books, Platon claimed an insufficient knowledge to be able to judge them properly. Yet, as most scholars have noted, Platon was an immensely learned man, whose knowledge of and participation in the intellectual life of Moscow was extensive and well known. A man of his erudition certainly knew about the local masons and Rosicrucians, and his demurral probably reflects his unease with the business of making reports on old and trusted friends.

Other officials did not share Platon's attitude, however. The Synod chancellery never stopped fretting about the Freemasons, and in 1785 it demanded the censure of a Russian translation of Johann Arndt's pietistic tract, *On True Christianity (O istinnom khristianstve)*, first published in 1605, that had been published in 1784 by Lopukhin's

press. Arndt's book had been known to a number of Russian Freemasons for a long time and had been a standard and rather popular
book among the German reading public in the seventeenth and early
eighteenth centuries.[27] The book, in other words, was neither new nor
especially threatening. But the Synod expressed outrage at its mystical,
Protestant, and anti-Orthodox content, and it demanded unsuccessfully that the entire press run be confiscated.[28] The Synod's distress
apparently remained unassuaged; in January 1786 Count Bruce sent
Novikov a stiffly worded letter (on Catherine's instructions) reminding
him that his presses existed in order to publish useful books and not
in order to start a new church schism.[29] This letter must have alarmed
Novikov, since Platon had just completed his interrogation and had
found Novikov's faith to be sound.[30]

This steady trickle of complaints, ad hoc investigations, and warnings made a deep impression on Catherine, and by the late 1780s she
began to pay more heed to the advice of the Synod and of the Moscow
police. The first sign of just how worried she had become came in July
1787, when she informed all the relevant civil and religious authorities
that, since the appearance of antireligious books had continued unabated, the Synod was being empowered to check every bookshop
and publishing house in the empire to ensure that no one printed or
sold unapproved or offensive religious books.[31] This order initiated a
two-year search of bookshops and printing houses in every province
of the Russian empire that, for a time, brought the book trade to a
halt.

The story of the book raids has been told in bits and pieces in
various published accounts. However, all the relevant documentation
was gathered by the Synod into a single archival volume, making it
possible to know in some detail what happened in various places.[32]
In most towns, the review of publishing was a rather simple matter.
Bookshops were few in number and small in size, so that a local cleric
could conduct his survey in perhaps a few minutes. But experiences
could vary considerably. Since neither the government nor the Synod
issued explicit instructions about how to proceed, what to look for,
whether to close the shops, or whether to seize the books, local religious and police officials were on their own. Some reports indicate
that they examined several books but found none that were offensive
or irreligious. Elsewhere, however, the entire collections of book dealers were registered, presumably to be on the safe side, and damning
comments were made about titles that had been in circulation for
years, such as operas, Voltaire's stories, and even some grammars and
works of natural science.

The purpose of the exercise was so vague that some clerics continued to send in lists years after the search was ordered, while others considered their job done after a single perfunctory review. The psychological consequences for publishing and bookselling, however, were chilling. Since no one knew what was wrong, everything became suspect. In addition, clerics were under orders to curtail the sale of offensive books until the appropriate authorities could make a final disposition. Thus, the book trade in effect became impossible for several months.

In Moscow, the thoroughness of the raids caused bookshops to close for almost half a year. The city authorities registered 313 titles and over 142,000 volumes.[33] Most of these came from private presses, in particular the Typographical Company and Lopukhin's press. But several books on the list had been published a decade or more earlier by institutional and academic presses and had never received any previous undue attention.

Once the lists had been prepared, the Synod went through them to determine which books required confiscation and which were harmless. Only fourteen offensive titles were found; all of them were removed from the bookshops, and the rest went back to the dealers, who could then reopen their doors. But still no one knew why the raids had taken place or whether there would be similar visits in the future.

Novikov, for one, became much more cautious about what he printed, issuing very few martinist works after 1787.[34] One can surmise, moreover, that his apparent vulnerability was sufficiently visible to his patrons and dealers that many of them now became more wary of conducting business with him. It may be, therfore, that the book raids compounded his financial problems and thereby brought about his downfall. Some scholars have gone so far as to insist that that was a large part of what Catherine had in mind when she approved the raids in the first place. Catherine, it is argued, had been privately hostile to Novikov's outspoken "liberal opposition" for several years. The issue of illegal religious books was merely a pretext to permit her to institute a full-fledged system of censorship with which to bring Novikov (and other "progressive" publishers) under control.[35]

The problems with this view should by now be evident. There is no evidence that Catherine held such secretly hostile views or that she had a long-term plan in mind at the time. Surely she would have been unlikely to allow private and nearly unrestricted publishing in 1783 if she was planning to increase censorship. Moreover, if the book raids were merely a pretext, why were only fourteen books—all of them

222

deemed to be harmful to faith rather than to the state—taken, several of which found their way back into booksellers' catalogues a short time later?[36] Why, for that matter, should she even need a pretext? And if the goal of the raids was a censorship system, why was it followed by a two-year period of relaxation and relative tolerance?

A less harsh variant of this view suggests that Catherine genuinely changed her mind during the second half of her reign, gradually moving from tolerance to unremitting suspicion. According to this argument, the violent excesses and disorders of the Pugachev revolt and the French Revolution were the main catalysts for this change of heart.[37] There can be little doubt that Catherine was becoming more suspicious in the late 1780s or that Pugachev's revolt and the storming of the Bastille had an influence on matters such as bureaucratic reform and the judicial system. But their impact on censorship is more problematical. These two events occurred sixteen years apart, during which time independent publishing was expanding; and the book raids took place two years before the outbreak of the French Revolution. Thus, any change in Catherine's outlook toward books must have arisen from other causes.

Some historians have argued that the book raids and the events leading up to them involved a specific assault on the masonic movement rather than a more general attack on all forms of free expression. Most of the memoranda and warnings that led up to the book raids, these historians point out, centered on the possible ill effects of masonic literature. The main victims in the raids, the Moscow bookstores and Novikov's circle, were the unquestioned centers of the most mystically inclined and secretive lodges, and Catherine's distaste for the ritualism of the Rosicrucians had been a matter of public knowledge for some time.[38] But if Freemasonry were the target, why take such stern measures? Freemasonry had been around for years without posing any noticeable threat. Furthermore, although Moscow was the center of Russian Freemasonry, there were many lodges in St. Petersburg, with numerous prominent senators among their members—yet the records of the Synod say nothing about a book raid having taken place in the capital. Most perplexing of all in this context is the fact that the raids were directed against bookshops rather than publishing houses. Would it not have been easier and more effective to issue a simple ban on printing masonic books, or to declare masonic presses illegal?

In an attempt to answer some of these questions and to dispel some of the old notions concerning censorship, V. A. Zapadov has recently argued that the book raids were not intended as a general assault on literature and were only indirectly an attack on the Masons. To be sure, he comments, the few books that were temporarily seized did have a masonic character, but it was not the books per se that bothered Catherine but the conspiratorial nature of the group that produced them. In itself harmless, Masonry became dangerous to Catherine when it became entwined with court politics and threats of palace coups. Zapadov's evidence of the connection between censorship and court politics consists essentially of the relationships between Novikov and the party that favored the investiture of Paul as emperor. Allegedly, the periods during which Novikov suffered the most—1785, 1787, and 1792—were the times of his most active contacts with Paul's party.[39]

Zapadov's argument contains some supportive features that are noticeably lacking elsewhere. Family politics clearly was an ever-present problem, even if Catherine had long since domesticated most of the circles at court. Obviously the lodges provided a special problem in that regard because of their secrecy, and—as Paul was to learn after he had succeeded Catherine—the combination of Masonry and court politics could be dangerous. But the connections between censorship and the activities of the pro-Paul group are pure conjecture on Zapadov's part. There is no basis for connecting Novikov with court politics in the 1780s and no documentation that would link the investigations of Novikov with fear of a court conspiracy. If Catherine did fear a conspiracy, it would seem that the St. Petersburg lodges would have been a more prominent target. And why go to so much effort to control the book trade nationwide if the problem was court politics?

Despite his effective debunking of some of the old mythologies, therefore, Zapadov holds firm to the old idea that the book raids were part of a long-term and methodical plan involving issues that had little to do with mystical books or violations of faith. But if even so diligent a scholar as Zapadov is unable to find documentation on which to rest this notion, perhaps it is time finally to abandon it in favor of a more direct, if less imaginative, explanation.

This explanation must begin by acknowledging that since no one has been able to find evidence of a well-ordered plan of censorship germinating in the back of Catherine's mind, no such hidden agenda existed. The acts of censorship and control of books were manifestly unsystematic and unrigorous in the 1780s, and so it seems far more likely that Catherine was responding to events in an ad hoc manner rather than anticipating them. The irony is that the events to which she was reacting were generated almost entirely by her own officials.

The concentration on Moscow and the Masons, for example, is best understood as a consequence of the views and the zealous character of Moscow's police officials. Three important officials—Bruce, Eropkin, and Prozorovskii—disliked the Masons, and they bombarded the capital with a barrage of communications that warned of their pernicious influence. The Synod chancellery was even more strident in its opposition to the Masons, and her distance from Moscow impeded Catherine's ability to judge the situation independently. Under these conditions, the active dissemination of masonic ideas through presses that were located almost exclusively in Moscow made those presses appear to be more dangerous than they were in actuality.

A more difficult problem arises in explaining why *any* of the presses should have been objects of suspicion. Why, in particular, did Catherine give an increasingly sympathetic hearing to reports of unspecified ominous goings-on when, in fact, she knew the allegedly dangerous people very well, had worked with them for years, and knew them to be politically tame? Just a few years earlier she had virtually ignored such warnings and, as late as 1785, Archbishop Platon had reminded her of the harmless and inoffensive character of the masonic lodges and of Novikov in particular. Why was she eventually less inclined to listen to him and more inclined to listen to Prozorovskii?

Certainly the isolated cases of monopoly rights and the publication of a small number of mystical books did not, in themselves, amount to sufficient challenges to warrant an action as extensive as the book raids. Their significance was magnified, however, by the fact that the books in question all came from the network of private publishing that was rapidly taking over printed communications in Russia. The hyperbolic and ominous tone of some of the reports opened her eyes to the extent to which private publishing was taking over and to her limited authority over it. These presses, she discovered, could print more or less what they wanted, and the government could react only after the fact. In the absence of any regular review of private printing, she truly did not know whether any dangerous books had appeared, and this realization, reinforced by the warnings of some of her highest police officials, brought about a minor panic. If all she could do was to react after the fact, she decided to sanction a measure which would at least tell her how much damage had been done.

The fact that so few books ultimately were banned indicates that the panic was momentary and that Catherine uncovered very little damage indeed. Her unwillingness, moreover, to create any permanent mechanism for overseeing publishers or for imposing more severe censorship rules suggests that she was satisfied, at least for the moment, that private printing was harmless. But the experience raised the specter of a publishing system that could get out of control, and it made her more likely to take more decisive steps to assert her political authority over publishers and writers in the future.

THE 1790s

Russian publishers and booksellers recovered very rapidly once the bookshops reopened, and the late 1780s became the most bountiful years that Russian publishing had ever known. But with the outbreak of the French Revolution, Catherine began an determined assault on the independence of the press. Between 1790 and 1795 several writers and publishers, Novikov and Radishchev among them, were arrested and placed in prison.[40] Books were confiscated, printing houses were closed, and the life of a writer became rather hazardous. Even a proposed new edition of Voltaire's works was scrapped because of Catherine's opposition.[41]

Catherine became convinced that the excesses of the Enlightenment had led to the French Revolution and, later, to the execution of Louis XVI. The writings of the *philosophes* therefore became seditious in her mind. Her fears of a secret Jacobin plot on her own life were so deep that she forbade the importation of French books and newspapers or books that even mentioned France. She barred the publication of a traveler's diary, for example, because it contained a single reference to the execution of Louis XVI. In 1794 she ordered all copies of Shakespeare's *Julius Caesar* removed from the bookstores because of the theme of regicide.[42]

Although she did not put the book trade through a new round of convulsive raids and surveys, Catherine did give free rein to the police to conduct periodic checks for proscribed books. Many formerly acceptable titles were now forbidden, and some proscribed books of the 1780s had come back on bookstore shelves. Police officials therefore had little difficulty in finding contraband. Most book dealers managed to weather these periodic storms with, at most, a loss of some of their stocks, but occasionally a bookseller suffered penalties as severe as those imposed upon some writers and publishers. Thus, in 1793 Prozorovskii found I. P. Glazunov selling some proscribed books, including several of Novikov's forbidden publications, and as a consequence Glazunov went to prison for a short time; even after his release, his business languished for about two years.[43]

The empress's fears did not cripple the press as much as they might have, however, because, even at this point, she did not create new institutional controls over printing. The number of books published annually, which had risen from an average of about 240 a year in the late 1770s to about 390 in the late 1780s, remained high. To be sure, the number of published titles fell after 1788, when nearly 500 books appeared, but the last five years of Catherine's reign, despite all the harrassment, still saw the press producing about 375 books a year (see table 4.1).

In the last months of her reign, however, Catherine ensured that the repressive atmosphere of the previous few years would outlive her by issuing a new edict, the infamous Act of October 11, 1796, which revoked the right of individuals to operate their own presses.[44] Henceforth, only those publishers who had received special privileges to publish before January 1783 were to be allowed to continue to publish privately. More than any other act, this new law drastically constricted the ability of writers to get their works into print. Overnight the number of active private presses dropped from sixteen to four, and by the end of the eighteenth century the number had fallen to three. The effect upon the rate of book production was equally severe. In 1797 only 212 civil orthography books appeared in Russia, compared to 320 the previous year, and the lowest total since 1777. Although production rose somewhat during the next three years, Russia averaged only about 300 books a year in the late 1790s. The crowning blow of this assault on the presses came when, for a brief period in 1800, Paul closed several institutional publishing houses altogether.[45]

Here, then, was a full-fledged and direct crackdown on the independence of publishing, but even this assault did not bring about formal a priori censorship per se. Rather, it closed off most avenues of publication other than those that were subject to formal in-house review. Certainly, institutional presses were far more cautious in the new atmosphere than they had been in the past, and in any case, the government was now much more aggressive in reviewing what came out and banning anything that offended it.

These acts demonstrated how fearful and defensive Catherine had become in her last years. But even if acknowledging how deeply the events in France shook her, many of her actions remain puzzling. One can, perhaps, understand the banning of specific books whose themes were now suspect and the arrest of writers such as Radishchev whose books posed genuine political challenges. But why did the French Revolution lead her to close the private presses and why only at the end of her life, by which time the reign of terror in France had ended?

At one level, one might suggest that she feared that Paul was too inept to maintain vigilance on his own, and rather than risk his losing control over national politics to clever literati, she simply closed most of their presses. Ultimately, however, this answer simply begs the question: Why had she come to fear private printing? Her old nemeses, such as Novikov and Radishchev, after all, had lost their presses and had been either imprisoned or otherwise silenced. None of the other private publishers, moreover, had been any more troublesome to her than the scholastic presses had been, and most had caused her no trouble at all. If the problem with private publishing had been expressly political, surely there were simpler and more effective controls, such as public censors, and more obvious targets, such as the masonic lodges. The target, however, was not individual; somehow the very existence of a system of private printing had become ipso facto dangerous.

The source of that danger, it appears, lay precisely in private printing's independence. Operating on their own, private publishers had moved printing into a world that was separate from the world of the empress. No longer was she a central figure or even the leading patron of literary life, and writers, publishers, booksellers, and private patrons conducted their business without her intervention or support. The success of private printing, in other words, brought with it a certain separation of intellectual life from political life, and whether or not individual writers or publishers were dangerous or in opposition was less important than the fact that a large portion of intellectual life was institutionally emancipated. For an empress who for so long had been inseparable from the leadership of literary life and whose philosophy of rulership presupposed the virtue of the government's active intervention in civil society, the emancipation of intellectual life must have been hard to take. That it organized itself around institutions that could regulate themselves was simply intolerable.

Catherine's wavering and ad hoc approach to policing books in the 1780s and early 1790s failed to address the core of the problem. Private printing and intellectual life remained outside her reach. Closing the presses, therefore, became her means of reasserting control and bringing the writers back within her orbit before they went the way, perhaps, of the French.

Looked at in this way, the law of October 1796 represents Catherine's failure to anticipate or to understand the changes which private printing had brought about. It also demonstrates her unwillingness to alter the laws to reflect an institutional relationship between government and the press that conceded the separation while establishing the absolutist government's authority over the actual communications process. From the perspective of "the well-ordered police state," therefore, the law of 1796 did not mark the establishment of systematic censorship but the failure to establish it.

After Catherine's death, Paul continued to impose heavy-handed, erratic, and unsystemized controls over books. His bans on books after they came out followed no clear patterns, although hints of republicanism, anti-Orthodoxy, or other offensive ideas usually sufficed to cause a book's confiscation.[46] Criteria were, if anything, less uniform than under Catherine, and some important new writers, including Ivan Pnin, managed to bring their work into print during Paul's reign. Remarkably, several new translations of Rousseau's works, including the *Confessions* and *Emile*, passed the censors.

In the provinces, the situation was still more muddled. Prior to the 1790s, provincial censorship had been as episodic as it had been in the major cities. To be sure, the Old Believers in Klintsy and Rakhmaninov in Kazinka had felt the brush of governmental harrassment, and the insecurity of the authorities in a number of other provincial areas had created conditions for publishing that were more stringent than those in either Moscow or St. Petersburg. But more frequently, the close association between governmental and literary circles had precluded anything beyond a system of de facto self-censorship with, at most, the formal approval of the local governor.[47] Even the book raids of 1787–88 failed to prevent the emergence of provincial publishing. But the series of repressive edicts passed between 1795 and 1798 had a marked, if inconsistent, effect on local presses.

Although the closing of private presses put a large number of publishers out of business, local presses proved to be more adept at circumventing the law than publishers in the major cities. Some private printers, including Nikita Sumarokov in Kostroma and Vasilii Kornil'ev in Tobolsk, overcame the new restrictions by selling their presses to public institutions and continuing to operate them as employees or lessees.[48] In three other towns—Smolensk, Vladimir, and Nikolaev—the new legislation actually brought new publishers—Sytin, Selivanovskii, and Ponomarev, respectively—from Moscow and St. Petersburg. Still, the overall effect of the laws on provincial publishing was decidedly negative. Publishers in Tobolsk, Yaroslavl, Tambov, Kaluga, and elsewhere, regardless of whether they were private or institutional, found that the atmosphere of apprehension greatly inhibited their activities. Thus, despite the fact that nearly as many presses were in operation after 1796 as before, the number of titles that were published in the provinces fell from 130 between 1791 and 1795 (an average of 26 a year) to 95 between 1796 and 1800 (19 a year). Three-quarters of the books printed in the latter five years, moreover, came from only four towns (Vladimir, Nikolaev, Smolensk, and Voronezh).

Paul's censorship system thus nearly destroyed the network of private printers, and this action markedly redrew the topical profile of published books. An examination of the subject matter of the books published at three key points in the last quarter of the eighteenth century demonstrates the extent of the effect. As table 8.1 shows, the percentage of titles in the humanities—history, philosophy, and belles-letters—rose between 1777 (42 percent of all titles) and 1787 (60 percent of all titles). But during the height of censorship in 1797 their proportion fell to one third of all titles. On the other hand, infor-

TABLE 8.1

Subject Composition of Russian-Language Publications, 1777, 1787, and 1797

Subject	Number			Percentage		
	1777	1787	1797	1777	1787	1797
Laws, manifestoes, and regulations	19	5	30	11	1	13
Official information and notices	10	10	23	6	3	10
Religion	22	69	39	12	17	17
Military affairs (excluding laws and regulations)	7	4	6	4	1	3
Calendars	8	6	4	4	2	2
Journals	4	17	6	2	4	3
Alphabet, grammar, and language	4	13	11	2	3	5
History and geography	19	55	16	11	14	7
Technology	5	8	6	3	2	3
Science and mathematics	2	22	12	1	6	5
Secular philosophy	18	65	18	10	16	8
Belles-lettres	37	120	42	21	30	18
Odes	23	3	20	13	1	9
Total	178	397	233	100	100	103[a]

Sources: Based on data in *Svodnyi katalog* and in Zernova, *Svodnyi katalog kirillovskoi pechati*.

[a] Figures do not add up to 100 because of rounding error.

mational, technical, legal, and military titles, which had been declining proportionally since the 1720s, continued to fall between 1777 (24 percent of all titles) and 1787 (7 percent), but in 1797 these categories of books rose to account for 29 percent. Odes, which had fallen into disfavor in publishing in the 1780s, rebounded in 1797 to form 9 percent of all titles. "Instrumental" titles, including language, scientific, and religious works, also made up a higher proportion in 1797 than they had previously.

Foreign-language books did not escape scrutiny, either. Another law of 1796 established censorship committees, first in the port cities of Riga and Radziwillowa and later in St. Petersburg, Moscow, and Odessa, to review all books that were imported into the empire.[49] These committees employed censors from the church, the state, and an academic institution, each of whom was paid quite well; the academic censors in St. Petersburg and Riga, for example, received 1,800 rubles a year. The law, however, failed to delineate the scope of the committees' responsibilities. Performances consequently varied considerably from city to city. Between 1797 and 1799 the censors in Moscow, St. Petersburg, Odessa, and Radziwillowa banned the importation of 87 titles altogether but the police censor in Riga, Fedor Tumanskii, seemed to be especially vigorous. In his first 166 days of work he examined 195 titles.[50] He established local censorship committees in all the Baltic territories to deal with non-Russian works,[51] and he even hired two Jews from Riga, Moses Hekel and Ezekiel David Levy, to censor all Yiddish and Hebrew books.[52] Between 1797 and 1799 his agents in Riga banned a total of 552 titles.[53] Included in the list were works by Swift, Goethe, Schiller, Herder, Wieland, Kant, and other formerly acceptable writers. Apparently pleased with Tumanskii's success, Emperor Paul arranged to have censorship committees operating at every port in the country.[54] As a final touch, on April 18, 1800, Paul forbade the importation of all foreign books or sheet music into Russia.[55]

For writers and publishers, the combined impact of closing private presses, banning foreign books, and occasionally censoring domestic ones was decidedly depressive. For the reading public, the impact presumably was also negative, although the book trade's vitality in the 1790s and the government's disinterest in continuing or institutionalizing its oversight of bookshops probably permitted readers to find all but the most recently published contraband. Older restricted books, as Zapadov noted, usually found their way back into the market.

Paul's successor, Alexander I, viewed the press in a more sympathetic light, and on March 31, 1801, three weeks after assuming the throne, he repealed all the repressive printing laws that had been enacted in the previous six years.[56] But the damage to publishing was such that it did not regain the vitality of the late 1780s until several years after the controls had been eased.[57] Paradoxically, shortly after Alexander lifted the ban on private printing and the import of books, he put into law Russia's first systematic censorship, which institutionalized prior review by the government of all published books. Alexander thus succeeded where Catherine and Paul had failed in establishing a new symbiosis, at least temporarily, between the government's political authority and the endeavors of writers and publishers to be a part of an intellectual life that, thanks to private printing, educational reform, and the book trade, had put itself permanently outside of the halls of power.

CONCLUSION

ALEXANDER'S REOPENING of the private presses and his systematizing of censorship represented the final acts in the institutional restructuring of Russian intellectual life. As a result of the evolution of printing toward independence and self-sustenance, a formal, if still fluid, division of social and cultural relations and responsibilities now existed within intellectual life, and this division governed the relationships among serious writers, hacks, publishers, booksellers, readers, and officialdom.

The most basic change was the separation of intellectual life from political life. Begun in the mid-1720s, with the transfer of control over printing from the emperor to the Academy of Sciences and the Synod, this separation had proceeded in fairly rapid succession to give ever more control over publishing to representatives of civil society, from the proliferation of scholastic presses in the 1750s and 1760s until most of the institutions of public communications fell into private hands altogether in the two following decades.

Most writers and translators continued to exist simultaneously in both the intellectual and the political spheres of public life, at least through the first half of the nineteenth century, in part because the market could not yet support them as professional journalists or writers. But the overseers of each realm were now quite different individuals, with distinct occupations and interests. The intellectual sphere was dominated increasingly by merchants, artisans, and persons who were able to devote themselves more or less full-time to writing, while the political sphere confined to function as the province of the state and its servitors. The necessity of moving back and forth between the two tended to undermine the compromise of being a literator, for whom literature and service were either part of a single moral endeavor or were, at the worst, complementary activities. By the end of Catherine's reign, the leading writers were coming to look ever more like full-fledged intellectuals, albeit ones who, for the most part, continued to serve.

Even within intellectual life itself, a certain duality had arisen between private deliberations and public expression which, while not requiring of the literati any separation of work or deliberate choices about careers, nevertheless exposed the ambiguities involved in moving from one to the other. Regardless of how deeply students and graduates immersed themselves in German pietism and mysticism while they were in the comfortable and intimate confines of their private lodges and circles, they invariably became voices of French thought, rationalism, moralism, and entertainment when they involved themselves in publishing. In the process, they witnessed the maturation of a Russian Enlightenment that would be marked by an irreconcilable, if not terribly antagonistic, tension between spiritual or inner virtue and civic improvement. To develop this characterization of the Russian Enlightenment more fully would entail a lengthier discussion of texts and ideas than has been possible here. But this study does suggest that the polarization that usually has been reflected as a historiographic disagreement between the defenders of a rationalist and secularizing view of the Enlightenment and the proponents of a moralistic, traditionalist, spiritual, and even faith-centered one can be viewed as a tension that was inherent in the intellectual institutions and ideas of the time and the growing separation of roles.

For the merchants and artisans who presided over the material side of communications, this division of labor was a natural and highly desirable one. Free of the administrative and financial complexities of institutional publishing and bookselling, they could conduct their activities strictly as a business, responding to the government as their customer or as a guaranteed market rather than as an employer. It also became their choice whether to patronize literature, whether to accept patronage from educated society, and whether to respond exclusively to the market. Most of them, it appears, tended to follow the path that was most likely to yield a secure income in what remained a very tight market. But because printing presses were now affordable to well-to-do writers, the opportunities for literary or personally gratifying publishing continued to exist.

The government, for its part, was now deprived of its status as the sponsor and organizer of intellectual life, and although many individuals within officialdom continued to participate in literary activities, officialdom's institutional role of censor lay fundamentally outside of intellectual life.

Readers, in turn, had also carved out a separate multilayered realm, providing an ample national market for devotional and utilitarian books, somewhat smaller markets for romances, adventure stories, and child-centered books, and a very small and mostly cosmopolitan audience for the more serious products of the Russian Enlightenment. By the 1780s it was becoming clear to publishers, booksellers, and writers alike that readers knew quite well what they wanted from the presses and that only occasionally did their demands correspond with the preoccupations of the literati.

These developments left the literati in an odd and perplexing situation that, on one hand, manifested many of their achievements but, on the other hand, left them with few options and only a limited influence on public morality. The achievements derived from their success in making literary activity much more their own independent domain, especially in the journals and lodges, than it had been earlier. The literati could be pleased, further, that the most abiding concerns of the cosmopolitan reading public—law, status, service, and child-rearing—had some affinities with their own concerns, if in more simplified and entertaining form than they would have liked. But hardly any of this had provided them with the national audience that they desired even among the literate population, and it in no way had given them a voice that was equal to that of church or state.

Still more disquieting was the realization that the emergence of a privately run communications system simply exacerbated the popular preeminence of frivolous books. In the last analysis, it was not the serious literati who reaped the rewards of publishing but those writers and translators who, like Aleksei Komarov, produced books that met the lowest common denominator of public taste. Even in the very realm that they had taken a hand in creating, the literati were finding themselves outflanked by an unfavorable convergence of hacks, merchants, and public taste.

Thus, after all the articles in which Nartov, Novikov, Chulkov, Taubert, and others spoke optimistically of the lively literary interests and voracious consumption of useful books by the common people, and all the polemics in which they contended that merchants, *meshchan'e*, and *raznochintsy* would eagerly buy and read literature if only it were available, the literati now had to face the possibility that most readers—who were, after all, an elite in themselves—were not much interested in what the literati had to offer.

For many writers, to be sure, the receptivity of the common people to the ideas of the writers remained an open question. Thus, Karamzin could write in 1802 with great hope that merchants and townsmen and even the poorest people were pooling their money to buy newspapers, useful books, and cheap novels. But implicit in his enthusiasm was the recognition that others held a more pessimistic view to which he felt obliged to respond. That view did not rejoice at popular reading habits; rather, it bemoaned the fact that the popular embrace of modern literature began and ended with romances that were bad for the heart and morally degrading, that set poor examples, and that stood far below the level of intellectual cultivation of the literary world of the big cities. Karamzin conceded that the common people were not reading what the educated society read or wrote. But to him the very act of reading was a bridge which readers might one day cross to enter the more sublime world of the literati.

> Every pleasant bit of reading has an influence on the intellect, without which neither the heart is able to feel nor the imagination to create. In the worst of novels there is already some kind of logic and rhetoric: whoever reads them will speak more coherently than a complete ignoramus who has never opened a book in his life. Besides, today's novels are rich in all kinds of knowledge.[1]

Most of Karamzin's contemporaries, however, were less sanguine about the uplifting power of romances and less sure of their own ability to transform the hearts of the common people than they had been earlier. For many years the literati had spoken hopefully of building institutions that reached out into the nation and that would open new avenues of moral service to the Russian people. Yet by 1800 it seemed either that the literary path was being muddied or blocked by the money-grubbing pandering of booksellers or, more disturbingly, that the people were simply uninterested. Either way, these reflections challenged the more optimistic assumptions that had informed the literati's longstanding participation in publishing and communication. From a psychological perspective, the maturation of printing may very well have contributed to the heightened sense of isolation that came to characterize intellectual life in the nineteenth century.

Certainly from the middle of the reign of Alexander I onward, writers and journalists were keenly aware and usually scornful of the mediating role between themselves and the public that the booksellers and publishers played, and they produced a profusion of articles that usually raged over—but sometimes appreciated—the domination of the men of the marketplace.[2] They also watched with keen interest the occasional commercial success of recognized authors, such as Krylov, Pushkin, and Zagoskin, in hopes that at least someone was reaching through to the wider readership and thereby breaking down the cultural barriers between them and the common readers that the book trade had come to symbolize.[3] By this time, however, the public was definitely something anonymous, even alien, and the life of letters, itself largely a creation of eighteenth-century printing, was now well on its way to becoming a life apart.

NOTES

AAN   Arkhiv Akademii nauk (Archives of the Academy of Sciences)

ChIOIDR   *Chteniia v Imperatorskom obshchestve istorii i drevnostei ros-siiskikh* (Readings of the Imperial Society of Russian History and Antiquities)

PSPR   *Polnoe sobranie postanovlenii i rasporiazhenii po vedomstvu pravoslavnogo ispovedeniia* (Complete Collection of the Decisions and Decrees of the Department of the Russian Orthodox Faith)

PSZ   *Polnoe sobranie zakonov Rossiiskoi imperii* (Complete Collection of the Laws of the Russian Empire)

RO GBL   Rukopisnyi otdel, Gosudarstvennaia biblioteka imeni Lenina (Manuscript Division of the Lenin State Library, Moscow)

RO GPB   Rukopisnyi otdel, Gosudarstvennaia publichnaia biblioteka (Manuscript Division of the State Public Library, Leningrad)

S. K.   *Svodnyi katalog russkoi knigi grazhdanskoi pechati XVIII veka, 1725–1800* (Union Catalogue of the Russian Civil-Orthography Book, 1725–1800)

TsGADA   Tsentral'nyi gosudarstvennyi arkhiv drevnykh aktov (Central State Archive of Ancient Acts)

TsGIA   Tsentral'nyi gosudarstvennyi istoricheskii arkhiv (Central State Historical Archives, Leningrad)

ZhMNP   *Zhurnal Ministerstva narodnogo prosveshcheniia* (Journal of the Ministry of Public Education)

Introduction

1. The roots of Russian book studies go back to Vasilii Sopikov's multivolume *Opyt russkoi bibliografii*, which came out at the very beginning of the nineteenth century. The field reached a peak, however, in the early twentieth century in the journal *Russkii bibliofil*, with contributions by N. M. Lisovskii, V. P. Semennikov, and dozens of other literary historians, bibliographers, and antiquarians. In the Soviet period, the history of the book has received attention especially in the late 1920s and early 1930s and from about 1960 until the present day.

2. Among the major fruits of this project are: S. P. Luppov, *Kniga v Rossii v XVII veke* (Leningrad, 1970), *Kniga v Rossii v pervoi chetverti XVIII veka* (Leningrad, 1973), and *Kniga v Rossii v poslepetrovskoe vremia* (Leningrad, 1976); M. I. Slukhovskii, *Russkaia biblioteka XVI–XVII vv.* (Moscow, 1973); S. P. Luppov and N. B. Paramonova, eds., *Knigotorgovoe i bibliotechnoe delo v Rossii v XVII–pervoi polovine XIX v.* (Leningrad, 1981);

A. A. Zaitseva and S. P. Luppov, eds., *Knizhnoe delo v Rossii v XVI–XIX vekakh* (Leningrad, 1980); A. A. Sidorov and S. P. Luppov, eds., *Kniga v Rossii do serediny XIX veka* (Leningrad, 1978); and E. L. Nemirovskii, *Vozniknovenie knigopechataniia v Moskve: Ivan Fedorov* (Moscow, 1964).

3. See, for example, Luppov, *Kniga . . . v XVII veke*, pp. 12–13ff.

4. See, for example, Luppov, *Kniga . . . v pervoi chetverti*, pp. 8–10ff.

5. Luppov, *Kniga . . . v XVII veke*, pp. 31–32.

6. This observation applies to most of the work being done by historical bibliographers in Leningrad and Moscow, who by training and profession have shown a far deeper intrinsic interest in the facts of book history than in engaging in theoretical debates.

7. On eighteenth-century manuscripts, see M. N. Speranskii, *Rukopisnye sborniki XVIII veka* (Moscow, 1963); M. I. Slukhovskii, *Bibliotechnoe delo v Rossii do XVIII veka* (Moscow, 1968); and V. V. Bush, "Drevnerusskaia literaturnaia traditsiia v XVIII veke," *Saratovskii gosudarstvennyi universitet: Uchenye zapiski* 4 (1925): 5.

8. Elizabeth Eisenstein, *The Printing Press as an Agent of Change*, 2 vols. (Cambridge, 1979).

9. Robert Darnton, *The Business of Enlightenment: A Publishing History of the Encyclopédie, 1775–1800* (Cambridge, Mass., 1979); Lucien Febvre and Henri-Jean Martin, *L'apparition du livre* (Paris, 1958); Robert Mandrou, *De la culture populaire aux 17e et 18e siècles: La bibliothèque bleue de Troyes* (Paris, 1964); Robert Altick, *The English Common Reader: A Social History of the Mass Reading Public, 1800–1900* (Chicago, 1963); Miriam Usher Chrisman, *Lay Culture, Learned Culture: Books and Social Change in Strasbourg, 1480–1599* (New Haven, 1982); Robert Escarpit, *Sociologie de la littérature* (Paris, 1968); *Livre et société dans la France du XVIIIe siècle* (Paris, 1965); and many others.

10. Marshall McLuhan, *The Gutenberg Galaxy: The Making of Typographical Man* (Toronto, 1962).

11. Eisenstein, *Printing Press*, especially pp. ix–xxi and 6–136.

12. Ibid., p. 75.

13. Ibid., pp. 31–32.

14. For a further discussion of this issue, see Gary Marker, "Russia and the 'Printing Revolution': Notes and Observations," *Slavic Review* 41 (Summer 1982):266–84.

15. Mandrou, *De la culture populaire*, pp. 84ff.

16. Jeremy D. Popkin, *The Right-Wing Press in France, 1792–1800* (Chapel Hill, N.C., 1980), pp. 54–83.

17. Altick, *English Common Reader*, p. 5.

18. Jürgen Habermas, *Strukturwandel der Öffentlichkeit* (Berlin, 1971), pp. 28–41, 43–46.

19. Ibid., pp. 112–26, 278–86.

20. Marc Raeff, *Origins of the Russian Intelligentsia: The Eighteenth-Century Nobility* (New York, 1966), pp. 158ff.

21. Edward Shils, *The Intellectuals and the Powers, and Other Essays* (Chicago, 1972); Lewis Coser, *Men of Ideas: A Sociologist's View* (New York, 1970); Ian Watt, *The Rise of the Novel* (Berkeley, 1957), chaps. 1 and 2; and A. S. Collins, *Authorship in the Days of Johnson* (Clifton, N.J., 1973), and *The Profession of Letters* (London, 1928).

22. Eisenstein, *Printing Press*, chap. 4; Febvre and Martin, *L'apparition*, pp. 400–438.

23. Robert Darnton, "Reading, Writing and Publishing in Eighteenth-Century France: A Case Study in the Sociology of Literature," *Daedalus* 100 (Winter 1971): 226.

24. Darnton, *Business of Enlightenment*, pp. 38–93. See also E. P. Goldschmidt's categorical and manifestly ahistorical statement that "there has never been a book that went to press unless the printer, rightly or wrongly, believed he would make a profit." E. P. Goldschmidt, *Medieval Texts and Their First Appearance in Print* (London, 1943), p. 13.

25. *Svodnyi katalog russkoi knigi grazhdanskoi pechati XVIII veka, 1725–1800*, 6 vols. (Moscow, 1962–75) (hereafter cited as *S.K.*).

CHAPTER ONE

1. Figures for the seventeenth century come from Luppov, *Kniga . . . v XVII veke*, p. 29, and A. S. Zernova, *Knigi kirillovskoi pechati, izdannye v Moskve v XVI-XVII vekakh: Svodnyi katalog* (Moscow, 1958).

2. Luppov, *Kniga . . . v pervoi chetverti*, pp. 3–5.

3. Ibid., pp. 6–55.

4. E. I. Katsprzhak, *Istoriia pis'mennosti i knigi* (Moscow, 1955), pp. 152–55. The first Russian books printed between the mid-1550s and the mid-1560s came from as yet unidentified presses. The first identifiable printing shop in Muscovy opened in Moscow, in 1564, was the press of Ivan Fedorov and Peter Mstislavets. For a fuller description of their activities, see Nemirovskii, *Vozniknovenie knigopech ataniia*.

5. Luppov, *Kniga . . . v XVII veke*, pp. 35–36; V. Ia. Adariukov, ed., *Kniga v Rossii*, 2 vols. (Moscow, 1924), 1:99–120; F. Titov, *Tipografiia Kievopecherskoi lavry: Istoricheskii ocherk, 1606–1721* (Kiev, 1916), pp. 402–4; T. N. Kameneva, "Knigopechatanie v Chernigove (1648–1818)," in A. I. Andreev, A. N. Nosov, and A. A. Novosel'skii, eds., *Problemy istochnikovedeniia* (Moscow, 1959), 8:267–313.

6. Luppov, *Kniga . . . v XVII veke*, p. 29; TsGIA, *fond* 796, *opis'* 58, no. 43, pp. 1–13.

7. Luppov, *Kniga . . . v XVII veke*, p. 17.

8. On manuscript books and woodblock prints (*lubki*), see Speranskii, *Rukopisnye sborniki*, pp. 29–31, 157–59; V. I. Malyshev, *Ust' Tsilemskie rukopisnye sborniki XVI-XX vv.* (Syktyvkar, 1960); Bush, "Literaturnaia traditsiia," pp. 1–2; N. A. Baklanov, "Russkii chitatel' XVII veka," *Drevnerusskaia literatura i ee sviazi s novym vremenem* (Moscow, 1967), pp.

158–59; and V. I. Sreznevskii, *Opisanie rukopisei i knig sobrannykh dlia Akademii nauk v Olonetskom krae* (St. Petersburg, 1913).

9. For more details on this argument, see Marker, " 'Printing Revolution,' " pp. 273–75.

10. Luppov, *Kniga . . . v XVII veke*, p. 93; Richard Hellie, *Enserfment and Military Change in Muscovy* (Chicago, 1971), pp. 188, 356–57.

11. V. I. Guerrier, *Otnosheniia Leibnitsa k Rossii i Petru Velikomu po neizdannym bumagam Leibnitsa* (St. Petersburg, 1871), pp. 74–77; Alexander Vucinich, *Science in Russian Culture: A History to 1860* (Stanford, 1963), p. 46.

12. *Khrestomatiia po istorii russkoi knigi, 1564–1917* (Moscow, 1965), p. 25; Adariukov, *Kniga v Rossii*, p. 130.

13. Adariukov, *Kniga v Rossii*, p. 134; A. N. Pypin, "Knizhnaia deitatel'nost' vremen Petra Velikogo," *Vestnik Evropy* 7 (July 1898): 254–55; B. O. Unbegaun, "Russian Grammars before Lomonosov," *Oxford Slavonic Papers* 8 (1958):106; T. A. Bykova and M. M. Gurevich, *Opisanie izdanii napechatannykh kirillitsei, 1689–Ianvar' 1725* (Moscow, 1958), pp. 318–26; A. Solov'ev, *Gosudarev pechatnyi dvor i sinodal'naia tipografiia v Moskve* (Moscow, 1903), pp. 52–53; E. N. Brailovskii, "Fedor Polikarpovich Polikarpov-Orlov, direktor Moskovskoi tipografii," *ZhMNP*, 1894, no. 295:6–12; Max Okenfuss, "The Jesuit Origins of Petrine Education," in John G. Garrard, ed. *The Eighteenth Century in Russia* (Oxford, 1973), p. 14; *Khrestomatiia*, pp. 27–29; A. V. Borodin, "Moskovskaia grazhdanskaia tipografiia i bibliotekari Kiprianovy," *Trudy Instituta knigi, dokumenta, pis'ma* 5(1936):53–109.

14. Luppov, *Kniga . . . v pervoi chetverti*, pp. 62–64; P. Pekarskii, *Nauka i literatura v Rossii pri Petre Velikom* (Moscow, 1862), 2:659–60; A. V. Gavrilov, *Ocherki istorii St. Peterburgskoi sinodal'noi tipografii* (St. Petersburg, 1911), p. 3; S. F. Ogorodnikov, *Tipografiia morskago ministerstva (istoricheskii ocherk)* (St. Petersburg, 1899), p. 30; R. M. Tonkova, "Peterburgskie tipografii pervoi chetverti XVIII veka, vkliuchaia akademicheskuiu," *Trudy Instituta knigi* 5(1936):117.

15. Luppov, *Kniga . . . v pervoi chetverti*, p. 63.

16. According to Gavrilov (*Ocherki istorii*, p. 117), there were fourteen printing presses at the Moscow Press in 1725—eleven new-type, two old-type, and one for engraving. By that time, however, the availability of several other new-type presses freed Peter from exclusive dependence on the old-type printing presses.

17. Peter went to some lengths to impose restrictions on the monastic presses. In 1720, for example, the monastic presses in Kiev and Chernigov were forbidden to publish new books without permission from the Collegium of Church Affairs (*Dukhovnaia Kollegiia*). The Chernigov press, in fact, was temporarily closed for failure to conform to synodal instructions. *PSZ*, 1st ser., no. 3653; *PSPR* 1:34 and 121–22 and 4:116.

18. N. Karamyshev, *Kratkiia istoricheskiia svedeniia o peterburgskikh tipo-*

grafiiakh s 1711 i statisticheskiia svedeniia o zavedaniiakh pechati za 1868–1895 gg. (St. Petersburg, 1895), p. 3; James Cracraft, *The Church Reform of Peter the Great* (Stanford, 1971), p. 116.

19. See the documents preserved in the collection of the *Prikaz knigopechataniia* at the Central State Archive of Ancient Acts (TsGADA), *fond* 1182—in particular, *opis'* 2, *delo* 113, 116, 123, 128, 148.

20. The references are to Georg Rimpler, *Rimplerova manira o stroenii krepostei*, translated from the German and published by the Moscow Press in December 1708 and January 1709, nos. 11 and 15 in T. A. Bykova and M. M. Gurevich, *Opisanie izdanii grazhdanskoi pechati, 1708–Ianvar' 1725* (Moscow, 1955); and Anton Ernst Borgsdorf, *Poverennye voinskie pravila kako nepriiatel'skie kreposti siloiu brati*, originally written in German but while Borgsdorf was in Russia and intended only for Russian readers, and published by the Moscow Press in January and February 1709 (Bykova and Gurevich, *Opisanie izdanii grazhdanskoi pechati*, nos. 14, 16, and 17).

21. *Geometricheskaia kniga*, published by the Moscow Press in December 1709. This was the third edition of the book (Bykova and Gurevich, *Opisanie izdanii grazhdanskoi pechati*, no. 18).

22. *Pis'ma i bumagi Imperatora Petra Velikogo* (Leningrad, 1958) 9, part 1:12–13.

23. Guido de Columba, *Istoriia v nei zhe pishet o razorenii grada Troi . . .* , published by the Moscow Press in June 1709 (Bykova and Gurevich, *Opisanie izdanii grazhdanskoi pechati*, no. 20) and republished twice during the rest of Peter's reign.

24. Leonhard Christoph Sturm, *Arkhitektura voinskaia*, translated from the German and Latin, *Architectura militaris hypotetica et eclectica*, and published by the Moscow Press on March 13, 1709 (Bykova and Gurevich, *Opisanie izdanii grazhdanskoi pechati*, no. 19). This book had been originally published in Nuremberg only seven years earlier.

25. *Pis'ma i bumagi Imperatora Petra Velikogo*, 9:31–32.

26. See the listings in Zernova, *Knigi kirillovskoi pechati*, pp. 41, 42, 69, 78, and elsewhere. On print runs, see Luppov, *Kniga . . . v XVII veke*, pp. 56–67.

27. The difficulties associated with arriving at reliable figures for the number and types of books published annually are particularly acute for the Petrine period. There have been at least three separate attempts to list them—by Pekarskii, Luppov, and Bykova and Gurevich. Luppov's figures (*Kniga . . . v pervoi chetverti*, pp. 86 and 98) are the most recent, but they are consistently much higher than the figures one gets from analyzing the catalogues of the other two. He has not provided the actual titles along with his calculations, nor has he said how he arrived at his figures. In addition, he has considered each separate issue of *Vedomosti*, the Petrine newspaper, to be a separate title, whereas the other two have treated it as only one number per year. If the additional numbers of *Vedomosti* are subtracted from Lup-

pov's figures, they become much more comparable to the other two. Even with this adjustment, however, his figures are higher.

Pekarskii, *Nauka i literatura*, did not tabulate annual figures himself, but he did compile a catalogue that listed books specifically, rather than publications of all kinds. The other catalogues, by contrast, have included laws and public notices in their figures. If the totals for these latter types of publications are added to the figures in Pekarskii's catalogue, they prove to be very close to the corrected version of Luppov's figures. However, Pekarskii's work is over a hundred years old. In the interim, several mistakes have been discovered in his dating and several titles unknown to him have been found. These discoveries are understandable, since Pekarskii worked essentially alone and used basically only the collections of the two major libraries in St. Petersburg. Nevertheless, Pekarskii's commentaries are still the most extensive ones available and his catalogue is the richest in references. But because of the various errors in it, his catalogue must be considered outdated for the present purpose.

The third source is the three-volume catalogue of Petrine books compiled by the Soviet bibliographers Bykova and Gurevich: *Opisanie izdanii napechatannykh kirillitsei, Opisanie izdanii grazhdanskoi pechati*, and *Opisanie izdanii napechatannykh pri Petre I: Dopolneniia i prilozheniia* (Moscow, 1965). Their data are the most reliable, since they provide all the titles left out by Pekarskii as well as correcting many of his mistakes. However, their figures are considerably lower than the others' for the first several years of Peter's reign. One reason is their exclusion of all books "narrowly relating to the church service in its traditional form," most prayer books, catechisms, and works of "pure theology" (Bykova and Gurevich, *Opisanie izdanii napechatannykh kirillitsei*, pp. 6ff.). Fortunately, this gap—which does not exist in Pekarskii's catalogue—can be filled by using the appropriate sections of still another catalogue: A. S. Zernova, comp. and ed., *Svodnyi katalog russkoi knigi kirrilovskoi pechati XVIII veka* (Moscow, 1968). This catalogue includes religious works published in the old orthography but does not include laws, notices, or any other publications that do not qualify as books. Although it, too, is far from complete for the century as a whole, most Soviet specialists believe that it is reasonably accurate for the Petrine period.

What I have done, then, is to make my own calculations based on the Bykova and Gurevich volumes and the one compiled by Zernova. For the rest of the chapter, the figures for total publications that appear in the text and the tables are those that I have calculated myself.

28. On the change from "holy tsar" to "emperor," see Michael Cherniavsky, *Tsar and People: Studies in Russian Myths* (New York, 1969), pp. 44–101.

29. S. L. Baehr, " 'Fortuna Redux': The Iconography of Happiness in Eighteenth-Century Russian Courtly Spectacle," in A. G. Cross, ed., *Great Britain and Russia in the Eighteenth Century: Contacts and Comparisons* (Newtonville, Mass., 1979), pp. 109–14; B. W. Maggs, "Firework Art and Lit-

erature: Eighteenth-Century Pyrotechnical Tradition in Russia and Western Europe," *Slavonic and East European Review* 54 (1976):24–40. The classic source on fireworks remains D. A. Rovinskii, *Opisanie feierverkov i il-liuminatsii 1674–1891 gg.* (St. Petersburg, 1903).

30. Baehr, " 'Fortuna Redux'," p. 110.

31. *PSPR* 1:252; *PSPR* (St. Petersburg, 1873), 2:670; T. S. Maikova, "Petr I, 'Gistoriia Sveiskoi voiny,' " in N. I. Pavlenko, ed., *Rossiia v period reform Petra I* (Moscow, 1973), pp. 103–32.

32. See, for example, TsGADA, *fond* 1182, *opis'* 2, nos. 113–16, 128; Pekarskii, *Nauka i literatura* 2:645-650; *PSPR* 1:97, 526, 669.

33. Pekarskii, *Nauka i literatura* 2:664–65.

34. Ibid., pp. 677–80; Max J. Okenfuss, *The Discovery of Childhood in Eighteenth-Century Russia: The Evidence of the Slavic Primer* (Newtonville, Mass., 1979), pp. 11ff; TsGIA, *fond* 796, *opis'* 58, no. 43, pp. 13–23.

35. Okenfuss, *Discovery of Childhood*, pp. 43–56.

36. *Zakonodatel'nye akty Petra I* (Moscow, 1945), pp. 42, 84, 126; Pypin, *Knizhnaia deiatel'nost'*, p. 260.

37. *Vedomosti* is considered by most specialists to have been the first Russian newspaper. Other scholars, however, argue that a seventeenth-century journal, *Vesti-Kuranty*, in which public notices and announcements appeared deserves that status. *Kuranty*, however, came out very irregularly over several decades and then only in manuscript. Technically, therefore, it was neither a periodical nor a publication. Substantively, moreover, it was available in so few copies that its readership can hardly have included more than a handful of people. For a different opinion, see A. N. Shlosberg, *Nachalo periodicheskoi pechati v Rossii* (Leningrad, 1958), p. 58.

38. S. M. Tomsinskii, *Pervaia pechatnaia gazeta Rossii (1702–1727 gg.)* (Perm, 1959), pp. 54–55, 126–53.

39. *Vedomosti vremeni Petra Velikogo, 1702–1719* (Moscow, 1906), 2:61.

40. *PSZ*, 1st ser., no. 1921.

41. Tomsinskii, *Pervaia pechatnaia gazeta*, p. 41.

42. Ibid., pp. 69, 97.

43. Ibid., p. 41; P. N. Berkov, *Istoriia russkoi zhurnalistiki XVIII veka* (Moscow, 1952), p. 46.

44. *Vedomosti vremeni Petra Velikogo* 2:86.

45. Tomsinskii, *Pervaia pechatnaia gazeta*, p. 41.

46. Berkov, *Istoriia russkoi zhurnalistiki*, p. 46.

47. *Vedomosti vremeni Petra Velikogo* 2:79–84. In theory, the available figures could be used to develop general information on the percentage of newspapers sold, the percentage given away, and the percentage undistributed. Unfortunately, too often the figures presented in the sources do not add up properly. Thus, for all but two issues printed in 1709, the totals given for sales, handouts, and remainders do not equal the number given for the total size of the editions. In most cases, the last figure is considerably lower than the sum of the others. For example, issue no. 8 of 1709 shows

150 copies printed, with 168 distributed at no charge, 23 sold, and 55 remaining, a total of 246. Issue no. 9 of the same year shows 500 copies printed, with 278 distributed at no charge and 318 sold, a total of 596. It is likely that the numbers given for total copies are incorrect, since in each case the difference is about 100. But that is only a guess.

48. James R. Sutherland, "The Circulation of Newspapers and Literary Periodicals, 1700-1730," *Library*, 4th ser., 15 (1943):111–16.

49. For a fuller discussion of military books, see E. E. Kolosov, "Russkaia voennaia kniga petrovskogo vremeni," *Kniga* 16 (1968):113–28. On Peter's involvement, see *Khrestomatiia*, pp. 38–42.

50. On the role of history books under Peter, see Pypin, *Knizhnaia deiatel'nost'*, pp. 264–67.

51. J. L. Black, *Citizens for the Fatherland: Education, Educators, and Pedagogical Ideals in Eighteenth-Century Russia* (New York, 1979), p. 63; Okenfuss, *Discovery of Childhood*, pp. 43–56.

52. Okenfuss, "Jesuit Origins," p. 14.

53. N. P. Kiselev, "O moskovskom knigopechatanii XVII veka," *Kniga* 2 (1960):130–36.

54. Pekarskii, *Nauka i literatura* 2:677–80.

55. Gavrilov, *Ocherki istorii*, pp. 113ff.; Pypin, *Knizhnaia deiatel'nost'*, pp. 260–61.

56. Luppov, *Kniga . . . v pervoi chetverti*, pp. 3–5.

57. Ibid., p. 155.

58. Ibid., pp. 8, 154–55.

59. Gavrilov, *Ocherki istorii*, p. 168; Luppov, *Kniga . . . v pervoi chetverti*, pp. 116–18.

60. Gavrilov, *Ocherki istorii*, p. 63; Luppov, *Kniga . . . v pervoi chetverti*, pp. 79–80, 119.

61. Solov'ev, *Gosudarev pechatnyi dvor*, p. 75.

62. Pekarskii, *Nauka i literatura* 1:677–80.

63. Ibid., p. 641.

64. Ibid., p. 663; Luppov, *Kniga . . . v pervoi chetverti*, p. 76.

65. Scattered sources give some indication of the cash value of these books. See Pekarskii, *Nauka i literatura* 2:680, which shows the Moscow Press sending over 8,000 rubles worth of books to various governmental bodies between 1721 and 1724 without receiving payment.

66. This information comes from Luppov's chart, but it excludes the value of books given out in wages. Luppov, *Kniga . . . v pervoi chetverti*, p. 199.

67. Ibid., p. 114.

68. Whether this decline reflects a diminished volume of book purchases depends in part on the course of book prices. As a rule, prices reflected costs of production, which were high, both in the seventeenth century and during Peter's reign. Most books cost between fifty kopeks and one-and-a-half rubles, clearly more than most people could pay. But some, such as the primers, sold for as little as three kopeks. These prices do seem to show a decline from the seventeenth century, but *not* during the course of Peter's

reign itself. On prices, see Luppov, *Kniga . . . v XVII veke*, pp. 54–73; Luppov, *Kniga . . . v pervoi chetverti*, pp. 146–54; V. Adrianova, *Materialy dlia istorii tsen na knigi v drevnei rusi XVI–XVIII vv.* (Moscow, 1912).

69. Pekarskii, *Nauka i literatura* 2:677–88; Gavrilov, *Ocherki istorii*, appendix 1; Luppov, *Kniga . . . v pervoi chetverti*, pp. 76, 114–15, 135–45.

70. Pekarskii, *Nauka i literatura* 2:683–88; Luppov, *Kniga . . . v pervoi chetverti*, p. 137.

71. Luppov, *Kniga . . . v pervoi chetverti*, pp. 140–41.

72. Luppov, *Kniga . . . v XVII veke*, pp. 93, 124, 183; Speranskii, *Rukopisnye sborniki*, p. 158.

73. Luppov, *Kniga . . . v pervoi chetverti*, p. 131. Luppov does not describe the listings of religious books.

74. Pekarskii, *Nauka i literatura* 2:677–80.

75. Ibid., pp. 664–65.

76. Ibid., p. 665.

77. Evidence of the continued vitality of hand copying under Peter comes from Speranskii, *Rukopisnye sborniki*, pp. 16ff.; N. N. Rozov, *Russkaia rukopisnaia kniga* (Leningrad, 1971), pp. 87–103; A. S. Myl'nikov, "Kul'turno-istoricheskoe znachenie rukopisnoi knigi v period stanovleniia knigopechataniia," *Kniga* 9 (1964):39–41; A. N. Pypin, "Dlia liubitelei knizhnoi stariny," *Sbornik Obshchestva liubitelei rossiiskoi slovesnosti na 1891 g.* (Moscow, 1891), pp. 194–276.

CHAPTER TWO

1. Gavrilov, *Ocherki istorii*, pp. 113–14.

2. Luppov, *Kniga . . . v pervoi chetverti*, p. 75.

3. Luppov, *Kniga . . . v poslepetrovskoe vremia*, p. 139.

4. Tonkova, "Peterburgskie tipografii," p. 115.

5. Gavrilov, *Ocherki istorii*, p. 129.

6. Ibid., p. 129; *PSZ*, no. 5175. The existing records show that the Senate also maintained its Moscow Press despite the terms of this order.

7. The figures presented in this chapter and in the rest of this study come from a handful of catalogues. The most important of these is the five-volume *Svodnyi katalog* and the volume of additions and corrections, *Svodnyi katalog russkoi knigi grazhdanskoi pechati XVIII veka, 1725–1800: Dopolneniia razyskivaemye izdaniia utochneniia* (Moscow, 1975) (hereafter cited as *S.K.*, vol. 6). Neither of these catalogues lists one-page notices or short individual laws. They do, however, list law codes and collections of laws, as well as lengthy statutes, and regulations. As the titles suggest, neither catalogue contains books published in the old orthography. Such books are listed in Zernova, *Svodnyi katalog . . . kirillovskoi pechati*.

The six-volume *Svodnyi katalog* is the latest and most comprehensive catalogue of eighteenth-century Russian publications, but it is by no means the only one. Until it was published in the mid-1960s, scholars depended on a similar catalogue prepared in the first quarter of the nineteenth century by Vasilii Sopikov, *Opyt rossiiskoi bibliografii*, 5 vols. (St. Petersburg, 1813–21). Sopikov was an important bookseller and bibliographer in his day, and there will be occasion to talk about him later. The annual figures one gets from his catalogue are very close to those one gets from *Svodnyi katalog* and the curves one gets from the two sets of figures are virtually identical. See V. V. Sipovskii, "Iz istorii russkoi literatury XVIII veka (opyt statisticheskikh nabliudenii)," *Izvestiia otdeleniia russkago iazyka i slovesnosti Imperatorskoi Akademii nauk* 6 (1901):120–65. Because the figures from the two catalogues are so similar, I have quoted only those from the *Svodnyi katalog*. See Luppov, *Kniga . . . v poslepetrovskoe vremia*, p. 55, for somewhat different figures.

8. S. M. Troitskii, *Finansovaia politika russkogo absoliutizma v XVIII veke* (Moscow, 1966), pp. 240–45.

9. Vucinich, *Science in Russian Culture*, p. 89; K. V. Ostrovitianov, *Istoriia Akademii nauk SSSR*, 2 vols. to date (Moscow, 1958–), 1:430–35.

10. G. N. Sokolovskii et al., eds., *Akademicheskaia tipografiia, 1728–1928* (Leningrad, 1928), p. 8.

11. Some sources give 1727 as the founding date, others give 1728. Recently, Soviet bibliographers have found a couple of Academy publications that they have been able to date to 1727, so that this uncertainty seems to have been resolved. See *S.K.* 3, no. 7450, and 4, no. 349. On the question of the founding date, see *Akademicheskaia tipografiia*, p. 10, and S. N. Sredinskii, *O vremeni osnovaniia akademicheskoi tipografii* (Baku, 1929), p. 250.

12. *Akademicheskaia tipografiia*, p. 11.

13. Luppov provides figures that cover the period from 1725 to 1740. Judging from his numbers, the Academy printed just over half (309 out of 616) of all titles in that time and about 60 percent of all books between 1727 and 1740. At that point, the academy's percentage declines somewhat, but it is nevertheless about half for the entire thirty-year period. Luppov, *Kniga . . . v poslepetrovskoi vremia*, p. 50.

14. For a fuller discussion of the relations between the conference and the chancellery, see Vucinich, *Science in Russian Culture*, pp. 82–89.

15. Ibid., p. 75; P. Pekarskii, *Istoriia Imperatorskoi Akademii nauk*, 2 vols. (St. Petersburg, 1873), 1:x–xii.

16. Unfortunately, there are no complete catalogues of the German- or Romance-language books published at the Academy. This absence impedes the determination of the amount of activity in which these presses engaged. However, catalogues of books for sale at the Academy's bookshop in the 1730s and 1740s show that almost all scientific works sold there were published in Latin, in German, or in a joint Russian-German edition; *S.K.* 3, nos. 8842, 8843, and 8844. Also, a German-language edition of the official newspaper, *St. Peterburgskiie vedomosti*, was published at the Academy of Sciences Press.

17. Traditionally, it has been argued that instruction in Latin was the major barrier to prospective Russian students and that the language of instruction

became a bone of contention between the Academy and the educated public. Recently, it has been shown that students in Russia's religious academies were taught in Latin and that those few Russians who did enroll in the academy university classes or gymnasium were graduates of these academies. The scholar responsible for these findings was unable to find any complaints from educated Russians about instruction in Latin. Okenfuss, "Jesuit Origins," pp. 125–26. These observations bring the traditional view into question. Still, the large and persistent dropout rate of Russian students from the Academy, as well as declining enrollments (the number of entering students declined from 114 in 1727 to 19 in 1737), implies that major barriers, whether cultural or linguistic, inhibited the educational process. Vucinich, *Science in Russian Culture*, pp. 78–79.

18. Quoted in Vucinich, *Science in Russian Culture*, p. 85.

19. Ibid., p. 84.

20. Eduard Winter, "Euler und die Begegnung den deutschen mit russischen Aufklärung," in *Die Deutsch-Russische Begegnung und Leonhard Euler* (Berlin, 1958), pp. 1–18; Eduard Winter, *Halle als Ausgangs punkt der Deutschen Russlandkunde im 18-Jahrhundert* (Berlin, 1953).

21. It was replaced in 1748 by a new series, the *Novi commentarii.*

22. N. V. Zdobnov, *Istoriia russkoi bibliografii ot drevnogo perioda do nachala XX veka* (Moscow, 1944), p. 33. See also Luppov's discussion of the translation, in which he speculates that the Academy deliberately excluded from the Russian translation the more difficult essays in the natural sciences, in an effort to minimize the lack of understanding. If that is so, then Müller's observation is all the more reflective of the Academy's dilemma. Luppov, *Kniga . . . v poslepetrovskoe vremia*, p. 68.

23. Vucinich, *Science in Russian Culture*, pp. 92ff.

24. *S.K.* 4:63–66.

25. A. V. Zapadov, *Russkaia zhurnalistika 30-kh–60-kh godov XVIII v.* (Moscow, 1957), pp. 4–6; V. G. Berezina, *Istoriia russkoi zhurnalistiki XVIII–XIX vekov* (Moscow, 1963), p. 23.

26. This conclusion runs counter to the frequently made suggestion that, during his tenure as editor of the newspaper after 1748, Lomonosov increased the number of translations that appeared in it and saw to it that all translations were written in a style that people could understand. See *S.K.* 4:62; Berezina, *Istoriia russkoi zhurnalistiki*, p. 23; Zapadov, *Russkala zhurnalistika*, pp. 4–6; A. G. Dement'ev et al., *Russkaia periodicheskaia pechat', 1702–1894* (Moscow, 1959), p. 19. A scanning of selected issues from before and after 1748 does not reveal any increase in the number of translations, nor does there appear to be any change in the type of articles that were translated.

27. *PSZ*, no. 8529.

28. Ibid., no. 9903.

29. *Mesiachnye istoricheskie, genealogicheskie, i geograficheskie primechaniia v Vedomostiakh* (St. Petersburg, 1728–48).

30. Zapadov, *Russkaia zhurnalistika*, pp. 9–11; *S.K.* 4:170–71; Luppov, *Kniga . . . v poslepetrovskoe vremia*, pp. 63–64.

31. Zapadov, *Russkaia zhurnalistika*, p. 10; G. Balitskii, "Zarozhdenie periodicheskoi pechati v Rossii," *ZhMNP*, new series, part 17 (1908), pp. 65–86.

32. Under Peter the Great, translators had worked either for the College of Foreign Affairs or the Slavonic Academy in Moscow.

33. *Istoriia Akademii nauk* 1:54.

34. Some recent Soviet scholarship has given that title to the seventeenth-century monk and religious thinker, Simeon Polotskii. Because of his position as the overseer of the so-called upper press (*verkhniaia tipografiia*) of the *pechatnyi dvor*, his interest in disseminating and propagandizing his own, secretly Catholic, theology, and his particular desire to develop a religious literary language as an alternative to Church Slavonic, Polotskii has at times been dubbed Russia's first professional writer.

Without denying that Polotskii was an extremely important figure in seventeenth-century Russian culture, and without minimizing the extent to which some of his ideas about language and the printing press anticipated those of eighteenth-century figures, I nevertheless doubt whether he can be linked very closely to some sort of cultural modernity, at least in so far as language and printing are concerned. Though he authored a primer, he never attempted to create a genuine literary vernacular to conform more closely with spoken Russian. With the exception of the primer, moreover, his writings did not gain much circulation outside of the Orthodox church. Indeed, it is not at all clear that he ever thought of the laity as his primary or desired audience. Even his role in the upper press was a modest affair, in which he printed very few books and was, in general, quite careful not to challenge the positions set forth by the church. See A. N. Robinson, "Simeon Polotskii i russkii literaturnyi protsess," in A. S. Demin, ed., *Simeon Polotskii i ego knigoizdatel'skaia deiatel'nost'* (Moscow, 1982), pp. 7–45.

35. Pekarskii, *Istoriia Imperatorskoi Akademii nauk* 1:2, 4, 6.

36. *S.K.* 3, no. 7130.

37. Quoted in P. N. Berkov, *Lomonosov i literaturnaia polemika ego vremeni, 1750–1765* (Leningrad, 1936), pp. 20–21.

38. Pekarskii, *Istoriia Imperatorskoi Akademii nauk* 2:43; V. N. Peretts, "Italianskaia intermediia 1730-kh godov v stikhotvornom russkom perevode," in V. N. Peretts, ed., *Starinnyi teatr v Rossii XVII–XVIII vv.: Sbornik statei* (St. Petersburg, 1923), p. 147.

39. For a competent English-language summary of this debate, see Rimvydas Silbajoris, *Russian Versification* (New York, 1968), pp. 1–35.

40. Trediakovskii's speech can be found in many collections; see, for example, A. Kunik, ed., *Sbornik materialov dlia istorii Imperatorskoi Akademii nauk*, 2 vols. (St. Petersburg, 1865), 1:10–15.

41. Berkov claims that Trediakovskii himself had abandoned his slavicisms by the time he returned from Paris in 1730 and that, in spite of his theories,

few examples of them can be found in his subsequent work. P. N. Berkov, "Des relations littéraires franco-russes entre 1720 et 1730: Trediakovskij et l'abbé Girard," *Revue des études slaves* 35 (1958):7–14.

42. *Materialy dlia istorii Imperatorskoi Akademii nauk*, 10 vols (St. Petersburg, 1885–1900), 8:77 (hereafter cited as *Materialy*).

43. Ibid. 8:6.

44. *S.K.* 3, no. 7708 and p. 209.

45. The relevant documents are in *Materialy* 2:45, 3:506, and 5:86. Anne patronized a history of Japan that consisted of a three-part translation of three different French histories of Japan. It was published in 1734 in an edition of 1,250 copies under the title of *Opisanie o Iapone* (*S.K.* 2, no. 4961). A volume on Peter II, entitled *Raspolozhenie uchenii E. I. V. Petra Vtorago*, was written by Georg Bilfinger and was published in 1731 in a print run of 1,200 copies (*S.K.* 1, no. 575). Apparently, some stories and plays written in French were ordered by Elizabeth (*Materialy* 8:94, 565), but I could find no examples of her ordering books in Russian.

46. RO GPB, *fond* 1105 (Shamrai Collection), no. 37, pp. 1–3, 16.

47. A. D. Bochagov, *Knizhnaia palata Akademii nauk, 1728–1740* (St. Petersburg, 1893), p. 10.

48. See Stählin's report on the book trade in 1756, in RO GPB, *fond* 871 (Stählin Collection), no. 108, p. 2. In 1748, Johann Taubert made several reports from abroad of foreign markets for Russian books and of Russian markets for foreign books. *Materialy* 8:606, 9:366–74, and 10:260–65.

49. *Materialy* 5:640–42.

50. See, for example, reports of 1736 which called for a more systematic communication of academy listings in the provinces: *Materialy* 2:803; I. S. Beliaev, "Izdaniia Akademii nauk v 1736 g.," *ChIOIDR* 3(1896):36–37.

51. The catalogues came out every two to three years in the 1730s and 1740s, listing titles in alphabetical order. Begun with only 55 titles in 1735, they grew to include more than 150 by the 1750s.

52. Translators' salaries ran from 120 to 200 rubles a year in the mid-1740s, but bonuses for best sellers enabled some translators to enhance their salaries substantially. See the salary list in *Materialy* 8:77.

53. Marcus Antonius Aurelius, *Zhitie i dela Marka Avreliia Antonina, Tsesaria Rimskago, S.K.* 1, nos. 45 and 46, translated from the German and published in 1740 (the size of the edition is unknown); Baltasar Gracian y Morales, *Gratsian, pridvornyi chelovek, S.K.* 1, no. 1613, translated from the French and published in an edition of 1,250 in 1741; and Franciscus Philippus Florinus, *Florinova Ekonomia, S.K.* 3, no. 7826, translated from the German and published in 1738 (the size of the edition is unknown).

54. *Materialy* 8:526–27, 531. Aesop's Fables, *S.K.* 3, no. 8548, was published in an edition of 1,200 in 1747; Jean Baptiste Morvan de Bellegarde, *Sovershennoe vospitanie detei, S.K.* 1, no. 477, translated from the French and published in 1747 (the size of the edition is unknown); and Hilmar Curas, *Vvedenie v general'nuiu istoriiu, S.K.* 2, nos. 3355 and 3356, trans-

lated from the German and published in editions of 1,200 each in 1747 and 1750.

55. Vasilii Lebedev's translation of *The Travels around the World of Admiral Lord Anson* was accepted for cash by the academy and published in a print run of 1,700 copies. *Materialy* 8:526–31, 9:17,63–64, and 305, and 10:339–40.

56. *Materialy* 7:483–84.

57. Raeff, *Russian Intelligentsia*, p. 139; Berkov, *Lomonosov*, p. 77.

58. *Materialy* 9:533 and 10:678.

59. TsGIA, *fond* 796, *opis'* 58, no. 43, pp. 24–39.

60. In the 1720s, the Senate Press evolved into little more than a house organ, publishing only the most official kinds of publications—largely laws and regulations—tempered occasionally with a mathematics or engineering text. But the Senate was not really very active in the publication of any sort of books. Of the seventy-five titles it issued between 1725 and 1755, thirty-one were published before 1732. In other words, for the last twenty-four years of this period, the Senate was publishing fewer than two titles a year.

61. Perhaps the most active scholastic user of the Academy Press at this time was the gentry Cadet Infantry Academy. Among the books published or reissued at its request were various grammars and history texts. In addition, the Infantry Academy requested the publication of several books in foreign languages so that its German students, who apparently did not read Russian, would have something to use. Books ordered for these students included poetry collections, literature, history texts, and a German Bible. *Materialy* 2:572, 7:55 and 449, and 9:308 and 404; and AAN, *fond* 3 (Papers of the Academy Chancellery), *opis'* 1, no. 79, pp. 157–69.

62. On laws, see Luppov, *Kniga . . . v poslepetrovskoe vremia*, pp. 58–61.

63. Ibid., pp. 88, 142–43.

64. TsGIA, *fond* 796, *opis'* 58, no. 43, pp. 24–39.

65. *PSPR* 5:401 and 7:21–28; Zernova and Kameneva, *Svodnyi katalog*, no. 2; Kameneva, "Knigopechatanie v Chernigove," p. 305; and T. A. Bykova, "Knigopechatanie v Rossii vo 2-oi chetverti XVIII v. (Fevral' 1725–Oktiabr' 1740 gg.)," *Kniga* 4 (1961):231.

66. *PSPR* 5:401.

67. Ibid. 9:159–60.

68. Ibid. 5:337 and 10:232 and 346.

69. Luppov, *Kniga . . . v poslepetrovskoe vremia*, pp. 142–43.

70. These figures are derived from Zernova, *Svodnyi katalog . . . kirillovskoi pechati*, which remains the most complete catalogue of eighteenth-century books in the old orthography. Over the past decade, however, Soviet bibliographers have shown that Zernova's catalogue is far from complete; there are at least several hundred publications from the years between 1725 and 1800 that she missed. Unfortunately, we do not yet have an updated and authoritative catalogue to replace it, and, as a consequence, I have been forced to depend upon Zernova for data on old-orthography books, even

though her figures are now out of date. See T. A. Bykova, *Katalog russkoi knigi kirillovskoi pechati peterburgskoi tipografii XVIII v.* (Leningrad, 1971), and T. A. Afanas'eva, "Svetskaia kirillicheskaia kniga v Rossii v XVIII veke (Problemy izdaniia, repertuara, rasprostraneniia, chteniia)," Candidate's diss., Krupskaia Institute of Culture (Leningrad, 1983), pp. 1–10.

71. *PSPR* 10:576–79.
72. Gregory L. Freeze, *The Russian Levites: Parish Clergy in the Eighteenth Century* (Cambridge, 1977), pp. viii, 147–83.
73. *PSPR* 11:152.
74. Zernova, *Svodnyi katalog*, nos. 1390 and 1397.
75. TsGIA, *fond* 796, *opis'* 58, no. 43, pp. 1–39.
76. Bykova, "Knigopechatanie v Rossii," p. 236.
77. *PSPR* 2:121.
78. Ibid. 2:207.
79. Luppov, *Kniga . . . v poslepetrovskoe vremia*, p. 93.
80. Vucinich, *Science in Russian Culture*, pp. 87–88.
81. *PSPR* 10:250; *Materialy* 7:341; Luppov, *Kniga . . . v poslepetrovskoe vremia*, pp. 93–100; *Akademicheskaia tipografiia*, pp. 17–18; *PSZ*, nos. 6240 and 7715.
82. *Materialy* 7:398; Luppov, *Kniga . . . v poslepetrovskoe vremia*, p. 94.
83. *PSPR* 10:250.
84. *PSZ*, no. 7715.
85. Ibid., no. 8832.
86. Ibid., no. 9794.
87. Ibid., no. 9805.
88. *Akademicheskaia tipografiia*, p. 25; *PSZ*, no. 8832.
89. The regulations are reprinted in *Istoriia Akademii nauk* 1:446.
90. D. V. Tiulichev, "Tsenzura izdanii Akademii nauk v XVIII v.," in *Sbornik statei i materialov po knigovedeniiu*, 3 vols. (Leningrad, 1970), 2:79–84.

CHAPTER THREE

1. Walter Gleason, *Moral Idealists, Bureaucracy, and Catherine the Great* (New Brunswick, 1981), p. 3.
2. See, for example, Nicholas V. Riasanovsky, *A Parting of Ways: Government and the Educated Public in Russia, 1801–1855* (Oxford, 1976), p. 25; Andrzej Walicki, *A History of Russian Thought from the Enlightenment to Marxism* (Stanford, 1979), pp. xvi–xvii; William Edward Brown, *A History of Eighteenth-Century Russian Literature* (Ann Arbor, 1980), pp. 160ff.
3. Of course, there were several, often highly prominent, exceptions to this rule: Lomonosov was the son of a peasant and Chulkov was the son of a merchant. But the fact remains that most of the leading literary figures came from the gentry. Even some of Shtrange's "democratic intelligentsia" were gentry. M. M. Shtrange, *Demokraticheskaia intelligentsiia Rossii v XVIII veke* (Moscow, 1965), pp. 9–28; Raeff, *Russian Intelligentsia*, p. 9; David

Ransel, *The Politics of Catherinian Russia: The Panin Party* (New Haven, 1975), pp. 211–26; Gleason, *Moral Idealists*, pp. 114–15.

4. Gleason, *Moral Idealists*, pp. 57, 92–94; G. Makogonenko, *Denis FonVizin: Tvorcheskii put'* (Moscow, 1951), p. 4; Marc Raeff, "Les Slaves, les Allemands, et les 'Lumières'," *Canadian Slavic Studies* 1 (1967):521–51; Riasanovsky, *Parting of Ways*, p. 22.

5. Shtrange, *Demokraticheskaia intelligentsiia*, pp. 4ff.

6. Black, *Citizens for the Fatherland*, p. 35.

7. Okenfuss and Cross have shown that the impact of education abroad was significantly greater than previous scholarship has believed. But the number of students abroad, even by their estimates, was not very great. In any event, foreign education did not begin to satisfy the government's growing demand for trained servitors. A. G. Cross, *By the Banks of the Thames: Russians in Eighteenth-Century Britain* (Newtonville, Mass., 1980), pp. 92–145; Max J. Okenfuss, "Russian Students in Europe in the Age of Peter the Great," in Garrard, *Eighteenth Century*, pp. 131–45.

8. Shtrange, *Demokraticheskaia intelligentsiia*, pp. 32–33.

9. Ibid., p. 23; Freeze, *Russian Levites*, p. 88; Luppov, *Kniga . . . v poslepetrovskoe vremia*, pp. 28–29; P. Znamenskii, *Dukhovnye shkoly v Rossii do reformy 1808 goda* (Kazan, 1887), p. 185.

10. Shtrange, *Demokraticheskaia intelligentsiia*, p. 11.

11. Ibid., p. 11.

12. Ibid., p. 21; *Istoricheskoe obozrenie gosudarstvennogo kadetskogo korpusa* (St. Petersburg, 1862), pp. 85–100.

13. Shtrange says that 4,000 soldiers received such training in the 1730s. By the mid-1770s the figure had risen to 10,000. Shtrange, *Demokraticheskaia intelligentsiia*, p. 16.

14. M. T. Beliavskii, *M. V. Lomonosov i osnovanie Moskovskogo universiteta* (Moscow, 1956), pp. 1–10; *Istoriia Moskovskogo universiteta*, 2 vols. (Moscow, 1955), 1:30.

15. Nicholas Hans, *History of Russian Education Policy, 1701–1917* (London, 1931), p. 16; *Istoriia Moskovskogo universiteta* 1:67.

16. Shtrange, *Demokraticheskaia intelligentsiia*, p. 53.

17. The lists of students attending the gymnasia were published once or twice a year as supplements to the *Moscow News*. N. N. Mel'nikova, *Izdaniia napechatannye v tipografii Moskovskogo universiteta, XVIII veka* (Moscow, 1966), pp. 446–47.

18. Hans, *Russian Educational Policy*, p. 64; Black, *Citizens for the Fatherland*, pp. 152–71.

19. Beliavskii, *Lomonosov*, p. 121; *Biograficheskii slovar' studentov Imperatorskogo Moskovskogo universiteta i chlenov gimnazii blagorodnoi s 1756 po 1760* (Moscow, n.d.).

20. Raeff, *Russian Intelligentsiia*, p. 138.

21. At the Infantry Corps, for example, 34 out of 43 instructors taught courses

in the liberal arts. At the Naval Corps, the figures were 20 out of 22. Shtrange, *Demokraticheskaia intelligentsiia*, p. 79.

22. Similar ideas regarding modern universities as thresholds of culture and civilization can be found in several contemporary sociological studies of intellectual life; see, e.g., Talcott Parsons, *Essays in Sociological Theory* (New York, 1935); Edward Shils, *The Intellectuals and the Powers and Other Essays* (Chicago, 1972); Reinhard Bendix, *Embattled Reason: Essays on Social Knowledge* (New York, 1970).

23. See the index of publishing houses in *S.K.* 5:278–90. The other new publishing houses of this period were the Military College Press (1763), two small military presses (1764 and 1774), and a new civil-orthography press for the Synod in St. Petersburg (1764).

24. Ogorodnikov, *Tipografiia morskago ministerstva*, p. 5; RO GPB, *fond* 1105, no. 24, pp. 1–2.

25. Ogorodnikov, *Tipografiia morskago ministerstva*, pp. 6, 7.

26. D. D. Shamrai, "Tsenzurnyi nadzor nad tipografiei sukhoputnogo shliakhetnogo korpusa," *Vosemnadtsatyi vek* 2 (1940):294.

27. Ibid., p. 302; Ogorodnikov, *Tipografiia morskago ministerstva*, p. 7.

28. The Artillery and Engineering Corps, although similar to the other corps in many ways, differed from them in the management of its press. Between 1765 and 1775 it maintained its official character, publishing few books and eschewing outside support. As a consequence, the artillery cadets involved themselves rather actively in the work of the other cadet presses. In the late 1770s, however, the Artillery Corps changed its course entirely by leasing its press to private concerns, which gained almost complete authority in editorial affairs. At that point, the Artillery Corps Press began to publish a large number of privately patronized literary manuscripts.

29. The exact figure for the Naval Cadet Press is 130 books published between 1763 and 1775.

30. Shamrai, "Tsenzurnyi nadzor," pp. 311–28.

31. A number of title pages make reference to patrons. For example, a translation of Voltaire's *Zadig* was published by the Naval Cadet Press in 1765 "on the account of the press's manager, Kostelev." *S. K.* 1, no. 1099. Indirect verification also comes from the fact that the subsidy to the press remained constant during the years in which publishing was expanding rapidly.

32. Raeff has made a similar point about the cadet corps and translated literature. However, he places its center in the literary circle of the 1740s of Sumarokov, Kheraskov, I. P. Elagin, and Peter Panin. But if one focuses upon the rate at which cadets produced translations and published them, the 1760s look far more impressive. Raeff, *Russian Intelligentsia*, p. 139; Gleason, *Moral Idealists*, p. 61; M. Khmyrov, "Ocherk zhizni i literaturnoi deiatel'nosti Sumarokova," in V. Pokrovskii, ed., *Aleksandr Petrovich Sumarokov* (Moscow, 1905), p. 17; *S.K.* 1, nos. 1099, 1104, 1299, and 2, nos. 4305, 4317.

33. Published in 1764 by the Infantry Corps Press.

34. S. P. Pisarev, "Instruktsiia o vospitanii, 1772–1775," *Russkaia starina* 31 (1881):660–61.

35. A Senate report of 1775 states that the cadet presses have been allowed to publish books for general use in the past and should be allowed to do so in the future, as long as the books are not offensive. It made no other recommendations. TsGADA, *fond* 17, no. 259, pp. 1, 2.

36. Shamrai, "Tsenzurnyi nadzor," pp. 311–29; RO GPB, *fond* 1105, no. 20, pp. 58, 77–82.

37. Shtrange, *Demokraticheskaia intelligentsiia*, pp. 85–109; Iu. Ia. Kogan', *Prosvetitel' XVIII veka Ia. P. Kozel'skii* (Moscow, 1958), p. 42.

38. Shtrange, *Demokraticheskaia intelligentsiia*, p. 108.

39. *S.K.* 2, no. 4289, published in 1766. See also the listings in Shtrange, *Demokraticheskaia intelligentsiia*, p. 284.

40. *S.K.* 1, nos. 262 and 844, and 2, nos. 2109–2112, 2297; Shtrange, *Demokraticheskaia intelligentsiia*, p. 292.

41. For a discussion of the amateur writer in seventeenth-century France, see David Pottinger, *The French Book Trade in the Ancien Régime, 1500–1791* (Cambridge, 1958), pp. 90–94.

42. The first of these catalogues appeared in 1761. Between 1764 and 1776 five additional Infantry Press catalogues were published. Between 1771 and 1774 the Naval Press issued three catalogues. *S.K.* 3, nos. 8947–8952, 8902–8904.

43. Only occasionally does it appear that privately financed books were excluded from the catalogues. In those instances, presumably, the author or patron received the entire edition.

44. *PSZ*, no. 10346.

45. N. A. Penchko, *Osnovanie Moskovskogo universiteta* (Moscow, 1953), p. 67.

46. Mel'nikova, "Izdanniia napechatannye," p. 3; I. Snegirev, "Ocherki istorii tipografii Moskovskogo universiteta s 1755 po 1812 god," *Moskovskiia vedomosti*, 1854, no. 111:1395; Stepan Shevyrev, *Istoriia Imperatorskogo Moskovskogo universiteta* (Moscow, 1855), p. 23.

47. B. P. Orlov, *Poligraficheskaia promyshlennost' Moskvy* (Moscow, 1953), p. 79. The ratio of workers to press depended on the particular operation and type of press involved. In general, the ratio ranged between 7:1 and 14:1.

48. S. A. Pokrovskii, *Politicheskie i pravovye vzgliady S. E. Desnitskogo* (Moscow, 1955), p. 154.

49. See the lists of books sent to students directly from the press in *Dokumenty i materialy po istorii Moskovskogo universiteta vtoroi poloviny XVIII veka*, 3 vols. (Moscow, 1958–63), 2:25–29 and 3:35–36, 351–52 (hereafter cited as *Dokumenty*). Letters from the teachers to the press are in *Dokumenty* 2:177–78 and 3:169, 373–79.

50. *PSZ*, no. 10515.

51. Mel'nikova, *Izdaniia napechatannye*, p. 4; *Dokumenty* 1:39–40, 42–43, 67, 79–80, 83–86; *S.K.* 4, nos. 8907–8915.

52. TsGADA, *fond 359*, no. 4, pp. 1–5.

53. TsGADA, *fond 17*, no. 39, pp. 1ff.

54. Mel'nikova, *Izdaniia napechatannye*, nos. 601, 611, 613, and others.

55. *Dokumenty* 1:208.

56. *Sobranie luchshikh sochinenii k rasprostraneniiu znaniia* (1762); *Poleznoe uveselenie* (1760–62); *Svobodnye chasy* (1763); *Nevinnoe uprazhnenie* (1763); *Dobroe namerenie* (1764); and *Journal des Sciences et Arts* (1761).

57. Berkov and others have characterized the members of Kheraskov's group as officers and cadets from the Infantry Corps who were brought to the university solely because of their contacts with Kheraskov, who had been an officer himself. However, most of these officers had, by 1760, attended classes at the university's gymnasium either as enrolled students or as auditors. In almost every case, attendance at the gymnasium preceded involvement in the journals. See, among others, Berkov, *Istoriia russkoi zhurnalistiki*, p. 124.

58. A. V. Zapadov, *Russkaia zhurnalistika XVIII veka* (Moscow, 1964), p. 34.

59. Gleason, *Moral Idealists*, p. 58.

60. *S.K.* 2, no. 5164; P. N. Berkov, "Histoire de l'Encyclopédie dans la Russie du XVIII siecle," *Revue des études slaves* 44 (1965):47–68; N. V. Revunenkova, "O perevodakh Entsiklopedii na russkii iazyk," in A.D. Liublinskaia, ed., *Istoriia v Entsiklopedii Didro i D'Alembera* (Leningrad, 1978), p. 257.

61. Mel'nikova, *Izdaniia napechatannye*, nos. 608 and 747 (Gellert), 114, 1116 (Genlis), and 313 (Fénelon). The Infantry Corps Press's edition of Gellert's *The Life of the Swedish Countess G.* was translated and paid for by the captain of the corps and noted literary figure Ivan Rumiantsev. *S.K.* 1, no. 1299.

62. Mel'nikova, *Izdaniia napechatannye*, nos. 74, 233, 399, 446, and 699.

63. The quality of instruction in all the language classes has been subjected to some derision in the literature. In the lower classes, for example, courses were often taught by older students rather than by members of the faculty. Denis FonVizin claimed that one professor would indicate the correct answers to examination questions by pointing to certain buttons on his jacket. Yet just a few lines later FonVizin admitted that he had learned Latin and German very well. Furthermore, it is known that many lectures were delivered in foreign languages, and the very fact that many students ultimately did translate books shows that they must have gained proficiency in at least one foreign language. Certainly the curriculum could not have emphasized language study more strongly. Upwards of twenty-five class hours a week were spent studying languages. In one required course on Russian stylistics, students were expected to translate contemporary European literature into Russian. The role of the teacher was to assist in refining the students' style

and improving their use of syntax. One would be hard pressed to find a more practical training for future intellectual endeavors. S. V. Rozhdestvenskii, *Ocherki po istorii sistemy narodnago prosveshcheniia v Rossii* (St. Petersburg, 1912), p. 220; Denis FonVizin, *Sobranie sochinenii,* 2 vols. (Moscow, 1959), 2:87–88; *Dokumenty* 3:373.

64. *Dokumenty* 3:86–88, 130–31.

65. Katsprzhak, *Istoriia pis'mennosti,* p. 204. On the fuller consequences of the plague, see John T. Alexander, *Bubonic Plague in Early Modern Russia: Public Health and Urban Disaster* (Baltimore, 1980).

66. *Akademicheskaia tipografiia,* p. 33; RO GPB, *fond* 1105, no. 26, pp. 1, 29–31.

67. By 1767 the Academy Press had become large enough to be divided into two separate operations. It is not clear whether this change had any effect on the direction of the press, but the "new" press seems to have been used primarily for privately submitted and patronized books. AAN, *fond* 3, *opis'* 1, no. 283, p. 84; no. 537, p. 913; no. 542, p. 702.

68. *Akademicheskaia tipografiia,* p. 32; D. D. Shamrai, "Prodazha v gubernskikh i provintsial'nykh gorodakh Akademiei nauk svoikh izdanii (1767–1769)," *Trudy Instituta knigi,* Vol. 5 (1936), p. 138.

69. Books published at the expense of private individuals were given special scrutiny, because of the concern that the relative autonomy of the press would allow something illegal to be published accidentally. AAN, *fond* 3, *opis'* 2, no. 554, p. 3.

70. AAN, *fond* 3, *opis'* 1, no. 298, pp. 250–51, and no. 308, p. 14.

71. There are several examples of Lebedev and Volchkov parceling out translations. See, among others, AAN, *fond* 3, *opis'* 1, no. 215, p. 340.

72. *Akademicheskaia tipografiia,* p. 39.

73. AAN, *fond* 3, *opis'* 1, no. 221, p. 236; no. 226, p. 200; and no. 263, p. 234.

74. For example, in 1761 a Senate translator, Iakov Trusov, presented to the Academy a translation of Defoe's *Adventures of Robinson Crusoe.* AAN, *fond* 3, *opis'* 1, no. 265.

75. AAN, *fond* 3, *opis'* 1, no. 267, p. 147, and no. 215, p. 340.

76. V. P. Semennikov, *Sobranie staraiushcheesia o perevode inostrannykh knig* (St. Petersburg, 1913), p. 64.

77. Ibid., pp. 65–89.

78. AAN, *fond* 3, *opis'* 1, no. 541, p. 199.

79. Semennikov, *Sobranie staraiushcheesia,* p. 18.

80. Ibid., p. 19.

81. AAN, *fond* 3, *opis'* 4, no. 29/2, p. 1.

82. Semennikov, *Sobranie staraiushcheesia,* pp. 19–20.

83. AAN, *fond* 3, *opis'* 1, no. 544, p. 330.

84. P. N. Berkov, ed., *Satiricheskie zhurnaly N. I. Novikova* (Moscow, 1951), pp. 439–41.

85. Ibid., p. 585.

86. Ibid., p. 41.

87. AAN, *fond* 3, *opis'* 1, no. 338, pp. 115–16.

88. See, among others, AAN, *fond* 3, *opis'* 1, no. 544, p. 3.

89. V. P. Semennikov, "Rannee izdatel'skoe obshchestvo N. I. Novikova," *Russkii bibliofil*, 1912, no. 5:43.

90. Semennikov, "Rannee izdatel'skoe obshchestvo," pp. 9–17; Adariukov, *Kniga v Rossii*, 1:354–55.

91. Zapadov, *Russkaia zhurnalistika XVIII veka*, pp. 28–31.

92. Ibid., pp. 51–55.

93. N. M. Lisovskii, *Bibliografiia russkoi periodicheskoi pechati, 1703–1900 gg.: Materialy dlia istorii russkoi zhurnalistiki* (Petrograd, 1915), pp. 3, 4; Michael VonHerzen, "Catherine II Editor of Vsiakaia Vsiachina? A Reappraisal," *Russian Review* 38 (1979):284ff.

94. Semennikov, *Russkie Satiricheskie zhurnaly, 1769–1774* (St. Petersburg, 1914), pp. 80–83.

95. Lisovskii, *Bibliografiia russkoi periodicheskoi pechati*, p. 4.

96. Millionaia Ulitsa was a main thoroughfare in St. Petersburg on which most of the publishing houses, bookbinders, and book shops were located.

97. *Zhivopisets*, part 1, no. 6 (1771), quoted in Berkov, *Satiricheskie zhurnaly*, pp. 439–43.

98. *S.K.* 3, nos. 7416 and 7417. They were published in overlapping serials running from 1763 to 1774.

99. Mel'nikova, *Izdaniia napechatannye*, nos. 299, 265, and 1243.

100. *Opyt istoricheskogo slovaria o rossiiskikh pisateliakh*, published in a print run of 600 copies by the Academy Press.

101. A. N. Neustroev, *Istoricheskoe razyskanie o russkikh povremennykh izdaniiakh i sbornikakh za 1703–1802 gg.* (St. Petersburg, 1875), pp. 182–83.

102. Semennikov, *Russkie satiricheskie zhurnaly*, p. 83.

103. Berkov, *Satiricheskie zhurnaly*, pp. 439–43.

104. Among the prominent writers who were forced to pay their own way were Ippolit Bogdanovich, Vasilii Ruban, Mikhail Chulkov, Fedor Emin, and Iakov Kozel'skii. The only major exception was Sumarokov, whom Catherine agreed to patronize after 1763. The archival references to these financial arrangements are voluminous. See, as a small sample, the following: for Bogdanovich, AAN, *fond* 3 *opis'* 1, no. 541, p. 672; for Ruban, AAN *fond* 3, *opis'* 1, no. 534, p. 513; for Chulkov, AAN, *fond* 3, *opis'* 1, no. 542, p. 174; for Kozel'skii, AAN, *fond* 3, *opis'* 1, no. 534, p. 60; for Emin, AAN, *fond* 3, *opis'* 1, no. 282, p. 323; and for Sumarokov, TsGADA, *fond* 17, no. 6, p. 1.

105. D. D. Shamrai, "Prodazha izdanii," pp. 140–51. The evidence for what was sold in the bookshop comes from the bookshop's catalogues.

106. Once again, the sources are too numerous to list. See, for Stroganov, AAN, *fond* 3, *opis'* 1, no. 253, p. 130; for Trusov, ibid., no. 532, p. 357;

for Bestuzhev-Riumin, ibid., no. 533, p. 285; for Betskoi, ibid., no. 533, p. 388; and for Panin, ibid., no. 537, p. 7.

107. AAN, *fond* 3, *opis'* 1 no. 323, pp. 1–3, and no. 312, pp. 106–107.

108. See, for example, AAN, *fond* 3, *opis'* 1, no. 303, p. 64.

109. Novikov and Sumarokov ultimately found backers, but Emin was less successful. The Academy impounded three-quarters of his print run until, in 1772, a St. Petersburg bookseller, Sergei Kopnin, bought about half of it. See the commentaries in *S.K.* 3, no. 8634.

110. Sipovskii, "Iz istorii russkoi literatury," pp. 162–66.

111. Ibid., pp. 164–65.

112. Watt, *Rise of the Novel*, p. 290.

CHAPTER FOUR

1. TsGADA *fond* 17, no. 257, pp. 1–2; Orlov, *Poligraficheskaia promyshlennost'*, p. 102.

2. AAN, *fond* 3, *opis'* 1, no. 309, p. 45; TsGADA, *fond* 17, no. 258, p. 1, and no. 259, pp. 2–3; *PSZ*, no. 13572; S. R. Dolgova, "O pervykh vladel'tsakh chastnykh tipografii v Rossii (I. F. Gartung i I. K. Shnor)," *Kniga* 32 (1976):179.

3. Hartung's status as the first private printer requires some clarification, since there were several other private printers in the empire before him that catered to non-Russian communities. In 1737, for example, Crown Prince Vakhtang of Georgia opened a Georgian press just outside of Moscow. In its seven years of operation, this press produced, in addition to original Georgian works, several translations of Russian religious tracts, including the writings of Feofan Prokopovich and Stefan Iavorskii. As far as is known, however, Vakhtang published no Russian books, and his editions circulated only among the Georgian colony near Moscow. D. L. Vateishvili, *Russkaia obshchestvennaia mysl' i pechat' na kavkaze v pervoi treti XIX veka* (Moscow, 1973), p. 34.

4. Hartung's experience paved the way for other foreign-language presses in Russia for older established communities and for some new ones, such as the Armenians and Swabians. The circumstances surrounding the founding of the Armenian press in Russia are most obscure. A Persian Armenian merchant, Gregor Khalduriants, had brought a press from London to St. Petersburg in 1781. Although there is no record of his having applied for a publishing privilege, he was allowed to keep the press until the mid-1780s, when the Armenian Archbishop Joseph, and other Armenian officials in Nakhichevan, told Khalduriants to register the press with the proper authorities. In 1789 the press was sent to Nakhichevan, and later to Astrakhan, where it was taken over by the Armenian church authorities. *S. K.* 5:284; V. B. Barkhudarian, *Nor Nakhijevani Haikakan gaghut'i patmut'ium (1779–1861 t't'* (Erevan, 1967), p. 435. I would like to thank Mr. Sarkis Shmavonian for translating the Armenian sources.

5. *PSZ*, no. 14495.

6. A convenient summary of the documents can be found in V. A. Zapadov, "Kratkii ocherk istorii russkoi tsenzury 60–90-x godov XVIII veka," in B. F. Egorov, ed., *Russkaia literatura i obshchestvenno-politicheskaia bor'ba XVII–XIX vekov* (Leningrad, 1971), p. 106.

7. *PSZ*, no. 15615; TsGADA, *fond 255, opis'* 1, no. 70, p. 15.

8. *PSZ*, no. 15634.

9. V. O. Kliuchevskii, "Vospominaniia o N. I. Novikove i ego vremeni," in his *Sochineniia*, 8 vols. (Moscow, 1959), 8:224–25.

10. The principal defenders of this interpretation include N. G. Malykhin, *Ocherki po istorii knigoizdatel'skogo dela v SSSR* (Moscow, 1964), pp. 113–20; D. D. Shamrai, "Iz istorii tsenzurnogo rezhima Ekateriny II: Arkhivno-bibliograficheskie razyskaniia, 1762–1783," Candidate's dissertation, Leningrad State University (1947); and I. M. Polonskaia, "I. G. Rakhmaninov—izdatel' sochinenii Vol'tera," in *Gosudarstvennaia Publichnaia Biblioteka: Trudy* 7 (1965):127ff. For a slight variance on this view, see V. A. Zapadov, "K istorii pravitel'stvennykh presledovanii N. I. Novikova," in G. P. Makogonenko, ed., *N. I. Novikov i obshchestvenno-literaturnoe dvizhenie ego vremeni* (Leningrad, 1976), pp. 37–48.

11. Semennikov, *Sobranie staraiushcheesia*, pp. 65–77.

12. Zapadov, "Kratkii ocherk istorii tsenzury," p. 107.

13. T. I. Kondakova, who has written several recent articles on the professionalization of Russian printing, has summarized the careers of Russian publishers in the following way: "Regarding the possible paths of development of this profession . . . one can indicate the following: bookseller to publisher, and writer, educator to publisher." T. I. Kondakova, "K istorii formirovaniia poniatiia 'izdatel' ' v sviazi s professionalizatsiei izdatel'skoi deiatel'nosti v Rossii v XVIII v. (postanovka problemy)," in A. A. Sidorov and S. P. Luppov, eds., *Kniga v Rossii do serediny XIX veka*, p. 182. See also T. I. Kondakova, "K voprosu o formirovanii professii izdatelia v Rossii v XVIII v.," in *Gosudarstvennaia Publichnaia Biblioteka: Trudy*, vol. 14, *Istoriia knigi* (Moscow, 1978), p. 166.

14. The leading publishers in this group were Johann Schnoor, Christian Klein, Bernhard Hecke, Bernhard Breitkopf, Friedrich Brunkow, Johann Weitbrecht, Friedrich Meier, Otto Gustav Meier, Gregor Weiss, Friedrich Hippius, Isaac Zederban, Christopher Claudia, Christian Rüdiger, Emelian Vil'kovskii, Fedor Galchenkov, Vasilii Okorokov, Matvei Ovchinnikov, Semen Selivanovskii, and the Ponomarevs.

15. Synodal documents refer to Otto Meier as a native of Lapland and an experienced typesetter. Breitkopf was a publisher and a bookseller. Brunkow had had experience as a bookbinder. Weitbrecht, Schnoor, Rüdiger, and Claudia had been bookbinders and booksellers; Hippius and Friedrich Meier, press operators and booksellers. Zederban, a native of Sweden, had been an ensign in the Russian navy; it is not known whether he had any experience with books. Klein had come to St. Petersburg from Mecklenberg in the 1750s to work as a typesetter for the Academy of Sciences. Hecke had arrived from Lower Saxony in 1773 to work as a bookbinder. Weiss's

occupational background is not known. TsGIA, *fond* 796, *opis'* 63, no. 512, p. 1, and *opis'* 62, no. 1, p. 1; *fond* 730, *opis'* 1, no 170, p. 7; *S.K.* 2, nos. 3260 and 3637; RO GPB, *fond* 871, no. 119, p. 4; Erik Amburger, "Buchdrück, Buchhandel und Verlage in St. Petersburg im 18. Jahrhundert," in Herbert G. Gopfert et al., eds., *Buch und Verlagswesen im 18. und 19. Jahrhundert, Beitrage zür Geschichte der Kommunikation in Mittel- und Östereuropa* (Berlin, 1977), p. 204; Kondakova, "K voprosu o formirovanii professii izdatelia," p. 167; M. I. Martynova and I. F. Martynov, "Peterburgskii knigoizdatel' i knigotorgovets XVIII v. E. K. Vil'kovskii i izdanie uchebnykh posobii dlia narodnykh uchilishch," in A. I. Kopanev et al., eds. *Istoriia knigi i izdatel'skogo dela* (Leningrad, 1977), p. 92; and I. F. Martynov, "Peterburgskii knigotorgovets i knigoizdatel' XVIII veka Iogann Iakob Veitbrekht," in A. I. Kopanev et al., eds., *Knigopechatanie i knizhnye sobraniia v Rossii do serediny XIX v.* (Leningrad, 1979), pp. 39, 49.

16. On Breitkopf's career and his links with the family firm in Leipzig, see Carl B. Lorch, *Die Druckkunst und die Buchhandel in Leipzig durch Vier Jahrhunderte* (Leipzig, 1879), pp. 11, 114–15, and Ulf Lehman, "Der Verlag Breitkopf in Leipzig und die Petersburger Akademie der Wissenschaften in der 60er und 70er Jahren des 18. Jahrhunderts," *Zeitschrift für Slavische Literatur* 8 (1963):25–33.

17. Martynova and Martynov, "Vil'kovskii," pp. 63–72.

18. Ovchinnikov's career has been described in I. F. Martynov, "Knigotorgovets i knigoizdatel' XVIII v. M. K. Ovchinnikov," *Kniga* 24 (1972):103–14. The major primary sources are in AAN, *fond* 3, *opis'* 1, no. 328, pp. 113–55; TsGIA, *fond* 796, *opis'* 67, no. 110, p. 87; and TsGADA, *fond* 7, no. 2813, pp. 204–205. These all refer to him either as "merchant" or "petty burger."

Vil'kovskii's career can be traced through Academy sources. Born in the Ukraine, he served in the Yaroslavl provincial government between 1765 and 1775. His name began to appear in 1775 as the assistant manager of the bookstore. By the late 1770s he had become an active private financier of books through the Academy of Sciences Press. In May 1781 he replaced Zboromirskii as manager of the bookstore, and he worked there until 1784, when the Academy fired him over a series of petty disagreements. Most documents referred to him as an Academic employee, but some referred to him as "college secretary." AAN, *fond* 3, *opis'* 1, no. 551, p. 207; no. 338, p. 23; no. 548, p. 443; and no. 551, p. 274; TsGIA, *fond* 796, *opis'* 67, no. 110, p. 88, and *opis'* 63, no. 332, p. 1; and *fond* 730, *opis'* 1, no. 170, p. 10. See also Martynova and Martynov, "Vil'kovskii," pp. 63–77.

For Galchenkov, very little source material exists. He had come to St. Petersburg in 1763 to work as a translator for the Academy of Sciences. According to Martynov, his metier was lowbrow literature, mostly fantasies and erotica. From the *Svodnyi katalog* one learns that he and Vil'kovskii had cooperated on translations of Goethe's *Young Werther* and several other works. He also had done a translation with Peter Bogdanovich. This suggests that a certain camaraderie existed among Academic employees who later went on to own their own presses. Galchenkov's social origins are unknown, but shortly after he entered into business with Vil'kovskii, he received the title of college assessor. TsGIA, *fond* 796, *opis'* 67, no. 110, p. 88; Zapadov, "Kratkii ocherk istorii tsenzury," p. 106; *S.K.* 1, no. 1425.

The Ponomarev family and Reshetnikov began to advertise books for sale in their bookshops a few years before they started publishing. In addition, each began to subsidize books in other people's presses at least a couple of years before they began to publish on their own. In 1784, for example, Stepan Ponomarev financed a book in Hippius' press, and Egor Ponomarev translated and financed a book in Lopukhin's press. *S.K.* 1, nos. 993, 1659, 1761, 2228, and 2257; 2, no. 5538; and 3, no. 8201.

19. The only exception to this rule was Vasilii Plavil'shchikov, who was the son of a merchant but devoted his adult life to intellectual pursuits. F. A. Brockhaus and I. A. Efron, eds., *Entsiklopedicheskii slovar'* (St. Petersburg, 1890–1904), 46:789.

20. Rakhmaninov's career has been the subject of a fair amount of study. The most complete biography is B. Martynov, *Zhurnalist i izdatel' I. G. Rakhmaninov* (Tambov, 1962). See also I. M. Polonskaia, "I. G. Rakhmaninov— izdatel' sochinenii Vol'tera," *Gosudarstvennaia Publichnaia Biblioteka imeni Lenina: Trudy* 7 (1965): 126–162; and I. M. Polonskaia, *A. N. Radishchev: Materialy i issledovaniia* (Moscow, 1958), pp. 227–30. Most of the relevant documents have been collected in a single archival volume, "O zapechatanii tipografii Brigadira Rakhmaninova po sluchaiu izdaniia im sochinenii Vol'tera, 1794 g.," TsGADA, *fond* 7, no. 2837.

21. The bibliography on Krylov as a poet and fablist composes a volume in itself, but surprisingly little has been written about his publishing enterprise. One can find all the known documents concerning the membership and financial and intellectual goals of his publishing coterie in N. Bystrov, "Tipografiia Krylova s tovarishchami," *Severnaia pchela*, 1847, no. 289: 1155–56. Commentaries on these documents can be found in S. M. Babintsev, *I. A. Krylov: ocherk ego izdatel'skoi i bibliotechnoi deiatel'nosti* (Moscow, 1955), pp. 8–33, and I. M. Polonskaia, "K biografii I. A. Krylova," *Gosudarstvennaia Publichnaia Biblioteka imeni Lenina: Trudy* 2 (1958): 69–85.

22. A summary of the main lines of Bogdanovich's career can be found in I. F. Martynov, "Knigoizdatel', literator, i bibliograf XVIII veka Petr Ivanovich Bogdanovich," *Kniga* 21 (1970):89–104. Additional material can be found in Nikolai Storozhevskii, "Delo o P. I. Bogdanoviche, tipografshchike i perevodchike 'Montiuglevoi Istorii matematiki' (iz arkhiva Poltavskoi politsii 1783)," *Kievskaia starina* (1891), no. 11: 308–12. The relevant documents are in AAN, *fond* 3, *opis'* 1, no. 331, pp. 343-53; RO GPB, *fond* 341, no. 385, pp. 1–3; and TsGADA, *fond* 7, no. 2894 ("Delo o kollezhskom assessore Petre Bogdanoviche vyslannom iz Sankt Peterburga v Poltavu, 1796").

Almost nothing is known about Sytin except that his closest associates, Aleksei Komarov and Ivan Vinogradov, were active translators and poets. Whether the famous late nineteenth-century publisher of the same name was his descendent is not known. E. I. Katsprzhak, "Tipografiia I. Ia. Sytina v. Peterburge (1791–1794 gg.)," *Gosudarstvennaia Publichnaia Biblioteka imeni Lenina: Trudy* 2 (1958):53.

23. Martynov, "Bogdanovich," p. 90.

24. The figures for intellectual publishers reflect the enormous impact of Novikov, who alone printed more books than all of the other intellectual publishers combined. But the pattern of brief careers and relatively high outputs applies to most of the others as well.

25. TsGADA, *fond* 7, no. 2894, pp. 50ff.

26. AAN, *fond* 3, *opis'* 1, no. 328, pp. 113–27.

27. *PSZ*, no. 16048; Martynov, "Veitbrekht," p. 54.

28. Hippius rented the Moscow Senate Press from 1780 to 1784. Between 1783 and 1792 he operated a private press, and between 1787 and 1789 he rented the press of the Moscow province administration. Reshetnikov operated a private press from 1786 to 1797, after which time he rented the Moscow province press until 1805. Okorokov rented the Moscow Senate Press from 1787 to 1800 and the Moscow University Press from 1789 to 1793. Galchenkov opened a private press in 1783, and in 1785 he entered into partnership with Vil'kovskii, with whom he worked until 1788. In that year Galchenkov left the operation to Vil'kovskii, who operated the press alone until 1795 then reopened it at the beginning of the nineteenth century. Otto Meier rented the Moscow Senate Press in 1778 and 1779. In 1783 he opened a private press that ran for two years. Christopher Claudia had a private press between 1783 and 1795, and between 1794 and 1801 he leased Moscow University Press in partnership with Rüdiger. *S.K.* 5:278–90; *PSZ*, no. 15615; TsGADA, *fond* 359, no. 15, p. 11, and *fond* 255, *opis'* 1, no. 70, p. 15.

29. After Plavil'shchikov bought Krylov's press, he worked as a private publisher for several years. In 1796 he sold the press to the St. Petersburg province administration, which allowed him to operate it on his own, without paying a fee, into the nineteenth century. *St. Peterburgskiia vedomosti*, Nov. 25, 1797, p. 187.

30. Kondakova, "K voprosu o formirovanii professii izdatelia," pp. 166–69; Martynov, "Veitbrekht," p. 48.

31. Martynova and Martynov, "Vil'kovskii," pp. 68–77; Martynov, "Veitbrekht," pp. 43ff.: Martynov, "Ovchinnikov," pp. 103–14; A. A. Zaitseva, "Novye materialy o Sanktpeterburgskom knigotorgovtse i izdatele I. P. Glazunove," in Kopanev, *Knigopechatanie*, p. 72.

32. A report in 1811 concerning Moscow publishers listed Selivanovskii as having ten presses; Ponomarev, four; Zederban, one; and Liuba (a former lessee of Moscow University Press), four. Plavil'shchikov became the most celebrated publisher of Alexander I's reign and is considered by many to

have been the inspiration for Alexander Smirdin, the philanthropic publisher of Nicholas I's reign. He also formulated one of the first bibliographic systems for the use of public libraries and book stores. Other records show that Reshetnikov, Claudia, Vil'kovskii, Schnoor, Sytin, Weitbrecht, Brunkow, and Breitkopf continued to publish at least into the early years of the nineteenth century. *S.K.* 5:280–89; TsGIA, *fond* 730, *opis'* 1, no. 86, pp. 89ff., and no. 170, p. 7; Orlov, *Poligraficheskaia promyshlennost'*, p. 117.

33. Quoted in Pavel N. Miliukov, "Educational Reforms," in Marc Raeff, ed., *Catherine the Great* (New York, 1972), p. 111. See also Max J. Okenfuss, "Education and Empire: School Reform in Enlightened Russia," *Jahrbucher für Geschichte Östeuropas* 27 (1979):41–68.

34. Rozhdestvenskii, *Ocherki po istorii prosveshcheniia*, pp. 552–59.

35. TsGIA, *fond* 730, *opis'* 1, no. 170, pp. 39–40.

36. Okenfuss, "Education and Empire," p. 56.

37. TsGIA, *fond* 730, *opis'* 1, no. 166, pp. 1–6, and no. 79, pp. 1–3.

38. *Opisanie del arkhiva Ministerstva narodnogo prosveshcheniia* (Petrograd, 1917), pp. 162–63; TsGIA, *fond* 730, *opis'* 1, no. 72, pp. 3, 17–18, 21–22, 25–26.

39. TsGIA, *fond* 730, *opis'* 1, no. 114, pp. 4–50.

40. TsGIA, *fond* 730, *opis'* 1, no. 166, p. 4; no. 78, p. 17; and no. 140, pp. 15–18; Gavrilov, *Ocherki istorii*, pp. 239–40.

41. I. M. Polonskaia, "Russkaia izdatel'skaia oblozhka i pereplet XVIII v.," *Kniga* 38 (1979):152–61.

42. J. Michael Hittle, *The Service City: State and Townsmen in Russia, 1600–1800* (Cambridge, Mass., 1979), pp. 198–200.

43. Bystrov, "Tipografiia Krylova," pp. 1155–56.

44. *S.K.* 3, nos. 8873, 8932, 8943.

45. Katsprzhak, *Istoriia pis'mennosti*, p. 58.

46. *S.K.* 1, nos. 165, 578, 855, and 1183.

47. *S.K.* 1, no. 1427.

48. *S.K.* 2, nos. 5421–5425.

49. Darnton, *Business of Enlightenment*, p. 302.

50. *S.K.* 2, nos. 5651 and 5648.

51. *S.K.* 2, nos. 5646, 2898, and several others.

52. S. A. Klepikov, "Russian Block Books of the Seventeenth and Eighteenth centuries," *Papers of the Bibliographic Society of America* 65 (1971): 217–24.

53. Raeff, *Russian Intelligentsia*, pp. 153ff.

54. *S.K.* 2, nos. 3030 and 3039, and 3, no. 8155.

55. A memorandum from the chancellery to President Dashkova, dated July 19, 1783, expresses that concern. AAN, *fond* 3, *opis'* 1, no. 334, p. 166, and no. 555, p. 85.

56. AAN, *fond* 3, *opis'* 1, no. 334, p. 166.

57. See, for example, AAN, *fond* 3, *opis'* 1, no. 2150, which discusses the

distribution of books in 1791, and no. 552, p. 207, on management of the bookshop.

58. AAN, *fond* 3, *opis'* 1, no. 556, p. 603.

59. G. P. Makogonenko, *Nikolai Novikov i russkoe prosveshchenie XVIII veka* (Moscow, 1952), pp. 7ff.

60. Raeff, *Russian Intelligentsia*, p. 161; M. N. Longinov, *Novikov i moskovskie martinisty* (Moscow, 1859); W. Gareth Jones, "The Morning Light Charity Schools, 1777–1780," *Slavonic and East European Review* 56 (January 1978):49–60; In–Ho Ryu, "Moscow Freemasons and the Rosicrucian Order," in Garrard, *Eighteenth Century*, pp. 205–20; Gilbert McArthur, "Catherine II and the Masonic Circle of N. I. Novikov," *Canadian Slavic Studies* 4 (1970):529–46

61. Adariukov, *Kniga v Rossii*, 1:354–55; V. P. Semennikov, *Knigoizdatel'-skaia deiatel'nost' N. I. Novikova i tipograficheskoi kompanii* (St. Petersburg, 1921), pp. 14–17.

62. AAN, *fond* 3, *opis'* 1, no. 547, pp. 268, 421; and no. 550, p. 76.

63. Jones, "Morning Light Charity Schools": 49-60; G. J. Marker, "Novikov's Readers," *Modern Language Review* 77 (October 1982):894–905.

64. Hans Rogger, *National Consciousness in Eighteenth-Century Russia* (Cambridge, Mass., 1960), p. 115; V. Ia. Stoiunin, "Trudy 'Vol'nogo Rossiisskogo Sobraniia' byvshego pri Moskovskom universitete," *ZhMNP*, nos. 10 and 11 (1854), pp. 1–40. Martynov has recently suggested that Novikov traveled to Moscow frequently in the 1760s and 1770s on behalf of the Izmailovskii regiment and that on these trips he established a working relationship with Christian Wever, a Danish-born bookseller who had just come to Moscow. If this is so, it would indicate a much greater and unbroken intimacy with Moscow's literary world than has been thought. Martynov unfortunately does not present any evidence. I. F. Martynov, *Knigoizdatel' Nikolai Novikov* (Leningrad, 1981), pp. 9–13.

65. *S.K.* 1, nos., 91–92.

66. Semennikov, *Knigoizdatel'skaia deiatel'nost'*, p. 15; *S.K.* 1, no. 2709, and 2, no. 3825; Gleason, *Moral Idealists*, pp. 121–22.

67. A. V. Zapadov, *Novikov* (Moscow, 1968), p. 78.

68. Martynov, *Novikov*, p. 78.

69. L. V. Svetlov, *Izdatel'skaia deiatel'nost' N. I. Novikova* (Moscow, 1946), p. 32.

70. Ibid. The lease has been reprinted in A. V. Mashtafarov, ed., "Neizdannyi dokument ob arende N. I. Novikovym tipografii Moskovskogo universiteta," *Kniga* 28 (1974):152–56.

71. M. N. Longinov, *Novikov i Shvarts: Materialy dlia istorii russkoi literatury v kontse XVIII veka* (Moscow, 1857), p. 6.

72. Ibid., pp. 6–11; M. Poludenskii, "Materialy dlia istorii Druzheskago uchenago obshchestva, 1782," *Russkii arkhiv*, 1863, no. 3:204–5.

73. Mel'nikova, *Izdaniia napechatannye*, pp. 188–251.

74. Martynov, *Novikov*, p. 63.

75. Andrei Bolotov, *Zhizn' i prikliucheniia Andreia Bolotova*, 3 vols. (Moscow, 1931), 3:277.
76. Longinov, *Novikov i moskovskie martinisty*, p. 23; Kliuchevskii, "Vospominaniia o Novikove," pp. 224–25.
77. RO GBL, *fond* 41, *opis'* 77, no. 2, pp. 18–20. Most of these letters appeared in *Russkii arkhiv*, 1864, no. 8: 737–47.
78. Rozenberg counted twenty provincial outlets for Novikov's books, and Martynov has discovered a dozen more. V. A. Rozenberg, *N. I. Novikov, podvizhnik russkoi knigi* (Berlin, 1921), pp. 60–61; Martynov, "Kniga v russkoi provintsii 1760–1790-x gg.: Zarozhdenie provintsial'noi knizhnoi torgovli," in Sidorov and Luppov, *Kniga v Rossii do serediny XIX veka*, pp. 118–24.
79. Martynov, *Novikov*, pp. 47–52.
80. Nikolai Tikhonravov, ed., *Letopisi russkoi literatury i drevnosti*, 5 vols. (Moscow, 1862), 5: 6–7; V. F. Liasov, "Vozniknovenie rynka podpisnykh izdanii v Rossii i knigorasprostranitel'skaia deiatel'nost' N. I. Novikova," *Kniga* 36 (1978):73–80.
81. Nikolai Karamzin, "On the Book Trade and the Love of Reading in Russia," in Harold B. Segel, ed., *The Literature of Eighteenth-Century Russia: A History and Anthology*, 2 vols. (New York, 1967), 1:449 (originally published in *Vestnik Evropy*, 1802, no. 9).
82. Sources differ on how many presses the university owned. Some leases listed twelve, others fifteen, still others twenty. By the beginning of the nineteenth century, sources agree, Moscow University Press had twenty-four presses.
83. Bolotov, *Zhizn' i prikliucheniia*, 3:276–80.
84. Tikhonravov, *Letopisi russkoi literatury*, 5:4–5.
85. Ibid., p. 22.
86. Ibid.
87. Ibid., p. 15.
88. Novikov apparently treated the money as an outright gift, whereas Pokhodiashin considered it a loan. M. M. Gromyko, "G. M. Pokhodiashin v 'Druzheskom uchenom obshchestve' N. I. Novikova," in O. N. Vilkov, ed., *Goroda Sibiri* (Novosibirsk, 1974), pp. 266–72.
89. Tikhonravov, *Letopisi russkoi literatury*, 5:23.
90. R. N. Kleimonova, "Izdatel'skaia deiatel'nost' Moskovskogo universiteta v pervoi chetverti XIX veka," *Kniga* 42 (1981):80–81.
91. Inventories taken in 1792 list dozens of titles that Novikov had published at the Typographical Company with quantities that often ranged into the thousands. Stocks of this sort suggest that Novikov regularly printed books in very high print runs.
92. Svetlov, *Izdatel'skaia deiatel'nost' Novikova*, pp. 76–77.
93. Jones, "Morning Light Charity Schools."
94. Gromyko, "G. M. Pokhodiashin," p. 271.
95. Martynov has identified ninety authors who published original works with

the Moscow University Press during Novikov's stewardship. If one were to include those authors who wrote for the Typographical Company, the figure undoubtedly would be much higher. Martynov, *Novikov*, p. 63.

96. Raeff, *Russian Intelligentsia*, p. 166.

97. Several previous scholars have claimed that they discerned a more precise ideological characterization of Novikov's books. Longinov, for one, emphasized the presence of a large number of mystical works, but argued that these works were consistent with the Russian Enlightenment. Svetlov, by contrast, saw Novikov as leader of a liberal opposition, and thus he barely mentioned Novikov's masonic connection. Another specialist, L. Fridberg, criticized Svetlov for underplaying the role of Freemasonry but argued that the deistic theology of Novikov's masonic books made them consistent with the Enlightenment and with opposition to the traditional establishment. None of these characterizations accounts for the great variety of Novikov's repertoire, a fact which is essentially conceded by Martynov. Longinov, *Novikov i moskovskie martinisty*, p. 123; Svetlov, *Izdatel'skaia deiatel'nost' Novikova*, p. 61; L. Fridberg, "Knigoizdatel'skaia deiatel'nost' N. I. Novikova v Moskve (1779–1792)," *Voprosy istorii* 1948, no. 8:27–33; Martynov, *Novikov*, p. 71.

98. Longinov, *Novikov i moskovskie martinisty*, p. 123; Kliuchevskii, "Vospominaniia o Novikove," pp. 224–25; Martynov, *Novikov*, pp. 76–105.

99. T. I. Kondakova, "Tipografskie i izdatel'skie marki v russkikh knigakh XVIII veka," *Kniga* 39 (1979):76–80.

100. See Platon's questions to Novikov in 1785 and his subsequent report, in "Voprosnye punkty, predlozhennye N. I. Novikovu Mitropolitom Platonem," in Tikhonravov *Letopisi russkoi literatury*, 1:23–28.

101. According to Vernadskii, the various organs of the upper civil and military administrations had staffs of which between 17 and 33 percent were Masons. G. V. Vernadskii, *Russkoe masonstvo v tsarstvovanie Ekateriny II* (Petrograd, 1917), p. 90.

102. See the sampling of introductions in I. V. Malyshev, ed. *Novikov i ego sovremenniki* (Moscow, 1961), pp. 324–36.

Chapter Five

1. N. D. Chechulin, *Russkoe provintsial'noe obshchestvo vo vtoroi polovine XVIII veka* (St. Petersburg, 1889), p. 57.

2. Ibid., pp. 57–58.

3. Ibid., pp. 61–62.

4. V. P. Semennikov, "Literaturnaia i knigopechatnaia deiatel'nost' v provintsii v kontse XVIII i nachale XIX vekov," *Russkii bibliofil*, 1911, no. 6:15,21; and V. P. Semennikov, "Dopolnitel'nye materialy dlia istorii provintsial'nykh tipografii XVIII i nachala XIX veka," *Russkii bibliofil*, 1913, no. 7:68–78.

5. A. V. Blium, "Izdatel'skaia deiatel'nost' v russkoi provintsii kontsa XVIII–nachala XIX vv.," *Kniga* 12 (1966):138ff.

6. Ibid., p. 139; and A. V. Blium, "Massovoe chtenie v russkoi provintsii kontsa XVII–pervoi chetverti XIX v.," in I. E. Barenbaum, ed., *Istoriia russkogo chitatelia*, 4 vols. to date (Leningrad, 1973–), 1:39–44.

7. Blium, "Izdatel'skaia deiatel'nost'," pp. 138–39.

8. Raeff, *Russian Intelligensia*, pp. 85–93; and Arcadius Kahan, "The Costs of Westernization in Russia: The Gentry and the Economy in the Eighteenth Century," *Slavic Review* 25 (March 1966):65–66.

9. Chechulin, *Provintsial'noe obshchestvo*, pp. 85–90.

10. Kameneva, "Knigopechatanie v Chernigove," p. 305.

11. A. M. Lazarevskii, "Gde i kak prodavalis' izdaniia Chernigovskoi Il'inskoi tipografii v proshlom veke," *Kievskaia starina*, 1889, no. 4: 199–200.

12. Semennikov, "Literaturnaia i knigopechatnaia deiatel'nost'," p. 16.

13. V. P. Semennikov, "Bibliograficheskii spisok knig, napechatannykh v provintsii so vremeni vozniknoveniia grazhdanskikh tipografii po 1807 g.," *Russkii bibliofil*, 1912, no. 2:48.

14. Semennikov, "Literaturnaia i knigopechatnaia deiatel'nost'," p. 19.

15. Chechulin, *Provintsial'noe obshchestovo*, p. 62.

16. Semennikov, "Literaturnaia i knigopechatnaia deiatel'nost'," p. 19.

17. *S.K.* 5:289–90.

18. V. M. Khoromanskii, *Stoletie tipografii Saratovskogo gubernskogo pravleniia, 1794–1894* (Saratov, 1895), pp. 6–12.

19. Ia. Grakhov, "O pokhodnoi tipografii kniazia Potemkina–Tavricheskago," *Zapiski Odesskago obshchestva istorii i drevnostei* 4 (1858):470.

20. *S.K.* 1, nos. 121, 126–29, and 2, nos. 2805–7, 2810.

21. *S.K.* 1, no. 262, and 2, nos. 5497, 5541.

22. Grakhov, "O pokhodnoi tipografii," p. 471.

23. *PSZ*, no. 16517.

24. *S.K.* 1, nos. 210, 1606, and 3, no. 6413.

25. V. G. Utkov, "Sibirskie pervopechatniki Vasilii i Dmitrii Kornil'evy," *Kniga* 38 (1979):78.

26. Blium has also calculated the subject composition of provincial books through 1806. Although his categories diverge somewhat from mine, and his dates are a little different, the overall conclusions are nearly identical. Blium, "Izdatel'skaia deiatel'nost'," p. 142.

27. Blium argues (ibid.) that the percentage of translated volumes was significantly higher in the provinces than in the country at large, but according to my calculations, he has understated the percentage of translated books coming out of the presses in the major cities.

28. *S.K.* 1, nos. 1086, 1300, and 2209; Blium, "Izdatel'skaia deiatel'nost'," p. 143.

29. *S.K.* 1, no. 2064.

30. N. M. Lisovskii, Russkaia periodicheskaia pechat', 1703–1900: Bibliografiia i graficheskaia tablitsa (Petrograd, 1915), pp. 1–9.

31. E. V. Avdoshenko, *Poet G. R. Derzhavin v Tambove* (Tambov, 1962), p. 14.

32. L. Trefolev, "Pervyi russkii provintsial'nyi zhurnal 'Uedinennyi poshe-khonets,' " *Russkii arkhiv*, 1879, no. 9:93.

33. Ibid., pp. 98–99, and S. Zolotarev, Pisateli Iaroslavtsy (Yaroslavl, 1920), pp. 45–49.

34. Trefolev, "Pervyi provintsial'nyi zhurnal," p. 115.

35. A. I. Dmitriev-Mamonov, "Pechat' v tobol'skom namestnichestve v kontse XVIII stoletiia," *Pamiatnaia knizhka tobol'skoi gubernii na 1884 god* (To-bolsk, 1884), pp. 268–69.

36. Utkov, "Sibirskie pervopechatniki," p. 284.

37. Dmitriev-Mamonov, "Pechat' v tobol'skom namestnichestve," p. 320.

38. The high incidence of inactivity was a result of the entire range of problems that had hampered Russian publishing throughout the century, but financial barriers proved to be the most refractory. In Saratov, for example, the provincial government had to make a series of collections from the local gentry and merchantry to raise the 1,000 rubles necessary to purchase the press. This assessment left barely enough money to pay the printers' salaries and nearly nothing to finance the actual publication of books. The press apparently limped along in this manner until 1812, when the local admin-istration agreed to provide an annual budget for publishing books. Kho-romanskii, *Stoletie tipografii*, pp. 6–12, and *Saratovskii krai: Istoricheskii ocherk, vospominaniia, materialy* (Saratov, 1893), pp. 266–72.

39. P. K. Simoni, "N. E. Struiskii: poet, metroman, i ego sel'skaia tipografiia," *Starye gody*, 1911, no. 1: 39.

40. *S.K.* 1, no. 313, and 2, nos. 5019, 5537.

41. Simoni, "Struiskii," p. 40.

42. Between 1786 and 1793 twenty-one of his works were published in Mos-cow or St. Petersburg. *S.K.* 3, nos. 6898–6929.

43. *Moskovskiia vedomosti*, 1789, no. 6: 55.

44. N. Guberti, "Pervaia tipografiia v Sibiri kuptsa Kornil'eva," *Bibliografi-cheskie zapiski*, 1892, no. 11: 861; *Rospis' rossiiskim knigam i landkartam prodaiushchimsia v Kaluge . . . u Kotel'nikova* (Kaluga, 1795).

45. *S.K.* 1, nos. 840, 1170, and several others.

46. Ivan Kalugin, "Neskol'ko slov o klintsovoi tipografii," *Bibliograficheskie zapiski*, 1858, no. 5:157.

47. Existing catalogues list very few titles printed in Klintsy, but the press's sub rosa existence probably precluded its books from appearing in the major institutional libraries that were the basis for the catalogues. Narratives, by contrast, describe a high level of activity, but they do not provide figures or lists of titles. One scholar has estimated that the Klintsy press and a related one in Poland together printed over seventy titles in the eighteenth century. Iu. A. Labyntsev, "Pamiatniki drevnerusskoi pis'mennosti v izda-niiakh staroobriadcheskikh tipografii XVIII–XX vv.," *Kniga* 39 (1979):173–78.

48. Ibid., p. 174.

49. G. V. Antiukhin, *Ocherki istorii pechati voronezhskogo kraia, 1798–1917* (Voronezh, 1973), pp. 10–11.

50. Ibid., p. 8.

51. D. Speranskii, "Uchenaia deiatel'nost' Evgeniia Bolkhovitinova, mitropolita kievskogo," *Russkii vestnik*, 1885, no. 176:526.

52. *S.K.* 1, no. 392, and 2, nos. 5007 and 5009.

53. Avdoshenko, *Derzhavin*, p. 13; G. R. Derzhavin, *Zapiski* (Moscow, 1860), pp. 280–86.

54. Avdoshenko, *Derzhavin*, pp. 13–14.

55. Semennikov, "Literaturnaia i knigopechatnaia deiatel'nost'," p. 21.

56. *S.K.* 1, no. 1798.

57. Avdoshenko, *Derzhavin*, pp. 15–22.

58. *S.K.* 1, nos. 272, 1306, and 2274, and 3, no. 6703.

59. *S.K.* 1, no. 2235; 2, nos. 5649, and 3, nos. 7707 and 8606.

60. Zolotarev, *Pisateli Iaroslavtsy*, pp. 45–53.

61. A. G. Cross, "Printing at Nikolaev, 1798–1803," *Transactions of the Cambridge Bibliographic Society* 4 (1974):150–51.

62. Ibid., p. 151.

63. Semennikov, "Literaturnaia i knigopechatnaia deiatel'nost'," p. 21.

64. Blium, "Izdatel'skaia deiatel'nost'," p. 143; and *Materialy dlia istorii Vladimirskoi gubernskoi tipografii, 1797–1897* (Vladimir, 1898), pp. 3–11; *S.K.* 5:289–90.

65. Martynov, *Rakhmaninov*, pp. 46–59; TsGADA, *fond* 7, no. 2837, pp. 6–16.

CHAPTER SIX

1. Luppov, *Kniga . . . v poslepetrovskoe vremia*, p. 108.

2. *PSPR* 11:121, 207, 267.

3. Luppov, *Kniga . . . v poslepetrovskoe vremia*, pp. 88, 125; *PSPR* 7:427, 9:93–96, and 11:152.

4. Luppov, *Kniga . . . v poslepetrovskoe vremia*, pp. 117ff.

5. Ibid., p. 127.

6. Monthly income figures for the period between 1731 and December 1740 are reproduced in ibid., p. 121.

7. In this context, Luppov (ibid., p. 122) holds fast to his distinction between traditional and "purely religious" books, on the one hand, and books that came from religious presses but had a nonreligious character or function, on the other. Thus, he categorizes teaching psalters, church primers, and some Books of Hours on sale at the Moscow bookshop as secular in content. As was pointed out in chapter 2, though, this distinction introduces a misleading notion of the chronological development from traditionalism to secularism. It ignores, moreover, the manifest typographical differences between church books and other books. It is unlikely, therefore, that anyone saw the educational books at the Moscow bookshop as signifying anything particularly secular.

8. Bochagov, *Knizhnaia palata*, pp. 4–5.

9. Luppov, *Kniga . . . v poslepetrovskoe vremia*, p. 112.

10. Ibid., p. 113; Bochagov, *Knizhnaia palata*, p. 11; Borodin, "Moskovskaia grazhdanskaia tipografiia," pp. 97–105.

11. Luppov, *Kniga . . . v poslepetrovskoe vremia*, pp. 113ff.

12. *Materialy* 2:803; Beliaev, "Izdaniia Akademii nauk," pp. 36–37.

13. *St. Peterburgskiia vedomosti*, 1728, no. 102.

14. *Materialy* 2:56–57; Bochagov, *Knizhnaia palata*, p. 10.

15. *Materialy* 2:499.

16. In the autumn of 1739, when Clanner decided to settle accounts with the Academy, an inventory was taken at the book shop, and the Academy determined that its current stocks were worth 72,000 rubles. This included almost 50,000 rubles worth of books published at the Academy's expense, 9,700 rubles worth of books published abroad, and laws and notices published at the expense of other individuals and institutions worth about 12,000 rubles. Another document from this period shows that Clanner had inherited 13,000 rubles worth of books that had accumulated prior to his arrival. Thus, the accumulation for his stay amounted to 59,000 rubles worth of books. Ibid., 4:226, 264.

17. Luppov, *Kniga . . . v poslepetrovskoe vremia*, pp. 112, 116.

18. *Materialy* 4:372.

19. Bochagov, *Knizhnaia palata*, p. 23.

20. *Materialy* 5:376, 430, 848, 868, and 7:123, 140–41; AAN, *fond* 3, *opis'* 1, no. 79, pp. 157–79.

21. *Materialy* 10:434–36.

22. Ibid., 10:505.

23. Ibid., 1:560–61, 590–91.

24. Ibid., 1:156, 164.

25. Ibid., 1:450, 583, 590.

26. Ibid., 2:182.

27. *PSZ*, no. 6240; *Sbornik postanovlenii i rasporiazhenii po tsenzure s 1720 po 1862 god* (St. Petersburg, 1862), pp. 11–13; *Materialy* 2:298–99.

28. Bochagov, *Knizhnaia palata*, p. 20; *Materialy* 7:269–70 and 8:110–11.

29. *Materialy* 4:172, 5:445–48, and 8:518, 537.

30. Ibid., 8:465.

31. Ibid., 8:606.

32. Ibid., 9:366–74.

33. Ibid., 8:673–74 and 9:29–30; Amburger, "Buchdrück," p. 203.

34. *Materialy* 10:150, 184.

35. Ibid., 10:260–65.

36. P. I. Bortenev, ed. *Arkhiv Kniazia Vorontsova*, 40 vols. (Moscow, 1870), 1:357. See also Luppov's chart on the profile of private libraries: *Kniga . . . v poslepetrovskoe vremia*, pp. 290–99.

37. S. P. Luppov, "Spros na akademicheskie i zarubezhnye izdaniia v Peter-

burge i Moskve v seredine XVIII veka (Iz proshlogo russkoi knigotorgovli)," *Knizhnaia torgovlia* 7 (1980):179.

38. Ibid., pp. 154–58.

39. *Materialy* 9:329.

40. Ibid., 9:387.

41. Ibid., 9:453, 481–83, 510–11, 521.

42. Ibid., 9:706.

43. Ibid., 9:650, 705, and 10:211.

44. RO GPB, *fond* 871 (Stählin collection), no. 108, p. 2.

45. Ibid., pp. 39–42.

46. Luppov, "Akademicheskie i zarubezhnye izdaniia," p. 178.

47. Ibid., pp. 163–69, 176. See also N. A. Kopanev, "Zarubezhnye izdaniia prodavavshiesia v Moskovskoi knizhnoi lavke Akademii nauk v 1749–1753," in Luppov and Paramonova, *Knigotorgovoe i bibliotechnoe delo*, pp. 24–26.

48. I. F. Martynov, "Knizhnaia lavka Moskovskogo universiteta v XVIII v.," *Knizhnaia torgovlia* 6 (1979):145.

49. Martynov, "Veitbrekht," pp. 39–42.

50. *S.K.* 5:278–90.

51. Semennikov, "Rannee izdatel'skoe obshchestvo," pp. 9–17.

52. Martynov, "Veitbrekht," p. 48.

53. *S.K.* 3, no. 8953.

54. Ibid., no. 8887; AAN *fond* 3, *opis'* 1, no. 914, p. 90; RO GBL, *fond* 31 (Bulgakov family archive), *opis'* 17, no. 2, p. 9. In later sources, Perepletchikov is referred to as a "merchant," but in the 1770s he worked as a bookbinder. See Tikhonravov, *Letopisi russkoi literatury*, 5:6; *S.K.* 3, no. 8925, and several other entries.

55. Pavel Simoni, *Knizhnaia torgovlia v Moskve XVIII–XIX stoletii: Moskovskie knigoprodavtsy Kol'chuginy v ikh knigotorgovoi deiatel'nosti i v bytovom obstanovlenie* (Leningrad, 1927), pp. 21–22.

56. *S.K.* 3, nos. 8875–85, 8932, and 8935; AAN, *fond* 3 *opis'* 1, no. 924, pp. 155–56. Among the more prominent Russian-born booksellers were the Glazunovs, Polezhaev, the Ponomarevs, Ovchinnikov, Reshetnikov, Sopikov, Kruglov, Zaikin, Zverev, Sokolov, Rakov, Klosterman, and Kozovlev. See *S.K.* 3, no. 8946; *Kratkii obzor knizhnoi torgovli i izdatel'skoi deiatel'nosti Glazunovykh za sto let, 1782–1882* (St. Petersburg, 1883), p. 1; AAN, *fond* 3, *opis'* 4, no. 29/1, p. 72, *opis'* 1, no. 924, p. 230, no. 928, p. 29, and no. 923, pp. 14, 142, 233; A. A. Zaitseva, "Novye materialy o russkikh knizhnykh lavkakh v S. Peterburge v kontse XVIII–nachale XIX v., " in *Knizhnoe delo v Rossii v XVI–XIX vekakh* (Leningrad, 1980), pp. 116–43.

57. Simoni, *Knizhnaia torgovlia v Moskve*, pp. 21–22.

58. *S.K.* 3, nos. 8918–24, and 6, nos. 293, 304, and 329.

59. G. I. Porshnev, "Istoriia knizhnoi torgovli v Rossii," in M. V. Muratov and N. N. Nakoriakov, eds., *Knizhnaia torgovlia* (Leningrad, 1929), p. 98.

60. Zaitseva, "Novye materialy o knizhnykh lavkakh," p. 120.

61. AAN, *fond 3, opis'* 1, no. 921, p. 118.

62. *S.K.* 1, no. 1089; AAN, *fond 3, opis'* 1, no. 2150, p. 1.

63. For examples of this, see *S.K.* 1, nos. 582 and 693.

64. A. A. Zaitseva, "Kabinety dlia chteniia v Sankt Peterburge kontsa XVIII–nachala XIX veka," in D. V. Ter Avanesian, ed., *Russkie biblioteki i chast-nye knizhnye sobraniia XVI–XIX vekov*," (Leningrad, 1979), pp. 43–45.

65. A list of the known catalogues can be found in *S.K.* 3, nos. 8842–8956, and 6, nos. 283–330. In addition, archival references discuss other catalogues that have not survived. See R. M. Tonkova, "Dopolnitel'nye svedeniia o knizhnykh rospisakh XVIII veka (po materialam Akademii nauk)," *Trudy instituta knigi* 5 (1936):49–52; A. I. Malein, "Knizhnye rospisi XVIII veka (otdel'nye zamechaniia)," *Trudy instituta knigi* 5 (1935): pp. 29–48; D. V. Ul'ianinskii, *Sredi knig i ikh druzei*, part 1 (Moscow, 1903); V. O. Osipov, *Knigotorgovaia bibliografiia* (Moscow, 1973), pp. 23-31.

66. These figures are very approximate, based upon material from a variety of primary and secondary sources, the most informative of which were booksellers' catalogues, newspaper advertisements, and notices printed in books and journals.

67. On Plavil'shchikov, see his catalogues, which continued into the 1820s, years after he had given up the press. On Brunkow, the information comes from his orders to the Academy of Sciences Press: AAN, *fond 3, opis'* 1, no. 922, pp. 125ff.

68. On the Glazunov firm, see *Kratkii obzor knizhnoi torgovli*; S. M. Babintsev, "Russkie knigoizdateli i knigotorgovtsy XVIII–XX v.," *Kniga* 2 (1960):376–83; N. M. Lisovskii, *Kratkii ocherk stoletnei deiatel'nosti tipografii Glazunovykh v sviazi s razvitiem ikh knigoizdatel'stva, 1803–1903* (St. Petersburg, 1903); Zaitseva, "Novye materialy o Glazunove," pp. 76–97.

69. S. Ogorodnikov, "A. I. Fomin (po neizdannym dokumentam)," *Izvestiia Arkhangel'skogo obshchestva izucheniia russkogo severa*, 1910, no. 3:21.

70. Ibid., p. 25.

71. *S.K.* 1, no. 2151.

72. AAN, *fond 3, opis'* 1, no. 541, p. 211.

73. D. D. Shamrai, "K istorii tsenzurnogo rezhima Ekateriny II," *XVIII vek* 3 (1958):198.

74. By way of comparison, publishers today figure that 40 to 50 percent of the wholesale price of a book goes to cover overhead expenses. Approximately the same percentage goes to cover production costs, leaving a profit of about 3 to 6 percent. In addition, the retail outlet marks up the price by two-thirds on most books. If such a formula had been used in Russia, books would have cost at least twice as much to the buyers as they actually did.

75. *S.K.* 3, no. 8552; AAN, *fond 3, opis'* 1, no. 536, p. 282.

76. AAN, *fond 3, opis'* 1, no. 535, p. 211, and no. 548, p. 88.

77. TsGADA, *fond* 17, no. 34; "O knigakh pechatannykh v Akademii nauk

i soobshchennykh iz kommissii o perevodakh 1779 g." This document reveals, among other things, that the Academy was so anxious to unload the Translation Society's books that it sold them at very small profit margins and, in at least one instance, even took a loss of 9 percent just to be rid of the book.

78. Martynov, "Veitbrekht," p. 42.

79. Ibid., pp. 42–43.

80. RO GBL, *fond* 1105, no. 114, pp. 15–23; AAN, *fond* 3, *opis'* 4, no. 29/1, pp. 72–77; Martynova and Martynov, "Vil'kovskii," p. 66.

81. AAN, *fond* 3, *opis'* 1, no. 926, pp. 288–332.

82. See the references to arrangements made by merchants in Leipzig and Amsterdam, in AAN, *fond* 3, *opis'* 1, no. 326, p. 293.

83. Ibid., no. 338, pp. 220–22, 321, 343–46.

84. Ibid., no. 383, pp. 24–38.

85. Tikhonravov, *Letopisi russkoi literatury*, 5:6–7.

86. Ibid., p. 7.

87. AAN, *fond* 3, *opis'* 1, no. 2150, pp. 1ff.

88. See the notations on their catalogues referring to the opening of new stores. *S.K.* 3, nos. 8876–85, 8932–35, 8944–46; Zaitseva, "Novye materialy o knizhnykh lavkakh," p. 122.

89. AAN, *fond* 3, *opis'* 1, no. 2162, pp. 14, 36, 38, 40, and no. 555, pp. 105, 473, and 533.

90. Martynov, "Veitbrekht," p. 57.

91. *Kratkii obzor knizhnoi torgovli*, p. 86.

92. *S.K.* 1, nos. 333, 582, and 693, and 4, p. 182.

93. AAN, *fond* 3, *opis'* 1, no. 384, pp. 274–80; no. 340, p. 240; no. 2162, p. 40.

94. Martynov, "Veitbrekht," pp. 44–47.

95. Watt, *Rise of the Novel*, pp. 42–43; Hilda Hamlyn, "Eighteenth-Century Circulating Libraries in England," *Library* 1 (1946):197.

96. Martynov, "Veitbrekht," p. 46.

97. I. M. Polonskaia, ed., *Spisok razyskivaemykh izdanii ne voshedshikh v Svodnyi katalog russkoi knigi grazhdanskoi pechati XVIII veka 1725–1800* (Moscow, 1969), no. 796.

98. Zaitseva, "Kabinety dlia chteniia," p. 32; Annelies Lauch, *Wissenschaft und kulturelle Beziehungen in der Russischen Aufklärung, Zum Wirken H. L. Ch. Bacmeisters* (Berlin, 1969), pp. 216–43.

99. N. G. Martynova-Poniatovskaia, "Materialy k istorii frantsuzkoi knizhnoi torgovli v Moskve," *Sobranie biblioteki Lenina*, 1928, no. 1:115.

100. T. Tastevin, *Histoire de la colonie française de Moscou depuis les origines jusqu'à 1812* (Paris, 1908), p. 70.

101. Ibid., p. 71; Martynova-Poniatovskaia, "Materialy k istorii frantsuzkoi knizhnoi torgovli," p. 126; N. V. Zdobnov, *Russkaia knizhnaia statistika* (Moscow, 1959), p. 67; Zaitseva, "Kabinety dlia chteniia," p. 43.

102. Zaitseva, "Kabinety dlia chteniia," pp. 33–39.

103. *S.K.* 6, no. 954.

104. Zaitseva, "Kabinety dlia chteniia," pp. 34–35.

105. Darnton, *Business of Enlightenment*, p. 302.

106. According to Darnton, "it cost twice as much to send a letter from Neuchatel to St. Petersburg ... as to buy an ordinary book in the STN's [Société Typographique de Neuchatel's] home office." Ibid., p. 303.

107. Ibid., pp. 302–3.

108. Giles Barber, "Books from the Old World and for the New: The British International Trade in Books in the Eighteenth Century," *Studies on Voltaire and the Eighteenth Century* 156 (1976):213–18.

109. Bernhard Fabian, "English Books and their Eighteenth-Century Readers," in Paul J. Korshin, ed., *The Widening Circle: Essays on the Circulation of Literature in Eighteenth-Century Europe* (Philadelphia, 1976), pp. 144, 166–67; Lehman, "Verlag Breitkopf," pp. 25–33; C. Grau and P. Hoffman, "Zur Verbreitung der Peterburger Akademie Publikationen in Deutschland im 18. Jahrhundert," in Helmut Grasshof and Ulf Lehman, eds., *Studien zur Geschichte der Russischen Literatur des 18. Jahrhunderts* (Berlin, 1968), pp. 123–34.

110. Martynov, "Veitbrekht," p. 41.

111. AAN, *fond* 3, *opis'* 1, no. 309, p. 210; no. 310, p. 341; no. 315, p. 130; and Tonkova, "Dopolnitel'nye svedeniia," pp. 50–53.

112. Bolotov, *Zhizn' i prikliucheniia*, 2:188–89.

113. Martynova-Poniatovskaia, "Materialy k istorii frantsuzkoi knizhnoi torgovli," p. 115.

114. *Reestr rossiiskim knigam ... prodaiutsia pri Imp. Moskovskom universitete* (Moscow, 1774, 1775, 1779); Darnton, *Business of Enlightenment*, p. 302; Martynov, "Knizhnaia lavka," p. 143.

115. Martynova-Poniatovskaia, "Materialy k istorii frantsuzkoi knizhnoi torgovli," p. 115.

116. Ibid., pp. 115–16.

117. Tastevin, *Colonie française*, p. 72.

118. Ibid., pp. 70–72; Martynova-Poniatovskaia, "Materialy k istorii frantsuzkoi knizhnoi torgovli," pp. 117–22.

119. Tastevin, p. 70; Martynova-Poniatovskaia, "Materialy k istorii frantsuzkoi knizhnoi literatury," p. 120.

120. Martynova-Poniatovskaia, "Materialy k istorii frantsuzkoi knizhnoi torgovli," pp. 124–28.

121. P. Stolpianskii, "Kniga v starom Peterburge," *Russkoe proshloe*, 1923, no. 1:132; Darnton, *Business of Enlightenment*, p. 303. In a letter to the STN, Müller claimed to do business with "all the readers of this country," a remark to which Darnton gives much credence.

122. A. A. Zaitseva, "Inostrannye knigotorgovtsy v Sankt Peterburge v kontse XVIII–nachale XIX v.," in Luppov and Paramonova, *Knigotorgovoe i bibliotechnoe delo*, p. 30; Zaitseva, "Kabinety dlia chteniia," pp. 33, 43–45.

123. Stolpianskii, "Kniga v starom Peterburge," pp. 132–133.

124. Rozenberg, *Novikov*, pp. 60–61; *Rospis' . . . knigam . . . kotoryia pro-daiutsia . . . v universitetskoi knizhnoi lavke . . . i v Rige u g. Gartknokha* (Moscow, 1783).

125. AAN, *fond* 3, *opis'* 1, no. 923, p. 194, and no. 326, p. 293. Eighteenth-century import figures reveal that prior to 1760 London imported about four pounds worth of books annually from Russia but between 1760 and 1780 the annual average was about fourteen pounds. Barber, "Books from the Old World," pp. 207–11.

126. Martynov, "Veitbrekht," p. 40.

127. Ibid.

128. AAN, *fond* 3, *opis'* 1, no. 921, p. 18. Other copies went into storage.

129. Ibid., pp. 49–51.

130. Martynova-Poniatovskaia, "Materialy k istorii frantsuzkoi knizhnoi tor-govli," pp. 124–25.

131. D. D. Shamrai, "Prodazha izdanii," p. 140.

132. Ibid.

133. Ibid., pp. 145–46.

134. Ibid., pp. 143, 148.

135. TsGADA, *fond* 359, no. 4, pp. 1–5.

136. Martynov, "Kniga v russkoi provintsii," pp. 120–24.

137. See, for example, *Rospis' rossiiskim knigam prodaiushchimsia . . . v universitetskoi knizhnoi lavke . . . a v drugikh gorodakh mozhno poluchit' sii knigi cherez vse pochtovye kontory* (Moscow, 1789).

138. For a fuller discussion of provincial subscribers, see Gary J. Marker, "Publishing and the Formation of a Reading Public in Eighteenth-Century Russia" (Ph.D. diss., University of California at Berkeley, 1977), pp. 369–98. The subject of reading and the reading public will be discussed in a forthcoming monograph on which I am currently working.

139. Martynov, "Kniga v russkoi provintsii," pp. 118–24.

140. Karamzin, "On the Book Trade," pp. 450–52.

141. TsGADA, *fond* 359, no. 4, pp. 1–5.

142. Ibid., pp. 6–7.

143. TsGIA, *fond* 796, *opis'* 68, no. 290, pp. 153–55.

144. Ibid., pp. 157, 188, 202, and several others.

145. Ibid., pp. 153, 170, 173, 201, 202, 203, and Martynov, "Kniga v russkoi provintsii," pp. 120–24.

146. I. D. Koval'chenko, ed., *Russkie pis'mennye i ustnye traditsii i dukhov-naia kul'tura* (Moscow, 1982), pp. 25, 31–36, 46.

147. Zaitseva, "Novye materialy o Glazunove," pp. 85–95.

148. For a further discussion of Karamzin's literary contacts, see A. G. Cross, *N. M. Karamzin: A Study of His Literary Career, 1783–1803* (Carbondale, Ill., 1971), pp. 1–65.

149. TsGADA, *fond* 17, no. 34.

150. AAN, *fond* 3, *opis'* 1, nos. 921–29.

151. Martynova and Martynov, "Vil'kovskii," p. 68.

152. Okenfuss, "Education and Empire," pp. 41–68.

153. *Opisanie del arkhiva Ministerstva narodnogo prosveshcheniia*, pp. 161–62.

154. H. R. Plomer et al., *A Dictionary of the Printers and Booksellers Who Were at Work in England, Scotland, and Ireland from 1726 to 1775* (London, 1932).

CHAPTER SEVEN

1. AAN, *fond* 3, *opis'* 1, nos. 922–29.

2. For a discussion of the reception of printing in the Renaissance, see Rudolph Hirsch, *Printing, Selling, and Reading, 1450–1550* (Wiesbaden, 1974), pp. 61–153.

3. On European almanacs, see Bernard Capp, *English Almanacs, 1500–1800: Astrology and the Popular Press* (Ithaca, N.Y., 1979).

4. Unless otherwise noted, the basic information on publishers, editions, and print runs of calendars comes from *S.K.* 4, nos. 264–523.

5. Not included in this figure are the several thousand German calendars that the Academy produced annually.

6. *S.K.* 4, nos. 264–69, 297, 325–27, 335–37, 384–91, 426–27, 483–88, 520–21.

7. *S.K.* 4, nos. 345–422.

8. *S.K.* 4, nos. 335–44.

9. For example, a *Calendar for Children* was published in 1776 and a calendar of church holidays in 1795.

10. In November 1792, for example, Ivan Glazunov ordered over 3,500 calendars of various types. In January 1790 Rakov ordered 1,000 calendars, and in 1798 Glazunov and Sopikov together ordered over 13,000 calendars. AAN, *fond* 3, *opis'* 1, no. 923, p. 15, and no. 924, p. 205; *S.K.* 4, no. 419; and AAN, *fond* 3, *opis'* 1, no. 383, p. 28.

11. AAN, *fond* 3, *opis'* 1, no. 924, p. 104. In a situation that was not unusual, Sopikov was still ordering additional calendars in June 1792, six months after they had been published.

12. AAN, *fond* 3, *opis'* 1, no. 336, p. 180.

13. AAN, *fond* 3, *opis'* 1, no. 928, pp. 6–63. This document lists all of the small orders for 1793; about three-quarters of them requested either maps or calendars.

14. *S.K.* 4, nos. 416 and 417.

15. The population of the Russian empire in the 1790s was about thirty-seven million, but about nine million of these people lived in territories that had been added during the eighteenth century, which had mostly non–Russian-speaking inhabitants. I am including, therefore, only those people who lived within the borders of 1709. V. M. Kabuzan, *Izmeneniia v razmeshchenii naseleniia Rossii v XVIII–pervoi polovine XIX v.* (Moscow, 1963), p. 10.

16. Okenfuss, *Discovery of Childhood*, p. 11.

17. Ibid., pp. 57–58 and 62.

18. Afanas'eva, "Svetskaia kirillicheskaia kniga," p. 77.

19. TsGIA, *fond* 730, *opis'* 1, nos. 17 and 27; *S.K.* 3, nos. 6190–94.

20. TsGIA, *fond* 730, *opis'* 1, no. 111, pp. 1–9; *S.K.* 3, nos. 7085–87.

21. *S.K.* 2, nos. 4739–44. For a thorough discussion as well as a complete translation of this book, see Black, *Citizens for the Fatherland*, pp. 209–66.

22. TsGIA, *fond* 730, *opis'* 1, no. 86, p. 55, and no. 119, p. 6.

23. Ibid., no. 133.

24. *Rospis' rossiiskim knigam . . . prodaiushchimsia . . . u knigoprodavtsa K. V. Millera* (St. Petersburg, 1774).

25. *Rospis' rossiiskim knigam kotoryia prodaiutsia u M. Ovchinnikova* (St. Petersburg, 1787).

26. AAN, *fond* 3, *opis'* 1, no. 923, pp. 225, 73, 143, 158, and 225; and no. 924, p. 156.

27. *S.K.* 2, nos. 3774–80.

28. Ibid., nos. 3743–49.

29. Ibid., no. 3369.

30. Ibid., nos. 3232–40.

31. In the 1792 inventory, Professor Teil's found 1,244 copies of this grammar. This number probably was close to the number of copies printed in the most recent (1790) edition. If this is the case, and if 1,200 represented the average print run of this book, then 6,000 copies had been sold before 1790. Once Novikov's property was impounded, these 1,244 copies disappeared from the market. Their absence apparently caused a shortage, because three subsequent editions came out before 1800. Svetlov, *Izdatel'skaia deiatel'nost' Novikova*, p. 86; *S.K.* 2, nos. 3238–40.

32. *S.K.* 3, nos. 7184–85; AAN, *fond* 3, *opis'* 1, no. 922, p. 76, and no. 923, pp. 73–74.

33. *S.K.* 1, nos. 1319–23.

34. AAN, *fond* 3, *opis'* 1, no. 924, pp. 134, 155, 177, and several others.

35. *S.K.* 2, nos. 3213–18, and 3, nos. 8092–98; AAN, *fond* 3, *opis'* 1, no. 923, pp. 225–26.

36. AAN, *fond* 3, *opis'* 1, no. 536, p. 653, and no. 537, p. 6.

37. Luppov, *Kniga . . . v XVII veke*, p. 93.

38. Luppov, "Akademicheskie i zarubezhnye izdaniia," pp. 156, 158, 163.

39. *S.K.* 3, nos. 7521–30.

40. In the bookstore orders for 1790, demand for the *Ulozhenie* ran very high. Most dealers ordered between 20 and 100 copies, and reorders of a similar magnitude were common. ANN, *fond* 3, *opis'* 1, no. 922, pp. 62, 77, 126, 134, 234, 291, 331, and others.

41. See the numerous citations in ibid., nos. 922–26; *S.K.* 2, nos. 4724–33.

42. *S.K.* 3, nos. 7566–73 and 7575–77.

43. *S.K.* 3, nos. 7454–60; AAN, *fond* 3, *opis'* 1, no. 924, pp. 135–36, and no. 922, pp. 38, 77, 126, 134, 233, and others.

44. *S.K.* 2, nos. 3296–3300.

45. Richard Wortman, *The Development of a Russian Legal Consciousness* (Chicago, 1976), p. 31–33.

46. Ibid., p. 26.

47. *S.K.* 2, nos. 5139–5144. Medical books of all kinds sold relatively well in Russia during Catherine's reign, attesting perhaps to the tremendous concern over disease and epidemics in such a plague-prone country. In the 1790s, for example, a volume entitled *A Description of Diseases in the Army* attracted a great deal of interest from booksellers.

48. Viscount Goschen, *The Life and Times of Georg Joachim Goschen, Publisher and Printer of Leipzig, 1752–1828,* 2 vols. (London, 1903), 1:90–95.

49. W. H. Bruford doubts the accuracy of these figures, citing an unidentified English source to the effect that a very popular English book entitled *Mrs. Rundell's Domestic Cookery* sold only between 5,000 and 10,000 copies a year. But A. S. Collins mentions several books that sold more than 10,000 copies a year in eighteenth-century England; Price's *Observations on the Nature of Civil Liberties,* for example, sold 60,000 copies in four months. W. H. Bruford, *Germany in the Eighteenth Century: The Social Background of the Literary Revival* (Cambridge, 1971), p. 280; Collins, *Profession of Letters,* p. 21.

50. A. I. Khodnev, *Istoriia vol'nago ekonomicheskago obshchestva s 1765 do 1865 goda* (St. Petersburg, 1865), pp. 390–91.

51. Lists of subscribers appeared at the end of each volume.

52. Wortman, *Russian Legal Consciousness,* p. 97.

53. The first German edition of *Young Werther* appeared in 1774, the first Russian one in 1781. *S.K.* 1, no. 1425.

54. Karamzin, "On the Book Trade," pp. 447–51.

55. *S.K.* 4:51–114.

56. Martynova and Martynov, "Vil'kovskii," p. 68.

57. *S.K.* 2, nos. 5615–19.

58. *S.K.* 2, nos. 3653–59.

59. *S.K.* 2, nos. 3058–63, 3037–40, and 4576–78.

60. TsGADA, *fond* 71, no. 34, p. 5.

61. *S.K.* 1, nos. 1108–12.

62. Ibid., 2, nos. 4249–57.

63. TsGADA, *fond* 17, no. 34, pp. 3–7. Sales figures stop in 1779, when the Academy's survey was completed. But few of the novels went into second printings in the final twenty years of the century and bookshop orders continued to be sparse.

64. *S.K.* 1, nos. 1844–46. Karamzin seems to have been aware of this situation when he wrote so optimistically of the sale of romances and so wistfully about the sale of important books.

65. AAN, *fond* 3, *opis'* 1, no. 551, p. 452; Martynova and Martynov, "Vil'kovskii," p. 72.

66. Russian translations of Molière's plays are listed in *S.K.* 2, nos. 4305–

21. The 1792 inventory showed that Novikov had substantial quantities of these plays. Four years earlier he had published twelve plays by Molière. The print runs are not known, but the remainders numbered between 950 and 1,200 copies for each play. Svetlov, *Idatel'skaia deiatel'nost Novikova,* pp. 93–95.

67. V. P. Semennikov, *Materialy dlia istorii russkoi literatury i dlia slovaria pisatelei epokhi Ekateriny II* (Petrograd, 1915), pp. 104–5.

68. AAN, *fond* 3, *opis'* 1, no. 355, pp. 146–93. This document contains an inventory from 1876, in which Sumarokov's plays are listed in quantities ranging up to several hundred copies each.

69. *S.K.* 2, nos. 2813–15; AAN, *fond* 3, *opis'* 1, nos. 922–26.

70. See, for example, *S.K.* 3, no. 6974, which lists the supposed fourth edition of Sumarokov's comedy, *Narcissus.* The play had originally appeared in 1769 and was not reissued until Novikov's new edition in 1786. The 1792 inventory shows that between 350 and 500 copies of each of Sumarokov's plays remained in stock. Since the initial print runs are not known, it is impossible to determine whether sales had been good or bad. But the reluctance of dealers to take these books at auction and the unwillingness of other publishers to reprint Sumarokov's works after the confiscation of Novikov's inventory suggest that Sumarokov had not yet struck a responsive chord among readers. Svetlov, *Izdatel'skaia deiatel'nost' Novikova,* pp. 87, 93–95.

71. *S.K.* 3, nos. 8547–53, and AAN, *fond* 3, *opis'* 1, no. 924, pp. 11, 23, 36, 51, 103; no. 923, p. 73; no. 922, p. 125; and no. 914, p. 186.

72. *S.K.* 2, nos. 3322–23.

73. Ibid., nos. 4060–66; AAN, *fond* 3, *opis'* 1, no. 924, pp. 36, 51, 134.

74. *S.K.* 3, nos. 7709–10 and 7712–13.

75. Ibid., 1, nos. 2036–41.

76. Ibid., 3 nos. 8631–33. Emin's *Fables* first appeared in 1764, in a print run of 1,316 copies. After a hiatus of twenty-five years, Bogdanovich printed two new editions within a span of four years. The success of the first of these editions can be inferred from the fact that the prominent bookseller Ivan Glazunov was willing to finance an additional printing. The more ponderous and religious *Path to Salvation* went through seven editions from five separate publishers between 1780 and 1798. *S.K.* 3, nos. 8638–45.

77. Sixteen of Levshin's books appeared in the eighteenth cenutury, but only one, *The Complete Hunter,* went into a second printing. Ibid., 2, nos. 3545 and 3546.

78. Okenfuss, *Discovery of Childhood.*

79. Ibid., 1, nos. 1670–77 and 903–9. The Hübner work was published by the Moscow University Press, Hippius, Ponomarev, and the Typographical Company; Father Benjamin's stories by the Academy of Sciences and Moscow University Presses.

80. Ibid., 1, nos. 2508–12; AAN, *fond* 3, *opis'* 1, no. 312, p. 155.

81. *S.K.* 2, nos. 4037–40.

82. Ibid., 1, no. 669; 2, no. 3738; 3, nos. 7161 and 8646. None of these histories went into a second printing in the eighteenth century.
83. *S.K.* 3, nos. 8525 and 8526; AAN, *fond* 3, *opis'* 1, no. 924, pp. 51, 134, 204, and no. 923, pp. 73, 99, 142.
84. *S.K.* 1, nos. 1263–68, 2711, 2713–21.
85. Ibid., nos. 45–50.
86. *S.K.* 1, nos. 903–9, and 2, nos. 5029–31.
87. TsGADA, *fond* 17, no. 34, pp. 1–7.
88. Ibid., pp. 1–3; *S.K.* 2, nos. 4834–36; AAN, *fond* 3, *opis'* 1, no. 543, p. 250.
89. *S.K.* 1, no. 1549.
90. Ibid., 2, no. 4332.
91. Ibid., 3, nos. 6219–21.

Chapter Eight

1. "Doklad Sviateishago Sinoda Imperatritse Elisavete Petrovne o knigakh protivnykh vere i nravstvennosti," *ChIOIDR*, pt. 1 (1867), pp. 7–8; P. N. Berkov and D. D. Shamrai, "K tsenzurnoi istorii 'Trudoliubivoi pchely'," *XVIII vek* 5 (1962): 400–1; P. P. Pekarskii, "Redaktor, sotrudniki i tsenzura v russkom zhurnale 1755–1765 godov," *Zapiski Akademii nauk* 12 (1867):47–56.
2. TsGADA, *fond* 3, *opis'* 2, no. 219, pp. 248–305.
3. V. A. Zapadov has uncovered a secret memorandum of December 1775 that forbade the sale of Russian letters for use in printing presses owned by private individuals. Zapadov believes that this policy was intended to control the spread of illicit private presses. But there is no evidence showing any pirate Russian publishing in this period. Rather, the Senate was probably trying to ensure that the foreign-language presses did not contravene their charters. Zapadov, "Kratkii ocherk istorii tsenzury," p. 104; TsGIA, *fond* 796, *opis'* 56, no. 612, pp. 10–16.
4. Shamrai, "K istorii tsenzurnogo rezhima," p. 187.
5. Ibid., p. 186; K. A. Papmehl, *Freedom of Expression in Eighteenth-Century Russia* (The Hague, 1971), p. 37.
6. V. P. Semennikov, "K istorii tsenzury v Ekaterinskuiu epokhu," *Russkii bibliofil*, 1913, no. 1:58.
7. Ibid., p. 57.
8. *S.K.* 3, no. 6324; Zapadov, "Kratkii ocherk istorii tsenzury," pp. 96–97; Shamrai, "Iz istorii tsenzurnogo rezhima Ekateriny II," p. 126.
9. *S.K.* 3, no. 6227.
10. Shamrai, "K istorii tsenzurnogo rezhima," pp. 185ff.
11. Tiulichev, "Tsenzura izdanii Akademii nauk," pp. 94, 107–8.
12. Zapadov, "Kratkii ocherk istorii tsenzury," pp. 97–98.
13. Papmehl, *Freedom of Expression*, pp. 34, 97–99, 112–19.
14. Wolfgang Gesemann, "Grundzüge der russischen Zensur in 18. Jahrhundert," in *Buch und Verlagswesen*, pp. 66–69.

15. *PSZ*, no. 14985.

16. *Opisanie del arkhiva Ministerstva narodnogo prosveshcheniia*, 1:166–67.

17. TsGIA, *fond* 796, *opis'* 1, no. 280, pp. 1–37.

18. AAN, *fond* 3, *opis'* 1, no. 551, p. 263.

19. *PSZ*, no. 15634.

20. TsGIA, *fond* 796, *opis'* 68, no. 299, pp. 1–2, 9–11, 39.

21. *PSZ*, no. 16086.

22. Longinov, *Novikov i moskovskie martinisty*, p. 245.

23. Ibid., p. 250.

24. Ibid., pp. 258–60; Longinov, *Novikov i Shvarts*, pp. 25–26; S. Smirnov, "Tsenzurnaia vedomost' 1786–1788 godov s predisloviem," *Osmnadtsatyi vek* 1 (1869):492–502.

25. TsGIA, *fond* 796, *opis'* 67, no. 110, pp. 78–88.

26. Longinov, *Novikov i moskovskie martinisty*, p. 261.

27. Albert Ward, *Book Production, Fiction, and the German Reading Public, 1740–1800* (Oxford, 1974), p. 4.

28. TsGIA, *fond* 796, *opis'* 66, no. 11, pp. 1–7.

29. Longinov, *Novikov i moskovskie martinisty*, p. 261.

30. Tikhonravov, *Letopisi russkoi literatury*, 1: 23–28.

31. *PSZ*, nos. 16556 and 16564; AAN, *fond* 3, *opis'* 1, no. 559, p. 527; TsGIA, *fond* 796, *opis'* 68, no. 290, p. 1.

32. The whole matter can be found in TsGIA, *fond* 796, *opis'* 68, no. 290, pp. 1–294. Curiously, these documents lack any reference to a search for books in either St. Petersburg or Kiev. Church authorities in those two cities received the same instructions as all other churchmen, but for some reason there is no indication that they conducted searches.

33. Zapadov, "Kratkii ocherk istorii tsenzury," p. 113.

34. Longinov, *Novikov i moskovskie martinisty*, pp. 280–88.

35. The scholars who have held this position include a majority of Soviet specialists, such as D. D. Blagoi, K. V. Sivkov, and A. V. Zapadov.

36. Zapadov, "K istorii pravitel'stvennykh presledovanii," pp. 41–45.

37. This somewhat older view is often described as the "liberal" position. Its most noted defender was A. A. Kizevetter, who expressed it in several works; see e.g., "Imperatritsa Ekaterina II kak zakonodatel'nitsa," in his *Istoricheskie ocherki* (St. Petersburg, 1912), pp. 215–17.

38. McArthur, "Catherine II," pp. 529–46; Ryu, "Moscow Freemasons," pp. 210–20.

39. Zapadov, "K istorii pravitel'stvennykh presledovanii," pp. 41–47.

40. See L. V. Svetlov, "A. N. Radishchev i politicheskie protsessy kontsa XVIII v.," *Izvestiia Akademii nauk SSR, Seriia istorii i filosofii* no. 5 (1949), pp. 446–453 for a review of all the trials of the last years of Catherine's reign.

41. Polonskaia, "Rakhmaninov," p. 137.

42. N. G. Vysotskii, "Zapreshchennyia pri Ekaterine Velikoi knigi," *Russkii arkhiv*, 1912, no. 10:252–55. Several other similar cases can be found in TsGIA, *fond* 7, no. 2797, "O zapreshchennyh knigakh 1793," pp. 1–33,

and "Pis'mo po povodu vysochaishago poveleniia ob otobranii iz knizhnykh lavok, pod vedomstvem Moskovskogo universiteta, sostoiashchikh vrednago i nepozvolennago soderzhaniia knig, v reestrakh oznachennykh," *ChIOIDR* Vol. 3 (1871), pp. 7–8.

43. Zaitseva "Novye materialy o Glazunove," p. 81.

44. *PSZ*, no. 17523.

45. Orlov, *Poligraficheskaia promyshlennost'*, p. 114.

46. TsGADA, *fond* 7, no. 3153, p. 592; Zapadov, "Kratkii ocherk istorii tsenzury," p. 133; P. P. Karatygin, "Tsenzura vremen Imperatora Pavla I," *Istoricheskii vestnik* Vol. 22 no. 10 (1885), pp. 154–60.

47. Blium has taken the oversight responsibilities of the local governor more seriously than I take them. He seems to believe that knowledge of the possibility for censorship inhibited local publishers. But lacking any concrete suggestions that anyone expressed these feelings (other than Rukavishnikov and Rakhmaninov, whose cases were unique), such an interpretation seems dubious. Blium, "Izdatel'skaia deiatel'nost'," pp. 154–55.

48. *S.K.* 5:289; Dmitriev-Mamonov, "Pechat' v Tobol'skom namestnichestve," p. 347.

49. *PSZ*, no. 17811.

50. V. V. Sipovskii, "Iz proshlago russkoi tsenzury," *Russkaia starina*, 1899, no. 5:443.

51. Ibid., p. 436.

52. *PSZ*, nos. 18186 and 18265.

53. Papmehl, *Freedom of Expression*, p. 137.

54. *PSZ*, nos. 18524, 18738, 18939, and 19010.

55. *PSZ*, no. 19387.

56. *PSZ*, no. 19807.

57. M. N. Kufaev, *Istoriia russkoi knigi v XIX veke* (Leningrad, 1927), p. 51.

Conclusion

1. Karamzin, "On the Book Trade," p. 452.

2. The polemics over the roles of publishers and booksellers in determining the fate of literature went on throughout the first half of the nineteenth century. For example, on the interchange between the conservatives and the early Westernizers during the reign of Nicholas I, see S. Shevyrev, "Slovesnost' i torgovlia," *Moskovskii nabliudatel'* 1 (1835):10–26, and V. G. Belinskii, "Literaturnye i zhurnal'nye zametki 1842," *Polnoe sobranie sochinenii*, 8 vols. (St. Petersburg, 1914), 6:449–54.

3. Paul Debreczeny, "The Beginnings of Mass Literature in Russia: Early Imitations of Pushkin's Narrative Poems," *Canadian Slavic Studies* 5 (Spring 1971):1–21.

BIBLIOGRAPHY

To COMPOSE a complete roster of all the sources that I have consulted for this book would be a relatively unprofitable venture, since the secondary literature, for the most part, consists of a voluminous but extremely disparate array of small or specialized studies that individually provide a great deal of information but collectively do not amount to a coherent body of literature. In any event, those sources that have been directly relevant to the writing of this book are discussed in the notes and their authors are listed in the index. Several authors, of course, such as V. P. Semennikov, S. P. Luppov, I. F. Martynov, and V. A. Zapadov, deserve particular mention for having made lasting contributions to the more significant aspects of eighteenth-century Russian printing history, but they have been discussed at length both in the notes and in the text.

What are listed below, then, are the archival sources, printed catalogues, and those selected primary sources, such as documentary collections, that have contributed in a significant way to my research.

1. Unpublished Sources

Leningrad

Archives of the Academy of Sciences (AAN)
    Fond 3   Academic Chancellery
Central State Historical Archive (TsGIA)
    Fond 730   Commission on the Establishment of Primary Schools in Russia
    Fond 796   Chancellery of the Holy Synod
Manuscript Division of the State Public Library (RO GPB)
    Fond 341   N. A. Kartavova Collection
    Fond 539   V. F. Odoevskii Collection
    Fond 568   P. Pekarskii Collection
    Fond 871   Ia. Ia. Stählin Collection
    Fond 1105   D. D. Shamrai Collection

Moscow

Central State Archives of Ancient Acts (TsGADA)
    Fond 3   Secret Chancellery
    Fond 8   Private Offices of Catherine II
    Fond 17   Collection on Literature, Science, and Art
    Fond 255   Moscow Senate Press Collection
    Fond 359   Moscow University Press Collection

283

Fond 1182   Office of Publishing, 1700–1721 (*Prikaz knigopechataniia*)
Manuscript Division of Lenin State Library (RO GBL)
Fond 41   Bulgakov Family Collection
Fond 233   P. Stolpianskii Collection

2. Catalogues and Other Reference Material

Alfavitnyi sluzhebnyi katalog russkikh dorevoliutsionnykh gazet. Leningrad, 1958.

Bykova, T. A., and Gurevich, M. M. *Opisanie izdanii grazhdanskoi pechati, 1708–Ianvar' 1725.* Moscow, 1955.

Bykova, T. A., and Gurevich, M. M. *Opisanie izdanii napechatannykh kirillitsei, 1689–Ianvar' 1725.* Moscow, 1958.

———. *Opisanie izdanii napechatannykh pri Petre I: Dopolneniia i prilozheniia.* Moscow, 1972.

Gennadi, Grigorii. *Literatura russkoi bibliografii.* St. Petersburg, 1858.

Izdaniia grazhdanskoi pechati vremeni Imperatritsy Elisavety Petrovny, 1741–1761. Vol. 1, *1741–1755.* Moscow, 1935.

Katalog izdanii Imperatorskoi akademii nauk. St. Petersburg, 1912–24.

Knigi grazhdanskoi pechati XVIII veka. Kiev, 1956.

Lisovskii, N. M. *Bibliografiia russkoi periodicheskoi pechati, 1703–1900 gg.: Materialy dlia istorii russkoi zhurnalistiki.* Petrograd, 1915.

———. "Periodicheskaia pechat' v Rossii, 1703–1903 gg. Statistiko-bibliograficheskii obzor russkikh periodicheskikh izdanii." In *Sbornik statei po istorii i statistike russkoi periodicheskoi pechati, 1703–1903.* St. Petersburg, 1903.

———. *Russkaia periodicheskaia pechat', 1703–1900: Bibliografiia i graficheskaia tablitsa.* Petrograd, 1915.

Malein, A. I. "Knizhnye rospisi XVIII veka (otdel'nye zamechaniia)." *Trudy Instituta knigi, dokumenta, i pis'ma* 5 (1936): 29–48.

Mashkova, M. V., and Sokurova, M. V. *Obshchie bibliografii russkikh periodicheskikh izdanii, 1703–1954.* Leningrad, 1956.

Mel'nikova, N. N. *Izdaniia Moskovskogo universiteta, 1756–1779.* Moscow, 1955.

———. *Izdaniia napechatannye v tipografii Moskovskogo universiteta XVIII veka.* Moscow, 1966.

Mez'er, A. V. *Slovarnyi ukazatel' po knigovedeniiu.* St. Petersburg, 1924.

Neustroev, A. N. *Istoricheskoe razyskanie o russkikh povremennykh izdaniiakh i sbornikakh za 1703–1802 gg.* St. Petersburg, 1875.

"Podlinnye reestry knigam vziatym po vysochaishemu poveleniiu, iz palat N. I. Novikova v moskovskuiu dukhovnuiu i svetskuiu tsenzuru." *Chteniia v Imperatorskom obshchestve istorii i drevnostei rossiiskikh pri Moskovskom universitete* 3 (July-September 1871).

Polonskaia, I. M., ed. *Spisok razyskivaemykh izdanii ne voshedshikh v svodnyi katalog russkoi knigi grazhdanskoi pechati XVIII veka, 1725–1800.* Moscow, 1969.

Riss, F. *Catalogue du cabinet de lecture*. Moscow, 1836.

Rodosskii, Aleksei. *Opisanie knig grazhdanskoi pechati XVIII stoletiia khra-niashchikhsia v biblioteke St. Peterburgskoi dukhovnoi akademii*. St. Pe-tersburg, 1896.

———. *Opisanie staropechatnykh i tserkovoslavianskikh knig khrania-shchikhsia v biblioteke St. Peterburgskoi dukhovnoi akademii*. St. Pe-tersburg, 1894.

Semennikov, V. P. "Bibliograficheskii spisok knig napechatannykh v provintsii so vremeni vozniknoveniia grazhdanskikh tipografii po 1807 g." *Russkii bibliofil* 2 (1912):47–77 and 2 (1912):36–58.

———. "Dopolnitel'nye materialy dlia istorii provintsial'nykh tipografii XVIII–nachala XIX veka." *Russkii bibliofil* 7 (1913):58–83.

Sokolov, A. P. *Russkaia morskaia biblioteka, 1701–1851: Ischislenie i opi-sanie knig rukopisei i statei po morskomu delu za 150 let*. St. Petersburg, 1883.

Sokurva, M. V. *Bibliografiia russkoi bibliografii*. Vol. 1, *Obshchie bibliografii knig grazhdanskoi pechati, 1708–1937*. Leningrad, 1944.

———. *Obshchie bibliografii russkikh knig grazhdanskoi pechati, 1708–1955: Annotirovannyi ukazatel'*. Leningrad, 1956.

Sopikov, Vasilii. *Opyt rossiiskoi bibliografii*. 5 vols. St. Petersburg, 1813–21.

Svodnyi katalog russkoi knigi grazhdanskoi pechati, XVIII veka, 1725–1800. 6 vols. Moscow, 1962–75.

Tonkova, R. M. "Dopolnitel'nye svedeniia o knizhnykh rospisakh XVIII veka (po materialam arkhiva Akademii nauk)." *Trudy Instituta knigi, doku-menta, pis'ma* 5 (1936):49–52.

———. "Iz materialov arkhiva Akademii nauk po literature i zhurnalistike XVIII v." *Vosemnadtsatyi vek* 1 (1935).

Ul'ianinskii, D. V. *Biblioteka D. V. Ul'ianinskogo*. 2 vols. St. Petersburg, 1913.

Zernova, A. S., ed. *Svodnyi katalog russkoi knigi kirillovskoi pechati XVIII veka*. Moscow, 1968.

In addition to the titles cited above, there are approximately 180 surviving catalogues (*rospisi* or *reestry*) of libraries and booksellers of the eighteenth century. I consulted all that were available in public libraries in Moscow and Leningrad (approximately 130 of them). Obviously, they are too numerous to list here, but a complete listing of all known catalogues can be found in *Svodnyi katalog*, vol. 3, nos. 8842–8956, and vol. 6, nos. 283–330.

3. Selected Published Primary Sources

Adrianova, V. *Materialy dlia istorii tsen na knigi v drevnei rusi XVI–XVIII vv*. Moscow, 1912.

Biograficheskii slovar' studentov Imperatorskogo moskovskogo universiteta i chlenov gimnazii blagorodnei s 1756 po 1760. Moscow, n.d.

Bolotov, Andrei. *Zhizn' i prikliucheniia Andreia Bolotova, 1738–1793.* 3 vols. Moscow, 1931.

"Cherty iz istorii knizhnago prosveshcheniia pri Petre Velikom." *Russkii arkhiv* 7 and 8 (1868): 1041–1057.

Derzhavin, G. R. *Zapiski.* Moscow, 1860.

"Doklad sviateishago sinoda Imperatritse Elisavete Petrovne o knigakh, protivnykh vere i nravstvennosti." *Chteniia v Imperatorskom obshchestve istorii i drevnostei rossiiskikh pri Moskovskom universitete,* Vol. 1 part 5. Moscow, 1867, pp 7-8.

Dokumenty i materialy po istorii Moskovskogo universiteta vtoroi poloviny XVIII veka. 3 vols. Moscow, 1958–63.

Fon Vizin, Denis. *Sobranie sochinenii,* vol. 2. Moscow, 1959.

"Gosudarstvennye dokhody i raskhody v tsarstvovanie Ekateriny II." *Sbornik Imperatorskogo russkago istoricheskago obshchestva* 5 (1870): 217–230.

Guerrier, V. I. *Otnosheniia Leibnitsa k Rossii i Petru Velikomu po neizdannym bumagam Leibnitsa.* St. Petersburg, 1871.

Istoricheskiia svedeniia o tsenzure v Rossii. St. Petersburg, 1862.

Istoricheskii ocherk i obzor fondov rukopisnogo otdela biblioteki Akademii nauk. Vol. 1, XVIII vek. Moscow, 1956.

Karamyshev, N. *Kratkiia istoricheskiia svedeniia o peterburgskikh tipografiiakh s 1711 i statisticheskiia svedeniia o zavedeniiakh pechati za 1868–1895 gg.* St. Petersburg, 1895.

Khrestomatiia po istorii russkoi knigi, 1564–1917. Moscow, 1965.

Koz'min, B. P., ed. *Sbornik materialov k izucheniiu istorii russkoi zhurnalistiki.* Vol. 1, XVIII v. i pervaia polovina XIX v. Moscow, 1952.

Kunik, A. *Sbornik materialov dlia istorii Imperatorskoi akademii nauk v XVIII veke.* 2 vols. St. Petersburg, 1865.

Mashtafarov, A. V., ed. "Neizdannyi dokument ob arende N. I. Novikovym tipografii Moskovskogo universiteta." *Kniga* 18 (1974): 152–156.

Materialy dlia istorii Imperatorskoi akademii nauk. 10 vols. St. Petersburg, 1885–1900.

Materialy dlia istorii russkoi knizhnoi torgovli. St. Petersburg, 1879.

Ogorodnikov, S. "A. I. Fomin (po neizdannym dokumentam)." *Izvestiia Arkhangel'skogo obshchestva izucheniia russkogo severa* 3 (1910): 18–29.

Opisanie del arkhiva narodnago prosveshcheniia, vols. 1 and 2. Petrograd, 1917.

Pekarskii, P. P., ed. *Bumagi Imperatritsy Ekateriny II khraniashchiiasia v gosudarstvennom arkhive Ministerstva inostrannykh del,* vol. 1. St. Petersburg, 1871.

Pis'ma i bumagi Imperatora Petra Velikogo. 11 vols. St. Petersburg-Leningrad, 1887–1962.

Polnoe sobranie postanovlenii i rasporiazhenii po vedomstvu pravoslavnago ispovedaniia rossiiskoi imperii, vols. 1–4. St. Petersburg, 1872–76.

Polnoe sobranie zakonov rossiiskoi imperii s 1649 goda. St. Petersburg, 1830–1917.

Poludenskii, M. "Materialy dlia istorii 'Druzheskago Uchenago obshchestva,' 1782." *Russkii arkhiv* 3 (1863): 203–217.

Rogozhin, V. N. *Materialy dlia russkoi bibliografii XVIII i pervoi chetverti XIX stoletii.* Vol. 1, *Dela moskovskoi tsenzury, 1797–1802 gg.* St. Petersburg, 1902.

Sbornik postanovlenii i rasporiazhenii po tsenzure s 1720 po 1862 goda. St. Petersburg, 1862.

Semennikov, V. P. *Materialy dlia istorii russkoi literatury i dlia slovaria pisatelei epokhi Ekateriny II.* Petrograd, 1915.

Snegirev, I. "Dva materiala dlia istorii grazhdanskago knigopechataniia v Rossii." *Biblioteka dlia chteniia* 6 (1834): 38–46.

Tikhonravov, Nikolai, ed. *Letopisi russkoi literatury i drevnosti.* 5 vols. Moscow, 1862.

Tokmanov, I. "Materialy dlia istorii russkoi i inostrannoi bibliografii v sviazi s knizhnoi torgovlei." *Bibliograf* 4 (1885): 76–81 and 6 (1885): 105–11.

Ul'ianinskii, D. V. *Sredi knig i ikh druzei.* Moscow, 1903.

Vedomosti vremeni Petra Velikogo, 1702–1719. 2 vols. Moscow, 1906.

Voskresenskii, N. A. *Zakonodatel'nye akty Petra I.* Moscow, 1945.

INDEX

LIBRARY OF CONGRESS CATALOGING
IN PUBLICATION DATA

Marker, Gary, 1948-
  Publishing, printing, and the origins of intellectual
life in Russia, 1700-1800.

  Bibliography: p. 283.
  Includes index.
  1. Publishers and publishing—Soviet Union—History—
18th century.   2. Printing—Soviet Union—History—18th
century.   3. Soviet Union—Intellectual life—18th
century.   I. Title.
Z368.M27   1985   070.5′0947   84-42893
ISBN 0-691-05441-X (alk. paper)